COMMAND IN WAR

COMMAND
IN WAR

MARTIN VAN CREVELD

Harvard University Press
Cambridge, Massachusetts
and London, England

LIBRARY OF CONGRESS CATALOGING IN PUBLICATION DATA

Van Creveld, Martin L.
Command in war.

Bibliography: p.
Includes index.
1. Command and control systems—History.
2. Command of troops—History.   I. Title.
UB212.V36   1985   355.3′3041   84-12934
ISBN 0-674-14440-6 (alk. paper) (cloth)
ISBN 0-674-14441-4 (paper)

To Leon and Greta van Creveld
with respect and love

PREFACE

A BOOK the size of this one cannot be written without aid and support from a great many people, most of whom will have to remain unmentioned for lack of space. Among those who deserve more than the usual credit are Amnon Sella of the Hebrew University, Jerusalem, who first suggested a history of C^3 at a time when I scarcely knew what the initials meant; Edward Luttwak of Washington, D.C., who knew how to say the right words at a time of despair; Steven Canby, also of Washington, D.C., who supported the project from the beginning; and Andy Marshall, who was not put off by my early strange peregrinations but waited patiently for the work to be completed. Several of my colleagues at the Hebrew University, including Benjamin Kedar, David Asheri, and Amnon Linder, have read part or all of the manuscript and gave me the benefit of their advice. I have enjoyed many splendid discussions with, and the hospitality of, among others, Stephen Glick, Seth Carus, Irving and Florence Glick, David Thomas, and Aviva Hay. Blessed with such friends, a man is blessed indeed.

Finally, Dvora has seen me through the publication of this book during what were by no means always easy years. Without her good will, encouragement, and love it would never have seen the light of day. My debt to her is immense.

CONTENTS

Contents

It was not the legions which crossed the Rubicon, but Caesar.

—NAPOLEON BONAPARTE

1

INTRODUCTION: ON COMMAND

THIS BOOK INVESTIGATES the historical evolution of a function of war that acquired its name only a decade or so ago: that is, C^3 (Command, Control, Communications). I am no admirer of jargon, however; so instead of constantly writing out the full term or using the abbreviation, I will use the word "command" throughout in much the same way as people commonly use the term "management" to describe the manifold activities that go into the running of a business organization.

That the concept of C^3 should be so recent is, at first glance, surprising. The problem of commanding and controlling armed forces, and of instituting effective communications with and within them, is as old as war itself. A Stone Age chieftain had to devise the optimal organization and find the methods and technical means to command the forces at his disposal. From his day to ours, failure to consider and to solve the problem was to court disaster—indeed, to make it impossible for the forces to exist.

Though the problem is anything but new, its dimensions have grown exponentially in modern times, especially since 1939. This growth is due to a number of factors: (a) the increased demands made on command systems[1] by present-day warfare; (b) technological developments that have multiplied the means at the disposal of command systems; (c) changes in the nature of the command process, resulting from the interaction of factors (a) and (b); (d) the appearance of new weapons systems that, when coupled with

1

structural changes inside command systems themselves, have increased the vulnerability of command systems; and (e) the rise in costs, caused by factors (a) through (d). I will discuss each factor in turn.

(a) The increase in the demands made on command systems is due to the greatly enhanced complexity, mobility, and dispersion of modern armed forces. The enormously swollen number of specialized troops, units, functions, and pieces of equipment that make up a modern technological army—a present-day Bundeswehr division, for example, contains some nine hundred different Military Occupation Specialties (MOS), as compared to only forty in a 1939 Wehrmacht infantry division—has made overall coordination and control both more important and more difficult. Simultaneously, the speed and the range of modern weapons have reduced the time in which to exercise coordination and control to a fraction of what it was only a few decades ago, in some cases to the point where command functions—intercepting missiles or low-flying aircraft, for example—can only be performed automatically, by machines whose capacity for fast, accurate calculation far exceeds that of the human brain. Conversely, the speed and the range, coupled with greatly increased striking power, have compelled armies to spread out over enormous areas; a battalion may easily hold a front ten times as wide as did its predecessor two hundred years ago, and its deployment in depth may mean that the space it occupies is hundreds of times as large.[2]

(b) The second factor that has revolutionized command is the development of communications and data processing technology. Over the last thirty years, a large number of new devices have been put into the hands of man, among them television and computers, mobile telephones and data links, and image intensifiers and remote-controlled sensors. Two questions—really two sides of a single coin—have arisen: What is the effect of the new devices on existing methods, and how can the devices best be put to use?

The significance of the technological revolution for the problems of command is even clearer when it is seen that the last three decades have produced, for the first time in history, artificial devices capable of reproducing or amplifying the functions not merely of man's limbs and sensory organs but, to a growing extent, those of his brain as well. This has given birth to a host of questions for which little or no precedent existed. Which are the strong points of man, and which are those of the new machines? How, in consequence, should the burden of work be divided among them? How should communication ("interface") between man and machine, as well as among the machines themselves, be organized?

(c) The increasingly complex demands made by modern forces and by modern warfare, on the one hand, and the appearance of technical devices capable of meeting that demand, on the other, together have led to an explosion in the amount of data processed by any given command system to carry out any given mission. As the quantity of data rose, the difficulty of interpreting it in preparation for decision-making grew, causing staff to be piled upon staff and computer upon computer. New techniques, from operations research and systems analysis to cybernetics and games theory, were developed in order to cope with the flood of data. The growing size and sophistication of command systems led to new and difficult problems of management; learning to master them has turned into a lifelong job. As anyone familiar with the size and modus operandi of modern staffs will realize, the danger of command becoming an end unto itself is a real one indeed.[3]

(d) It has always been necessary to protect command systems and enable them to function effectively under the adverse effect of enemy action, but this problem too has assumed new dimensions in recent years. The size of headquarters and the signature that they leave in the form of electronic emissions make them prime targets for the precision-guided munitions (PGMs) now coming into use. Moreover, the dependence of command systems on electronically transmitted data flows has rendered them vulnerable to electronic warfare designed to interrupt those flows.[4] Growing reliance on formal computer languages, even though it increases speed and precision, also leads to a loss of the flexibility and redundancy of normal language, which raises nagging questions about the system's ability to survive the elimination of some of its parts. The attempt to solve this problem by providing an increased number of communication nodes, and by the automatic switching of data flows from one to another, leads to further complexity. And so the cycle continues.

(e) A very important outcome of these developments, and one

3

that renders their study imperative, is the exponential rise in costs. Regarded as a fraction of the army's overall costs, the price of command systems was traditionally almost negligible. A relatively small staff (even Moltke's General Staff in 1870 numbered only approximately seventy officers, as against close to a million men that it controlled during hostilities against France), some wagons with filing cabinets and maps, a pool of mounted orderlies, and such technical contrivances as field telescopes, standards, trumpets, drums, and pigeons (later supplemented by telegraph and telephone) formed the sum total of command systems.

Beginning in World War II, however, and increasing in pace thereafter, the situation changed. Organizations and devices associated with the gathering, storage, and transmission of information began to eat into the inside of armed forces, so to speak. This has reached the point that they now form by far the most important component of the price tag of airborne and naval weapons systems, and their share in those of land-bound systems is also rising year by year. Paradoxically, even as the per-bit cost of data processing fell by a factor of ten over each of the three decades from 1950 to 1980,[5] the cost of command systems rose so much that it now threatens to swallow up entire defense budgets. Something, it appears, has gone radically wrong—so wrong, indeed, that the continuation of the same trend may soon lead to a point where command systems, for the first time in history, will be perfect simply because there is nothing left for them to command.

These developments, for all the dangers of unmanageability and even catastrophic failure that they entail, present a source of opportunities as well. Precisely because the complexity of armed forces and the multiple missions that they must perform (from counterinsurgency to nuclear deterrence) make overall coordination more important than ever, and owing to the unprecedented range of gadgets at its disposal, the role that command may play in determining the outcome of present-day military conflict is crucial. By making possible a faster, clearer reading of the situation and a more effective distribution of resources, a superior command system may serve as a force multiplier and compensate for weaknesses in other fields, such as numerical inferiority or the politically induced need to leave the initiative to the enemy. Which, to use a primitive example, is more cost effective: another nuclear-powered aircraft carrier, or a communications and data processing system that will enhance the effectiveness of existing ones? Should money be invested in additional tanks, or is it perhaps better spent on a computer to model their employment? Such questions will never be easy to answer, but the very fact that they can be—and increasingly are—asked points to the growing importance attributed to command systems. Given the problem of rising costs, the dilemma is likely to become even more important in the future.

To take part in the debate concerning the command requirements of present-day military forces, or to prescribe solutions for those requirements, is beyond the purpose of this book. My purpose here is to consider Western military history on land, already analyzed from so many different points of view, in terms of the evolution of command systems and the way in which such systems operated. Such a study will certainly not eliminate the command problems facing modern armies; however, it may well shed some additional light on their nature, identify the main factors involved and the way they interact through change, and help indicate the direction in which reform should move. In making the attempt, moreover, I am doing no more than previous historians have. No sooner was materialism turned into dogma by Karl Marx than history, previously considered the domain of politics and battles (not to mention royal bedrooms), began to be recast in terms of production and consumption. No sooner had the unconscious been unveiled by Freud than history came to be rewritten in terms of an Oedipus complex. The case of command is similar. To look at old facts through new glasses, then to make use of the facts in order to gain a better understanding of those glasses—that, after all, is just what makes history worthwhile.

THE NATURE OF COMMAND

Command may be defined as a function that has to be exercised, more or less continuously, if the army is to exist and to operate. The definition is a happy one, since it serves to bring out the extraordinary importance of command; few other functions carried out by, or inside, the armed forces are as important in both respects, existence and operation.

The need for command arises from, and varies with, the size, complexity, and differentiation of an army. A one-man army requires no command, at least not in the sense that a hundred-man army does. An army operating as a single, solid, homogeneous block (phalanx) of men would be, and was, comparatively simple to command—to the extent, that is, that its unwieldiness and the limited repertoire of missions that it could fulfill allowed it to be commanded at all. Once a force of any size is subdivided into several subunits, however, the problem of assigning a specific mission to each, and of ensuring proper coordination among all, becomes much more difficult. These difficulties grow with the number of units, the power and range of their weapons, the speed at which they move, and the size of the spaces over which they operate. Should the units in question become specialized—that is, acquire different characteristics and missions—the difficulty of coordinating the various factors while maintaining the cohesion of the whole grows further still.[6] The role of command, in other words, increases with the sophistication of the forces—which, as has already been said, helps account for the attention paid to it in recent years.

The responsibilities of command, apart from the obvious and often by no means trivial job of looking after itself, are commonly divided into two parts. First, command must arrange and coordinate everything an army needs to exist—its food supply, its sanitary service, its system of military justice, and so on. Second, command enables the army to carry out its proper mission, which is to inflict the maximum amount of death and destruction on the enemy within the shortest possible period of time and at minimum loss to itself; to this part of command belong, for example, the gathering of intelligence and the planning and monitoring of operations. The first type of responsibility we shall term function-related, the second output-related. That the two are mutually dependent and by no means entirely distinct—can an army exist without intelligence? or defeat the enemy without its own justice system being in good order?—is a matter of course. The classification, nevertheless, is a useful one, as is shown also by the fact that in practice the two functions are frequently entrusted to separate parts of the organization.

Another and equally useful way of looking at command is to ask not what its responsibilities are but what it does. The exercise of command in fact involves a great many things, not all of which can be clearly separated from each other. There is, in the first place, the gathering of information on the state of one's own forces—a problem that should not be underestimated—as well as on the enemy and on such external factors as the weather and the terrain. The information having been gathered, means must be found to store, retrieve, filter, classify, distribute, and display it. On the basis of the information thus processed, an estimate of the situation must be formed. Objectives must be laid down and alternative methods for attaining them worked out. A decision must be made. Detailed planning must be got under way. Orders must be drafted and transmitted, their arrival and proper understanding by the recipients verified. Execution must be monitored by means of a feedback system, at which point the process repeats itself.

This presentation of the process of command as a cycle oversimplifies things insofar as it fails to recognize that, in practice, the incoming information is of inconsistent value; 99 percent of it is likely to disappear without a trace, whereas the remaining 1 percent may have a profound effect on operations—though whether this means that the 1 percent would be of value even without the 99 percent is a different question altogether.[7] The various stages are not fixed: some authors differentiate them into a larger number, others condense them into a smaller one.[8] The neat charts in books on business administration notwithstanding, the stages have borders that are not easy to draw in practice, and they are likely to be carried out, in part at least, simultaneously rather than in succession. Finally, far from being governed solely by the objective requirements of the situation, they interact and influence each other so that the beliefs underlying interpretation (for example) may well determine the way data are gathered and classified. Nevertheless, the description does present a fairly good theoretical picture of what command is all about.

A most interesting way of looking at the functions of command is to try to work out the qualities of an imaginary, "ideal" command system, an approach that will make it possible to extrapolate back toward reality in much the same way that Newtonian mechanics worked out the movements of actual bodies from those of imaginary ones moving along (nonexistent) straight lines in (nonexistent)

7

empty space at (nonexistent) constant speed. An ideal command system, then, should be able to gather information accurately, continuously, comprehensively, selectively, and fast. Reliable means must be developed to distinguish the true from the false, the relevant from the irrelevant, the material from the immaterial. Displays must be clear, detailed, and comprehensive. The mental matrix, individual or collective, against which information is analyzed and transformed into an estimate of the situation must correspond to the actual world rather than to one that existed twenty-five years previously or not at all.[9] The objectives selected must be both desirable and feasible, two requirements that are not always compatible. The alternative ways of action presented to the commander and his staff should be real, not just subterfuges presented as a matter of form. (As Moltke remarked to his aides, the enemy always seemed to have three alternatives open to him and he usually chose the fourth.) Once made, the decision must be firmly adhered to in principle, but not under any and every circumstance. Orders should be clear and unambiguous; they must tell subordinates everything they should know, but nothing more. Monitoring should be close enough to secure reliable execution, but not so close as to undermine the authority and choke the initiative (or even, as sometimes happens, the very ability to act) of subordinate commanders at all levels.

As this discussion implies, differences between various command systems can often be resolved into the various ways in which they approach these problems. The methods used for dealing with increasing complexity; the relative attention paid to function-related and to output-related responsibilities; the emphasis laid on any given part of the command process; and the specific strengths and weaknesses displayed in relation to the ideal—taken together, these qualities will go far toward defining the nature of any given command system. Whatever the solution adopted, the demands made on command systems are clearly of the utmost importance. With everything operating as it should and the manifold parts nicely balanced and meshing with each other, command may act as a force multiplier; Napoleon's presence on the battlefield was said by some of his enemies (this is attributed variously to Blücher and to Wellington) to be worth a corps of forty thousand men. Conversely, a failure at any point may put the entire chain in jeopardy—when, for

8

instance, a decision is based on an out-of-date piece of information. It is quite possible for errors made at more than one point to reinforce each other or, if the commander is lucky, to cancel each other out. War being by nature confused and the process of command complex, it is virtually certain that some breaks and errors will occur, a fact that a wise commander will take into account and provide for. While failure to do so may well result in catastrophe, it is equally true that not even the greatest victories in history resulted from anything like a perfect command system; in many cases, indeed, victories were won in spite of, rather than because of, the way the army's command system operated. So it has been in the past; and there is little doubt that, the introduction of modern communications and data processing systems notwithstanding, it will be so in the future.

THE EVOLUTION OF COMMAND

The functions of command, as I have said, are eternal. Provided he had a force of any size at his disposal, a Stone Age chieftain would have been confronted with them—all of them—just as much as his present-day successor is. Insofar as the forces at his command (and those of the enemy) were very much smaller, simpler, and slower in action, the functions of command were also simpler to carry out. On the other hand, the chieftain in question would hardly even have had writing materials, not to mention a pair of binoculars or an adding machine, to assist him in exercising those functions, which in turn would have placed very close limits on the size and effectiveness of the forces he could command. In balancing the task facing the Stone Age chieftain against the means that were available to him for carrying it out, there is little reason to believe that the exercise of command as such has become more difficult since Alexander showed how it should be done.

Although the functions of command are thus not subject to change (it is certainly conceivable for the way in which they are carried out to vary, however, and for their relative importance and relationship to each other to do the same), the means at its disposal as we know them today are, without exception, the result of long and continuous development. A useful method for classifying these

9

means is to divide them into three categories: organizations, such as staffs or councils of war; procedures, such as the way in which reports are distributed inside a headquarters; and technical means, ranging from the standard to the radio. The combination of these three should make it possible, in principle, to describe the structure of any command system at any given time and place.

The evolution of command systems does not take place in a vacuum, however. Their development is partly a response to changing requirements. A modern mechanized brigade, capable at a pinch of covering 150 miles per day, obviously cannot be commanded by the same technical means as a Napoleonic cavalry brigade capable of no more than a fifth of that distance. An invader reaching from the English Channel to Verdun, to use the example of World War I, cannot be perceived, much less countered, by means of personal observation such as was employed by commanders in past centuries. Developments in weapons, tactics, strategy, and a host of other factors will require command systems to match. The latter are thus reflections of the art of war as it exists in any given period; they are affected by, and in turn affect, the state of that art.

Like other parts of the art of war, however, command also has its own history, which is to a limited extent autonomous and independent of other components. In particular, since the means at its disposal are diverse, a development in any one of them almost always entails a change in the rest. For example, it was the procedure of submitting daily detailed strength reports, established toward the end of the eighteenth century, that created the requirement for specialized personnel and thus gave birth to the first general staff. Once staffs existed, pen and paper, not to mention desks and filing cabinets, became much more important than they had previously been. The switch from oral to written operational command, largely accomplished within the century from 1750 to 1850, meant that far more attention could be paid to systematic analysis. Thus, the various elements of command systems interact with each other and with the processes of command, and they push development along.

Finally, developments in command have often been stimulated by outside factors, particularly technological ones. The employment of the telescope, for example, enabled Frederick the Great to establish his headquarters at a fixed location overlooking the battlefield rather than having to rush around it, as was the practice of Gustavus Adolphus a century before. Samuel Morse hardly had the U.S. Army in mind when he invented the telegraph, but once the tele-graph existed its military significance was soon appreciated. The same holds true for the telephone (originally invented as a by-prod-uct of research aimed at providing aids for the deaf) and the radio. The effect on organization and procedures, and indeed on the con-duct of war, of all these inventions has been profound.

The evolution of command, in brief, is as complex as that of any other part of the art of war. Moreover, its study presents some unique problems, which form the theme of the next section.

THE STUDY OF COMMAND

To understand the evolution of command through time, it is first of all necessary to work out a matrix into which it will be possible to fit the command system employed at any given time and place. What, one might ask, were the demands made on a given command system by the existing state of the art of war? In what ways were these de-mands met? What organization, if any, was provided for the pur-pose? What technical means (even an arm being waved up and down constitutes a technical means) and what procedures were em-ployed? How was intelligence procured and processed, and in what manner were plans arrived at? What means of communication ex-isted, and how did their characteristics affect the transmission of in-formation? How was the execution of orders monitored, and what control, if any, did the commander exercise over the course of events? As one writer has pointed out, existing military literature makes surprisingly few efforts to answer these questions, if indeed it asks them in the first place.[10] While books on management and "de-cision-making theory" have multiplied promiscuously in recent years, works on command as here understood are, for one reason or another, rare. Save perhaps for the occasional intercepted or misun-derstood message or the broken-down radio, it is indeed possible to study military history for years and hardly notice that the problem exists. A possible explanation may perhaps best be put in terms of a homely analogy. Few people pay any attention to long-distance tele-phone calls unless they are exceptionally difficult (or easy) to make.

11

That vast organizations, as well as billions of dollars in equipment, are necessary to make the call possible at all is something of which most of us are only dimly aware.

The treatises written on the problem of command as here defined tend to fall into two categories. At one end of the scale are works that insist that a plan should be "good," that is, conform to a few normally quite ill-defined principles of strategy. On the other end are the handbooks and manuals that explain, most learnedly, the difference between a "memorandum" and a "staff paper" (the former is an informal version of the latter, or vice versa) and insist that place names should always be typed in capital letters. The former are commonly associated with superficial research, the latter the result of a divorce between command systems and the things that must be commanded. Either generalities or banalities—whereas I am concerned with everything in between.

History, unlike the social sciences, deals with the specific rather than with the general, and in any case generalization is nowhere more hazardous than in the infinitely complex interaction of thought and action that constitutes the process of command. It is quite possible for a command system, when operated by different men, to function in very different ways; accordingly, in order to capture the process of command rather than merely the external shell of the means at its disposal, it is necessary to ask not merely how things could have been done on the basis of the available means but also how, on this or that occasion, they were in fact done. However old-fashioned such an approach may appear at a time when historians are increasingly reluctant to consider armies as military instruments,[11] a study of command cannot avoid asking the down-to-earth questions: who ordered whom to do what, when, by what means, on the basis of what information, what for, and to what effect. On pain of becoming a mere theoretical exercise, in other words, a study of the development of command must include a great deal of plain operational history.

To find out who did what, and why—that, no doubt, is a very tall order, and one that can be made as difficult by an abundance of information as by its absence. Worse still, to concentrate on a few cases of "decision making"—an approach often followed by political scientists—is to distort reality. To paraphrase Northcote Parkinson, 90 percent (at least) of good command consists of things that never happen.[12] The division does not disintegrate on its march from Y to Z; it is not taken by surprise, at least not regularly; no more than a few detachments lose their way every day, and lack of maintenance does not cause more than (say) a third of its vehicles to be immobilized at any given time. These things are often taken for granted, yet in fact nothing is more remote from the truth. In war as in business life, the operation of Murphy's Law (everything that can go wrong, will) cannot be avoided except at the price of constant vigilance and great effort. As Moltke once wrote, in war with its enormous friction even the mediocre is quite an achievement;[13] yet to go into the tens of thousands of individual decisions that make even mediocrity possible is utterly impossible. The vast majority of them are in any case only made semi-consciously and as a matter of routine. A good battalion commander does not have to "decide" to post pickets at night any more than a reasonably competent corps commander has to "decide" to take his maps along. Yet in the long run, and given a reasonable amount of luck, it is precisely this kind of thing that makes the difference between competence and incompetence, victory and defeat.

A study of the way command has been exercised through history, to sum up, is faced with a plethora of methodological and conceptual difficulties. To make the task manageable, it is necessary to limit the analysis to the purely military side of things. This means, however, taking a somewhat blinkered view of reality, given that political, economic, and social (and, increasingly, technological) factors have always affected military command. It is clear, furthermore, that only very brief periods can be dealt with—in general, because of the superabundance of information, they tend to become even briefer as we approach recent times—and only at the level of fairly high headquarters: the commander in chief, his principal subordinates, and a few of those immediately subordinate to them. It is also obvious that no reference can be made to each of the myriad routine decisions any commander has to make, except by means of a very general description of their nature and of the way they were dealt with. Finally, unfashionable though such an approach may be, a historian can only write of things for which source material is available. This means, a priori, that it is possible to analyze only history's

13

most "important" command systems. The duke of Brunswick's thoughts and actions during the 1806 Jena Campaign may be quite as illuminating as Napoleon's, but no thirty-two volumes of his correspondence have been published.

These considerations, combined with the desire to take the long view and thus gain the perspective and riches that constitute Clio's greatest forte, have dictated the outline of this book. Its chapters are designed to illustrate the most important stages through which military command has passed from ancient Greece to the present day. Following the introduction, chapter 2 provides an analysis of command as it was organized in the "antediluvian" age before 1800, welded into a unity by the fact that means of communication changed hardly at all over a period of centuries. In chapter 3 there follows an account of Napoleonic warfare, chosen because it appears to constitute the greatest single revolution ever wrought in the art of command—and one, moreover, that owed little to technological advances. Chapter 4 discusses command as exercised by the German General Staff, the first and for a long time the best among such organizations, on the basis of the telegraph. Chapter 5 focuses on the problems of command in World War I; particular attention is paid to the effect of machine warfare and wire-bound communication systems. Chapter 6 deals with "modern" mobile warfare as exemplified by some of its best practitioners, the Israeli Defense Forces (IDF) in 1967 and 1973. Finally, chapter 7 tries to assess the influence of modern technology—the helicopter and the computer—and modern organization on command as exercised by the U.S. forces in Vietnam.

To provide a reasonably complete picture, each chapter opens with a description of the "state of the art"—the fundamental characteristics of warfare in a given place and time. This is followed by comments on the commander's personality (where relevant) and on the nature of the command system through which he made his influence felt. An analysis of the system's actual functioning on campaign and during battle is provided wherever possible; this analysis is as detailed and as rigorous as the available sources allow. Wherever something is not known—and this is often the case—an explicit statement to that effect is made.

Although the division of the book into chapters followed naturally once the role of technology in shaping command systems was granted (or, rather, assumed), the selection of the campaign to be studied in each was more problematic. An error in selection may of course render the study useless if the case chosen is not "typical," but I am at a loss to think of a method by which "typical" ones may be found. One way to solve this problem would have been to include numerous campaigns and to study only the salient characteristics of each, but this would have been to risk a superficiality that is as inimical to history as it is to command. As a matter of fact, all that can really be said in favor of the cases actually presented is that their selection was governed by the above-mentioned considerations (the availability of source material, brevity, and the like) and not by any desire to illustrate a particular point of view. They are probably no more, but also no less, representative of their age and stage of development than any others that could have been chosen.

Contrary to the procedure employed in many writings on military history, the case studies here presented do not show both sides of the picture (except to the extent that is absolutely necessary for the reader's understanding), for to do so would be to use information not available to commanders at the time. Instead, the course of events will be followed, as far as possible, through commanders' eyes and from behind their desks (or, before they became desk-bound, between their horses' ears). This, no doubt, is another distortion or at least a narrowing of history as it actually happened. Any analysis is.

What will result from such a study? By analyzing historical command systems at work we may hope to gain a better idea of how it was done, successfully or otherwise. We may reasonably expect to deepen our understanding of the effect of technological and other change on command systems, and of the role of command itself among the other factors that give war its shape. Even without firm conclusions, the discussion itself may be valuable. Studying the past may be a matter of marginal utility only, but the past is us and it is on the past alone that all decision making is inevitably based. If systematic study of the past is taken away, only personal experience, hearsay, and intuition remain. Military history may be an inadequate tool for commanders to rely on, but a better one has yet to be designed.

So far I have spoken of command as if it were solely a rational process (or, rather, a combination of processes) in which information is used to orchestrate men and things toward performing their missions in war. This is not strictly true, however, since war is an irrational business par excellence. The men engaged in armed conflict require motivation as well as coordination. It being the quintessential task of commanders to send men to their deaths, the incentives associated with the gainful pursuit of peace often do not apply and must be replaced by an appeal to irrational motives.[14] As any number of lost battles in history will testify, it is quite possible for the very drives that cause men to fight to render them unamenable to effective command. Even when this is not the case, there is a contradiction between the two functions: motivating is best carried out by a commander who positions himself way out front among his troops, whereas coordinating typically requires his presence at a fixed and detached point in the rear. Finally, motivating differs from coordinating in that it does not consist, at any rate not entirely, of the tricks of the trade. To motivate others a commander must be motivated himself, or else cheat all of the people all of the time. War, to quote Clausewitz, is a clash of moral forces above all. This book, it is true, is not primarily concerned with moral forces. Not to bear their importance in mind at all times, however, would be to misunderstand completely the nature of command.

2

THE STONE AGE OF COMMAND

REFLECTING ON command as he would have liked it to be, Moshe Dayan once rhapsodized, "Where, oh where are the good old days of the simple wars when, as the hour of battle approached, the commander got on his white horse, someone blew the trumpet, and off he charged towards the enemy."[1] Dayan, whose hostility toward drawn-out discussions and "management" was notorious, was thinking of a period before the distinction most fundamental to any organization, that between the leading and the led, had extended into the battlefield and before the functions of the commander became specialized to the point that he no longer fought with weapon in hand. By and large, it will be seen, this change came at a surprisingly late moment in history. Not until the second half of the seventeenth century did senior commanders habitually start taking their place behind, rather than in front of, their men, and Frederick the Great was probably the first commander in chief regularly depicted as wearing a suit of linen rather than of armor.[2] From his day to ours the physical location of the commander in relation to his troops has undergone many peregrinations.

The commander's actual place, of course, is determined by his functions or lack of them. Obviously, a commander who wielded a spear in the front ranks of his army cannot have exercised much more than the—admittedly very important—moral functions of his job. Armies that were commanded in this way either could not be subjected to close control during battle or else were so simple in

17

structure and function that no such control was required. This simplicity, in turn, was both cause and effect of the fact that millennia passed without the technical means of communication undergoing any fundamental change, however numerous and important the developments in every other field. Seen from our rather special point of view, these millennia form a clear unity that I have termed the Stone Age of command. It is the limitations imposed on command by the technical means available, but above all the ways in which those limitations were occasionally overcome, which constitute the period's relevance to the present.

THE PARAMETERS OF STRATEGY

Did strategy—and, by implication, strategic command—exist before 1800? The question will probably come as a surprise to some military historians, bent as they are on quarrying their examples from every campaign from Marathon (490 B.C.) onward. In this chapter I argue, however, that strategy in the sense that Napoleon, Jomini, and Clausewitz made classic hardly existed before their time, and that this was due above all to the fact that strategic command was all but impossible to exercise.[3]

There is, of course, a sense in which strategy has always existed. Commanders in chief have always had a number of alternatives. The decision to go to war having been made, commanders had to choose between taking the offensive (seeking out the enemy) and staying on the defensive (waiting to receive his blow or perhaps avoiding it altogether). It was possible to fight the enemy with all one's might, seeking to force a decision in battle, or else to try and wear him down gradually by a process of attrition. It was possible to determine what kind of terrain to fight in and what to avoid, which in turn presupposed some knowledge of the country and the resources that it might make available. A commander's decision as to which of these courses to take would presumably depend on the information at his disposal—information concerning the state of his own forces and the enemy's, their respective countries, the climate, and so on. In this sense, strategy—or should one rather speak of grand strategy?—is eternal and has changed hardly at all from the Stone Age to our own time.

Seen as parameters that govern strategy, these factors have one thing in common: they are relatively slow to change. Few countries in history could double their forces overnight, nor could they alter those forces' methods of fighting without prolonged—possibly very prolonged indeed, since tactics are usually the product of social and economic factors rather than of purely military ones—training and preparation. Terrain and climate are notoriously slow to change; if they do, they do so only in the course of many generations. There have been exceptions, it is true; as a rule, however, it was precisely the fact that the principal parameters of strategy are relatively resistant to change that made it possible for information about them to be usefully gathered and transmitted by the primitive means in existence.

Consider a commander before 1800, sitting in his capital and preparing to launch a war.[4] The sources of strategic intelligence open to him included books—Napoleon, for example, is known to have read every available description and military history of Italy before setting out to conquer it in 1796, and Caesar ("The whole of Gaul is divided into three parts . . .") probably did the same—as well as maps, however primitive; from these and from the newspapers that began to be published early in the seventeenth century one could glean general information concerning the theater of operations, its resources, its climate, and the nature of the people inhabiting it. This written information was supplemented—or in some periods (such as the almost bookless early Middle Ages) replaced—by oral sources, the tales of traveling merchants, artists, pilgrims. To obtain more specific geo-military information about such things as roads, fords, bridges, and fortresses and about the enemy's moves and intentions, it was necessary to rely on diplomats and spies. The two were often indistinguishable, and still are.[5]

As even a cursory glance will reveal, each of these sources had its own strengths and weaknesses. Some were insufficiently specialized to bring in the specific information that a commander might need, while others were of questionable reliability. Intermittent at the best of times—Napoleon, setting out to conquer Palestine in 1798, used as his main source François Volney's *Voyage en Egypte et en Syrie* published in Paris thirteen years before—the flow of information was likely to be reduced still further upon the actual outbreak of hostilities, though the absence of continuous front lines and the inability of armies to police extensive tracts of territory meant that it was unlikely to dry up altogether.

In the absence of telecommunications and often of regular mail service as well, the speed at which information was able to travel varied greatly. Rumor, especially concerning "great events" such as a battle lost or won, moved fastest of all—speeds in excess of 250 miles a day are on record—but only at the price of the subject matter being neither selective nor reliable. On the other hand, books, maps, and travelers could hardly be expected to move at more than a walking pace, say ten or fifteen miles a day over extended periods. Somewhere in between these extremes came the reports that agents, stationed in friendly or hostile territory or else reporting on the moves of some neutral ruler, sent back to their employer. When properly utilized and taken together, such sources were often able to present a commander with a fair basis for strategic planning. But their limitations—especially in regard to speed—were such that their usefulness for operational purposes in the field was always questionable.

Rapid, long-distance information-transmission systems were not, it is true, entirely unknown even before 1800. Extensive relay systems, dependent on mounted couriers and sometimes also on the human voice traveling from outpost to outpost across the desert, were a notable feature of the Persian Empire.[6] They were subsequently copied by the Hellenistic monarchies and by the Roman emperor Augustus, whose *cursus publicus*—carriages driving from station to station along strategic roads—survived for several centuries.[7] Recorded performances of these systems show that they were capable, at their best, of transmitting information at 150 to 200 miles a day, though it must be kept in mind that the very recording of such performances is itself proof of their exceptional nature and that reliability rather than speed was frequently the most important objective.[8] Financed either centrally or by the local population in the form of compulsory services, such systems invariably required a strong, stable government as well as very good control over and policing of extensive tracts of territory, the absence of which probably explains why no such system is recorded in western Europe during any period between the fall of the Roman Empire and the end of the sixteenth century.

Side by side with courier relay systems, optical telegraphs based on fire or smoke signals are frequently mentioned in Greek and, to a lesser extent, Roman sources.[9] Such systems were employed by the Scots until the end of the sixteenth century and in Montenegro right down to the beginning of the twentieth. They may consist either of a simple beacon—a bonfire on top of some mountain announcing a predetermined piece of information, such as the appearance of a hostile army or fleet—or of long chains of fires like those that, according to legend, swiftly informed Queen Clytemnestra in Mycenae that her husband Agamemnon had finally conquered Troy. Either way, the information transmitted had to be both simple and prearranged, a severe limitation that the ancients, despite many ingenious attempts, never succeeded in overcoming.[10] Often employing symbolic languages with low redundancy, and being dependent on good weather, the reliability of such systems is lower than that of couriers. For them to work it is necessary for the recipients to know a message is coming, and approximately when, or else the signals may pass unobserved.

What constraints did the technical characteristics of these systems impose on the nature of the military information that could be usefully transmitted? First, note that the systems were more easily employed behind an army than in front of it; thus their use for offensive warfare was fairly limited. Given the relatively low speed of courier systems, they were most useful in transmitting administrative and grand strategic information, where speed did not greatly matter; on the other hand, to try to use them in order to direct armies by remote control was likely to lead to the kind of petty strategy beloved of eighteenth-century commanders. Optical systems were capable of transmitting information faster, but they were tied to fixed points in space and had the further limitation that they were unable to transmit any but the most rudimentary types of information. Such systems, therefore, were used mainly for announcing the most outstanding of expected events—the outbreak of a war, or its conclusion (not accidentally, the latter was the first recorded use made of optical telegraphs both in classical antiquity and during the French Revolution). In short, they were more useful for conducting strategy than for directing operations in the field; to the defensive than to the offensive; and to the static defense than to the mobile one. This, of course, helps explain why the most extensive systems for which archaeological evidence has survived formed part of that masterpiece of strategically (not, however, tactically) rigid defense, the Roman *limes*.[11]

A ruler in his capital, then, might rely on messenger systems to exercise general supervision over his armies in the field. A provincial governor might use optical systems in order to summon reinforcements to a threatened sector, while a force garrisoning or besieging a town or camp might place signaling equipment on top of towers for the purpose of short-range tactical communications.[12] Neither courier nor optical systems were at all suitable for the direction of operations in the field, however, and indeed there is no evidence of any historical attempt to employ them in this task. To enable a field army to operate at all, its commander had to be on the spot and possessed of wide latitude to do as he thought fit; conversely, for the ruler to insist on being consulted about every detail was ipso facto to render the conduct of war all but impossible. One solution was to have the ruler accompany the army, acting either as its actual commander in chief—as did Alexander and, two millennia after him, Frederick the Great—or in a symbolic, supervisory capacity, as was often the case until the middle of the nineteenth century. Where a ruler was sufficiently competent to exercise command, or at least to refrain from so doing, this solution could lead to the most brilliant results; otherwise it was worse than useless.

In any case, given the limits imposed by technology, the only place from which it was possible to exercise any kind of operational command was the army itself. Sitting in his tent and contemplating the situation, the commander's sources of enemy intelligence, as enumerated by Frederick the Great soon after the middle of the eighteenth century, were as follows: travelers, local inhabitants (that is, any halfway intelligent peasant), deserters, prisoners, and the spies occasionally sent out to explore the enemy's camp while disguised as merchants' servants.[13] Many of these, it has been pointed out above, traveled hardly any faster than the armies on whose movements they were reporting. The timeliness of intelligence depends on the relative speed of information and its subject matter, not on the absolute speed of each separately; therefore the problem of providing the slow-moving armies of old with up-to-date news was quite as acute as in the case of modern forces, whose mobility, however high, is nevertheless an infinitesimal fraction of the speed of light at which most messages are transmitted. This low ratio also imposed strict limits on the range at which active intelligence operations could be conducted; even under the best of circumstances, and barring any number of possible mishaps, such operations were only possible when the enemy was at most a few marching days away.

One other very important source of enemy intelligence that must be mentioned is the cavalry patrols sent ahead to reconnoiter. The use of such patrols is, surprisingly, attested to only from the end of the fifth century B.C.; earlier Greek commanders did not apparently understand their employment.[14] Nor does the fact that the idea is simple necessarily mean that it was invariably put into practice, and it would be possible to cite any number of armies that met with disaster for lack of a proper vanguard. Furthermore, though small groups of horsemen can travel much faster than armies, the advantage they enjoy should not be exaggerated. Either they had to be prepositioned in the enemy's way, which in itself presupposes some knowledge of his likely moves, or else they would have to travel forward and backward in their quest for information, thus cutting their effective range in half. Given these limitations, there appear to be few cases in history before 1800 in which armies were subject to direct observation by the enemy when more than twenty or so miles away.[15]

If obtaining long-range enemy intelligence always constituted a problem, so did communicating with one's own forces. In the present day of radiotelephone and data links it is difficult to recapture the sort of utter isolation that ensued until about 1900 (in the case of small units, until after World War I) whenever detachments were sent out or an army was separated into several forces. Hannibal in Italy, to cite one extreme example, is said to have had no idea of what the second Carthaginian Army under his brother Hasdrubal was up to until the Romans informed him by tossing Hasdrubal's severed head into his camp. Napoleon at Bautzen in 1813 could do nothing to communicate with Ney, on whose advance the outcome of the battle depended, even though their respective headquarters were less than ten miles apart. Even as late as 1866, Moltke, caught in a similar situation at Königgrätz, was powerless to communicate with the Prussian 2nd Army and spent a few extremely uncomfortable hours scanning the hills for a sign of its presence. For thousands of years before that, the speed at which field armies could communicate with each other was essentially limited to the speed of the horse—say no more than ten miles per hour on the average, given conditions that were not too unfavorable and over comparatively short distances.

The fact that communications were slow and insecure explains why commanders were always reluctant to send out detachments (the term, remaining in usage until the middle of the nineteenth century, speaks for itself): once detached, they would become all but impossible to control. Nor does the remedy—the establishment of proper strategic units capable of independent action—appear to have suggested itself before the end of the eighteenth century. A survey of Western military history before the French Revolution fails to bring to light any permanent formations of more than 3,000 men (that is, formations provided with their own titles or numbers rather than simply called after their generals, and in possession of some symbol of collective identity such as standards or flags). Among the largest on record were Eumenes' *Argryaspidae* (Bearers of the Silver Shields) around 300 B.C. and the Spanish *Tercios* some 1,900 years later, the latter so unwieldy that they were soon defeated and replaced by the smaller and handier Dutch and Swedish battalions. The limiting factor governing the size of such formations was presumably the number of men who, standing in dense array, could see and obey the same visual signal, itself of limited size owing to reasons of convenience. Even such units, however, were the exception rather than the rule; as late as the middle of the eighteenth century no European army had a permanent formation larger than the regiment, comprising up to 2,250 men.[16] Cavalry regiments, owing to the larger space they occupied and their greater mobility, never even numbered as many as 1,000 men. The size of these units alone is sufficient to show that their purpose was purely tactical; nor did any of them possess either the staff or the organic combination of all arms that could have made them suitable instruments for independent strategic use. Whatever units larger than this were required in battle, or to go on some "detached" mission away from the army's main line of operations, had to be put together on an ad hoc basis. As late as the middle of the eighteenth century this was done by means of

24

ordres de bataille published from time to time. It was only during the Seven Years War (1756–1763) that the first divisions were tentatively put together by de Broglie in Germany, and even then it took the idea another forty years to mature.

It is not true, nevertheless, that armies before 1800 never separated into two or more forces.[17] Alexander during his later campaigns in Bactria and Hyrcania; Antony during his Armenian campaign of 36 B.C.; the Crusaders in 1097 during one leg of their crossing of Asia Minor; Henry V on his way to Italy three years later—these and many others had their forces take different routes toward a common objective, usually some town whose location was known with reasonable accuracy. Yet a closer examination of each of these instances shows clearly that Alexander did not precede Moltke, as one historian has asserted, in inventing the principle of "march divided, fight united";[18] his moves were not intended to confuse, outmaneuver, or trap an enemy force but, on the contrary, were made possible solely because he expected to meet with only negligible opposition from mountain tribes. Furthermore, there is no positive evidence that Alexander's columns, the one under himself and the other under Parmenion, communicated with each other during their separate marches. How difficult a feat that could be is made sufficiently clear by the Crusaders' near-destruction at Dorylaeum in 1097 because their two columns, though no more than five or six miles apart, were unable to locate each other quickly.[19] In each of these cases, it was logistics rather than strategy that dictated the army's separation into parts; there were always limits on the number of men and animals that could find food along a single road, and this might easily be exceeded if the army was a large one and the country poor.[20] Also, siege trains and, after 1500, artillery were sometimes so heavy and cumbersome that they had to be transported by a shorter and better road (where possible, by water) than that taken by the rest of the army.[21] Such expediency was merely the product of necessity, however; there appear to have been few if any cases before 1800 when an army was deliberately split into separate forces as part of a successful strategic maneuver directed against the enemy in the field. Prussia's Frederick II is said to have been among the first to have made the attempt during his Bohemian campaign of 1757; he failed, though admittedly not for lack of strategic coordination, and contemporary military critics were not slow to condemn him for trying.[22]

The problem of long-range communications in the field was not, of course, the only reason why commanders were reluctant to split their forces and embark on strategy of the Napoleonic kind. The limited number of good roads that existed in any part of the world before the nineteenth century, making it impossible to move an army in parallel columns except across country; the fact that good maps, giving a correct two-dimensional representation of the theater of war, complete with roads and distances, were always scarce;[23] and the virtual absence of portable timekeeping devices until the end of the seventeenth century, forcing commanders to rely on difficult-to-use astronomical means instead[24]—these factors, taken together, all but compelled commanders to limit strategy to those operations that they could keep under their own direct control, that is, those that could be carried out by a single force marching more or less *en bloc* and covered, at best, by a vanguard in front and some detachments on both flanks.[25] Strategy thus consisted of attempts to take the enemy by surprise by utilizing some unexpected way of approach or by stealing a march at night; of marches and countermarches; of the taking of positions, the blocking of communications, the devastation of selected pieces of countryside in order to deny supplies to the enemy; in short, of all the maneuvers that made eighteenth-century warfare the peculiarly slow, cumbersome, indecisive process that it often was. Furthermore, as Clausewitz notes, armies operating in this way could normally deliver battle only by a kind of mutual consent between the opposing commanders in chief;[26] a challenge had to be put out and accepted, either formally by messenger, as was often done in the Middle Ages,[27] or else informally by parading and demonstrating in front of the enemy's camp, as was the practice of Julius Caesar and subsequent commanders all the way down to the eighteenth century. On the other hand, for such armies to make use of strategy in order to surround or outflank the enemy and put him in an impossible situation before the commencement of battle— which constitutes the essence of the Napoleonic *manoeuvre sur les derrières*—was all but impossible and is indeed said to have been carried out successfully only once in two millennia.[28] Strategy, the product of numerous factors, was impractical only to the extent that it depended on communications between, and the coordination of, forces engaged on mobile warfare over large distances; that, however, is saying rather a lot.

There is another way in which strategy after Napoleon differed from that before him. Since armies normally stayed close together, and since the power and range of weapons were limited to the point that a hostile force more than a couple of miles away might, for all its ability to inflict damage, as well be on the moon, there was a very real sense in which wars only got under way when the two sides' main forces, each normally under the direct orders of its commander in chief, confronted each other. To quote one well-known authority, wars were essentially "extended walking tours," or "rides" (*chevauchées*) and "marches into the field" (*Feldzüge*) that sometimes culminated in the carefully regulated tournaments known as battles.[29] This and the fact that they drew the bulk of their supplies from the surrounding countryside (whether by means of direct requisitioning and plunder or indirectly by forced contributions with which to pay the contractors) meant that the principal problem facing them for the greatest part of a campaign was not how to fight the enemy but how to exist in the field.[30] It was in order to deal with this problem that staffs and staff work were first invented.

THE NONEVOLUTION OF STAFFS

The word "staff" (formerly prefaced by "capital" rather than by the current "general") has a variety of meanings in English.[31] Used in its widest sense, the term has come to mean simply a body of assistants attached to any figure in the military, government, or business who wants to look at all important. A distinction may perhaps be drawn between staffers and servants; the former supposedly aid their boss in the line of duty, whereas the latter cater to his purely personal needs. As secretaries know, the difference is often blurred in practice. Furthermore, so loose is common usage of the word that a member of, say, the White House "staff" may be anyone from the humblest chambermaid to the second most powerful man in the land.

Even disregarding purely personal servants, a staff of any size appears to consist of two kinds of people: technical assistants (typists, telephone operators, filing clerks, and the like, whose duties are narrowly prescribed) on the one hand, and various researchers, planners, and managers on the other. To include all these under the single rubric of "staff" is historically misleading, for the former appear to have preceded the latter by many centuries.

To confine our discussion to military staffs alone, one way of looking at them—originating in the German system—is to distinguish between the "special" and "general" sections comprising them.[32] The former consists of technical experts such as the commanding officer of artillery and the commanding officer of engineers (signals, chemical warfare, trains, and so on) who are normally made to wear two hats and command the troops of their own arms as well as advise the commander in chief on their use; also included are the adjutant, the quartermaster, judge advocate, and the like. The members of the general section, on the other hand, include the intelligence officer, the operations officer, and, in the case of larger formations, officers responsible for those aspects of logistics and personnel administration most immediately tied up with the conduct of operations. As compared to those of the special section, the functions of the general section are broader, and, to the extent that they are dependent on the enemy's moves and not merely on their own (as food supply largely is, for example), they are also less predictable, less repetitive, and less subject to formalization by means of written rules. In a word, greater uncertainty is associated with the duties of the general section, which in turn calls for a different kind of organization and possibly also for a different type of personnel.

The origins of military staffs are unknown. It may safely be assumed that commanders, even prehistoric ones, have always employed some aides to relieve them of certain technical, time-consuming, or simply onerous duties. The history of these people, from grooms to copyists to the aide-de-camp responsible for catering to the general's mistress ("if he keeps one," as one eighteenth-century handbook puts it), is for the most part obscure, probably at no very great loss to us.

The earliest staffs about which anything at all is known are, as usual, Greek ones.[33] Xenophon speaks of the Spartan king (in the case of other city-states, this would be the elected general, or *strategos*) being surrounded by "those about the public tent," by whom he meant "such peers as share the royal tents, the prophets, the doctors, the officers of the army and any volunteers who are present."[34] To translate this into modern terms, a Greek army's staff—or perhaps one should rather speak of "headquarters"—consisted of (a) a few senior commanders, selected, presumably, on the basis of personal and political considerations as well as purely military ones; (b) technical experts, among whom the heralds should be included in addition to the above-mentioned specialists;[35] and (c) hangers-on. In this type of organization neither a special nor a general staff section is in evidence. Since the armies of Greek city-states were small, short-lived, logistically simple organizations, the absence of the former is readily explicable; from all that we know—and it must be remembered that staff work, until quite recently, has had a very nasty habit of leaving few positive traces upon history—it appears that there just wasn't that much administrative work involved.[36]

Owing to the nature of strategy, the functions of a general staff section were carried out only intermittently; such functions were usually performed partly in the commander's head and partly in councils of war. The former defies explanation except by post hoc rationalization; the latter were attended by the army's senior officers and called irregularly at the commencement of a campaign or on the eve of some major decision—for instance, when Alexander asked (or pretended to ask) his commanders whether to accept Darius' offer of ceding Asia west of the Euphrates in return for calling off the war.[37] The way in which business was transacted undoubtedly depended on the commander's personality and, since Greek armies were often made up of various contingents, his political standing as well. That all this involved much paperwork is difficult to believe; a Greek commander's correspondence seems to have been largely confined to letters to the government back home, often phrased with truly laconic brevity.[38]

To imagine the armies of Greek city-states, ad hoc organizations of citizen-soldiers, functioning without much of an administrative apparatus is one thing; to do the same for the forces of Alexander and his Hellenistic successors, however, is quite another. The running of these armies, consisting as they did of tens of thousands of professional fighting men who were mobilized on a permanent basis and often passed their profession to their sons as military colonists, must have required considerable administrative expertise and paperwork, not to mention any number of clerks, desks, filing cabinets, and archives. Alexander's army is known to have employed a secretary (*grammateus*), Eumenes of Caria, whose function was in fact less specialized than his title implies, since he was also used to transmit messages on the battlefield, turned into a famous cavalry commander, and finally emerged as one of the Successors. His department was responsible for keeping the *basileis ephemerides,* or royal diary,[39] and presumably also had a hand in paying the troops and in compiling the list of those who had wedded Asiatic wives.[40] Hellenistic armies certainly had their paymasters and secretaries, but since the papyri that are our sole source carry only their titles it is impossible to follow their work in any detail.[41]

Passing now from administration to the conduct of operations, all we really know is that Alexander had with him *bematists,* or surveyors, who presumably collected information on routes, economic resources, and camping grounds as well as measuring distances in the previously almost unknown, semi-mythological countries that the army traversed.[42] That these officials also busied themselves with enemy intelligence, at least in the sense of gathering all possible information on their numbers and military customs, is quite probable but cannot be proved; nor do the sources contain any hint that might reveal the existence of an operations department responsible for planning. The most that can perhaps be concluded is that, in the course of time, certain senior commanders such as Parmenion were entrusted with specialized functions such as transport on a semi-permanent basis and in addition to their other duties.[43]

How much paperwork, in any case, did all these armies require for the conduct of operations in the field? The answer, to go by what little positive evidence has survived, is, not very much. Alexander is known to have written a large number of letters, many of them addressed either home to Macedonia or else to some governor on his line of communications far in the rear. On one occasion he even replied to a letter from Darius.[44] That all of this was done on a very regular basis—Alexander's letters to Olympias, his mother, were private in nature—is difficult to believe, however, for such regularity would have entailed the establishment of a specialized information-transmitting system, of which there is no trace in the sources. Rarely if ever, furthermore, is there an explicit mention of a written missive of any kind sent to a commander in the field, or conversely of a subordinate commander addressing a written report to Alexander. Assuming subordinate commanders to have operated under the king's direct control for the most part—they often shared his tent—and taking into consideration the extreme difficulty of communications between mobile headquarters in the field, this is not surprising; and yet one cannot help but wonder.

It may be possible to draw similar conclusions from the fact that, out of several hundred Roman army documents preserved on papyri in Egypt, not a single one deals with intelligence or operational matters—though again it cannot be overlooked that there was little or no campaigning in Egypt after the time of the emperor Augustus, from whose reign the earliest extant documents are dated. What we do have are unit records of all kinds dealing with day-to-day garrison life: unit rosters, either complete or partial; special lists for guard duty or fatigues or the like; morning reports (*acta diurna*) on the number of men in a unit, with officers listed separately; monthly and annual strength reports; and correspondence concerning pay, promotion, discipline, and supplies. Units were apparently required to keep up regular journals. There also existed itineraria, standardized handbooks concerning all kinds of matters; the only ones that have come down to us consist of lists of feast days to be observed.[45] Clearly an army whose system of internal record-keeping was as sophisticated as this should have had no difficulty whatsoever in using written missives to plan, direct, and monitor operations in the field. Of such missives, however, there simply is no trace. The most that the sources attest to are sealed orders concerning destination that Caesar could have issued (but did not) to the fleet commanders before embarking from Sicily for Africa in 46 B.C.[46]

Everything considered, the organization and functioning of Roman army headquarters on campaign remains a mystery to us. Historians have identified dozens of different officers, indicating an elaborate and precise division of labor, but none who under modern practice would have been included in the intelligence or operations departments.[47] Nor are the literary sources of much help: it is only on the rarest of instances that we get a glimpse of the staff at work. Thus Appianus, writing early in the second century A.D. and describing Scipio's triumph three hundred years before, notes that the victorious commander was surrounded by "young men his own relatives . . . [and] those who had served him as secretaries, aides, and armor bearers."[48] Writing at the time of the emperor Claudius, Onasander advised the general to select his counselors either from among men accompanying the army specifically for the purpose or else from among "his most respected commanders." All that he has to say concerning their functions, however, is that "it is not safe that the opinions of one single man on his sole judgement should be adopted,"[49] presumably indicating the existence of councils of war in some form.[50] Other sources still identify the *praefecti fabrum*, enigmatic figures who may have acted as trusted couriers for top-priority long-distance messages,[51] and the *contubernales*, or tent companions, young men of good family taken along by the commander on a personal basis in order to enable them to serve their military apprenticeship.[52] That was all; or was it?

From Cicero's correspondence and the *Corpus Caesarianum* some modern authors have attempted to reconstruct the existence of a system of regular reports by subordinate commanders to the commander in chief and from the latter to the government at home. Cicero, however, during his governorship of Cilicia only sent private letters home, on one occasion even leaving it to his friend Atticus to decide whether or not to submit them to the Senate.[53] Caesar's correspondence with his subordinate commanders in Gaul was mainly limited to the winter season, which as a politician he spent weaving intrigues in Italy,[54] or else to the announcement of some success by a lieutenant on a "detached" mission. In the sources there is little trace of a regular reporting system, much less of a systematic use of written orders and operational staff work; such a situation made it possible for Pompey to occupy huge tracts of land in the Middle East without authorization from the Senate. Let it be noted, too, that a regular relay system for transmitting reports over long distances, the above-mentioned *cursus publicus*, was not established until the time when the empire had ceased to expand and its frontiers became stationary—until the time, in other words, when mobile offensive warfare for the most part had given way to day-to-day security and administration.[55]

Our knowledge of the intelligence organization of the Roman army at the time of its greatest military efficiency, during the late

Republic and early Principate, is equally fragmentary. The use of spies is occasionally mentioned, but since these things were as secret then as they are today the ones explicitly mentioned were almost invariably directed against the Romans.[56] Information from local inhabitants was as unreliable as it was important, and could, when a commander misjudged his sources, lead to the kind of disaster that overtook Crassus in Mesopotamia.[57] During the war that Caesar fought in Spain (49 B.C.) and undoubtedly in many other wars too, numerous deserters passed between the two sides and brought information along.[58] Cicero in Cilicia had *praesidia*,[59] and Caesar in Gaul *speculatores*,[60] both are perhaps best described as lookouts stationed or sent out to report on enemy moves, and the *speculatores* were treated as spies when caught.[61] Beyond this, both Cicero and Caesar sometimes formed massive cavalry vanguards of mounted troops specifically charged with following the enemy and reporting on his movements.[62] That all these different categories of troops came under their own commanders, at least for administrative purposes, may well be believed, but the sources are silent even on this. On the other hand, the existence of an "intelligence" department, responsible for systematically gathering and analyzing information, is nowhere mentioned and is indeed made unlikely by the fact that Caesar, like other commanders for millennia after him, habitually interrogated deserters, prisoners, and spies in person.[63]

What evidence survives, then, points to the conclusion that the elaborate staff organization in existence was responsible mainly for matters that, under modern practice, would belong to the province of the adjutant general, the paymaster, and often the quartermaster[64]—the reason, presumably, being precisely that these functions could be reduced to rules, exercised more or less on a routine basis and without resort to long-range communications between mobile headquarters. On the other hand, operational intelligence (including, often enough, the actual gathering of information by riding ahead and gazing at the enemy) and planning were carried out largely by the commander in chief aided by his secretaries and whatever councils of war he cared to call, a procedure whose persistence into the eighteenth century is itself proof that a specialized planning staff did not exist. In other words, the staffs that can be traced dealt with function-related matters above all. Alexander in his tent before Gaugamela and Caesar in his at Ruspina did their tactical planning in splendid isolation and then put their schemes, ready made, to their assembled senior commanders.

The millennium after the fall of the Roman Empire in the West (A.D. 476) was certainly not lacking in revolutions in warfare. Frankish axmen and Norman knights, English longbowmen and Genoese arbalesters, Swiss pikemen and Spanish sword-and-buckle men, followed each other in a bewildering kaleidoscope of weapons, tactics, and formations, only to be overtaken, and finally swept away, by the invention of gunpowder. Against the background of these changes, it is a remarkable fact that the technology of command changed not at all while armies' level of organization precipitously declined. Medieval armies were normally small, impermanent, and made up either of knights serving to meet their feudal obligations or, later, of mercenaries taking their place. Literacy was rarer than it had been in ancient times and the armies themselves were organized (to the extent that they were organized at all) on the basis of personal rather than political relationships. Under such conditions the only staffs that can be traced consisted of the princes' private households, which were put, so to speak, on a war footing.[65] A prince going on campaign would be surrounded by his principal vassals, whose advice he might seek in frequent councils of war, and by a few officials whose (original) functions may best be understood from their titles—the seneschal responsible for justice, the marshal who kept order in the ranks, and the constable or second in command. To the constable, the most important of the officials, the prince might sometimes delegate part of his own functions, such as the granting of permission to go on private raids.[66] What written staff work can be traced is concerned almost exclusively with questions of military law, logistics, and personnel, including above all pay, which in England was the responsibility of the Royal Wardrobe.[67] Of specialized departments dealing with intelligence and operations, on the other hand, there is no trace.

When staffs started reemerging from the darkness of the Middle Ages, toward the end of the sixteenth century, many of the conditions governing their employment in earlier periods still prevailed. The speed at which information could travel was still limited to that of man and horse, and the effectiveness of long-distance communications had, if anything, declined, owing to the deterioration in many places of stable government. Nothing new had been added to the methods for gathering intelligence,[68] nor were armies even now able to inflict damage on each other except when well within eyesight. The most important problem confronting them still remained how to exist at all, and it was to deal with this problem that the staffs of the period were clearly organized.

The staffs of the commanders Maurice of Nassau, Gustavus Adolphus, Wallenstein, and Cromwell were, from what we can glean of them, remarkably similar organizations, indicating a common origin.[69] All consisted essentially of a number of specialists, such as the provision master, wagon master (responsible for keeping the trains in order during the march), provost marshal, judge advocate, treasurer, and "enforcer" (*Generalbewaltiger*), an officer whose job it was to extract contributions from the country traversed and who thus exercised an early form of military government, together with their assistants. Some armies, notably the imperial Austrian one, also had a roadmaster in charge of the guides, who, in the absence of detailed maps, had to be locally recruited and kept honest by means of threats and promises. Then there was the adjutant general, responsible for officer personnel, and the commanders of the specialized troops—artillery, engineers, and sometimes cavalry as well. Such lesser figures as surgeons, soothsayers, and executioners completed the colorful picture.

Seventeenth-century headquarters did include one officer whose duties were destined to have a great future: this was the quartermaster, known in French as the *maréchal de camp*. Originally a petty naval officer responsible for the orderly loading of ships' holds,[70] the quartermaster in his military capacity is first mentioned in 1600 and had assumed the rank of "quartermaster general" by 1701. His duties, as the title implies, consisted of riding ahead of the army each marching day in order to select a suitable place for a camp, which he then proceeded to stake out by means of poles and ropes. These duties necessitated some knowledge of mathematics as well as the assistance of a small staff; and it was from this staff that the modern general staff was born.

Perhaps the best description of the duties of an eighteenth-century quartermaster general is provided by Pierre Bourcet in his celebrated work, *Principes de la Guerre des Montagnes.*[71] His first task is to reconnoiter the country ahead of the army, not merely in the manner of guides but "militarily," that is, taking into account all the possibilities and obstacles that it might present for marching and for battle. Riding ahead of the army in this capacity, the quartermaster general will naturally be entrusted with intelligence work, interrogating local inhabitants and deserters as well as intercepting friendly patrols on their way back from observing the enemy. He is, Bourcet says, responsible for coordinating all the correspondence addressed by members of the army to the commanding general (who in turn will have his hands full corresponding with the minister of war and with the governments of the countries in whose territories he operates) and also for preparing all marching orders and *ordres de bataille.* Finally, it is for him to inform the sutlers of the army's movements, its logistic requirements, the location of its magazines, and so on. To perform all these duties he must have a thorough knowledge not merely of geometry, topography, and the art of war but also of the idiosyncrasies of each commanding general and of the various arms whose characteristics, especially in regard to marches, may differ considerably from those of the army as a whole. To carry out his "innumerable duties" Bourcet suggests that the quartermaster general be furnished with all of four assistants. This number, he adds, should suffice, provided they are not taken away from him and put to other tasks.

The good quartermaster general, says Frederick the Great, "cannot fail to make his fortune, since he will gain, by practice, all the skills needed by an army general . . . the only exception is formed by the operational plans, but even these he will witness carried out, and will therefore be able to prepare them, provided he is possessed of good judgment."[72] None of this prevented him from disgracing his own quartermaster general, the famous Graf von Schmettau.

As Bourcet indicates, the staff working under the quartermaster general's direction was both modest and impermanent, being always in danger of falling victim to the commander in chief's parsimony; indeed, the second recorded use of the term in English (1781) has it that "the staff proper exists only in war."[73] The one established by Frederick the Great in the winter of 1756–57 (that is, after a summer of campaigning was already over; the king had another staff during the War of the Austrian Succession in 1740–1748, but it was later disbanded) consisted of the quartermaster general himself, a quartermaster general lieutenant, and four quartermaster lieutenants.[74] Of these officers the first was disgraced, the second killed soon after the battle of Prague in the summer of 1757. Successors, apparently, were never appointed, and the king following this brief experiment managed to do without them for the remainder of the war. It was only in 1768, when writing his *Military Testament,* that Frederick once again woke up to the usefulness of having a quartermaster general. He now suggested that the latter's staff should consist of one quartermaster, one quartermaster lieutenant, and five lieutenants attached to serve any useful purpose that might come to hand, a grand total of seven officers—this in an army sixty thousand men strong.

To select one historical quartermaster general, Marlborough's burly William Cadogan, he is found writing down his master's strategic plans; riding out to take up contact with the approaching allied imperial Austrian army under Prince Eugene; supervising the operations of a wing of the army in battle, not actually commanding himself but acting as the duke's high-powered messenger (when other messengers had failed, as happened at Ramilles in 1706: Orkney at the head of the right wing disregarded an order to fall back) and serving as his "eye"; reconnoitering a ford across a river to see whether it was passable; commanding the army in its winter quarters while Marlborough was away in England; commanding a strong vanguard charged with the task of improving roads, establishing bridges, and seizing a bridgehead across a river; leading the same vanguard into an (unforeseen, it is true) battle; commanding convoys, loaded with siege material, on their way past the French lines toward the town of Lille in 1709—all this in addition to discharging the normal quartermaster functions of planning marches, fixing the order of march, and locating camps and staking them out. Truly he was a man for all seasons, though on the whole perhaps more at home on horseback than behind a writing desk.[75]

The second key figure in any eighteenth-century headquarters—disregarding for the moment the various technical experts enumerated above—was the commander's secretary, a civilian who would normally be assisted by a few clerks. Originally appointed to assist the commander in his correspondence, the secretary's role expanded as more and more staff work came to be done in writing. Such secretaries as Marlborough's Adam Cardonnel, Frederick II's Eichel, and Ferdinand of Brunswick's Christian von Westphalen were normally civilian experts of long standing, hardly ever serving as soldiers; indeed, it was precisely the fact that they did not form part of the army that enabled them to follow their own private generals over the years.

The distribution of business among commander in chief, private secretary, and quartermaster general was nowhere laid down in regulations but varied in accordance with custom, circumstances, and the interplay of the personalities involved. An aggressive, fast-acting commander like Frederick II might well try to concentrate everything—intelligence, planning, operations, staff work—in his own hands, relying on his secretariat simply as a technical organ responsible for taking down his orders and allowing nobody to share his thoughts.[76] A commander who, for one reason or another, wished to postpone or evade responsibility might well bypass both secretary and quartermaster general and call his senior officers to frequent councils of war, which according to Prince Eugene could always be depended upon to decide to do nothing. Ferdinand of Brunswick (commander of the Hanoverian army during the Seven Years War) seems to have depended to an unusual degree on his secretary, the lawyer Westphalen, to whom he addressed as many as eight written messages a day and with whom he engaged in detailed games of question and answer ("contingency planning") as part of an attempt to guess the enemy's intentions.[77] De Broglie and his quartermaster general, the ambitious Pierre Bourcet, exchanged endless memoranda on all that the enemy, and they themselves, might or might not do.[78] Frederick's Eichel, by contrast, was sent on numerous special missions and also took a large hand in running the army, but did not share any of his master's operational plans. As might be expected, the more important the secretary, the fewer and more narrowly circumscribed the duties of the quartermaster general, and vice versa.[79]

Thus, eighteenth-century staffs were clearly organs in transition. On the one hand, there persisted the age-old tendency to concentrate all intelligence and operational matters in the hands of the commander in chief, assisted by a secretary (who was neither a military expert nor a member of the army, but rather a part of the boss's private household, the equivalent of the modern office manager) and by such councils of war as he cared to summon. On the other hand, there were in the quartermaster general's duties elements that made his office capable of almost infinite expansion; his mission of riding ahead of the army—to the place where enemy intelligence was naturally easiest to procure—and his knowledge of mathematics, considered to be the key to all warfare, worked in his favor. Regardless of whether it was the secretary or the quartermaster general whose functions were the more important in any given army, more and more staff work, including in particular personnel, logistics, and sometimes also operational contingency planning, now came to be done in writing. Written *ordres de bataille*,[80] marching orders,[81] and standing letters of instruction played an increasingly prominent role. More and more frequently, too, outposts transmitted their reports in writing.[82] Much of this was still done on an ad hoc basis, however. As many contemporary writings on what qualities a quartermaster general must have reveal, it was still the man, not the organization, that counted. A further indication of the unsettled state of things is the fact that no staff colleges were set up except on an experimental basis,[83] and that the publication of the first staff manual had to wait until the French Revolution.[84]

The expansion of paperwork made itself felt on the strategic plane of warfare also. Already in the sixteenth century, the incipient shift from feudal to absolutist and bureaucratic forms of government meant that the personal prowess of a ruler in war diminished in importance. Sovereign princes accordingly began to relinquish personal command, choosing instead to appoint lieutenant-generals under various titles and surrounding them by what were often closely drafted letters of instruction.[85] The separation between sovereign and commander in chief made the institution of a regular correspondence between them necessary, thus contributing to the rise of royal mail services. The spread of new administrative techniques, including decimal arithmetic, logarithms, and double-entry bookkeeping, enabled reformers such as Louvois in France to impose an unprecedented degree of central control over armies widely separated in space.[86] The upshot was that, by the middle of the eighteenth century, de Broglie in Germany was writing to Versailles twice a day, taking about a fortnight to receive a reply. Ferdinand of Brunswick went so far as to write Frederick II four times a day, and was gently admonished to ease the flood. Since the speed with which messages were transmitted over long distances had increased hardly at all, such close control meant that generals were bound hand and foot; as Schlieffen put it, they were not really authorized to make war at all, but merely to capture a province or lay siege to a town.[87] As had happened in the Roman Empire also, the attempt to exercise such long-range supervision inevitably acted as a strong brake on operations. It was one reason why strategy ran into a rut from which it took Napoleon to get it out again.

To sum up the history of military staffs over two thousand years of Stone Age command is a difficult task indeed. From the evidence that has survived, it appears that such staffs were originally designed mainly in order to relieve commanders of administrative detail and the day-to-day running of armies, and that such matters were taken care of by more or less specialized officers, in accordance with fixed rules and in writing, whenever and wherever armies were large or permanent. Also present from the earliest times on were specialist commanders, who were often made to wear double hats and advise their superiors on the use of their troops. On the other hand, the much greater uncertainty associated with operations, and the difficulty of reducing it to a set of rules, help explain why the modern general staff was so slow to develop; as late as the middle of the eighteenth century it was an open question as to whether its functions should be carried out by the traditional council of war, by the commander's secretary, by the quartermaster general, or simply in the commander's head. While the use of written general staff work certainly increased from about 1500 on, the organization to deal with it only developed in fits and starts. The growing use of written letters of instruction and the institution of a regular correspondence between courts and their commanders in the field enabled governments to impose strict controls on strategy, but only at the price of reducing it essentially to trivia. On the tactical level, moreover, communications had not improved a bit since Roman times. As a result, the main action was still almost invariably confined to the commander's own place; and it is to the place of the commander in action that I next turn.

THE CONDUCT OF BATTLE

Surprisingly, in view of the endless variety of weapons and tactics during the ages, the factors that have determined the way tactical command is exercised are few and easy to identify. The subdivision (or lack of it) of the army into units and the existence of a proper chain of superior and subordinate commanders subject to some kind of discipline; the nature of the available communications technology, including above all the constraints that it imposed; the nature of the predominant weapons in use (shock versus missile power); and, finally, the ethics of the period and its view of the commander's proper functions—these factors, in their manifold interactions and combinations, have determined the scope and effectiveness of tactical command from the beginning of recorded history to the present day.

Greek phalanxes were large bodies of heavily armed infantrymen. Even before 400 B.C. they occasionally numbered as many as ten thousand men and they fought eight deep, so that the front of an army took up approximately three-quarters of a mile. Packed closely together and sandwiched front and rear by the best available troops, the phalanx was designed not merely to maximize striking power but also to keep the half-trained citizen-soldiers under physical control. Though an elaborate hierarchy of subunits and a chain of command did exist, especially in the Spartan army,[88] on no occasion was any of these units seen to be doing anything on its own; this and the fact that they apparently possessed neither flags nor standards to symbolize their permanent identity suggest that their tactical importance was not great.[89] Given the rudimentary nature of the acoustical signals that formed the sole form of battlefield communication, the only way in which such a force could be controlled at all was to have it operate in solid blocks.[90] This in turn meant that the number of things it could do was rather limited: open ranks, close ranks, forward march, perhaps a few simple evolutions. To exercise any form of control, in other words, it was necessary to reduce the number of functions almost to the vanishing point.

A Greek commander going into battle first had to reconnoiter the terrain, which he did either by riding over it when the enemy was still at a distance or else by taking up a position on top of some convenient hill and observing. He would then try to determine the enemy's order of battle, which could usually be done by direct observation also. His next step was to decide on the order, from right to left, in which the various formations and contingents were to fight, a critical decision since it could hardly ever be changed during the battle itself. It was possible to make the phalanx wider or deeper than usual, but since the various forces often had their own traditions in this respect the decision belonged to the commander only to a limited extent. In the absence of good battlefield communications, it was vital to hold a meeting of the principal subordinate officers prior to action in order to create a shared base of knowledge and agree on a common plan—the inability to do so constituting one of the worst effects of being taken by surprise. After their meeting the officers rejoined their units, and the signal for the battle to begin was given by acoustical means so as to reach the whole army simultaneously. The two forces would then march, or rush, upon each other. Since the first clash almost always decided the issue, the use of reserves, in the sense of a separate force kept under the commander's own hand, was all but unknown. Once the armies had met and were, as the saying went, "pushing shield to shield," there was nothing more a commander could do; so he picked up his own shield and joined in the fray.[91] Of an attempt to coordinate various movements, much less to exercise control or change dispositions during the engagement itself, there could be no question whatsoever.

The ease with which Greek forces, owing to their small size and compact formation, were controlled, and the fact that control at all times was neither necessary nor possible, should not be taken as an indication that the commander's activities were of no consequence. Instead, precisely because he was always fully visible to his men, marching in their midst and fighting in their ranks, the motivating functions he exercised were supremely important. The sacrifice, review, and speech held before the battle; the example set during it; the trophy erected after it—all these were morale-building factors that, in modern armies, are either carried out at one remove by means of mass communications or else delegated to subordinate commanders. Their true significance is perhaps best shown by the fact that an army whose commander was killed in action could still conquer, as happened for example at Mantinea II in 361 B.C., but one deserted by its commander, as Darius' forces twice were, was irretrievably lost.

Early in the fourth century B.C. a refinement was introduced into this tactical system. Greek armies now started outflanking each other, first by accident and then by design. To do this commanders placed themselves at the head of a picked body of troops on the right wing, broke through the enemy's normally weak left, and then ordered their forces to wheel through ninety degrees so as to take the rest of the enemy in flank. The mechanics of this move are nowhere explained, but given disciplined troops two simple acoustical signals, one to halt the advance and dress ranks and one to make the force turn around, must have sufficed. By carrying out such a move, moreover, commanders often sacrificed control over their own left wing; at Coronea (394 B.C.) the Spartan commander, Agesilaos, only heard of the defeat of his left when "a man" (not, interestingly, a specialized messenger) reached him in the midst of a ceremony in which he was being crowned victor by the troops of his own right wing.[92]

Though Greek warfare became much more sophisticated during the two centuries following Coronea, incorporating various types of light infantry with cavalry and elephants in addition to the traditional phalanx, the basic dilemma confronting the commander remained the same. To have the greatest possible effect he had to position himself at the decisive point; standing at the decisive point, however, often meant losing all control over the rest of the battle even when fronts were as small as one or two miles. Forced to make a choice, most commanders followed Agesilaos' example by opting for the first alternative, preferring to exercise some control over some of their forces than trying to command all of them to no effect at all. At Mantinea II the victorious Theban commanders, Philopides and Epaminondas, both fought at the head of their decisive wing (in this case, the left) and both were killed without apparently having issued any orders to the army as a whole after the original deployment and signal for the battle to begin.[93] Both at the Granicus and at Issus, Alexander's role, apart from the usual personal reconnaissance and deployment of his forces, consisted of first giving the signal to attack and then looking out for some break to appear in the Persian line. Once the break appeared he stormed into it at the head of his companion cavalry, fought with great gusto, and was wounded on both occasions. That not even Alexander could do this and at the same time control the ten units forming part of his own right wing, much less the six comprising Parmenion's on the left, hardly requires saying; indeed, the very number of these units (the large "span of control," to use modern terminology) is itself a powerful argument against their being subject to any kind of close tactical control in battle.

Hellenistic battles generally followed a similar pattern. The commander in chief put on his armor—a significant act that helps put his role in perspective—and posted himself on what he hoped would be the decisive wing, normally but not necessarily the right. Though possibly no longer fighting in person (none of Alexander's successors is said to have been wounded during a major battle), these commanders nevertheless exercised direct control not only over the army as a whole but also over their own wing and, further down the ladder of command, over their companion cavalry, modeled after Alexander's. The other wing was invariably given to some experienced cavalry commander.[94] A council of war was usually held, in which the subordinate commanders received their instructions before being sent back to their units. From this point on, however, they were largely on their own. One signal would start the struggle of the light troops and elephants, another recall them so that the main business of the day could get under way. The commander in chief then stormed forward at the head of his wing in an attempt to force a decision. Sometimes a messenger would reach him from the other wing (where the same process would be taking place, only in reverse) warning him that it was in trouble, and the commander might then halt his troops by bugle and go to his subordinate's aid.[95] That he tried to control the army as a whole during the charge is nowhere asserted. On several occasions, in fact, Hellenistic commanders rode off the battlefield after having gained the upper hand in their own wing, thus giving the best possible proof of their concern, or lack of it, for the rest of their armies and incidentally losing the battles.[96]

There were, it is true, exceptions to this pattern. At Gaugamela, Alexander, standing on a low hill that overlooked the otherwise perfectly flat terrain, at first coolly fed in one unit after another to head off an attempted Persian outflanking movement on his right. Even when he finally did charge, he remained, if not in actual control, at least sufficiently aware of developments elsewhere on the battlefield to first refuse and then answer a call for help from Parmenion on the left.[97] Antigonus at Gabiene (316 B.C.) was unique in that he gave the decisive wing to his son Demetrios to lead, thus freeing himself to command the army as a whole and to direct a successful outflanking movement.[98] Yet even Antigonus ended up by leading a cavalry charge against Eumenes' phalanx. Tied to his own wing of the army, a commander was not free to move across the battlefield; at most, a commander whose wing had been defeated might extricate himself and renew the fight elsewhere, as did Eumenes at Gabiene and Ptolemy at Raphia.[99] On the whole, the functions of a Hellenistic commander in battle can be summed up as follows: deploy your forces according to what you can see of the enemy and of the terrain, place yourself at what you hope will be the decisive wing, and storm forward at the right moment, but never by any means go too far in case somebody else might cry out for help.

If early Greek commanders tried to solve the problem of control by limiting the number of units and functions that could be controlled (that is, by building a single, compact, and therefore unwieldy phalanx) and subsequent commanders by positioning themselves at the head of the decisive wing and thus limiting control to part of the army, Roman ones arrived at an extraordinarily effective solution by devising formations that could, and did, fight without need for overall direction. Too much has been written concerning the legion's checkerboard formation for a detailed account to be necessary here. For our purpose, the outstanding fact is that the legion was organized into compact, permanent units—century, maniple, or cohort, according to the period in question—each of which had its own commander, bugler, and standard.[100] The latter was no improvised contraption for issuing ad hoc signals but a permanent fixture, of symbolic as well as practical use, which made it possible to issue many different orders.[101] The combination of proper training, bugles, and standards made it possible first to call the men's attention and then to issue the exact order.[102]

Even more crucial than the technical means that enabled subordinate commanders to exercise proper control over their men was the checkerboard formation itself. By leaving open room for maneuver and allowing the centurions to see each other's units, the formation enabled them to come to each other's aid. There existed a well-rehearsed repertoire of tactical moves from the *cuneus* (wedge) to the *sera* (saw), capable of being carried out at a moment's notice and without further ado. Consequently, as has been remarked, Roman legions in battle scarcely needed a commander in order to gain victory; time and again (Zama, Cynoscephalae, Thermopylae, Magnesia, and Caesar's battle against the Belgians are good examples) the sources mention centurions, or else military tribunes, field-grade officers all, who "knew what to do" and "judging on the spur of the moment" came to their comrades' aid, or closed a legion's shattered ranks, or took a number of maniples and, apparently acting on their own initiative, carried out an outflanking movement. In most of these cases (Thermopylae was an exception; there the officer in question was none other than Cato, serving as a military tribune, who later boasted that whoever saw him on that day would agree that Rome owed more to him than he to her), not even the names of these people have survived, which may perhaps be taken as a further indication that their moves did not depend on orders from the commander in chief.

A point to be noted in this connection is that in no recorded case were these movements carried out by a legion as such. As Delbrück wrote, the legion was an administrative unit, not a tactical one; in any case, for it to move in any direction but forward and backward while keeping its checkerboard formation would have been all but impossible.[103] It was consequently the subordinate units, not the legion as a whole, that carried out tactical movements, and again their large number—sixty centuries, thirty maniples, and later ten cohorts—is a powerful argument against their being subject to any close control by the legion commander.[104] The latter's relatively low importance is also brought out by the example of Caecina's operations in Germany in A.D. 15. Though he had with him at least two legions, it was the tribunes and the centurions whom the commander in chief addressed when preparing to fight a battle.[105]

The Roman legion's solution to the problem of battlefield control, then, was to simplify it by means of standardized tactical drill coupled with a deployment that gave subordinate commanders at the lowest levels the means, as well as the opportunity, of exercising their own initiative and supporting each other. The two factors together, coupled with the fact that he was not in direct charge of any subordinate unit (except possibly a small bodyguard), untied the hands of the commander in chief; for the first time he was capable of free movement around the battlefield.[106] Whereas Roman commanders in the third century B.C. had stood on the wings and fought hand to hand in the manner of their Greek counterparts,[107] Scipio Africanus no longer did so.[108] Scipio Aemilianus in 146 B.C. is described by Polybius as touring the battlefield in the company of three shield-bearers, showing himself, assessing the situation, and taking advantage of whatever opportunities presented themselves locally.[109] Dressed in a red toga that clearly marked his location and incidentally suggests that he did not expect to be in serious personal danger, Caesar in his battle against the Belgians did the same.[110]

It would be possible to go on adducing examples forever, but a single one will suffice here. One of the best instances of battlefield command in the ancient world left to us is the battle of Ruspina (47 B.C.) when Caesar faced the Pompeians under Labienus in Africa. Caesar, marching out from camp over perfectly flat terrain, was informed by his scouts that the enemy was in sight. At the same moment a cloud of dust in the distance also signified their presence. He immediately rode ahead with a small party, sighted the enemy, and ordered a single line of battle (he did not have enough forces to keep a reserve) to be formed. He next instructed—by what means we are not told—the wings to take care not to be enveloped, a necessary precaution since that was just what the enemy with his superior cavalry proceeded to do. As the two armies came closer together, Caesar, from the point he was stationed at (Labienus at this juncture was riding up and down his front, encouraging his own men and coming close enough to Caesar's not merely to exchange taunts with them but to get his horse killed), "had the order passed down the ranks" that no soldier should advance more than four feet in front of the standards. After some skirmishing on both flanks, the enemy by virtue of his superior numbers was able to surround Caesar's army. In response Caesar with his standards ordered every alternate cohort to turn about, so that half his force now faced the rear, as he did himself. With a volley of missiles, which must have been delivered upon a signal from the commander in chief, Caesar's troops broke through the encircling ring of enemy soldiers. Still well in hand, they retired to find that their comrades behind had scattered the enemy also. Deciding to call it a day, Caesar started marching back to camp while still maintaining battle formation.[111]

The use of permanent, well-organized, integrated units; an efficient system of tactical communications at the lowest level, that of the century, maniple, and cohort; a deployment that enabled subordinate commanders to support each other and to make use of their initiative; and the consequent freedom enjoyed by the commander in chief—such were the elements of the tactical command system that for hundreds of years turned the legions into the symbol of victory in the field. Also of great importance was the standardized repertoire of tactical movements carried out by the various units, though in this case it is possible to argue that the very element that contributed to success also limited the legion's effectiveness when it came to fighting in unfamiliar terrain such as the deserts of Persia or the forests of Germany. Furthermore, the equation can also be turned around. It was precisely the stability and iron discipline of the Roman army as a whole that made tactical flexibility and the exercise of initiative at the lowest level possible. Only under conditions of long-term stability, coupled perhaps with a streak of conservatism, was it possible to create a body of officers who, as one author puts it, acted with that "impersonal efficiency" characteristic of the Romans, knew what to do without having to be told, and were capable of passing that knowledge down to the next generation.

Long-term political and organizational stability, however, was precisely what the Middle Ages lacked most. For most of Western Europe invasion was followed by invasion, one private war by another. Such large political structures as were established—for example, under Charlemagne—were usually short-lived and in any case unable to impose their control over the outlying provinces. The size of armies underwent a dramatic decline. Except possibly when the Crusaders marched through the Holy Land under unusually difficult circumstances, permanent units were almost unheard of until France's Charles VII started rebuilding them in the middle of the fifteenth century. Training, which the Greeks and Romans had carried out in organized units, now came to consist almost exclusively of individual exercises in arms, whether extending over a lifetime, as in the case of knights, or amounting to hardly anything at all, as in the case of their peasant following. Finally, there was the ethos of the period; whereas Hellenistic and Roman commanders were explicitly warned not to involve themselves in hand-to-hand combat,[112] similar behavior was unthinkable to medieval commanders who were essentially knights with exceptionally large followings. For them to fight constituted the supreme honor, the crowning glory of their existence as knights; to avoid fighting was to put both their personal and political standing at risk.

Medieval armies entering battle were arrayed on feudal principles, each knight gathering his followers under his own banner and in turn following that of his immediate lord. The commander in chief's normal place was right in the center, his location clearly marked by a banner larger than the rest and serving to attract danger to his person rather than as proof of its absence, as had been the case in Caesar's day.[113] Around him were his household knights—Harold's *Huyscarles,* Philip Augustus' *sergents*—and possibly also a few important barons. In well-organized armies, such as those of the Templars, these bodyguards were forbidden to leave their banner. This special restriction was often resented; it set the household knights apart from their brethren, who were free to hack away at any enemy they chose. In the absence of real-time battlefield communications it was very important to hold a preliminary council of war so as to create at least some common basis for action. A trumpet signal was given—the army contingents furnished by the various places normally included trumpeters on the scale of about one per one hundred men[114]—and the two sides charged each other. Since the army's organization was based almost entirely on personal bonds, and since the location of the opposing commanders in chief was clearly marked, it made sense for the two of them to fight each other. This happened at the very first recorded Frankish cavalry charge during the Saxon War of 626, when Clothar "put spurs to his horse and crossed the stream [the Weser], all the Franks following him and swimming through the water" to charge the Saxon leader Bertwald and kill him.[115] At Legnano in 1176 and at Bouvins in 1214, Emperor Frederick I and King Philip II of France, respectively, led charges and barely escaped with their lives.

The primitiveness of medieval battlefield command was not primarily due, it would seem, to any kind of technical backwardness. Even the most technically backward of warriors, such as the sixth-century Franks described in the *Strategicon,* must have been capable of using trumpets and banners and for all we know did so freely. The difficulty consisted rather in the unstable organization of these armies and the ethos of the period. For the exercise of command to be possible there must be somebody to obey orders; medieval armies, however, were made up purely of officers, or perhaps one should say that their most salient characteristic was precisely that the distinction between officers whose function is to lead or direct and men whose job is to kill and be killed was not recognized. Also, battles between knights were based purely on shock. Like the fights of earlier Greek phalanxes, they were liable to be decided at the first clash if not before (one side might turn and run) or else the struggling mass of men and horses would become utterly uncontrollable. Even if they had wanted to—and there are few signs that they did— there was no way in which medieval commanders could direct a battle once they had joined it. To fight in person and thus serve a moral function was the only thing to do.

Around the basic theme of clumps of knights hacking away at each other there were many possible variations. Perhaps the simplest was to have the three "battles" (vanguard, main body, rearguard) that invariably made up medieval armies fight not simultaneously, in line, but in succession as they arrived on the field. This must often have happened by accident and was, it seems, turned into a deliberate system by the semi-permanent, and highly efficient, armies of the First Crusade in Palestine. If the chronicles that serve as our sources concerning the battles of Antioch (three of them, in 1097 and 1098), Ramla (1101), Ramla II (1102), and Askalon (1105) make any sense at all, it would seem that the commander in chief invariably led the third and last division, and thus was able first to watch the vanguard engage, then to send the main body to its support, and finally to charge with his own rearguard at whatever point he thought most useful.[116]

Another type of variation was created when light troops (often mercenaries) took part in the battle, in which case it was necessary first to order them into action and then to recall them by some signal so that the knights could come to grips with each other. Such moves, requiring properly coordinated use of bugles and/or flags, were apparently carried out most successfully in 1066 at Hastings[117] and at

Arsouf in 1191, less so at Crecy in 1346 where the French knights tried to ride roughshod over their own retreating crossbowmen. As this last example shows, it was organization and discipline, not technology, that formed the critical limiting factors.

When the English in the fourteenth century introduced the longbow, shock was replaced by missile power as the decisive element in battle. In such battles the commander inevitably stood well back, if only because he was a knight himself and did not carry the despised bow. Consequently both Crecy and Poitiers witnessed the respective English commanders, King Edward III and the Black Prince, overlooking the field from a hill in the rear and communicating by messenger[118] with the commanders of the bowmen below.[119] Yet even these two, in the final resort, were nothing if not good knights; the Black Prince, and after him Henry V at Agincourt in 1415, ended up by personally charging the French, as knights should.[120]

This last example makes it clear that the nature of tactics is one crucial variant that helps determine the methods of battlefield command. The greater the reliance on shock, the shorter the duration of the engagement and the less subject to overall control it was; the more important the missile power, the easier it was for the commander to stand back at some point (think, for example, of Saladin, a non-Western commander with none of the knight's ethos, plucking his beard on the hill near Hattin in 1187) and direct his forces to engage or disengage. Since cavalry and shock action remained, by and large, the decisive and most prestigious battle-winning factors until the middle of the seventeenth century, it is not surprising that the knightly ethos prevailed and that many commanders continued to fight in person. Even at the time of Breitenfeld (1631) and Lutzen (1632), Gustavus Adolphus, as great a commander as any, is found storming forward at the head of his cavalry on the right wing in the manner of some Hellenistic king, acting as a kind of mobile fire guard and helping to raise morale at whatever point he made his appearance. Appropriately enough, he was killed as he rode, accompanied by a mere two followers, way ahead of his troops on a rescue mission to his hard-pressed left.[121]

Leading cavalry charges in the manner of Gustavus or his opponent, Pappenheim, was not the only method of conducting a battle open to early modern commanders in chief. Beginning in the sixteenth century, portable firearms began to play an increasingly important tactical role. At first harquebusiers and musketeers were employed with pikemen in the same tactical units, but the proportion of the latter gradually fell until the invention of the bayonet around 1660 combined fire with cold steel in the same weapon and caused the harquebus and pike to disappear altogether. With the multiplication of firearms, drill—an innovation of the late sixteenth century—became necessary in order to employ the new weapons to the greatest possible effect and prevent bodies of troops from firing upon each other. This in turn required tactical units better organized and disciplined than any that Europe had seen since the fall of Rome, and by the seventeenth century these were in fact everywhere being set up: companies, battalions, and regiments made their appearance in that order, each with its commander, second in command, trumpeters, and standard bearers (ensigns). To distinguish all these units from each other as well as from the enemy, gaudy uniforms were adopted around 1660 and not discarded until breechloading weapons and an open order of battle made camouflage both possible and essential some two centuries later. During the fifteenth century, drums, useful in carrying out the movements of drill, were added to the traditional signaling devices. Since permanent units larger than the regiment did not exist but had to be improvised as the occasion might demand, *ordres de bataille* became all-important, contributing in turn to the increase in the role of staff work.

The effects of all these changes on the way command was exercised were far reaching. Whereas medieval officers had simply been fighting men more brainy or brawny than the rest, distinguished from them merely by the greater cost and decoration of the arms they carried, officers now began to turn themselves into a separate class of professionals. To emphasize their separateness, they used the enlisted men's weapons as their own playthings: in order to show that their business was to lead and direct, not to kill, they adopted first the demi-pike, then the pistol, then the cane, and finally the model tanks and aircraft that decorate the desks of many present-day senior officers. Since killing was now carried out at a distance by bullets that failed to distinguish between nobleman and commoner, it had in any case ceased being fun. Beginning from the top, knights in shining armor gradually gave way to "chess players" like Maurice of Nassau or "military intellectuals" like Raimondo Montecuccoli.

As the knightly ethos declined, fewer commanders felt inclined to fight in person; Vendome at Oudenaerde (1708) and Charles XII at Pultava (1709) still did so, it is true, but they were members of a dying breed, and in both cases they ended up by losing the engagement. Marlborough at Ramilles led a charge in the course of which he was unhorsed and ridden over, but only in order to help repulse a French attack at a moment when no other commander was at hand. When Ney at Waterloo (1815) fought with musket in hand this was a clear sign of mental derangement. More typical of the dangers facing commanders during the early modern period was the case of Turenne at Sassbach in 1675: riding out to observe the situation on his right, he passed near a battery and helped sight it. As he was doing so a ball struck him on the chest and killed him on the spot.

The advent of firearms, and the revolution in tactics and in organization that it brought in its way, also affected the position of the commander in chief in another way. The reduced reliance on shock effect caused a gradual thinning-out of tactical formations, from the eight to ten ranks under Maurice of Nassau around 1600 to the four to five under Marlborough a century later right down to the two sometimes employed by Napoleon.[122] This thinning-out, together with the increase in the size of armies, meant that fronts frequently were extended to the point that they no longer formed single, coherent wholes that could be controlled by one man. Even when the terrain was perfectly flat and open, it was no longer always possible for a commander to watch his entire front without standing so far back as to make effective command impractical. Far better, then, to move about the front, or else concentrate on what one hoped would be the decisive point and rely on messengers (the first aides-de-camp properly speaking now make their appearance)[123] in order to communicate with the rest of the army. A third alternative consisted of trying to plan every move in advance, relying on highly trained troops and strict discipline to carry out the scheme as ordered.

Of all the eighteenth-century commanders, probably the most adept at moving about the battlefield was the duke of Marlborough. The march toward battle typically started two or three days in advance, when sources of some kind—their exact nature is never revealed—would tell him that the enemy was to be found somewhere not too far away. Riding ahead ten miles or so in his capacity as quartermaster general, Cadogan would locate the enemy and send word back to the duke. The latter then rode forward and, while waiting for the rest of his troops to arrive, made a personal reconnaissance of the terrain. Since the order in which the army deployed was already standardized (in this, it seems, the duke was well ahead of his time), there was no need to work it out afresh on each occasion. Where there was still time, as at Blenheim in 1704, Marlborough rode across his front to show himself. He then stationed himself on top of a hill close behind his center and ordered the battle to begin, using messengers (with written orders) to communicate with the wings and personally addressing the assembled commanders of the center. The battle having begun, the duke observed for a time and then rode to one of the wings to watch its attack progress, or else help close some gap in the line. All the while he kept in touch, by messenger, with the rest of his front. Where there developed an opportunity for a decisive stroke the duke was invariably to be found, assessing the situation and personally ordering the signal to be given. This system required a very good eye for terrain; an ability to guess, in general terms, how and where dangers or opportunities might develop; a body of messengers who, in the words of one contemporary expert, "understood how important it is to transmit an order exactly, correctly estimate the situation, and are sufficiently enterprising not to let a decisive opportunity pass by";[124] and, finally, a body of principal subordinates who could be relied upon to hold out without committing gross errors while the duke was away.[125]

Where the terrain prevented free movement across the battlefield an eighteenth-century commander might adopt the old system and follow his decisive wing in battle, thereby relinquishing control over the rest of his forces and simply hoping that things would work out as planned. The battle of Krefeld in 1758 is a perfect example of this method.[126] Here Ferdinand of Brunswick planned for one force under General Spörcken to hold the French while the main Hanoverian body carried out a wide outflanking movement to the right, crossing the ditch behind which the enemy troops were sheltering, in order to take them in the flank and rear. Having issued his orders on the previous day, Ferdinand himself joined his main force and, moving through rather close terrain, lost all ability to oversee the battle as a whole. An outlook left on the tower of a church was at least able to signal the movements of the French reserves, but all contact with Spörcken was lost and the French were consequently able to get away on time. Though Ferdinand remained in possession of the battlefield, the attempt was not a happy one.

Finally, Frederick the Great's battles were always offensive and always carefully thought out in advance, requiring precise, machinelike movements and highly trained, strictly disciplined troops to carry them out. The king as a rule would ride out ahead of the approaching army, observe the enemy at close quarters, and then assign each unit its direction as it passed by.[127] From this point on the machine was supposed to function automatically. At times it did so: at Leuthen in 1757 the movements (largely no doubt owing to the fact that a low ridge, unknown even to Frederick, prevented them from being observed by the Austrians) went off like clockwork. In others, such as Zorndorf in 1758, units—either because of the terrain or because they met with unexpected resistance—strayed from their assigned positions in the line and got in each other's way or else allowed gaps to open. On such occasions it was the Prussian cavalry, often acting on its commanders' own initiative without any orders from the king (Seydlitz at Zorndorf), which saved the day. On the whole, and despite some spectacular triumphs at Leuthen and Rossbach—the latter won by Seydlitz almost single-handedly— the system only worked moderately well and produced about as many defeats as victories. Thus Frederick's system of tactical command, one of the earliest in which a commander attempted continuous control of the whole army, and relying for this purpose on as robotlike a body of troops as has ever been put into the field, cannot be called an unqualified success even when wielded by its inventor's masterly hands. In those of his less competent successors it led directly to disaster.

CONCLUSIONS: MARS SHACKLED

Summing up two millennia of Stone Age command, the most important fact to be noted is perhaps that, owing to the primitive state of communications technology, the commander in chief had to take care of many things that he should be able to leave to subordinates; or, to turn the argument around, the most important moves could take place only in the commander's immediate presence. Alexander riding out with a small party before the battle of Gaugamela; Gustavus rushing about the battlefield in the capacity of a mobile fire brigade; and Marlborough moving hither and thither, helping to stem a French counterattack and personally giving the signal for the decisive stroke to begin—these are typical examples of the way things were done. That they could not be done without commanders' temporarily relinquishing control over the bulk of their forces is a matter of course.

Always unable to command the whole of their forces the whole of the time, commanders devised various solutions for dealing with the problem. One extreme, leaving a commander with little but his moral function, was to surrender virtually all control, as medieval princes did. Another, leading to not dissimilar consequences, was to enforce overall control by literally compressing the troops into a single block, or phalanx; the number of functions that could be controlled was thereby much reduced. Compromise solutions included commanding part of the army all of the time, in the manner of a Hellenistic king, or all of the army part of the time, as was Marlborough's method. Frederick II was among the first modern commanders to try to command all of his army all of the time, but this could only be achieved by turning it into a mindless, lifeless machine that was dependent for its triumphs on a set of exceptionally enterprising cavalry commanders. By far the most successful of these solutions, the only one that consistently produced victory over a period of centuries and almost regardless of the commander's personality, was the Roman one: that is, a command system, not based on any real technical superiority, that relied on standardized formations, proper organization at the lowest level, a fixed repertoire of tactical movements, and the diffusion of authority throughout the army in order to greatly reduce the need for detailed control. The hands of the commander in chief were thus untied.

The same problem that determined the methods of battlefield command also governed the commander's ability to conduct operations in the field. As long as rapid and reliable communication between mobile forces over considerable distances was regarded as impractical, the safety of armies depended on their staying closely together; and staying together in turn imposed strict limits on their size. Operational intelligence and planning consequently remained both intermittent and sufficiently simple to be carried out mainly by the commander himself until the eighteenth century and even beyond. "General" staffs, as distinct from those concerned with administration and logistics, were accordingly slow to develop. It was not until the middle of the nineteenth century that the traditional *coup d'oeil* with its implications of immediate personal observation gave way to the German-derived "estimate of the situation," implying map study and written reports.[128]

On the strategic level, the most important development was that sovereigns gradually ceased exercising personal command from the sixteenth century on. Two results were the institution of an extensive correspondence between court and commander in chief, and the sidetracking of strategy into a straitjacket from which it took several centuries to liberate itself. France being the best organized of any pre-1789 state, the peculiarly convoluted operations of Condé, Turenne, de Saxe, and de Broglie ensued. As had been the case in the Roman Empire, strategy on a grand scale remained possible mainly where a ruler and commander were united in a single person, as in the cases of Gustavus and Frederick the Great, or else where a commander's political and personal standing at court gave him an exceptionally large measure of freedom, such as was enjoyed by Marlborough (so long as his wife enjoyed the queen's confidence) and Eugene. On the whole, however, the attempt to run strategy by remote control had a stifling effect, culminating in the Seven Years War as fought in western Germany.

Even as the frustration at the strategic level was at its height, however, other factors were already at work on a lower level to liberate warfare from its shackles. One crucial factor, battlefield control, was to make little (if any) progress until the beginning of the twentieth century, but commanders in the years after 1700 at any rate no longer fought in person, and tactical organizations became both articulated and permanent. More and more staff work was coming to be done in writing, and in the quartermaster's staff commanders now possessed an instrument that was already beginning to show clear signs of promise. Here and there experiments were being made with staff colleges, these representing the first attempts at providing senior officers with a systematic training in war. The stage, in brief, was being set for the greatest revolution ever in the history of command to burst upon the scene.

3

THE REVOLUTION IN STRATEGY

FROM THE DAWN of recorded history until shortly before 1800, to recapitulate the essence of the argument so far, technology and organization placed limits on the ability of armies to gather, transmit, and process information and, consequently, on their size and the nature of the missions they could perform. Field armies numbering even as many as eighty thousand men remained exceptional throughout the period, and, once assembled, they often could not be effectively commanded. Although it was always possible to throw out detachments to perform tasks of secondary importance on the flanks and in the rear, these by definition were not subject to close control, and armies accordingly spent most of their time on campaign operating in single, fairly compact bodies directly under the eye of the commander in chief. Fronts being narrow, the pace of the advance was constrained either by congestion on the few available roads or else by the need to march across country,[1] and its direction in space was to some extent canalized by the fact that it was only possible to wage large-scale war in populous and prosperous districts.[2] Given the slowness and insecurity of long-distance communications, intelligence concerning the enemy's operational and tactical moves (though not necessarily concerning his strategic intentions, which could be discovered and announced by overt or covert agents) had to be obtained at ranges seldom exceeding 15–20 miles. Taken together, these factors placed very strict limits on an army's level of performance—that is, on what strategy could and

58

could not do. Under such circumstances no very elaborate "general" staff system was required, and in fact none is recorded in history before the time of the French Revolution.

These constraints did not constitute the only way in which the state of technological development helped shape strategy in the centuries before 1800, however. In an age when nine-tenths of all supplies (by weight) consisted of food and fodder and could be collected on the spot, when the relative backwardness of the banking system enabled large sums in cash to be levied directly from occupied towns and used to pay the troops or purchase their supplies, and when a soldier was supposed to require only one new coat every two years, it was possible to go on campaign without worrying too much about the rear. There existed, in other words, a chasm between the conduct of war in the field and national (or tribal or city-state) life, a chasm that was not completely bridged until the First World War led to the mobilization of entire societies. It was the existence of this chasm that made it possible for rulers from the earliest times to double as commanders in the field, as their titles show.[3] By and large, these conditions still prevailed in Napoleon's time. Though his armies often established lines of communication more extensive than anything previously attempted,[4] the link with the homeland remained fairly tenuous, and there was nothing to prevent the armies from breaking away from these lines for a while; thus the very technological backwardness that hamstrung strategic command in the field also allowed war to be self-supporting, at any rate temporarily and in part. Consequently the years around 1800 may be regarded as among the last in which the traditional union between ruler and commander was still possible, though this of course does not explain why this system in Napoleon's hands was so enormously successful. To put the matter in different words, Napoleon's ultimate secret may have been that he made use of the economic and technological backwardness of his time in order to exercise command in the field, yet at the same time found ways to liberate strategy from the limitations traditionally imposed on it by that very backwardness. To use existing technology to the limit and at the same time make its very limitations work for one—surely that is the hallmark of genius.

To present the revolution in strategy as entirely the emperor's creation would be to overshoot the mark, however, insofar as there were at work in eighteenth-century Europe other factors that made the revolution possible. Everywhere new roads and canals were being built, which facilitated travel and in many places made parallel roads available for the first time. A regular network of royal mail services, gradually established from the sixteenth century on and greatly expanded in the eighteenth, now linked all the main cities and enabled information to travel, by Napoleon's own estimate, about twice as fast as it had in Caesar's day.[5] Cartography—for the first time based on triangulation rather than on guesswork—had made great strides since 1700, and maps of all sizes and qualities were now at last freely available, though coverage of the Continent as a whole remained spotty and lacking in uniformity.[6] Finally, population density had increased to the point where many, if not most, regions could support armies,[7] thus decreasing the latter's dependence on magazines and convoys and making greater mobility possible.[8] Regarded from these points of view, the technological-economic foundation for a revolution in strategy was clearly being laid.

At the same time as the infrastructure, so to speak, of strategy was changing, the first attempts to improve the organization of armies were being made. Already in the middle of the eighteenth century Saxe had "dreamt" of permanently organized legions capable of carrying out independent operations.[9] Bourcet during the Seven Years War organized an invasion along several parallel axes (more novel as an exercise in coordination than in strategy, since commanders from the earliest times on had often hit upon the idea of dividing their forces in mountainous country) and later helped de Broglie in Germany to make the first attempt at organizing an army into divisions of all arms. Experiments along these lines continued, leading to the creation of the first corps, properly speaking, by the Assemblée Nationale in 1794. What the campaign of 1805 revealed to a startled world was a direct outgrowth of these experiments and yet, at the same time, completely new and unprecedented: an army 150,000 strong organized into eight numbered corps, each containing units of all arms and each provided with a uniformly structured, though not exactly permanent, staff to direct its operations—each a little army in its own right.

Perhaps the most important single characteristic of the new corps, and one that was critical in making the revolution in command possible, was their sheer size. A corps numbering 20–30,000 men could not, according to contemporary military wisdom,[10] be overwhelmed in an afternoon; a day or two would be required, by which time a well-developed communications system might pass the news along and bring another corps to the rescue. The time thus gained, and the fact that the corps were roughly interchangeable and able to exchange roles without further ado, cut the frequency with which information had to be passed between the army and its headquarters; or, which amounts to the same thing, made it possible to extend the range over which information could be usefully sent. An enhanced level of strategic performance was thus achieved. Instead of keeping close together, the army was now able to spread its corps at a distance of fifteen to thirty miles from each other and so avoid problems of supply and traffic control.[11] Each corps operated independently, yet all were also expected to respond to a single grand design and usually did so. Combining to create a predetermined formation with front, rear, wings, and center, the corps were supposed to be capable of changing their relative positions at a moment's notice, alternately acting as vanguard, pivot, or wing in relation to the army as a whole. Their roles, too, were subject to constant and endless variation; a corps might find itself acting as a hammer on one day, then serving as an anvil on the next. A corps employed to cover a strategic enveloping maneuver during the first phase of a campaign might well find itself in the vanguard of the advance in the second, only to be relegated to the role of an occupation force in the third. If a sudden summons arrived in the middle of the night, the same corps would find itself marching hell for leather on its way to take part in a decisive battle.[12] Under Napoleon the life of a corps or division commander was guaranteed to be strenuous and indeed dangerous, but it was seldom boring.

To keep an eye on the vast hordes that made up the army; to gather intelligence from all over the comparatively enormous theater of operations or even to form a mental picture of that theater; to maintain control over the large fronts, often extending over seventy miles or more; to transmit reports and orders over such distances; to exercise supervision over the movements of the various corps, as well as those of the countless columns and convoys traveling in both directions across a zone of communications that stretched, in 1805, from Austerlitz to the Rhine; to maintain the continuous flow of information that alone made possible the endlessly flexible combinations and maneuvers characteristic of Napoleonic warfare—all this required an apparatus of command, control, and communication more advanced than anything previously attempted. One's astonishment concerning the command system that made possible such an upheaval in strategy grows still further when it is understood that, except for the long-range communication service provided by the Chappe telegraph, which linked the army in the field to Paris, there were no technological advances of any kind.[13] While staffs and organizations made a great leap forward, horses were still horses and orders still had to be copied out by hand, laboriously and without the benefit of anything as sophisticated as carbon paper. In the last analysis, then, Napoleon's command system and indeed the entire revolution in warfare that he wrought cannot be understood simply on the basis of the techniques, organizations, and procedures in use. Rather, his revolution was the product of one of those rare explosions of human energy which, like supernovae, sometimes light up the course of history.

"THE GOD OF WAR"

It cannot be the purpose of the present study to analyze commanders' personal attributes (as Stalin once supposedly told his undersecretary for war, "we do not possess a pool of Hindenburgs"), but an exception must be made in Napoleon's case. More than any of his predecessors or successors he created the command system through which he worked; it was, so to speak, tailored to measure, cut to suit his own dimensions. That nobody but him could have made such a system work is probable; that his absence would have caused its collapse (as indeed happened in Spain, where he made only one brief personal appearance) is certain.[14]

Napoleon Bonaparte: the supreme egotist who sent hundreds of thousands to their deaths cheering. He was possessed of unlimited self-confidence coupled with tremendous optimism, the conviction that everything would turn out well; this quality does as much to explain his ability to deal with uncertainty as any technical aspect of his command system. And he was completely unperturbable under stress: "Few people can form an idea," he once wrote, "of the extraordinary moral force that is required in order to launch one of those battles that decide the fate of armies, countries, and thrones."[15] Finally, he had what he liked to call *le feu sacré,* the distinctive characteristic of the warrior, an utter determination to conquer or perish with glory.

Intellectually, Napoleon's most distinctive quality may well have been his vivid imagination, which not only endows many of his letters with high literary quality but also enabled him to envisage things as they would be after this or that series of moves were carried out. To this he joined a formidable capacity for calculation that, in at least one documented case, enabled him to accurately predict the location of a decisive battle several weeks before it took place.[16] "Napoleon always thinks faster than anybody else" was one contemporary comment;[17] *il sait tout, il fait tout, il peut tout* was another.[18]

A complete master of his profession, Napoleon—in his own words—could personally do everything connected with war. An iron constitution enabled him, at least until 1812, to be everywhere, see everything, and sustain the most amazing physical feats—spending ten days in a tent in subfreezing temperatures before Austerlitz, or covering 150 miles on horseback in forty-eight hours in Spain. Contrary to legend, Napoleon did need his sleep, but was able to distribute it around the clock and summon it at will—a few hours in the late evening, a few more early in the morning, perhaps a brief catnap during the day. Not one to be kept awake by even the most important of events, he spent the final hour before the battle of Waterloo, between ten and eleven o'clock on 18 June 1815, asleep.

Whenever he was not asleep Napoleon was at work—while he was in the bath, at the theater, at the hurriedly taken meals. Work, to quote his own words again, was the medium in which he lived.[19] On campaign he habitually worked eighteen hours out of twenty-four, but even this could be surpassed when the occasion demanded: on the eve of some important battle, such as Wagram in 1809, he would go virtually without sleep for several days on end. The daylight hours saw ceaseless and prodigious activity: traveling, inspecting, reviewing, meeting with subordinates and with other dignitaries, reconnoitering, gathering intelligence, questioning prisoners and local inhabitants, all of which enabled him to see and hear for himself and prevented him from becoming the prisoner of his staff. The nights, by contrast, were spent in the cabinet; it was at this time that reports were received and collated, plans hatched, orders issued, letters written, bulletins composed. Frequently dictating to four different secretaries on four different topics at one time, Napoleon would send off up to sixty missives a day. Commanding eight corps in the field in 1805, he still found time to write to his stepson in Italy two or three times every day, going into the greatest detail as to what was to be done, where, and how. Reading these letters, and appreciating the enormous powers of concentration and of memory behind them, is to experience at first hand the most competent human being who ever lived.

No examination of Napoleon's qualities as a commander can be even partially complete without a reference to his formidable abilities as a leader of men. A good understanding of the native qualities of the French soldier; a knack for resounding phrases; an encyclopedic memory for faces, often assisted by careful but well-concealed homework; and a talent for stage management—all these are indispensable for understanding why so many followed him for so long. A hard taskmaster, Napoleon was as sparing of praise as he was generous (and prompt) to reward when rewards were called for. A believer in keeping subordinates on their toes, he demanded the impossible so as to extract the possible. His frowns, not to mention his formidable outbursts of rage that were at least partly play-acted and never uncontrolled, were the terror of those around him. He often addressed subordinates in a joking, familiar tone, but he did not permit others to respond in kind. A businesslike military order—to Eugene de Beauharnais or to General Rapp, for example—would frequently end with a brief and idiosyncratic phrase advising the recipient as to his health or assuring him of the emperor's esteem. Instead of merely scrawling an "N" at the bottom, he once signed a message to Murat with the words *activité, activité, vitesse, je me recommande à vous.*[20] These measures worked; on the whole, few men were better served by their subordinates.

INSIDE IMPERIAL HEADQUARTERS

The first and probably most important fact to be noted about Napoleon's command system is that the emperor himself served as his own commander in chief. In an age when long-distance communications, despite many improvements, remained comparatively slow and uncertain, this was an inestimable advantage that exercised a strong liberating effect on strategy. Napoleon, moreover, was his own master; he did not have to summon endless councils of war or argue with royal hangers-on as did his opposite numbers in the Allied armies in 1805 or in the Russian one in 1812. This system of unified command meant that decisions could be made rapidly and without conflict; it also made everything dependent on a single man whose health, physical and possibly also mental, did not improve after 1809.

The structure of Napoleon's Imperial Headquarters, like that of similar top-level organizations before and since, was not permanent but changed from time to time as the occasion might demand. Nevertheless, from at least 1805 on, it always consisted of three principal parts: the emperor's Maison, the General Staff (État Major de l'Armée) under Marshal Berthier, and the Administrative Headquarters under Daru. The three parts were independent, the only formal link between them being the emperor himself. A curious amalgam of the old and the new, each component in the organization contained a private as well as an official element, which makes the analysis of the whole a very difficult task.

The Maison, as its name indicates, had originally been the part of a king's household that accompanied him on campaign. Revived by Napoleon during the Consulate, it consisted (in 1806) of some eight hundred men—grooms, valets, pages, cooks, and personal bodyguards—whose presence was required as much to surround Imperial Headquarters with a certain grandeur as to serve practical purposes in the field. Responsibility for this establishment was divided between two men, Duroc who ran the show and Caulaincourt who looked after the traveling arrangements.[21] Neither of these two, however, was simply a headquarters battalion commander; Duroc was often sent on missions requiring diplomatic finesse (including the procurement of females for his master), and Caulaincourt, a map attached to his coat button, invariably accompanied Napoleon on reconnaissance and during battle and took down whatever orders the emperor might dictate while traveling. Both men were among the empire's principal dignitaries who combined personal and command functions, or perhaps one should say that even under Napoleon the old view of command as the commander's private business had not yet been entirely superseded; and indeed the emperor often wrote of "my affairs" going well or otherwise.

Although Napoleon's principal attendants were given official command duties, the most important command organ in the Grande Armée was, paradoxically, a private institution. Forming part of the Maison, the emperor's cabinet was the direct heir of royal secretariats in ages past. It was not, strictly speaking, a military organization, but simply the technical apparatus through which the emperor worked. It was divided into three parts: the Secretariat proper, the Statistical Bureau, and the Topographical Bureau. Each of these merits a brief description.

The Secretariat was formed by a small number of shorthand secretaries, librarians, and archivists, all of them civilians, whose responsibilities corresponded roughly to those of the modern dictaphone operator, audio-typist, and filing clerk. Like the grander officials of the Maison, these men tended to be experts of long standing. Napoleon disliked new faces around him, and the permanence of the cabinet's personnel did as much as its formal organization to ensure its smooth and frictionless functioning.

Reporting directly to Napoleon, the Statistical Bureau obtained long-range strategic enemy intelligence (does the emperor of Austria intend to go to war? If so, what will the king of Prussia do?). It was normally led by one of the emperor's senior adjutant generals—Savary in 1805–1809, Bignon in 1812, d'Ideville in 1813. To obtain the information that was required, almost as many means were employed then as today: newspapers were systematically collected and translated, spies and agents were planted in every important city and used the imperial mail service for forwarding coded messages. Deciphered missives were also passed on by the so-called Black Cabinet, an organization founded by Colbert in the seventeenth century that specialized in opening the mail of lesser ambassadors who, unable to afford courier services, were forced to trust the mail and were derisively known as *les chifreurs* (the encoders).[22] Unlike subsequent intelligence organizations, however, the instrument in Napoleon's hands was not militarized and did not form part of the General Staff—another indication that the time-honored tradition which regarded such matters as the commander's private business had not yet lost all its force.

Operational intelligence originating in the corps' cavalry patrols (to anticipate our analysis somewhat) was passed to Napoleon by Berthier's General Staff; that organization also included a section under Colonel Blein responsible for interrogating local inhabitants, deserters, and prisoners who were often procured especially for the purpose.[23] Finally, Napoleon also had his own sources of intelligence in the adjutant generals and the *officiers d'ordonance* whom he sent on special missions and who usually reported back directly to him; on these, more will be said below.

Intelligence, though organized on a massive scale, had scarcely made any technical progress and still employed the age-old methods; as Napoleon once told Marmont, "You order the major to put a peasant at your disposal, arrest his wife as a hostage, have a soldier dress himself as the man's farm hand. This system always succeeds." The quality of the information thus procured varied very much, ranging from excellent during the early campaigns to abominable during the later ones when information became, owing to the intense nationalist feelings in Russia and Germany, much harder to obtain. Furthermore, as Jomini notes, the very kind of strategy made possible by all this intelligence also brought about a change in its nature.[24] The widely dispersed way in which armies now began to operate, combined with their sheer size, meant that reports coming from a single spy or even cavalry patrols on the movements from Y to Z of Corps X were not of much significance. To understand what the enemy was about, it became necessary to locate his central reserve and headquarters, which in turn became the subject of concealment. No longer could there be a question, as there had been in the eighteenth century, of opposing commanders in chief politely writing to each other and giving the exact location of their headquarters as part of the letterhead.

While the General Staff under Berthier was thus responsible for gathering the reports sent in by the corps, Napoleon's organization differed from modern ones in that he remained his own estimator in chief. That such a system was practicable at all is in itself proof that the amount of information to be processed was limited; it does not mean, however, that the job was much easier two hundred years ago than it is today. As the emperor himself wrote:

Nothing is so contradictory and nonsensical as this mass of reports brought in by spies and officers sent on scouting missions. The former see corps in place of mere detachments, the latter report weak detachments in places where corps are present. Often they do not even report their own eyesight, but only repeat that which they have heard from panic-stricken or surprised people. To draw the truth from this mass of chaotic reports is something vouchsafed only to a superior understanding; mediocre ones are lost therein, they tend to believe that the enemy is here rather than there, and proceed to evaluate available reports in accordance with their wishes. In this way they commit grave errors that are quite capable of wrecking entire armies and even countries.[25]

The fact that the emperor's brain served as the Grande Armée's central information-processing machine, thus eliminating numerous intermediate tiers, certainly helps explain the speed and decisiveness characteristic of Napoleonic warfare at its best; on occasion, however, it could mean snap decisions based on wishful thought, lack of thought, or afterthought.

The third and final part of the cabinet, to return to our analysis of its structure, was formed by the Topographical Bureau first created by Lazare Carnot. Under Napoleon it was headed by Bacler d'Albe, another civilian who followed his master for seventeen consecutive years. Probably the most indispensable of all Napoleon's collaborators, d'Albe was responsible for preparing the emperor's campaign headquarters for the day's (or rather, the night's) work. Arriving at a new location, a large table would be set up in the room, or tent, serving as the cabinet, and a situation map spread over it. Using information supplied by the Statistical Bureau concerning the enemy and by the General Staff concerning the Army's own positions and strength, as well as any reports sent in by the corps, d'Albe prepared the map for Napoleon's inspection by marking it with colored pins representing friendly and enemy formations. Special closets containing carefully arranged information, statistical and other, on the

Grande Armée and its opponents were always kept at hand. Four secretaries seated in the corners completed the scene, which at night was illuminated by about a score of candles.

If Napoleon's cabinet originated in the age-old royal secretariat, the Grande Armée's General Staff was of more recent origins. Following the close of the American Revolution in 1783, Ségur, then minister of war, feared that the dissolution of the army would lead to the loss of many experienced officers. He accordingly offered peacetime employment to sixty-eight officers—including Berthier, who had served as quartermaster general, officers in his own staff, and some others—in studying such professional military subjects as history, geography, reconnaissance, and practical science.[26] Inherited by the Revolution, the Staff Corps—which saw such men as Dessaix, Kléber, Soult, Ney, and Gouvion Saint Cyr pass through its ranks—was expanded and renamed several times. In 1792 the National Assembly drew on its members in order to provide each field army with a proper chief of staff (*chef d'état major*) for the first time. Berthier himself was assigned to the Army of the Alps; in 1796 he produced a *Document sur le Service de l'Etat Major Général à l'Armée des Alpes,* which he sent to Paris in the hope that it would serve as a model for other armies. Berthier's document divided the responsibilities of the General Staff into four sections, each under an adjutant general.[27] The chief of staff's duties were defined as dispatching orders, keeping the army's war diary, looking after the situation reports, keeping a situation map, keeping registers, and conducting inspections. More important than any of these, however, were the general principles expressed:

Though each adjutant general (there should be four assisting the chief of staff) is responsible for one particular part of the service, he must be informed about the state of business in general . . .

Nobody can send out anything in his own name; everything must come from the chief of staff who is the central pivot of all operations. All correspondence is addressed to him; he signs everything; in case he is absent he will issue special orders.[28]

As organized from 1805 on, the apparatus working under Berthier's direction possessed four functions—(a) to handle (that is, copy, register, and send out) the emperor's correspondence inside the army; (b) to expand and elaborate Napoleon's orders, and also independently to write to those of the marshals whose momentary tactical situation was not so important as to warrant the emperor's own attention (on the average between 10 and 13 October 1806, Berthier's letters to senior officers outnumbered the emperor's by four to one); (c) to supply Napoleon's cabinet with all possible information concerning the army's own situation, which made Napoleon call Berthier his "walking situation report"; and (d) to work out the enormous number of details of routine operations, including orders of the day, postal services, passwords, police, gendarmerie, supply columns, hospitals, prisoners of war, deserters, recruits, court martials, and civil government.[29] The extent to which these functions were still governed by the old scheme of things is brought out by the fact that the first three were the responsibility of Berthier's own Maison and cabinet, modeled on the emperor's, whereas the General Staff proper only dealt with the last function. Though the apparatus for handling "general" staff business had been greatly extended and articulated, the traditional view of these matters as basically the commander's private affair still persisted and is indeed reflected by the fact that the emperor invariably addressed his subordinates by name or by invented title ("my cousin"), never by their role in the formation they were in charge of.

Comparing Berthier's position to that of a modern chief of staff, it is easy both to overestimate and to underestimate his responsibilities. His access to enemy intelligence limited by the fact that he had no control over the Statistical Bureau, Berthier in no sense was an independent collaborator with Napoleon, much less a co-equal one, which was all to the good since the one occasion on which he was given the command of troops (in 1809) clearly showed him to be incapable of exercising it. On the other hand, to describe him merely as *l'expediteur des ordres de l'Empereur* (his own phrase to Soult)[30] is a gross underestimate both of the man and of the organization that he controlled. The Grande Armée, after all, was the first in history to radically decentralize the conduct of operations in the field and spread them over hundreds, later even thousands, of square miles of territory. Such a method of waging war required a two-way information transmission and processing system larger and more complex than anything previously attempted, and this system it was Berthier's responsibility to manage. By and large, and despite the rather primitive technical means at his disposal, he succeeded remarkably well until overwhelmed by distances, numbers, and his own failing health in Russia and Saxony. When Berthier was absent, moreover, as was the case during the 1815 Waterloo Campaign, the resulting muddle was monumental and led directly to the emperor's fall. "A goose that I have turned into an eagle of sorts" was the cruel but not inappropriate description Napoleon gave of his chief of staff.

The third element making up the headquarters of the Grande Armée, Daru's administrative-economic staff, was separated from Imperial Headquarters by dozens and sometimes hundreds of miles. Daru was responsible for running the entire vast zone of communications, which in 1813 consisted of half a continent. In this zone he levied contributions, made requisitions, established magazines and hospitals, directed the evacuation of the wounded and of prisoners, put local manufactories to work for the army, and oversaw endless similar matters. The personnel working under his command consisted entirely of civilians, as in prerevolutionary days.[31]

The structure of Napoleon's command system in 1813 is shown in Figure 1. The contribution of the various elements to the Grande Armée's success was rather uneven. Some of them, notably the emperor's Secretariat and his Topographical Bureau, were highly practiced organizations that performed their limited duties smoothly and efficiently. Berthier's Cabinet seems to have been just as efficient and generally performed well, except when the emperor's instructions were confused or absent. The intelligence provided by the Statistical Bureau varied from very good to very bad, and the same is true for the two-way reporting system inside the Grande Armée. In a period when many generals were still little but jumped-up subalterns (and this was even more the case in Napoleon's "democratic" armies than in those of his opponents) and did not possess a proper staff training, it is hardly surprising that many of them should have failed to understand the role of proper secretarial practices. The evidence reveals countless cases in which generals and even marshals were admonished for bypassing Berthier, for flooding the emperor with masses of useless trivia, for failing to number, date, and place

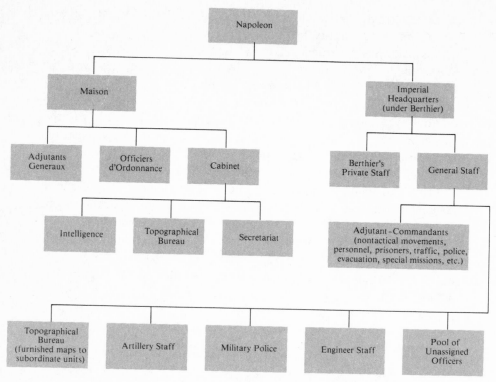

Figure 1. The organization of Imperial Headquarters, 1813

their missives, or even for misspelling place names.[32] At Waterloo, a famous chain of failures of just this kind led directly to Napoleon's defeat.[33] Furthermore, the Imperial Headquarters, which originally had been quite small, attracted more and more personnel until its establishment reached the enormous figure of ten thousand and came to resemble a small army in its own right—much of it useless ballast.

The real secret of Napoleon's command system, in any case, was not to be found at the Imperial Headquarters but rather in the Grande Armée's organization into divisions and corps. Each consisting of a properly balanced combination of the three arms and therefore capable of defending itself against superior numbers for a limited period of time, the corps and divisions were revolutionary in that they possessed their own well-organized general staffs. The di-

vision staffs, made up of eleven individuals, were rigidly standardized; the ones at the corps, consisting of any number between sixteen
and twenty-four, were less so. Both divisional and corps staffs were
organized into definite sections so that variations were limited to the
number of officers in each.[34] Unlike modern staffs, all these bodies
were only semi-permanent; they belonged to the commander rather
than to the formation. Soult leaving for Spain in 1813 and Ney taking over the Army of Berlin in the same year took along their own
staffs. Ney's staff in 1806 (a total of twenty-three officers) provides a
typical example of the organization.[35]

> Adjutant general (Jomini): one first aide-de-camp and seven other
>   ADCs
> Chief of staff (Dutaillis): two ADCs
> Employees of the general staff: six officers
> Attached to the general staff: five officers

Corps headquarters included the artillery and engineer inspector
generals, each with his own staff; a *commissaire ordonnateur en chef,*
responsible for supply; two *commissaires de guerre,* representing
Daru's organization; one *directeur des vivres pain,* one *directeur des
vivres viande,* one *directeur des forages;* one surgeon general; and one
director of mail services. Divisional staffs were built up on similar
principles, except that the adjutant commandant doubled as chief of
staff and thus made a considerably smaller establishment possible.

An important point to note about all these staffs, those of the subordinate formations as well as the emperor's own, is that their personnel received no specialized training. Bourcet's experimental staff
college at Grenoble was closed in 1765, and no real successor was
opened until 1818. In the Grande Armée commanding generals selected staff officers from among captains with at least two years' service, and after a probationary period these men were retained on the
staff. From here it was possible for them to work their way up into
Berthier's own organization. Despite the absence of a formal training program, and to some extent replacing it, the importance of rotating officers between staff and line was well understood; practiced
from the beginning, this system was formalized in 1813 when two
years' service were made mandatory for staff officers before promotion to major.

The system's first function was to place in front of the emperor the vast quantities of well-ordered information that he needed in order to control his widely dispersed forces. Apart from d'Albe's situation maps, described above, this information came in the following forms: (a) the *livrets de la guerre,* kept separately for each regiment in the army and including its commander's name and record, subordinate units, actual strength, number of sick and wounded, replacements on their way from the depots to the front, and a note on the men's regional origin; (b) territorial records of all military regions with names and credentials of commanders, staffs, senior officers, place commanders, units, bridging trains, police formations, garrisons, and military institutions; (c) records on the composition of the general staff; (d) the *feuilles de mouvement,* a record of all movements on their way from the rear to the front and from the front to the rear, complete with stages and dates; and (e) complete registers and records (campaigns, decorations, wounds, present post) of every officer in the army.[36] Updated daily and completely renewed every fortnight, these records formed the background against which the daily *états de situation,* prepared by the corps at the end of each day's operations and normally reaching Napoleon when he woke up around midnight, were evaluated. The reports, which were standardized, provided complete information about the corps' movements during the day: their location, additions to and subtractions from them, the state of uniforms, equipment, and arms, supplies at hand and available in the country, and the results of reconnaissances made, prisoners interrogated, and so on. To amplify these an *état de situation sommaire* had to be submitted every five days, and a *grand état de situation* every fifteen, both written out on special forms designed by Berthier. With all this information properly arranged and presented by his chief of staff, Napoleon was (or should have been, had the marshals always done their paperwork properly) in a position to really know what his forces—and those of the enemy, on whom similar records were kept by the Statistical Bureau—were doing.

Reports gathered and presented by the General Staff, on the one hand, and by the Statistical Bureau, on the other, thus constituted the most important sources of information at Napoleon's disposal. Climbing through the chain of command, however, such reports tend to become less and less specific; the more numerous the stages through which they pass and the more standardized the form in which they are presented, the greater the danger that they will become so heavily profiled (and possibly sugar-coated or merely distorted by the many summaries) as to become almost meaningless. To guard against this danger and to keep subordinates on their toes, a commander needs to have in addition a kind of directed telescope—the metaphor is an apt one—which he can direct, at will, at any part of the enemy's forces, the terrain, or his own army in order to bring in information that is not only less structured than that passed on by the normal channels but also tailored to meet his momentary (and specific) needs. Ideally, the regular reporting system should tell the commander which questions to ask, and the directed telescope should enable him to answer those questions. It was the two systems together, cutting across each other and wielded by Napoleon's masterful hand, which made the revolution in command possible.

As organized from 1805 on, Napoleon's system for cutting through established channels and for directly gathering the information he needed consisted of two separate parts. The first was a group of between eight and twelve adjutant generals; these were men selected unsystematically from among colonels who caught the emperor's eye, usually carried the rank of brigadier or major general, and were between ages thirty and forty and thus in the full flower of their mental and physical powers. Their duties varied enormously, from reconnoitering entire countries (Savary in 1805) to negotiating a surrender (Rapp in the same year) to spying out enemy headquarters under the cover of a truce (Rapp again, on the eve of Austerlitz) to commanding the cavalry or the artillery reserve in battle (Druot, Lauriston) to governing a province and commanding a garrison far from the main theater of operations. Such responsibilities called for practical *savoir faire* as well as diplomatic ability, the knowledge and talents of a military commander, and, last but not least, sheer physical stamina. The following instruction to Bertrand, issued on the eve of the 1806 Jena campaign, is typical of its kind:

Tomorrow at dawn you depart [from St. Cloud] and travel to Worms, cross the Rhine there, and make sure that all preparations for the crossing of the river by my guard are being made there. You will then proceed to Kassel and make sure that the place is being put in a state of defense and provisioned. Taking due security precautions, you will visit the fortress of Hanau. Can it be occupied by a *coup de main?* If necessary, you will visit the citadel of Marburg too. You will then travel on to Kassel and report to me by way of my *chargé d'affaires* at that place, making sure that he is in fact there. The voyage from Frankfurt to Kassel is not to take place by night, for you are to observe anything that might interest me. From Kassel you are to travel, also by day, by the shortest way to Köln. The land between Wesel, Mainz, Kassel, and Köln is to be reconnoitered. What roads and good communications exist there? Gather information about communications between Kassel and Paderborn. What is the significance of Kassel? Is the place armed and capable of resistance? Evaluate the forces of the Prince Elector in regard to their present state, their artillery, militia, strong places. From Köln you will travel to meet me at Mainz; you are to keep to the right bank on the Rhine and submit a short appreciation of the country around Dusseldorf, Wesel, and Kassel. I shall be at Mainz on the 29th in order to receive your report. You can see for yourself how important it is for the beginning of the campaign and its progress that you should have the country well imprinted on your memory.[37]

This is a Napoleonic directive at its best, succinct yet clear and detailed, leaving considerable discretion to his subordinate, and ending characteristically with a note assuring the recipient of his mission's extraordinary importance. It is as revealing for its indications of what the emperor knew as it is for indications of what he did not know (the maps he was using, it seems, were far from perfect). To quote another example, this time illustrating the use of the adjutant generals for the purpose of checking the veracity of a subordinate's report:

You [Lebrun] will first visit the corps of the duke of Regio [Oudinot] and inform me about his person. Has he recovered? Will he be capable of assuming command in the field? How are his divisional guns and where are they located? Who are his brigadier generals? You will supply me with a picture of his entire corps, but only a general one, without reviewing it. You are to review the cavalry only. You will report on the state of his infantry, artillery, trains, magazines, and hospitals, also the rumors circulating in and around the corps—in brief, anything that might interest me. You will go to Bayreuth, check the outposts there, and gather information about the road to Berlin and what is going on there . . . You will do the same at the other corps . . . You are to send all official messages to the major general [Berthier], all else directly to me.[38]

Accompanied by two or three *petits aides de camp,* the adjutant generals traveled all over Europe, from Spain to the Vistula and beyond, giving rise to respect and also, it seems, occasional resentment. In view of the nature of their missions, mobility in and out of the group was considerable; if an adjutant general did not get himself killed, he could expect to end up in command of a corps or with some equally important assignment.

Whereas the adjutant generals were given wide latitude to report "on anything that might interest me" and sent to inspect entire provinces and armies, the younger *officiers d'ordonance,* mostly lieutenants and captains, were sent on more limited missions involving either the transmission of messages to the corps or else the gathering of topographical information on roads, bridges, fortresses, and so on. Normally twelve in number, these officers were selected by the emperor from the scions of noble French (later also Polish) families. Two years' service with the troops was the only formal prerequisite, though artillerymen and engineers were given preference over the rest. The candidates had to be good horsemen and proficient in at least one language besides French. To meet the well-nigh incredible demands he made on them, exceeding even those required of their seniors, the emperor chose young men under twenty-four years of age. To these men the word "impossible" was unknown; frequently provided with only the haziest instructions concerning the whereabouts of a headquarters to which they were carrying a message, without maps, they rode day and night, covering as much as two hundred miles in forty-eight hours and arriving in a state of collapse. One of these young men, the Pole Desire Chlapowski, on one occasion traveled from Valladolid to Warsaw in nineteen days. In return for their extraordinary performance the emperor took good care of them: "Go and take your rest in one of Kaiser Francis' beds," he said to Lebrun on the latter's return from a mission on the eve of Wagram in 1809.

Though corps and divisions were provided with their own *officiers d'ordonance,* as was Berthier's General Staff, "young men whom one can make run in carrying orders" always remained in short supply.[39] The shortage was both cause and effect of a tendency among the various headquarters to retain each other's messengers, and sometimes made it necessary to employ local personnel for the transmission of reports and orders. On 5 May 1813 two critically important messages to Lauriston and Ney went out by way of Saxon gendarmes who were paid twenty napoleons each for their services. The use of such improvised means by Napoleon's army, in many ways the best organized that history had seen until then, is a telling comment not only on that army but on the entire history of command prior to his time.

1806: THE CAMPAIGN

To illustrate the actual working of the Napoleonic command system, I have selected the 1806 campaign against Prussia that culminated in the double battle of Jena-Auerstädt. That the campaign was "typical" can neither be proved nor disproved; in all probability it was so in some respects, less so in others. Though it certainly shows the emperor and his war machine at their superb best (one reason for selecting it), it was, with equal certainty, far from perfect. One thing working in its favor is its brevity, which allows a reasonably detailed analysis within the limited space available.

The cause of war was Napoleon's desire to sign a peace treaty with England, for which purpose he dangled Hanover as a bait for British eyes. In July 1806 news of this diplomatic move reached Berlin, which was already incensed by French arrogance (in 1805 Bernadotte's corps on its way to Ulm had crossed the Prussian possession of Ansbach without bothering to ask for permission) and at being compelled to cede morsels of territory for the benefit of Murat and Berthier. Pushed by the war party under the leadership of Queen Louise, Prussia started rearming. Late in August news of this reached Napoleon, who was at St. Cloud, and prompted him to start his preparations, although he still hoped to avoid war.

The first part of the emperor's job was purely mental. Using information supplied by the Statistical Bureau concerning the Prussian Army, and poring over his maps, he examined the alternatives open to him and formed a preliminary design for concentrating the

Grande Armée in the country around Bamberg; from there he intended to cross the Frankenwald (the Franconian Forest) and march north into Saxony. He communicated this plan to no one, however, and merely told Berthier (in his capacity as minister of war) to have the various corps, at that time scattered in cantonments throughout southern Germany, brought up to strength with recruits from France.[40] An *état de situation générale* of the army was asked for, and detailed contingency planning for the routes to be taken by each corps to its deployment area was put under way. On 5 September, too, a reconnaissance by engineer officers of the roads leading from the army's cantonments to Bamberg was ordered.[41] To obtain information on the movements of the Prussian forces, officers of the Statistical Bureau were dispatched to visit the French embassies at Leipzig and Berlin; they were to travel slowly and use their journeys to report on the country between Bamberg and their destinations. Orders also went out to Dejean, the army's chief of artillery who was responsible for the supply of ammunition, to start filling up gaps among the artillery and cavalry mounts.[42]

Having thus put preliminary preparations under way, the emperor turned his attention to securing his rear against a possible English landing and ordered Dejean to have Boulogne and Antwerp fortified.[43] On 9 September, still working from his study at St. Cloud, he was giving consideration to his future line of communications and was sending orders to Berthier to have the roads from Strasbourg to Mannheim to Mainz and Würzburg reconnoitered while paying particular attention to any fortresses on the way.[44] Berthier, stationed at Munich, was told to open secret negotiations with Napoleon's ally, the king of Bavaria, asking him to start provisioning the places around Bamberg and promising him that "if I fall out with Prussia, which I do not believe . . . , he will gain Bayreuth."

On 10 September a report on the state of supplies available in the fortresses along the Rhine was demanded from Dejean, and Caulaincourt was told to prepare the emperor's campaign headquarters—tents, baggage, wagons, and field telescope—for travel.[45] Throughout this time Napoleon was making conciliatory noises in the direction of Berlin, offering no concessions but telling the king of Prussia and the Prussian ambassador in Paris that he did not want war and ordering the French ambassador in Dresden to do the same.[46] The dice had now apparently been cast, however, for Marshal Bessières received the order to prepare the Imperial Guard for taking the field.[47] Finally, precautionary orders went out to Berthier to concentrate the corps of Ney, Augereau, and Davoût, as well as some other forces, at Würzburg the moment he (Berthier) was informed of a Prussian invasion of Saxony. News of the troop movements was to be sent to General Rapp in Strasbourg and from there by telegraph to St. Cloud. "An hour [after receiving it] I shall leave for Würzburg," Napoleon wrote. To make sure no news from the army would cross paths with the emperor on his way to Germany and be lost, Berthier was instructed "to arrange matters in such a way that I shall receive your reports at Mainz."[48]

Napoleon then turned his attention to administrative details. On 16 September he started gathering detailed information on the state of his corps, partly by talking to such of their commanders as were at hand (Davoût, for one) and partly by demanding written reports from Berthier. By that time Berthier's *état de situation* had arrived, revealing among other things a shortage of *officiers d'ordonance,* which the emperor at once set out to correct.[49] Now for the first time he revealed a little of his plans, telling Dejean and Berthier that Mainz was going to be "the pivot of operations" against Prussia.[50] Ney's corps was ordered to concentrate first at Ulm and then at Ansbach, and information to this effect was passed to Berthier.[51] Bernadotte's corps in its turn was ordered to Bamberg. Marshal Soult was instructed to make a tour of Bavaria's frontier with Austria, making sure that everything was ready for defense but ordering every officer "to spare no pains in dealing with the Austrians in the most friendly manner while remaining on guard."

Prussia invaded Saxony on 13 September 1806; the news must have reached Napoleon late on the 18th, for it was early on the 19th that the Guard was ordered to start marching for Strasbourg.[52] Unperturbed by the news of the invasion, the emperor busied himself with various details concerning the number of adjutants at headquarters, ordered additional reconnaissances, and—to show that he had time for everything—inquired into the hours a Paris museum was open.[53] On the 24th his equanimity was disturbed by a report from Berthier, apparently written on 19 or 20 September, that two Prussian armies had crossed the Elbe River and were now marching west on Hof and Hanover. Napoleon, who had not expected them to move so fast and feared a Prussian attack on his lines of communications that stretched toward the Rhine, at once sent Berthier the final deployment orders[54] and left for Mainz early the next day.

Up to this point Napoleon had acted as his own chief of staff. All plans came directly from his own head, the result of map study and whatever information there was on the Prussian intentions, which seems to have been little enough. To Berthier were left merely the details, including also the assignment of marching routes for each corps to reach its assembly place. The emperor had in the main divided preparations into two parts, corresponding with Dejean on the logistic details and with Berthier on the army's personnel and movements. Since it was Berthier who was actually present in Germany, enemy information, to the extent that it did not stem directly from the French embassies, also passed through his hands. Some of Napoleon's orders, but not many, apparently went directly to the corps, but the reasons for this were purely geographic and Berthier was informed in every case. It was also Berthier who arranged for the majority of reconnaissance journeys to be made, though again some of the most important ones—notably Lebrun's—were ordered by Napoleon in person. Using Berthier as a vehicle for transmitting and monitoring orders, Napoleon naturally bypassed him in whatever matters were not directly connected with the Grande Armée—the affairs of Italy or northwestern France, for instance—and in his dealings with foreign potentates. Yet on the other hand, and for no better reason than that he was present on the spot, Berthier was also employed on the delicate diplomatic mission of talking with Napoleon's Bavarian ally. There was no fixed system in all this; usually, however, Napoleon employed each man in his official capacity, never hesitating to bypass him—informing him, of course—or to use him elsewhere, if that seemed opportune.

Arriving at Mainz on 28 September after four days of travel, Napoleon at once became prodigiously active and spent three days dictating orders on everything from the army's organization to its mess kits. He left the town (and the empress) behind on the evening of 1 October, traveling through the night to reach Würzburg on the evening of the next day after making a stop at Aschaffenburg to see the "Prince Primate" of the Confederation of the Rhine. In Würzburg he received reports from Murat, whose cavalry patrols had located the Prussians, 150,000 strong, in the country around Erfurt in Saxony.[55] Here too he met Berthier and received his reports, and was shown the reports of the marshals concerning the state of their corps.[56]

While at Mainz, Napoleon sent a letter to his brother, King Louis of Holland, from which one can deduce how little he really knew of the Prussians and the extent to which his understanding of their intentions was based simply on map study.

It is my intention to concentrate all my forces on my extreme right, leaving all the country between the Rhine and Bamberg completely uncovered, in such a way as to have almost 200,000 men united on the battlefield. If the enemy [assumed to be moving slowly west from Erfurt] sends detachments into the area between Mainz and Bamberg I shall not be bothered, since my line of communications goes back to Forcheim, which is a little fortress close to Würzburg . . . [The enemy, who does not know this] believes my left to be on the Rhine and my right on the Bohemian border, and that my line of operations is thus parallel to my front; he may therefore try to attack my left, in which case I shall throw him into the Rhine.[57]

Here, then, was the plan of campaign in its grandest outline. Significantly, it went to the emperor's brother, not—so far as we can ascertain from the available evidence—to either Berthier or the marshals.

On 3 October at Würzburg, Napoleon officially assumed command of the Grande Armée by publishing a proclamation and having the marshals pass their corps in review. His 1st Corps (Bernadotte) was now at Lichtenfels, 3rd Corps (Davoût) at Bamberg, 4th Corps (Soult) at Amberg, 6th Corps (Ney) at Nuremberg, 5th Corps (Lannes) at Schweinfurt, 7th Corps (Augereau) and the Guard (Lefebvre) at Würzburg. The heavy cavalry reserve (Murat) was located behind Ney's corps. A number of reports from Bernadotte and Savary's spies arrived, showing that the enemy was marching slowly westward but had not yet reached Fulda.

Basing his plans on these dispositions and on this intelligence, the emperor on 5 October explained his intentions in a letter to Marshal Soult. The Grande Armée was to cross the Frankenwald in three columns; Soult followed by Ney and 10,000 Bavarians on the right;

Davoût, the Guard, and the Heavy Cavalry Reserve in the center; and Lannes followed by Augereau on the left.[58] Riding ahead of the center column were four brigades of light cavalry whose commanders were put under Murat's personal command and ordered to send their reports in duplicate, one to Murat as commander of the army's vanguard and one to Bernadotte as leader of the central column. Apart from this letter to Soult the emperor only wrote to Bernadotte and dictated a short note to Davoût, leaving it to Berthier to inform the remaining marshals. His orders, contrasting sharply with the far more detailed missives sent out during the period of preparation and also with those going to Eugene in his capacity as viceroy of Italy, were simple enough: they told the marshals only where to go at what time, what to do once they got there ("once at Hof, your first concern is to establish communications with Lobenstein, Ebersdorf, and Schleiz") and, in general, instructed them to pass on any intelligence and keep at hand as many supplies as possible. Given the enemy's presumed location, it was the left-hand column that stood in the greatest danger of being attacked. Nevertheless, Napoleon positioned himself with his center, secure in the knowledge that Lannes would be able to hold out or fall back until either Augereau or Bernadotte could come to his aid;[59] no longer could there be any question of the commander in chief always trying to do everything important himself.

To judge by his published correspondence, Napoleon sent out only a comparative handful of messages to the corps commanders between 5 and 10 October. This must have been due partly to the physical difficulty of maintaining communications across the forest roads, but partly also to Napoleon's realization that, once preparations were at an end and the campaign under way, the greater uncertainty associated with operations could best be dealt with by not putting too tight a leash on the individual marshals. We do catch a glimpse of one *officier d'ordonance* being sent back to Würzburg to take a last look at the base being established there (significantly, Napoleon did not wait for logistic preparations to be completed before starting the campaign) and another going out to report on the whereabouts of Soult's corps on the right. Missives also went out to the marshals, updating them on the progress of the various corps and carefully noting the locations where the emperor himself could be reached. "Send me news frequently," he wrote to Soult; "in a combined war such as the present one it is impossible to obtain good results except by means of very frequent communications. Put this at the top of your list of priorities."[60] It was the essence of Napoleon's command system, nevertheless, that it could and did make do without such communications for a limited time; on 10 October, for instance, the emperor on his way from Ebersdorf to Schleiz could hear a cannonade coming from the direction of Lannes's corps on the left, but this did not worry him even though it took some twelve hours to find out what was going on. "Since I no longer hear the sound of battle from Saalfeld," he wrote to Murat, "I presume the enemy has not defended it for long."[61]

Napoleon on campaign should not, in any case, be imagined as sitting behind a desk and dictating orders. Most days were spent actively searching for information, reviewing troops, and supervising the proper execution of his orders. Here and there the emperor would stop a formation of any size (all the way down to battalion), inquire into its recent doings, and single out some outstanding individual for the kind of promotion that would leave the rest of the troops gasping. Messengers carrying information reached him irregularly during the day; he himself normally issued his orders in writing and did most of his dictation in the evenings after reaching the place where Imperial Headquarters had been established by Caulaincourt. Retiring to bed at about 2000 hours, he would rise around midnight in order to study the detailed situation reports sent in by the corps. It was usually between then and about 0300 hours that the most important work of the day was done; his orders dictated, the emperor would return to bed for a few more hours' sleep while Berthier saw to it that the marshals received their orders in time for them to prepare the next day's movements.

On the morning of 8 October the leading columns of the Grande Armée, having already spent three days marching, crossed the Saxon border and thereby opened the campaign. That day no opposition was encountered, but on the morning of the 9th Murat with the vanguard met a Prussian force under Tauenzien at Schleiz and defeated it. News of the engagement was brought to Napoleon at Ebersdorf by his adjutant general, Rapp, who had been an eyewitness; from prisoners' reports the emperor now pieced together a new

THE JENA CAMPAIGN
October 1806

To Magdeburg

Leipzig

R. Saale

Naumburg   Weissenfels
Auerstädt

To Dresden →

3

1

Apolda
Dornburg   Zeitz

Eisenach   Gotha   Erfurt   Weimar
Köstritz
Jena
4   1

5
Roda   Gera
7   5   6

Kahla   Weida

SAXONY   0

Neustadt   Auma

Saalfeld   Schleiz

Meiningen   Ebersdorf   Saalburg

Gräfenthal   Lobenstein   Plauen

Coburg   FRANKENWALD   Hof

Kronach
Lichtenfels   4
1   Kulmbach
Schweinfurt   7   5   3   6
R. Main   6   Bav

Bamberg   Bayreuth   BOHEMIA

Würzburg

Forchheim

BAVARIA

Infantry

Cavalry

Nuremberg   Amberg

Miles
0   30

R. Regnitz

estimate of the enemy situation. "It seems clear to me," he wrote to Soult at 0800 hours on 10 October, "that the Prussians were planning to attack; their left was going to debouch through Jena, Saalfeld, and Coburg, commanded by Prince Hohenlohe at Jena and by Prince Louis at Saalfeld; the other column was going to proceed via Meiningen and Fulda. It thus seems you have nothing between you [at Plauen] and Dresden, perhaps not even 10,000 men." To this another note was appended: "I have just received your dispatch of 9 October, 1800 hours . . . The news that 1,000 Prussians are retreating from Plauen to Gera leaves no doubt in my mind that Gera is the meeting point selected by the enemy. I doubt whether they concentrate there before I get there first. I hope that the day will bring information that will give me a better idea of their plans."[62] Napoleon at this time had not yet reestablished contact with his left wing; nor did he know whether the Prussians intended to attack, defend, or take to their heels.

The day passed without further news of the enemy. "Once we arrive at Gera," Napoleon wrote to Soult at 1800 hours, "things will clarify themselves."[63] Meanwhile he acted on what little information he had, issuing a series of orders that would have led to the concentration of his forces in a semicircle around Gera by noon on 11 October. This proved a blow in the air, however; already on the next morning the cavalry, closely followed by Bernadotte's corps, entered Gera and found it empty. The day passed without further news of the enemy's whereabouts. It was only sometime late in the evening, around midnight, that two reports did arrive; one from Soult saying that the enemy who had left Gera were falling back on Jena, and one from Murat saying that a captured Saxon officer had placed the king of Prussia, with 200,000 men, at Erfurt. The Prussians, it now appeared, were not going to offer battle as far south as Napoleon had expected (and hoped), and might indeed be assembling their forces in preparation for beating a retreat to the north, in the direction of Magdeburg, or to the east, toward Dresden.

At this point, the advantages of Napoleon's one-man command system and large span of control (eight corps subordinate directly to the emperor) showed themselves. Between 0230 and 0600 on 12 October a series of curt orders went out to the marshals, swinging the entire army to the northeast and thus initiating, in the space of three and a half hours and on the basis of no more than two reports and a look at the map, the famous enveloping maneuver that was to lead to the destruction of the Prussian Army in the double battle of Jena-Auerstädt. From left to right, Lannes was ordered to march directly on Jena; Augereau to follow him as far as Kahla; Murat to go for Zeitz, on the way to Dresden, and Bernadotte to follow in his wake; Davoût to reach north in a forced march that was to bring him to Naumburg, so as to form the army's new right wing together with Bernadotte; and Soult and Ney to march west and so form the Grande Armée's new center at Gera-Neustadt. All this was communicated by a single comprehensive order to Berthier followed by individual orders to each of the four leading corps; the corps in the rear (Augereau, Bernadotte, Ney, Lefebvre) received letters only from Berthier.[64] It is apparent that there was a division of labor between the emperor and his chief of staff, enabling Napoleon to devote his attention to other matters that had to be dealt with that morning, such as a letter to his foreign minister Talleyrand, the Second Bulletin of the Grande Armée, and some administrative matters. On the other hand, it seems that none of the marshals was allowed a glimpse of the grand design underlying all these moves; to this extent command remained Napoleon's own exclusive concern and totally centralized. Each order, whether written by Napoleon or by Berthier, contained a few details only: the direction to be taken by the corps, the situation of its neighbors to the right and left, the expected location of Imperial Headquarters, and, in the case of the four leading corps, a general injunction to procure all possible information concerning the enemy's whereabouts and plans. More than that, apparently, was not required.

A point to be noted about all these orders, and one that certainly helps explain the "secret" of Napoleonic warfare, is the speed at which they were carried out. This is demonstrated by Table 1. As a glance at the map will show, the gap separating the army's two wings amounted to approximately forty miles, a distance not only considerable in itself but larger by far than that covered by almost any pre-Napoleonic field force. Although the orders themselves were communicated at an average speed of five and a half miles an hour, a speed that had hardly changed for millennia, the promptness

Table 1. The destination of Napoleon's orders, 11–12 October 1806

Corps	Location on the night of 11–12 October	Distance from HQ (in miles)	Departure of order	Arrival of order	Movement starts
Murat	Gera	19	0400 hrs	0715 hrs	0900 hrs
Bernadotte	Gera	19	0400 hrs	0715 hrs	0900 hrs
Davoût	Mittel	4.5	0500 hrs	0600 hrs	0700 hrs
Soult	Weida	11	0400 hrs	0600 hrs	0700 hrs
Lannes	Neustadt	8.5	0430 hrs	0600 hrs	1000 hrs
Ney	Schleiz	12	0300 hrs	0530 hrs	0600 hrs
Augereau	Saalfeld-Neustadt	20	0530 hrs	0815 hrs	1000 hrs

SOURCE: Vaché, *Napoléon en Campagne*, p. 49.

with which they were carried out—less than two hours on the average between reception and execution—is remarkable indeed, and shows the point not merely of having a flat-topped organization with a correspondingly large span of control but also of dividing the army into manageable, properly organized strategic units with their own permanent general staffs and messenger services, units that did not require mutual coordination in order to swing into action. The average interval from the time an order was issued to the moment it was carried out amounted to four hours; if another four hours are added as the average time that it took a report from the corps to reach the emperor, and assuming that the latter was not slow in making up his mind, one may conclude that it was possible in a twenty-four-hour period to issue the corps with three separate movement-orders and to have those orders carried out. This is a figure that present-day armies, for all their telecommunications equipment, can barely equal and certainly not improve upon.

Having dictated more letters, Napoleon at 0830 hours mounted his horse and rode toward Gera, where Imperial Headquarters was being established. He soon came across one of Davoût's divisions, which was marching toward Naumburg, and passed it in review. At 1230 he reached Gera and installed himself at the Ducal Palace. Waiting for news, he kept himself busy by writing a letter to "my brother," the king of Prussia; he may also have seen Soult, whose new headquarters was also located at Gera. He went to bed at 2000 hours and was waked up at midnight, when he found that no news from the corps had yet arrived. He thereupon wrote a letter to the empress ("I go to sleep at eight and rise at midnight; I sometimes think that you have not yet laid down") and went on to dictate the Grande Armée's Third Bulletin, designed to be published a fortnight after the events it described, as if the movements ordered on the previous day had already been carried out: [Murat] is between Zeitz and Leipzig, [Bernadotte] at Zeitz, Imperial Headquarters at Gera, the Guard and Soult at Gera, Ney at Neustadt, [Davoût] at Naumburg, and Augereau at Kahla ... The enemy, cut off from Dresden, was still at Erfurt on the 11th and was trying to recall his columns sent to attack Kassel and Würzburg."[65] Impatient for news from his wings, Napoleon now sent messengers to ask for it from Lannes and Davoût. He also ordered Murat and Lannes to make no fresh moves and rest their troops from the previous days' exertions. He himself, he added, would soon move to Jena.

Scarcely had these messengers gone on their way than three others arrived from the marshals. The messages they carried had been written late on the 12th or early on the 13th and had taken between eight and ten hours to reach the emperor over twenty-five miles of unfamiliar country at night. One messenger, coming from Augereau, reported that Hohenlohe was at Jena and falling back on Weimar in order to rendezvous with the main Prussian Army. The second, from Davoût, located that main army in the Erfurt-Weimar area and assured the emperor that the king of Prussia, traveling from Erfurt, had reached Weimar and that the country to the east (which his corps had traversed) was empty of the enemy. Finally, Murat sent Napoleon an agent of Savary's who likewise located the enemy in the Erfurt-Weimar area. Of these messages the second was the most important, showing as it did that the Prussians had abandoned whatever offensive projects they might have had. "The veil has been torn at last," Napoleon commented to Murat; "the enemy is beginning his retreat towards Magdeburg."[66] He also knew, as the Prussians did not, that Davoût at Naumburg was in a position to cut off his opponent's route. Thus everything was ready for the decisive act of the drama to begin.

1806: THE BATTLE

Like that of few commanders before or since, Napoleon's system of warfare was based on decisive battles. Not for him were either bloodless maneuvers (though the one he carried out at Ulm has remained deservedly famous) or protracted struggles of attrition, the latter in particular being a form of war in which neither his command system nor his own peculiar talents could be brought to bear to the best effect.[67] Battles dependent on mutual understanding—as had been the case during the Stone Age of command—were not for him; instead, he aimed at first pushing his opponent into a corner from which there was no escape, then battering him to pieces. On 13 October 1806 the first half of this purpose had been achieved.

Only the final preparations remained to be made. Murat was ordered "to betake yourself, as soon as possible and taking Bernadotte's Corps along, to Dornburg"; Murat himself was to report at Jena during the night. An *officier d'ordonance* was sent galloping back along the Auma road in order to speed up the arrival of the heavy cavalry. (This is the only occasion during the mobile phase of the campaign that Napoleon issued his orders directly to divisional units, and it can be explained by the absence of their commander, Murat, who was with the vanguard.) The army's Fourth Bulletin, describing the enemy as "caught in flagrant delict," was composed at 1000 hours. The emperor then rode forward to his center at Jena. Finding the normal route blocked by troops and trains, he made a detour through Köstritz, halted, and decided to have Soult march there so as not to have to march the whole way from Gera to Jena the next day; Berthier's order to the marshal went out at 1130 hours. Continuing his journey, the emperor around 1330 hours could hear the noises of shooting from the direction of Jena without knowing what it meant. At 1500 hours, with the emperor still three miles short of Jena, a messenger arrived from Lannes, whose troops were doing the firing, saying that he was engaged against 15,000 Prussian troops north of Jena with another 25,000 behind them. Napoleon at once jumped to the conclusion that Lannes was being attacked by the entire Prussian Army—a conclusion very different from what he had previously told Murat, and wrong to boot. Acting on the spur of the moment, he had Berthier take down orders for Lefebvre and Ney to march on Jena with all possible speed, adding that "an ADC should kill a horse, if necessary" in order to fetch Soult as well. Missives also went out to Davoût and Bernadotte, telling them of these developments and ordering them, in case they should hear the sounds of combat that day, to fall on the enemy's left; otherwise they were to wait for further orders to reach them during the night.

It was now shortly after 1500 hours. Napoleon, according to Generals Suchet (one of Lannes's divisional commanders) and Savary, who were eyewitnesses, rode forward to the plateau of Landgrafenberg west of the Saale River, where he found Lannes's headquarters. From there he made a personal reconnaissance of the enemy's positions, coming close enough to be shot at. The advance columns of the Guard now started arriving at the plateau, and Napoleon personally showed their generals the positions he wanted them to occupy during the night.[68] He supped with all the generals present and then went to see if Windknollen, a high point on the plateau whose occupation by Lannes's artillery was vital for defending against a possible Prussian attack, had indeed been taken. What he saw was not reassuring. The road was blocked by vehicles and the officers present were calmly taking their supper. Swallowing his anger, the emperor seized a lantern and personally directed the widening of the road, each battalion hacking away at the rocks for an hour and then marching away to its assigned position while another took its place. Napoleon remained on the spot until the first vehicle had passed through, then went to the bivouac that Suchet's grenadiers had prepared for him at the edge of the plateau.[69]

That evening Napoleon made another personal reconnaissance of the terrain, this time straying so far forward that he was shot at by his own outposts on his way back to camp. He returned to his bivouac and, shortly before 2200 hours, dictated the promised orders for Davoût. The marshal was told that a large Prussian army was deployed between Jena and Weimar and ordered to march on Apolda so as to fall on the enemy's left. He could take whatever road suited him, provided only that he participated in the combat. "If Marshal Bernadotte is still with you," the missive went on, "you may march together; but the emperor does hope he has taken up the position at Dornburg assigned to him." These were the last orders sent to either marshal until 0500 hours on 15 October—that is, until after the battle was over.

Having snatched several hours' sleep, Napoleon woke up at 0100 hours on the 14th and dictated his Order of the Day. He now had at hand two corps, those of Lannes and the Guard, west of the Saale on the Landgrafenberg Plateau; four more—from left to right, Augereau, Ney, Murat's heavy cavalry under their divisional commanders, and Soult—were converging on it. "At dawn," the emperor would "give the signal" for Lannes in the center to attack "the village on our right" (Closewitz) and thus enable Ney, coming up behind him, to deploy on the plateau. Ney in turn was to wait for the village to be captured, "then take himself to the right of Marshal Lannes." On the left Augereau was to fall on the enemy from the south, using Lannes's left wing as a line of orientation and apparently without waiting for further instructions. Soult, on the opposite wing, was to cross the Saale "by the road which has been reconnoitered," and take up positions so as to form the army's right. Finally, the Guard, which was already present, and the cavalry, "as soon as it arrives," were to be held "in reserve [on the plateau] . . . in order to go where circumstances may dictate." The corps' tasks having thus been enumerated (Napoleon's order is in fact far more rambling and disorganized than this summary would indicate), a few lines were added on the formation that each corps was to employ and on the importance, "today, of deploying completely; subsequently we shall make such moves as are dictated by the enemy so as to drive him from the positions that are necessary for our deployment."[70] An order as ill drafted as this one, based on a hopelessly mistaken idea concerning the enemy's strength and intentions, would surely have earned its author a failing grade at any present-day staff college. Whose fault this was, Berthier's or the emperor's own, is impossible to determine.[71]

In what manner the Order of the Day was communicated to the marshals is not entirely clear. Apparently no general meeting was held; instead, Lefebvre, who was at hand, probably received his instructions orally, as did Murat and Ney, who had been summoned to Jena on the previous day. An eyewitness informs us that Napoleon met with Lannes and Soult at 0400 hours.[72] Augereau probably received a written message (either a copy of the Order of the Day or else an extract containing the paragraphs pertaining to him), whereas Davoût and Bernadotte were left without orders at all. The Order of the Day, at any rate, was the last written directive issued on the 14th; from this point on the battle was commanded entirely by word of mouth.

It was now 0500 hours. Lannes had left Napoleon's tent, and the emperor was left with Soult alone. Suddenly shots rang out. "That's it, the affair is starting," he is recorded as having said.[73] Accompanied by some torch-bearing soldiers, he visited as many of Lannes's and Lefebvre's troops as were within reach, haranguing them and reminding them of the battle of Austerlitz in the previous year. Advancing under the cover of an early morning fog, Lannes's troops were for a time lost to the emperor's view. The mist lifted at around 0900 hours and revealed them in possession of Closewitz and pushing on to the northwest. Napoleon, from his command post at the edge of the plateau, where he was accompanied by Berthier, Caulaincourt, a few pages, and a number of adjutant generals and *officiers d'ordonance* drawn up a short distance behind, could now see an unexpected gap opening up between Augereau's troops, coming from the left, and Lannes's. Probably making use of his *officiers d'ordonance,* he threw into this gap the Guard artillery as well as some additional guns taken from Lannes and Augereau to form "the grand battery of the center." Near 1000 hours the guns of Soult's corps could be heard firing on the right; this took the Prussians facing Lannes in the flank, and enabled the latter to make steady if slow progress beyond Closewitz.

Feeling that the battle was going well, Napoleon soon shifted his battle headquarters in a northwesterly direction to the height of Dornberg (not to be confused with the village of Dornburg farther north, which had been assigned to Bernadotte as his objective) so as to follow Lannes's troops and oversee their action. It must have been during this time that Ney, who had been chafing in the rear while he waited for his troops to arrive, stormed forward at the head of his leading brigade, unobserved and without orders, passed to Lannes's left (instead of to his right, as ordered), advanced straight against a strong Prussian battery, and soon found himself isolated beyond the village of Vierzehn Heiligen and taking heavy casualties. Attacked by the formidable Prussian cavalry, he was compelled to form a square and would have been overwhelmed by the combination of fire and shock had not Napoleon, now again in command, observed what was taking place and ordered two Guard Cavalry Regiments under his adjutant general, Bertrand, as well as forces from Lannes's left, to come to his aid. These moves did relieve the pressure on Ney, but the fighting on this center-left side of the field remained indecisive.

Throughout these hours more forces of the Grande Armée were reaching the scene. To the left Augereau's forces had been arriving since 1000 hours, with Napoleon sending off one messenger after another to indicate an objective for each division and regiment. In the center more and more of Ney's troops were coming up. Further to the right, Murat must have been in place around noon, but it was only toward 1300 hours that Soult's rearguard (St. Hillaire's division) was ready. Now outnumbering the Prussians two to one, outflanking them on the south and threatening to do the same on the north, Napoleon sent out messengers to order a general advance. The Prussians facing Soult on the right gave way almost at once, and things there were all but over by 1400 hours. On Napoleon's center, however, Lannes was just starting to make progress when "numerous squadrons of imposing appearance showed themselves far away, apparently bent on taking Marshal Lannes in the flank." These, it turned out, were 15,000 Prussian cavalry under General Rüchel. The emperor from his vantage point thereupon dispatched Ségur to tell Lannes to form a square, and at the same time ordered the last of Lannes's troops who had been held in reserve (a brigade under General Vedel) to his aid. Seeing that they were not to be thrown into the fray, the Guard murmured in protest; they were silenced by a few sharp remarks from their master.[74]

Now facing overwhelming odds—Murat's cavalry was converging on them, in addition to the French infantry—Rüchel's troops broke and fled toward Weimar. It was now around 1500 hours, and only on the extreme French left were the Saxons still holding out against Augereau. The emperor now sent Ségur with orders for the division on Ney's left (General Marchand) to take this force in the rear, and by 1600 hours most of the Saxons had been taken prisoner. Proceeding slowly and issuing instructions to take care of the wounded, an exhausted Napoleon now rode across the battlefield to his former bivouac and from there to the castle of (or, some say, an inn at) Jena. The battle, one of the most smashing victories in world history, was over.

Napoleon's command of the battle of Jena is interesting in that it marks the end of an epoch in which it was possible for a commander in chief to overlook a field *and* take a direct part in the conduct of the engagement. Surrounded by a small staff and backed up by a much larger one whose functions were as much decorative as security-related, the emperor changed his command post only once during the battle. Relying on direct observation and using messengers, he ceaselessly intervened in the operations of those of the corps that he could see, unhesitatingly ordering about divisions and even regiments. On the other hand, Soult and possibly also Murat on the right received not a single order throughout the day. This may have been a mark of confidence in those marshals to whom the emperor felt closest (at Austerlitz he had laughingly remarked, "I and Soult understand each other"); it may, however, have reflected the fact that the heaviest fighting took place on the French left. But perhaps it was a case of out of sight, out of mind. As Napoleon is said to have remarked, every general tends to see the important point of a battle or campaign where he himself is situated.[75]

The battle had a curious aftermath. As he was taking up his quarters at Jena, Napoleon found waiting for him one Captain Tobriant, of Davoût's staff. This officer proceeded to impart the startling information that the Grande Armée's 3rd Corps had just beaten the main Prussian Army at Auerstädt. At first Napoleon refused to believe the tale: "Your marshal must be seeing double today," he snapped at the messenger. Gradually, however, the truth dawned on him. What Lannes's reports and his own observation had caused him to take for the main Prussian Army had in fact been a mere flank guard under Hohenlohe, behind which the commander in chief, with 60,000 troops, was retreating to the northeast. The main army ran straight into Davoût, who was marching from Naumburg to Apolda in conformity with the emperor's orders, and was soundly defeated by him. All the while, Bernadotte, though he had been at Naumburg with Davoût when the emperor's last order reached them, preferred to follow the previous order and sauntered leisurely to Dornburg, arriving too late to fight at either Jena or Auerstädt.

Thus Napoleon at Jena had known nothing about the main action that took place on that day; had forgotten all about two of his corps; did not issue orders to a third, and possibly to a fourth; was taken by surprise by the action of a fifth; and, to cap it all, had one of his principal subordinates display the kind of disobedience that would have brought a lesser mortal before a firing squad. Despite all these faults in command, Napoleon won what was probably the greatest single triumph in his entire career.

CONCLUSIONS: MARS UNSHACKLED

To properly appreciate Napoleon's command system and the way it worked, one must approach it from the viewpoint of the preceding centuries, not from the perspective of those that followed. Once the distorting effect of latter-day general staffs is taken away, things become very much clearer on both the tactical and the strategic levels.

As the battle of Jena shows, there was nothing particularly revolutionary in Napoleon's tactical command. Like Frederick II at Leuthen, he positioned himself on an overlooking hill from which he tried to supervise events. Like Marlborough at Ramilles, he relied on messengers to communicate with his forces in front and below. Like Carl XII at Pultava, he issued written orders on the eve of battle but not thereafter, and contrary to the recommendations of Maurice de Saxe he did take a hand in the detailed deploying of his troops rather than limiting himself to assessing and ordering the most important movements.[76] The tactical formations employed on the battlefield were not particularly novel.[77] As compared to Marlborough, Napoleon was, if anything, less successful in his role as a tactical commander; one reason for this was probably that the span of control, especially during the second half of his career, was too large for one man, however great his genius, to handle in the noise and confusion of battle. It may be for this reason that Napoleon is regarded by some as a lesser tactician than he was a strategist.[78]

It is when one turns from tactics to strategy, however, that the real nature of the revolution in command brought about by Napoleon becomes apparent. Unlike previous commanders in chief, Napoleon on campaign no longer attempted to keep the bulk of his forces concentrated under his own hand. No longer was the commander found doing everything important, such as riding forward to gather enemy intelligence and taking charge of the army's decisive wing. To the extent that these and similar functions were now left to the corps' staffs as a matter of routine, General Headquarters drastically cut down the burden of communicating and data processing that rested upon it. Since the corps were able to operate and hold out on their own, Imperial Headquarters could tolerate a far higher degree of uncertainty concerning the corps' momentary situation; this in turn made it possible to raise the level of performance to the point that it took the French armies only a few brief campaigns to overrun virtually an entire continent.

To make this decentralization in command possible, it was necessary (a) to organize the army into self-contained, mission-oriented strategic units, each with its own proper commander, staff, and balance of all arms; (b) to institute a system of regular reports from the corps to General Headquarters, and of orders from the latter to the corps; (c) to organize a headquarters staff capable of dealing with all the traffic thus generated; and (d) to prevent the commander in chief from becoming a prisoner of that staff, to institute a directed-telescope system that would enable him to cut through the regular command hierarchy and take a look, at will, at any part of the army or obtain any kind of information that might be required at the moment. The need for each of these changes was thoroughly understood by Napoleon; in one form or another, they were all present in the Grande Armée. In general, and despite a great many errors in detail, Imperial Headquarters functioned extremely well until the campaigns of 1812–1813 when it became overwhelmed by numbers and distances.

Quite as important as the above organizational and technical improvements was the confidence that was needed on Napoleon's part in the ability of his units and commanders to function independently for a limited period of time, and conversely the marshals' willingness to assume responsibilities far beyond those carried by the commanders of "detachments" in previous ages. Put at the head of very considerable forces, sometimes left without orders for days on end and yet expected to conform to an overall design, they functioned very well indeed if the triumphs of the years 1805–1809 are any guide. Even in the campaigns of 1812–1813 and 1815 it was often the personalities rather than the system that broke down. The selection of Jerome to command an army in Russia was undoubtedly an error (though one that, like Joseph's employment in Spain, may have been made inevitable by the marshals' unconditional refusal to serve under each other); and if Ney and Davôut had exchanged places in 1813—Ney to command Hamburg, Davôut to take charge of the flanking army at Bautzen—the campaign might well have ended differently.

Although the army's organization was thus decentralized, and despite the presence, for the first time ever, of a chief of staff who carried that title, there is a sense in which command remained an extremely centralized affair, with Napoleon going even further in this direction than many of his predecessors did. As has been pointed out by many modern authors who have taken the Prussian-German general staff system as their model, Napoleon neither wanted independent subordinates nor tried to educate them. He did not envisage a chief of staff as a co-equal collaborator but merely as a technical organ that might, at best, take over some functions regarded as insufficiently important to merit the emperor's own attention at any given moment. Napoleon, like Frederick II, did all his planning himself; it was only toward the end, with his self-confidence somewhat shaken, that the marshals were allowed an occasional comment on his designs. There is no positive indication that in 1806 any of them were given a glimpse of the underlying scheme like that afforded Napoleon's brother, King Louis, though some of them were at different times shown parts of it. To this extent, but to this extent only, is the accusation of overcentralization leveled at Napoleon by subsequent critics justified.

Centralization, however, also had its advantages. Combined with the large span of control—eight corps reporting directly to Napoleon by way of Berthier, with no intermediate headquarters—it is one explanation for the amazing speed at which many of the Grande Armée's operations were initiated and carried out. In passing judgment on the system, one should keep in mind the sheer genius that was needed to create it for the first time. In the final account, the very strong centralizing element in Napoleon's command system is perhaps best explained—leaving aside the emperor's idiosyncrasies—by the fact that, because the system was new and without precedent, nobody else could be expected to understand its workings nearly as well as its creator did. Another factor working against greater decentralization was the fact, already noted, that none of the marshals would defer to any of the others, sometimes with dire results, such as Bernadotte taking offense at being put in Davoût's wake and consequently missing the battle of Jena.[79] This, one might add, constituted part of the price to be paid for Napoleon's large span of control and for the speed and decisiveness that it helped make possible.

Contrary to much modern historical opinion, in any case, the worst accusation that can be leveled at Napoleon's command system is probably not overcentralization as such but rather a lack of method, of which overcentralization was both a cause and an outcome. As an analysis of the addressees and the contents of his missives will show, Napoleon on campaign sent out his orders with no kind of system whatsoever, writing to whomever he thought necessary at the moment, putting into his messages whatever part of his plan he thought fit, and informing those others whose names happened to occur to him. Frequently no attention was paid to the sequence in which orders should logically be dispatched—for example, for those orders to depart first whose recipients were the farthest away. Orders to the marshals and to the *officiers d'ordonance,* bulletins, letters to the government back home and to the enemy's head of government and to countless other dignitaries, streamed from his mouth to the secretaries' quills at a speed and variety that are as disconcerting as they are amazing. In sending forth the stream the emperor did not always distinguish between operational command and attention to detail; had he done so, he would have been able to concentrate on the former and leave more of the latter to subordinates, especially Berthier and Dejean. Further savings could have been made, and errors avoided, by systematically providing Berthier and the General Staff with a comprehensive order valid for all the corps and then leaving it to them to write to each marshal separately. The corps often received double and sometimes conflicting orders, one from Napoleon and one from Berthier; and Napoleon himself, habitually carrying a superhuman burden, was occasionally overworked to the point of feverishness.

Testifying to the enormous powers of concentration, calculation, and imagination behind them, the emperor's orders cannot but leave one wondering what miracles would have been achieved had there been behind them in addition a proper staff method. As it was, however, all Napoleonic management was management by exception.

The frequent absence of method in the emperor's correspondence must be put down partly to his impatient character, partly to the fact that he stood on the threshold between the age-old tradition of oral operational command and the new system of written staff work. Writing, as one author puts it, may be "the gunpowder of the mind," but it cannot be used without a price being paid.[80] Although a proper method in staff work might well have improved the Grande Armée's performance from a strictly practical point of view, such a method would inevitably have resulted in a dilution of the unique drive behind the emperor's dictated orders. Their highly idiosyncratic form was as important as their contents, if not more so. Taken as a whole and despite frequent errors and oversights, those orders are unequaled in the leadership qualities that they display. For even a capable staff to have written them out methodically, paragraph by numbered paragraph, might have improved them technically, but only at the expense of watering down or even doing away with this unique incisiveness. Nothing could be a greater error than to consider Napoleon's orders solely from the point of view of their "information content"—neatness, organization, conciseness, and so on—and thus to miss the very features that make those orders into masterpieces unsurpassed in the whole of military history.

Partly owing to this lack of method, but partly also because of the confusion that is inherent in war, the campaign of 1806 — brilliantly successful though it was—did not take place without any number of blunders in command. Corps were sent across each other's marching routes (Davoût and Bernadotte at the outset of the campaign), were left without orders (Augereau from 7 to 10 October), and failed to communicate with each other when such communication was vital (Augereau with Bernadotte during the same period). Intelligence concerning enemy movements and intentions was almost entirely lacking until the last moment and, when it finally did become available, badly misinterpreted on at least two separate occasions. That such blunders did not lead to defeat, or even to disorder greater than was normal during the emperor's campaigns, may have been partly due to Prussian lethargy and incompetence; in the main, however, it was made good by the wide discretion granted corps commanders and, above all, by their ability to operate without orders for a period of time.

Though this summary has concentrated on the reports that Napoleon received and on the orders that were issued by him, it would be a great mistake to regard him simply as a calculating machine that sat at General Headquarters and planned operations from behind a desk. As an examination of his daily routine will show, he spent most of his time either on horseback or in his carriage, traveling perhaps three times the distance covered by the average infantryman each day,[81] reconnoitering terrain, reviewing troops, and providing the kind of leadership that has rarely been equaled and never surpassed. These prolonged absences from headquarters, during which only occasional information about the state of the army as a whole could reach him, are in themselves proof of the fact that much could be left to corps commanders, and that the emperor was willing to forgo, or at least postpone, receiving certain kinds of messages in return for the ability to exercise supervision and see for himself.

Finally, a most important point to be considered is that the revolutionary system of command employed by Napoleon was the outcome not of any technological advances, as one might expect, but merely of superior organization and doctrine. The technical means at the emperor's disposal were not a whit more sophisticated than those of his opponents; he differed from them in that he possessed the daring and ingenuity needed to transcend the limits that technology had imposed on commanders for thousands of years. Whereas Napoleon's opponents sought to maintain control and minimize uncertainty by keeping their forces closely concentrated, Napoleon chose the opposite way, reorganizing and decentralizing his army in such a way as to enable its parts to operate independently for a limited period of time and consequently tolerate a higher degree of uncertainty. Rather than allowing the technological means at hand to dictate the method of strategy and the functioning of command, Napoleon made profitable use of the very

101

limitations imposed by the technology. That none of this would have been possible without an improvement in the infrastructure of strategy, as described above, is a matter of course, nor was the revolution in command entirely without its forerunners. Nevertheless, somebody had to put the puzzle together, and Napoleon Bonaparte was the man who did. To know what one can do on the basis of the available means, and to do it; to know what one cannot do, and refrain from trying; and to distinguish between the two—that, after all, is the very definition of military greatness, as it is of human genius in general.

4

RAILROADS, RIFLES, AND WIRES

IN THIS CHAPTER the command system employed by the Prussian Army during the 1866 Königgrätz campaign against Austria will be described and evaluated. This campaign provides the earliest example of the modern General Staff in action; in addition, its short duration makes possible a sufficiently detailed discussion within a limited space. That a description of the German campaign against France in 1870–71 would have revealed anything fundamentally different is unlikely; that it would have been much longer than the one presented here is certain.

Another consideration that governed the choice of the Königgrätz campaign pertains to the nature of command itself. In an age when new electronic marvels are being introduced almost daily and thus the gadgets in current military use are out of date, it is easy to forget (and it has in fact often been forgotten) that command, rather than being simply an assortment of technological marvels around which organizations and procedures are built, consists instead of a series of processes—each of them as old as war itself—by which the technological means at hand are pressed into service.[1] Were this not the case, a chapter on the American Civil War would have been more in place here, since it better illustrates the use of the telegraph. At a time when the Union and Confederate armies availed themselves of wire to span half a continent, the military use of the telegraph in Europe was still quite tentative.[2] This relative backwardness is nowhere better illustrated than in the Königgrätz campaign itself—

103

which, it must be added immediately, does not imply any underestimate of the importance of the telegraph. In this and the following chapter the role it played, and the limitations it imposed, on the conduct of war will be fully analyzed.

A WATERSHED IN TECHNOLOGY

During the middle years of the nineteenth century, the art of war was in a state of flux probably unequaled in any period before or since. New types of weapons, such as breech-loading rifles and rifled cannons (the latter made of steel rather than bronze), and new means of transport, the railways, were being introduced simultaneously, thus making necessary a complete reappraisal of the traditional methods. Even the stepchild of war—communications technology—in its capacity as the father of invention was finally showing signs of progress; after thousands of years during which long-distance communications had been carried out by mounted messengers, the telegraph now presented armies with a new and in some ways unprecedentedly effective means for transmitting information. In 1866 none of these inventions was completely new, and most had indeed already seen some early use in the wars of 1859, 1864, and 1861–1865. Nevertheless, none had as yet reached that stage of maturity in which the basic rules governing the employment of a new technology, and its effects, are no longer the subject of debate.

Added to these changes, and in some ways dwarfing them, was the sheer increase in army size. Montecuccoli around 1650 had regarded 30,000 men as the maximum number that could be controlled by a single commander. Turenne regarded a force of 50,000 men as "inconvenient for him who commands it and for those who compose it," whereas Gouvion Saint Cyr early in the nineteenth century reflected that to direct more than 100,000 troops "calls for such moral and physical strength that one cannot hope to find them combined in a single man."[3] That these figures were not figments of the imagination but presented very real limits is shown by Napoleon's own battles. At Austerlitz in 1805 the emperor commanded 85,000 men with great finesse, but at Jena in 1806 he lost control over one-third to one-half of his force of 150,000. At Leipzig in 1813 he commanded only one of the three battles that were being fought simultaneously by his 180,000 troops.[4] At Königgrätz in 1866, however, both sides together mustered 440–460,000 troops, which is slightly more than those who had met at the "Battle of the Nations" at Leipzig. It was, quite simply, the biggest battle ever fought until then.

To start with the last of these developments, the increase in the size of armies meant that they could no longer be kept permanently mobilized but had to be maintained as reserves and called at the outbreak of hostilities, to be hurled at the enemy like so many ballistic missiles emerging from their silos. Not only did the process of calling up men, forming them into units, giving them their equipment, and deploying them on the borders present unprecedented problems of management and administration, but the forces once assembled were, in Moltke's words, too large "either to live or to advance"; concentrated in a single mass they "could not even exist," their only remaining option being to fight.[5] The concentration of such forces, reasoned Prussia's chief of staff, was "in itself, a calamity," for the growth of major formations—the corps, which now numbered well in excess of 30,000 men each—had made it impossible to maintain any one of them along any given axis of advance.[6] Hence it had become imperative "to march separately but fight jointly," a method requiring strong self-contained formations, good advance knowledge of the enemy's movements, and excellent communications between forces widely dispersed in space.[7] Moltke's system of war, in short, could not be put into practice without a command system to match; or perhaps one should say that the nature of armies presented new problems in command which it was the task of the *Generalstab,* the General Staff, to solve.

Contributing to the spread of armies over space was another factor: the rise of the railways for war and conquest. Early experiments in the military use of rail—for instance, in 1848–49, when the revolutionaries in Baden used it to get away from the Prussian Army's clutches; 1851, when the Austrian mobilization against Prussia led to the latter's humiliation at Olmütz; and during the wars of 1859 and 1864—had shown the railways' usefulness to be confined almost entirely to the mobilization and deployment preceding the outbreak of actual hostilities. Given the finite capacity of each line, the speed with which it was possible to mobilize and deploy depended almost entirely on the number of lines that could be put into service. Since there was seldom more than one line connecting any two points, reliance on the railways thus necessarily meant spreading armies over wide fronts—this quite regardless of commanders' desires or of the fears that such a system inspired.[8] In the Königgrätz campaign, the side that emerged victorious was the side whose army had used five railways to deploy (as against only one used by its opponent), and whose front, consequently, spread over two hundred miles.

The railroad also affected command in another way. A purely technical device unaffected by either threats or promises, the railroad was less flexible than columns of men and horses, which could always be made to go another mile or find their way around. Consequently, reliance on the railroad implied an increased emphasis on scientific, mathematical calculation as opposed to the intuition of old. Coordinating men, weapons, supplies, and trains, as well as maximizing each railway line's capacity and preventing congestion, demanded a type of painstaking staff work not unfamiliar to the members of Berthier's *état major général* but raised to a new level of accuracy in both space and time.[9] To make such accuracy possible, the railway section tried to insure that the whole process would be free of enemy interference (achieved by detraining the forces well behind the borders) and thus turned war into an engineering matter only. As time went on this approach spread from the railway section, soon to become the most prestigious single department of general staffs everywhere, to other parts of the organization, sometimes with disastrous results; in 1866, however, this development was still in the future.

If several factors thus came together to make possible—indeed demand—new standards in the exercise of centralized control, contemporary developments in weapons technology had an opposite effect. During the early modern period, and sometimes during the Napoleonic wars also, entire companies and battalions had relied on salvos fired upon command, which was made possible by the tactic of having troops advance in paradelike fashion, slowly, in line or in column, and stand upright. By 1866, however, the defensive power of the new breech-loading rifles had been recognized by Moltke, and the number of men per yard of front was being reduced to present the enemy with less of a target.[10] Breech-loading made firing from a crouching or prone position practicable; thus troops were able to look for cover. In the absence of novel means of tactical communication, the spreading out of troops and the altered firing position led to a sharp decrease in the amount of control that junior commanders were able to exercise over their men. To put it another way, the advent of the new weapons—or rather their spread from a handful of *Jäger* and *chasseurs* (light infantry) to the infantry as a whole—meant that for the first time in history troops could no longer fight standing up, in full view of each other and of their own commanders. Entire armies turned into clouds of uncontrollable skirmishers, especially when on the attack. The situation was not to be fundamentally altered until the arrival of the portable radio in World War II.

The telegraph, the first real technological advance in the field of communications to take place in millennia, reinforced all these conflicting tendencies. It was dependent on wire, which meant that the stations had to be fixed in space, and was consequently more useful to the defense than to the attack. The unwieldiness of the equipment at hand (wagons, wires, spools, poles), as well as that of the apparatus needed for setting up the service in difficult terrain, confined its use almost exclusively to major headquarters and strategy; using it for tactical purposes other than those of siege warfare was difficult if not impossible. The telegraph line ran along the railways and the process of mobilization would have been inconceivable without its aid; once the railhead was left behind, however, the use of the telegraph became problematic, with the obstacles increasing in direct proportion to the mobility of the campaign.

In 1866, the Prussian military telegraph service was as good as that of any other continental country, but no better.[11] An optical system was being built between Berlin and the newly annexed Rhineland as late as 1835; experiments with the new invention, the telegraph, got under way during the 1840s and advanced rapidly thereafter. By the mid-1850s the most important European cities were already linked by wire, and a "remarkable expansion" of the Prussian Army's Telegraphic Institute—an early attempt to put the necessary paraphernalia into wagons and thus make it suitable for field use—was being reported.[12] By the end of the decade sufficient progress had been made for a corps of "telegraph and railway engineers" to be established for the purpose of installing, operating, and maintaining both kinds of lines, and joint training with other kinds of troops was under way.[13] By 1865 these developments, which were fully paralleled elsewhere, were to result in a Field Telegraph Service capable of linking field armies with general headquarters in the rear and, theoretically at any rate, also with each other. The construction of lines at two to three miles per hour was regarded as practicable, as was the transmission over them of messages at the rate of eight to ten words a minute. For the transmitters to function, however, the wagons on which they were mounted had to be stationary, a limitation which meant that service would be interrupted whenever headquarters moved.[14] The telegraph thus represented a temptation to commanders to keep in touch with the rear at the expense of the front, which may not be unconnected with the fact that, as we shall see, all but one of the major engagements in the Königgrätz campaign were fought without direction by army commanders.[15] The telegraph had an influence at the headquarters level, but corps and divisions, not to mention formations further down the ladder, still remained entirely dependent on messengers and optical and acoustic signals.

The way in which contemporaries appraised these developments, their excitement about the new technology and their understanding of its limitations, is best put in their own words. "The present author well remembers," an Austrian officer wrote in 1861,

the fear which seized him in 1859 when he heard that *Feldzeugmeister* Hess [commanding against the French in Italy] could be in direct telegraphic communication with Gyulay [in Vienna] . . . The author was worried lest this would lead to a revival of the blessed *Hofskriegsrat* [Royal Council of War] and this fear turned out to be well founded. A commander who is tied down in this way is really to be pitied; he has two enemies to defeat, one in front and another in the rear . . . everything combines to rob the commander of his force and independence, partly by accident, partly by design. To prevent the telegraph from doing too much damage in war it is necessary either to have a great prince on the throne or a courageous commander with a strong character who, unafraid to assume responsibility, will know how to disregard a dispatch from home.[16]

Although it had been suggested that the telegraph would make possible instantaneous two-way communication between commanders and detachments and thus reduce or eliminate uncertainty, our officer did not view things in quite such an optimistic light.

In tactical matters, too, one will do well not to rely on the telegraph, since it is so extraordinarily vulnerable and very unreliable ... the enemy, treason, one's own artillery fire, and even the weather are all capable of interrupting the service at any time. The more important the lines, the greater these dangers. In most cases, i.e. in the presence of the enemy, the telegraph can never replace personal messages ... the telegraph, like the railway, will only be of use to the tactician in the most exceptional of cases, and he will do well not to place too much trust in either. The same is not true for the strategist who ... will often be tempted to employ this modern means of rapid communication. Let him beware, however, not to go too far, or else the power of this difficult-to-control medium may turn against him.

As we shall have occasion to see, these warnings proved well founded. The telegraph's importance in commanding armies in the field—as opposed to the process of mobilization and deployment, and also to the maintenance of communications between the armies and a stationary general headquarters in the rear—proved marginal. Contrary to the predictions of some, its use did not significantly reduce "the fog of war." If the Prussians triumphed in 1866 this was due to the fact that, like Napoleon sixty years before, they devised means to overcome the limitations of the new instrument at the very time when they were exploiting its potentialities; and it is to those means that I now turn.

THE BIRTH OF A STAFF

Like other organizations of its kind, the Prussian General Staff had its origins in the eighteenth-century quartermaster staff.[17] Its earliest functions were the surveying and laying out of camps; fortification and reconnaissance were subsequently added. Originally established in wartime and disbanded upon the termination of hostilities, it was made permanent in the 1790s and received its officers from Frederick's Académie des Nobles. Its functions were laid down in writing, and somewhat expanded, by a General von Lecoq in 1800: in addition to the above-mentioned duties, the officers of the Quartermaster Staff were to lead columns on the march and in combat, act as their commander's ADCs ("and tender advice when asked"), administer the intelligence and espionage apparatus, and keep the war diary. The staff was branching out, in other words, from purely technical functions into intelligence and operations.

In 1802–3 the staff was reorganized by Colonel von Massenbach, who was later to be dismissed from the service as one of the authors of the Jena debacle. Staff business was now divided into "basic" (meaning strategic intelligence) on the one hand and "current" (the study of war, drafting regulations, and contingency planning) on the other. A policy of rotating officers between staff and line was instituted, and the staff itself divided into three parts—one for the western, one for the eastern, and one for the central theater of war. After 1806 General Gerhard von Scharnhorst carried on Massenbach's work, helped found the Kriegsakademie, and for the first time provided major formations with their own regular staffs under a chief of staff, thus laying the foundations for the subsequent *Truppengeneralstab,* or General Staff with the Troops. Throughout this period the staff remained subordinate to the War Ministry (whose Second Department it constituted from 1814 on) and thus was far removed from the king's ear; it was only in February 1866, following fifty years of by no means always harmonious relations between ministry and staff and *after* the war against Denmark had been fought and won, that King Wilhelm declared he would henceforth "transmit his orders regarding the operational movements of the deployed armies through the General Staff." Even so, as the wording shows, the General Staff's influence on army organization and armament in peacetime remained indirect at best.

In 1816 the Berlin General Staff had a "department" for each of the three theaters of war, plus a "section" for military history, a subject which had been introduced by Scharnhorst and which was later to have an extraordinary influence in molding German military doctrine and practice.[18] Trigonometry and topography were dealt with by "bureaus," printing by an "institute." Outside Berlin the *Truppengeneralstab* had four officers (including the chief of staff) with each corps and one with each brigade; a divisional organization

110

was adopted only in the 1830s. The structure remained substantially unaltered during the next fifty years. Under the surface, however, the Second (Central) Department expanded until it dealt with organization, training, mobilization, and deployment, whereas the Western and Eastern Departments were gradually reduced to intelligence-gathering, thus providing the foundations for the subsequent *Fremde Heere West* and *Fremde Heere Ost* (Foreign Armies West and East). Since its duties included mobilization and deployment, the Second Department also controlled the railways—an anachronism not corrected until the establishment of an independent Fourth Railway Department in 1869.

Throughout these reorganizations the General Staff remained rather modest.[19] From 1853 on its Berlin members included two generals in addition to the chief of staff, three colonels as Department leaders and one as chief of staff to the artillery inspector general, six staff officers, and six captains—a total of twenty-one. Outside Berlin each of the three Army Headquarters should have had (but did not, owing to a shortage of trained personnel) one general and six other officers; nine Corps Headquarters had one general and two other officers each; and eighteen Divisional Headquarters had one officer each. The *Truppengeneralstab,* then, numbered sixty-six men, and the General Staff as a whole eighty-seven. By contrast, a single U.S. Army corps staff in World War II had sixty-nine officers.[20]

The business of the General Staff in peacetime consisted of a painstaking gathering of information on possible opponents and theaters of war; of drafting and redrafting plans for mobilization (*Mobilmachung*) and deployment (*Aufmarsch*); of preparing regulations and standing orders for training purposes; of conducting war games (*Kriegspiele*) of the kind which the Austrians allegedly refused to learn because there was no money to be made in them; and of the annual staff rides, or *Generalstabsreise,* lasting three weeks and used to familiarize staff officers with one another and with the terrain over which they were likely to operate. The entire rather leisurely process did not result in as much homogeneity and unanimity of opinion as has sometimes been imagined by military historians— the notion of a staff consisting of human cogwheels, each precisely like every other, was left to Schlieffen to establish as an ideal—but it

111

did lead to the creation of a body of officers who were thoroughly familiar with each other's strengths and weaknesses and who could be relied upon to carry out their duties painstakingly and reasonably quickly.

As war approached in 1866, the Prussian chain of command had at its top King Wilhelm, sixty-eight, a crusty old soldier who, like all Prussian rulers, had spent much of his life in and around the army and would, had he been a quarter of a century younger, no doubt have made a good regimental commander. His principal adviser was chief of staff Helmut von Moltke, two years younger than his sovereign, a taciturn, somewhat sly man who combined common sense with a wide education that was unusual in a Prussian officer. A great organizer with an eye for detail, he had done outstanding staff work during the last stages of the 1864 war against Denmark, but had never commanded anything larger than a battalion, and that in peacetime.

Moltke's position in 1866, like that of the General Staff as a whole, was not yet as strong as it would become; even in 1862, indeed, it was still possible for a book on the Prussian Army to be published in which the staff received no mention at all.[21] The staff's relative importance may be gauged from the fact that its members occupied only one wagon in the six railway trains that moved Royal Headquarters from Berlin to the field; as one officer in a position to know commented, "A mass of do-nothings trying to look important is always repulsive, especially when they act friendly, wish you success, appear to agree with everything, yet feel duty-bound to comment on things they know absolutely nothing about."[22] Though Moltke was indeed the king's principal adviser, at least three other persons in important positions submitted their own plans for the campaign and had to be fobbed off. Calm and unprepossessing, Moltke succeeded for the most part in keeping the king's mind on the straight and narrow, which was by no means the least of his achievements.

Moltke's own chief advisers in the field[23] were General von Podbielski, his *Oberquartiermeister* whose position is best described as that of a deputy chief of staff, and von Wartensleben, the railway expert who was not too specialized to carry messages in the field.[24] There were the three department heads (Doering, Bergmann, Veith) as well as the artillery inspector general, the commanding general, engineers, two attached generals (*à la suite*), and six ADCs. None of these officers was as yet too important to handle any business that might come up, nor were most of them too specialized to step into each other's shoes when necessary. The result was a relaxed, friendly atmosphere that prevailed during the daily meetings presided over by Moltke.[25]

Immediately subordinate to General Headquarters was the 1st Army commander Prince Frederick Charles, a cautious, somewhat narrow-minded soldier not unlike his royal uncle. He had taken part in a few General Staff exercises and commanded (to the extent that princes can ever be said to command anything) units from company all the way up to corps. Late in the 1864 war he took over from Wrangel as commander in chief, with Moltke as his chief of staff. This time his chief of staff was General Voights-Rhetz, a difficult character who was jealous of Moltke and contemptuous of his plans. Consequently, the real powerhouse of 1st Army was the intelligent, ambitious, hard-driving *Oberquartiermeister* Stülpnagel, a close friend of Moltke's who sometimes acted as if his superiors did not exist.[26]

Very different was the setup at 2nd Army Headquarters. Its commander was Crown Prince Frederick Wilhelm of Prussia, three years younger than his cousin and like him the graduate of the royal Prussian military education; he also had an English wife, however, who helped him acquire an outlook wider than usual. Youthful and spirited, he and his enterprising chief of staff, General Blumenthal, breathed into 2nd Army an offensive spirit quite different from the creaking prudence prevailing at 1st Army. Their *Oberquartiermeister,* General von Stosch, was later to gain fame as the founder of the Prussian Navy but in this campaign was overshadowed by his superiors.

Finally, Elbe Army Headquarters was really a Corps Headquarters expanded and renamed at the last moment. The cautious commanding general, Herwarth von Bittenberg, and his chief of staff, Colonel Schlotheim, held independent command for only a very short time at the beginning of the campaign. Subsequently their army was subordinated to 1st Army and acted as an ordinary, if somewhat enlarged and detached, corps.

Thanks to the diary of Verdy du Vernois, an officer on Frederick Wilhelm's staff who was destined to become Prussia's minister of war, it is possible to watch an Army Headquarters in action. Its members included, in addition to the leading trio, the prince's two adjutants and his two orderlies; the artillery commander with two adjutants; two engineering officers with four adjutants between them; four (instead of the regulation six) General Staff officers, and four more adjutants. Add the Headquarters company commander with two deputies, three military police officers, and an intendant and a surgeon (both civilians) and the total rises to twenty-seven men, of whom twenty-five were officers, including six possessed of a full General Staff training. These figures exclude princely hangers-on, of whom there were several, each attended by his own orderlies and valets.

Though an Army Staff in the field fell into three separate departments that were in turn divided into sections,[27] the arrangements were sufficiently flexible for much of the actual business to be distributed by the chief of staff on an ad hoc basis. Since the number of General Staff officers was insufficient, the various adjutants were constantly being called upon to provide assistance and act in their stead.[28] The shortage of staff officers, in turn, was itself partly due to the fact that they were constantly being sent out to act as messengers and lookouts for their royal commander. All in all, the distinction between the two types of officer was by no means as clear as might have been expected; of a self-constipating command system of the modern kind, in which each officer works in his own enclosed space and does not communicate with the others except by radiotelephone or data link, there could be no question whatever.

Running between these headquarters, and between them and subordinate ones,[29] was a system of daily reports that had grown considerably in size and comprehensiveness since 1815; no longer was there much of a chance, as had often been the case in Napoleon's day, that a commander would address his subordinate as "my cousin" and receive an undated message in reply. Moltke's directives always carried date and hour of departure, were brief and to the point (partly, one suspects, because the low capacity of the telegraph made such brevity necessary) but, by that very token, somewhat colorless, without a trace of the drive that constitutes the true greatness of Napoleon's letters. Moltke supplemented his directives by an extensive private correspondence (in a sense, all of Napoleon's correspondence had been private) with his trusted men at both Army Headquarters, Stülpnagel and Blumenthal. With his forces spread over a front two hundred miles long, Moltke was unable to wield a directed telescope in the Napoleonic manner and had to have his "eyes" stationed permanently on the spot instead. The armies, however, did make extensive use of their staff officers and adjutants in order to monitor operations by subordinate units, on which use more will be said below.

To assess the staff system just described is a difficult task, half hidden as it is under the heaps of praise and opprobrium that have been piled on it ever since it gained its first triumphs.[30] As compared to the Napoleonic model to which it stood in large if unacknowledged debt, the greatest virtues of Moltke's staff appear to have been its compactness, its thorough peacetime training, and its organization, superior in some respects to Napoleon's (the Nachrichtenbureau, or Military Intelligence Service, was now at last clearly separated from the Secret Police and made into a regular part of the staff rather than a distinct body linked to it solely through the commander in chief). Fully as important as any of these, however, was the calm atmosphere at headquarters, which was the product both of Moltke's own personality and of the fact that he and his staff, unlike Napoleon and Imperial Headquarters, traveled only slowly and infrequently and did not strive to be everywhere at the same time. Relying on the telegraph, an instrument far superior to anything previously in existence, to communicate with the armies far away, the staff was able to take a detached view of events while at the same time refusing to panic even when news from them failed to arrive, as frequently happened. The calmness enabled Moltke to spend the period of mobilization lying on a sofa and reading a book—which forms a strange contrast with the frenetic overactivity that so often characterized Napoleon's headquarters. Moltke's three-line directives might not serve as an inspiration to his subordinates, but there was no danger that he would forget any of them, either.

1866: PLANNING AND DEPLOYMENT

Since no information concerning the workings of the General Staff's intelligence service has come down to us,[31] Moltke's knowledge of his Austrian opponents can only be reconstructed from the memoranda that he drew up from 1860 on. A knowledge of military geography and of the configuration of the Austrian railways led him to the conclusion that an Austrian offensive was possible either from Moravia, directed against Silesia, or from Bohemia against Berlin by way of Saxony. Also known to him was the mobilized strength of the Austrian Army: ten corps, of which eight would be left if the army had to guard against Italy also. Finally, in the spring of 1866 the news that the Austrians were establishing a single Army of the North under Feldzeugmeister Benedek led Moltke to the conclusion that they would try to attack either Silesia or Berlin, but not both. Which of these two alternatives would actually materialize remained to be seen, he thought—and in the end neither did.

Ignorant as he was of the Austrian plans, Moltke at first drew up and rejected several alternative plans of deployment,[32] finally deciding to concentrate his forces in a central position around Görlitz from which, it was hoped, it would be possible both to guard Silesia and to take an eventual Austrian advance on Berlin in the flank. His plans were rejected by the king, however, for the latter still hoped to avoid war altogether and refused to sign the order for mobilization, thus enabling the Austrians to gain a head start of three weeks. When the Prussian mobilization finally got under way it was necessary to use all five railways leading to the frontiers, thus resulting in a scattered deployment all along the Saxon and Austrian frontiers that had been neither foreseen nor intended.

As late as 25 May 1866 no intelligence had reached Moltke to enable him to decide which course the Austrians would take. An offensive against Berlin was considered more likely, however, for the alternative was to abandon Austria's Saxon allies (and the army corps that they could and did provide) to their fate. Moltke, accordingly, deployed his own main forces in the west also. Opposite Saxony, on the left bank of the Elbe between Dessau and Halle, was General von Herwarth's Army of the Elbe with one and a half corps (44,000 men). Frederick Charles's 1st Army with five corps (150,000 men) was deployed to the right of the river from Torgau as far east as Görlitz. Separated from it by a gap of some 60 miles, and covering Silesia, was Frederick Wilhelm's 2nd Army with two corps (60,-000 men). From west to east, the Prussian forces were thus spread along an arc over 200 miles long.

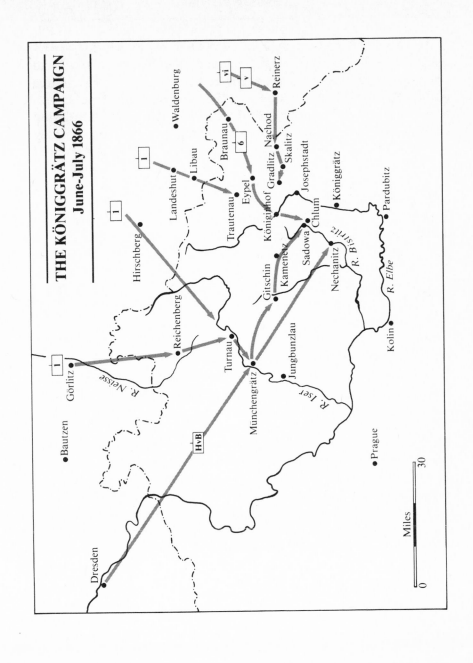

THE KÖNIGGRÄTZ CAMPAIGN
June–July 1866

By 3 June, relying on sources whose exact identity will forever remain unknown, the Prussians concluded that the enemy only had one corps west of Prague preparing to support the Saxons. Three additional corps were identified by the Nachrichtenbureau as getting ready near Pardubitz in Moravia. As an easy calculation showed, even if these three started marching west immediately they would not be able to confront 1st Army with superior forces, and that not before 15 June. On the other hand, "the entire deployment of the Austrian Army"—whatever was meant by that phrase—now suggested to Moltke that an offensive against western Silesia (the Landeshut-Waldenburg area) was in the cards. He accordingly transferred Ist Corps (General Bonin) on Frederick Charles's left to 2nd Army, so that the former was left with 120,000, the latter reinforced to 90,000 men.[33] Should the Austrians attack toward Silesia instead of through Saxony, it was the task of 1st Army to cross Saxony and march into Bohemia in order to "disengage" (Moltke's own phrase) the crown prince.

That this deployment, brought into being under the pressure of time and in accordance with what little information there was concerning the enemy's intentions, already contained the design of crushing the Austrians between two Prussian armies is possible but cannot be positively shown on the basis of the surviving evidence. Writing to the historian Heinrich von Treitschke twenty-five years after the event, Moltke declared: "The meeting of two hitherto separate armies on the battlefield I consider to be the highest goal that can be attained by strategy. It was therefore part of the plans for the campaign to voluntarily maintain the separation that had initially been inevitable, and to postpone direct cooperation until the moment of the encounter with the enemy's main forces."[34] By 1891, however, Moltke had been the recipient of a quarter of a century's adulation by a world that saw him as the inventor of a new strategic doctrine based on external lines. Being human, he may have come to believe in his own legend.

Whatever plans Moltke may have hatched for catching the Austrians between two fires, they were not understood by the rest of the Prussian High Command or even by his own closest confidants, who were following their master's moves with undisguised apprehension. At a meeting with the King on 11 May all those present (Voights-

Rhetz, the king's ADC Alvensleben, and Bernhardi, the Prussian representative in Florence and a "famous military author" who on this occasion was echoing the views of the Italian chief of staff) unanimously criticized the deployment as likely to cause each of the widely separated Prussian forces to be beaten in detail. A message to the same effect was submitted in writing by General von Steinmetz, commanding general of Vth Corps on the extreme Prussian left and a decidedly eccentric character, whereas Blumenthal's contribution to the discussion was to insist that Moltke carry out his own "beautifully simple" plan of concentrating in Silesia and marching from there straight upon Vienna. Even Doering, the head of the Central Department who was directly involved with the planning, insisted that the "limited number of roads cannot be decisive in regard to the number of corps that are to deploy," and for good measure added that the crown prince "was in a state of ignorance concerning the political and military situation." Those who would see in the Prussian command system a beautifully coordinated machine, operating in perfect accord with no friction among the well-oiled cogs, will have to look at some campaign other than the one of 1866.[35]

The truth of the matter appears to be that Moltke, compelled by circumstances to divide his forces, realized—as the rest of the Prussian commanders, each absorbed in the affairs of his own unit and steeped in Jomini's doctrine of internal lines, did not—that each of those forces was itself sufficiently strong and well organized to take on the Austrians for a time, and that no disaster would ensue even if one of them were forced back along its own line of communications until the other, moving laterally across the front, could come to its aid. Moltke's task therefore consisted of directing his armies toward a common meeting place—for which purpose the town that was indicated was Gitschin in Bohemia, selected on the basis of a simple calculation concerning the westernmost point that the Austrians could reach before clashing with 1st Army coming from the opposite direction[36]—and making sure that none of them went off on wild goose chases of their own.

As it turned out, it was the last part of this task that proved the hardest to accomplish. Scarcely had the railway deployment been completed than Blumenthal, on the "basis of all incoming information" and without requesting permission from above, moved 2nd

Army laterally to the east on 8 June, thus drawing it away from 1st Army on its right instead of helping to close the gap between them. This unexpected move provoked a little homily on the relationship between obedience and independence from Moltke's normally placid pen.[37] To counterbalance 2nd Army's move, with which he was compelled to acquiesce post facto, Moltke ordered the transfer of the Guard Corps from Frederick Charles to Frederick Wilhelm on 11 June.

Blumenthal, however, was not the only officer in the army with ideas of his own. Scarcely had Moltke finished dealing with the consequences of his subordinate's incomprehension (or rebellion, depending on one's point of view) than he was forced to take cognizance of another independent move, this time by 1st Army and likewise going in the wrong direction. Concluding from his loss of the Guard Corps that the center of gravity of the campaign was being shifted to Silesia (which was true in itself, if hardly part of Moltke's plan), Frederick Charles, now in command of the weaker of the two armies, with only 90,000 men (though he would still be able to call on Herwarth's 44,000, just across the Elbe), fearfully started shifting his own forces eastward in a flank march so as to get close to his royal cousin. Once again, Moltke had to leap into the breach, this time in order to prevent it from closing; he forbade 1st Army from extending its forces farther east than Hirschberg, which still left a 30-mile gap between it and the right wing of 2nd Army.

Even this, however, was not the end of the matter. On 13–14 June news reached Berlin that the Austrians were only sending two corps (First and Second) to aid the Saxons, instead of entering Bohemia with the bulk of their forces.[38] Emboldened by this development— together with Herwarth, he could now count on a superiority of over 50 percent—Frederick Charles now evidently decided that too close an association with 2nd Army would do nothing but rob him of whatever glory there was to be gained in Saxony and Bohemia. He accordingly used his own initiative to countermand his orders of 11 June and march his army west again, disregarding a directive from Moltke who did not see the need for such a move.[39] Within the space of a single week, therefore, there had taken place three independent moves by the armies, not one of which suited Moltke.

Subsequent historians, attempting to discover the General Staff's "secret," have seen in the opening moves of the 1866 campaign a masterful plan consistently carried out by subordinates who were of one mind with their commander; of this, however, there is no evidence in the sources. Rather, a picture presents itself of a deployment that was dictated above all by an old king's obstinacy and shaped under extreme time pressure. Whatever strategic design there may have been behind this deployment, it was definitely not understood by anybody except its author. Displays of initiative by subordinate commanders there were aplenty, to be sure, but they were without exception based on lack of comprehension—or worse—rather than on any profound agreement with Moltke's strategy.

The entire matter, however, can also be viewed from another angle. Though the purpose behind its mobilization and deployment plans was scarcely understood even by the most senior commanders, the Prussian Army sought certainty where certainty was a realistic goal and used railway and telegraph to carry out those plans with a brisk efficiency that left the rest of the world gasping. Once the armies were in place, however, the method of command changed. Telegraphic communication between General Headquarters and the field armies in the period prior to the crossing of the border seems to have functioned smoothly enough—which is not surprising, since the former was stationary in Berlin and the latter simply moved from one well-known country estate to the next[40]—but no further attempt was made to control the armies' movements in detail. Though Moltke was working with subordinates who were totally lacking in comprehension for whatever strategic plans he may have entertained and who on occasion abused the independence granted them, those plans were sufficiently flexible to accommodate errors; that is, a large safety margin was left to ensure that mistakes would not develop into catastrophes. In the absence of a reliable means of lateral communication between the armies, such a margin was to be had only by limiting Moltke's own span of control—even at the expense of reducing the influence that General Headquarters could bring to bear—and making each army separately strong enough to hold out until another came to its aid. By the same token, and leading to a further decrease in the influence of General Headquarters, it was necessary for the Prussians to make do without a central reserve, unlike Napoleon in 1806. Far from attempting to achieve certainty by fine-tuning his resources to their (largely unknown) missions, therefore, Moltke took the opposite tack: his entire deployment was meant to enable the army to operate without such fine-tuning, thus cutting down the amount of information needed to direct the campaign and in turn making those celebrated brief orders possible. As he himself later wrote, it was a simple plan. Its test would be in the execution.

THE CAMPAIGN IN BOHEMIA

On 15 June 1866 the German Diet in Frankfurt on the Main approved Austria's demand for the mobilization of all federal troops except for the Prussian contingent, and on the same day Moltke warned his commanders (Herwarth, Frederick Charles, and a few leading smaller contingents stationed in western Germany) to start the invasion of Saxony on the next day unless countermanding orders were issued. This method of "optional control" was typical of Moltke's command system in general; to make sure his messages were received the chief of staff also demanded confirmation of each one separately, adding that "the correct receipt of all coded telegrams, and of all other important telegrams dispatched from this Headquarters, is to be reported by return wire."[41] Thus freedom and independence were nicely balanced.

As Herwarth moved against the Saxon capital of Dresden from the west on the afternoon of the 16th, Moltke kept him informed of the moves of 1st Army, which was swinging its right wing (8th Division) into Saxony from the north; the movements of both armies were also reported to Blumenthal, who was given "no instructions from this Headquarters" (imagine a present-day formation of this size receiving no instructions for a full day!) but was warned not to cross into Austrian territory unless explicitly ordered to.[42] So light was Moltke's touch, and so tenuous his position as the army's de facto commander in chief, that Herwarth moving into Dresden on the 18th did not see fit to inform him. Left in the dark for twenty-four hours, Moltke finally telegraphed Schlotheim at noon on the 19th and received the reply that the king had already been informed of the town's fall on the previous day. Of the enemy, either Saxons or Austrians, there had been not a trace.[43]

This little misunderstanding cleared up, Moltke on 19 June wired permission for 2nd Army to cross the frontier into Moravia, then sent by rail and orderly one of his amplifying messages: "The Saxon Army has retreated into Bohemia. All reports [this must have been the Nachrichtenbureau again] indicate that 1st and 2nd Austrian Corps are concentrating near the Saxon border on both sides of the Elbe. 3rd Corps is marching on Pardubitz, 8th Corps is on its way to Brünn. 4th Corps too seems to be moving west. Everything, therefore, indicates that the enemy's main force is preparing to concentrate in Bohemia"—that is, not to invade Silesia, as Moltke had previously thought. Since Herwarth and Frederick Charles were already moving into Bohemia from the west and north respectively, it was Frederick Wilhelm's task to cross the mountain passes from Silesia into Moravia in order to help close the gap separating them from 1st Army, but leaving behind a corps to guard the Neisse. "The location of subordinate corps and divisions," Moltke added, "is to be reported to me daily by wire."[44]

At the same time as Moltke concluded that the Austrians were going to make a stand in Bohemia, Frederick Charles independently arrived at the same conclusion. The prince, said to be an assiduous student of Napoleon and Clausewitz, had borrowed from Clausewitz a cardinal maxim: "The best strategy is always to be very strong, first in general and then at the decisive point. Nothing should be detached away from the main force that is not urgently required to carry out some very important mission."[45] This profound idea he now proceeded to carry out, not by relying on two-way communications between headquarters and corps and on a fine calculation of time and space, as had been Napoleon's method, but by reverting to the earlier practice of keeping all his forces together. He consequently was able to move only very slowly toward the town of Reichenberg where, on the basis of topographical considerations—it was the nearest river shown on the map—and in the absence of any detailed enemy information, he expected the Austrians to make their stand.[46]

On 24 June the leading columns of 1st Army, marching forward blindly in dense array with the cavalry in the rear—the prince had still not been able to overcome the old idea of using his horse in the Napoleonic manner to deliver the final shock in battle—entered Reichenberg. A skirmish took place with a party of Austrian hussars who took to their heels after five horses had lost their lives; apart from this, no enemy was found.[47] Puzzled as to the enemy's whereabouts, Frederick Charles decided to give his troops a day's rest so that Herwarth on his right rear could catch up and the situation could clarify itself. He would have extended the pause in operations for another day had not a telegram from Moltke, dispatched on the 23rd but taking three full days to reach 1st Army, shaken him from his lethargy: "While it had been expected to meet the main Austrian Army at Reichenberg, this does not seem to be the case at present ... I fear 2nd Army will now draw the bulk of the enemy's forces upon itself. Only a strong move by 1st Army can disengage 2nd Army ... the Austrians are marching full speed to the north; the main point is to reach the Isar before they do. One hundred thousand men [Moltke was indulging in a slight exaggeration] under Prince Frederick Charles, with another 50,000 in reserve right behind him, offer the best guarantee for victory."[48]

As the delay in the arrival of Moltke's telegram—a top-priority one, if indeed a system of priorities did exist in 1866—shows, long-range communications within the Prussian Army were by no means satisfactory. The telegraph was still a novelty to most Prussian troops, who enthusiastically destroyed any Austrian installations they found on the way instead of preserving them for their own subsequent use. In the order of march the telegraph detachments and their heavily laden wagons often found themselves relegated to the rear of the columns, while the troops used what poles they found standing to make bonfires in their bivouacs and had to be forbidden to engage in this popular practice.[49] Consequently the time it took for messages from Berlin to reach 1st Army varied very much, from as little as four or five hours in some cases to as much as three days in others. The average, to judge by the hours of dispatch and arrival and by internal evidence relating to the sequence in which the various moves were carried out, was probably on the order of twelve to fourteen hours.[50] The interval must have been even longer in the case of 2nd Army, which maintained its forward telegraph station at Libau on Prussian territory throughout the campaign, relying on messengers to carry the cables between that place and headquarters.[51] Moltke's written supplements, which traveled by rail and ADC, sometimes reached their destination before the telegraphic messages, leading to misunderstandings.

Communications between the armies and General Headquarters were far from perfect, but those between the armies themselves were simply abominable. A Major Burg coming from 2nd Army Headquarters on 21 June asked Frederick Charles how 2nd Army could best assist him; Frederick Charles replied that it was necesary to arrange for a junction of the two armies to take place at the earliest possible moment, thus exposing the extent to which he still misunderstood Moltke's strategy.[52] On the 23rd there was another direct communication between the two armies, after which date all contact between them was apparently lost until the 29th. During much of the campaign 1st Army was therefore in ignorance of the moves of 2nd Army, which in turn had its hands full fighting the Austrians and could not be bothered about Frederick Charles's strange peregrinations in Bohemia.

Galvanized into action by Moltke's telegram of the 23rd, Frederick Charles on the 27th marched his 8th Division (General von Horn) toward Turnau on the Iser, it being again supposed that the Austrians would choose to make their stand somewhere along a river. Here he was confronted by a smaller Austrian force that inflicted a sharp reverse on him before retiring across the river, leaving the bridge intact.[53] Still ignorant of the Austrians' whereabouts, Frederick Charles decided to look for them farther south at Münchengrätz, also on the Iser.[54] He and Voights-Rhetz spent the 27th preparing for this maneuver, arranging for Herwarth—who was now once again in touch, communications with him having previously been interrupted for twenty-four hours—to attack the presumed Austrian concentration from the west while their own forces did the same from the north. At 0700 hours on the 28th, 100,-000 men accordingly opened a majestic assault on Münchengrätz, only to discover that the Austrians had made good their escape. Frederick Charles nevertheless sent a description of the "battle" to his royal uncle, receiving a congratulatory reply the next day.[55]

Thus 1st Army had, by 28 June, missed its prey three times in succession and was moreover moving south, away from 2nd Army, instead of east to support it, as Moltke had intended. It seems that Voights-Rhetz's expectation that the Austrians would be waiting for him behind the Iser had by this time turned into an *idée fixe;* having failed to find them at Münchengrätz, he now hoped to catch them even farther south at Jungbunzlau. Frederick Charles, though apparently less sure about the direction in which the Austrians had disappeared, allowed himself to be persuaded, and orders for the resumption of the southward advance were being prepared on the afternoon of the 28th. It was not until 1300 hours on the 29th, when a patrol sent to Jungbunzlau returned and reported that the place was unoccupied by the enemy, that Voights-Rhetz was finally persuaded that Benedek had retreated east rather than south.[56]

If 1st Army—and Moltke, who by this time was entirely dependent on his field armies for enemy intelligence, the Nachrichtenbureau having apparently lost all trace of the Austrian moves—had hitherto operated in blissful ignorance of the true strategic situation, a series of telegrams from 2nd Army, passed on to Reichenberg and from there on to Münchengrätz,[57] now proceeded to open their eyes. With mixed fortunes 2nd Army had spent the 27th and 28th of June fighting the Austrians; news of these battles was beginning to reach Berlin in the morning of the 28th. At 1300 hours on that day, therefore, Moltke wired Frederick Charles: "The debouching of 2nd Army from the mountain passes will be substantially facilitated by the advance of 1st Army." And again, at 0635 hours on the 29th, after a report from 2nd Army concerning the identity of the forces with which it was faced had reached Berlin: "The crown prince with only three corps [in fact he had four, but one of those, the VIth, had been left behind on the extreme left wing and took no active part in the campaign] has the passes behind him, 10th, 4th and 6th and 8th Austrian Corps in front, and 2nd [Austrian Corps] on his left flank. It seems imperative for 1st Army, which is facing [two Austrian and one Saxon] corps with five of its own, to disengage him." Still not confident that his orders would be carried out, Moltke had a third telegram dispatched at 0730 hours on the 29th over the king's signature: "His Majesty expects that 1st Army will rapidly advance to disengage 2nd Army, which finds itself in a difficult situation in spite of the series of victorious battles."[58] This done, he informed Blumenthal.[59]

Having received the first of these messages early on the 29th, Frederick Charles at 0930 hours issued orders to his forces to take the road east to Gitschin, instead of south along the Iser to Jungbunzlau as intended on the evening of the previous day. Before he himself left Münchengrätz he wrote a letter to his father from which it is clear that he still had no idea of the enemy's whereabouts and did not expect to fight him at Gitschin on that very day.[60] Lateral communications between 1st and 2nd Army were still thoroughly bad, and all messages passing between them had to be transmitted from Prausnitz (where 2nd Army Headquarters was located on that day) through Libau and Reichenberg to Münchengrätz, only the two middle places being connected by wire. Marching to Gitschin with 3rd Division (General von Werder) and 5th Division (General von Tümpling) in the van, the Prussians early in the afternoon encountered opposition from the Saxon corps under Prince Albert and an Austrian brigade under General Ringelsheim. A hot fight ensued, ending only at 2330 hours when Albert, receiving news from Benedek (who had no idea of the fight taking place) to the effect that the entire Allied force was going to make a stand in a position farther to the rear, decided to withdraw after first consulting with his Austrian colleague. In all of this Frederick Charles (much less Moltke in Berlin, who was informed only on the following day) had no share whatsoever; having been among the last to leave Münchengrätz the commander of 1st Army received his first inkling of the engagement, the largest fought by his troops before the battle of Königgrätz itself, after sunset, when the sound of gunfire was heard from afar but was mistaken for firing by 2nd Army owing to the great distance from which it seemed to come. It was only at 2200 hours, when the prince himself was approaching Gitschin, that verbal news arrived, in his own words, "as an obscure tale."[61]

Even the accidental battle of Gitschin, in any case, was not the last error in command to be committed by 1st Army Headquarters during this strange campaign. His cavalry still well to the rear, Frederick Charles had no means of keeping in touch with the retreating Saxons and lost all trace of them on the 30th. As the campaign drew to its climax, 1st Army therefore had behind it an entire series of intelligence failures; a period, lasting from 23 to 29 June (six days out of the fourteen that the campaign lasted before the decisive battle), during which it had only the foggiest idea of what 2nd Army was doing; and an encounter battle fought by accident without the knowledge, much less the direction, of its commanding general. To cap it all, the enemy, his whereabouts finally discovered, had succeeded in making good his escape once more—and all this in one of the most successful wars known to history.

THE CAMPAIGN IN MORAVIA

As we have seen, 1st Army advancing into Bohemia kept its forces together and thus failed to find the enemy except by accident; whereas the problem facing 2nd Army was exactly the opposite. Since Moravia can be entered from Silesia only by way of a number of widely separated mountain passes, the four corps forming 2nd Army were kept apart at the beginning and drew together later in the campaign. Separated as they were, they encountered the enemy and in most cases beat him, the combination of Prussian needle-gun fire with Austrian frontal attack causing the Austrians to lose more men even when they won. Distances were large and communications slow, however, so the Prussian corps managed largely without support from, or direction by, Army Headquarters.

Consisting, from right to left, of Ist Corps, the Guard, Vth Corps, and VIth Corps (which marched behind Vth Corps and did not fire a shot throughout the campaign), 2nd Army started its advance into Moravia on 25 June, six days after 1st Army had entered Bohemia and nine after the beginning of Herwarth's march into Saxony. Following plans prepared by Blumenthal on 22 June, Ist Corps marched through the westernmost pass leading from Landeshut toward Trautenau, the Guard took the central road from Eggersdorf to Braunau, and Vth Corps the eastern route from Reinerz to Nachod, so that twenty to twenty-five miles separated each of the corps from its neighbors. Following behind the Guard in the center was 2nd Army Headquarters, which thus effectively deprived itself from contact with, and control over, 75 percent of the forces under its command for as long as the crossing of the mountains lasted. Of the enemy nothing was known except that he was holding the passes with small cavalry detachments; it remained to be seen whether he would concentrate in Bohemia or whether he would exploit 2nd Army's dispersed condition to throw himself upon each of the corps separately as they emerged from the passes. Assuming, nevertheless, that the Austrians were informed of the Prussian movements—2nd Army Headquarters suspected, rightly, that the enemy was tapping the wires connecting it with Berlin—it was Vth Corps that appeared to be in the greatest danger (on 24 June "spies" had reported the presence of 18,000 Austrian troops at Nachod). Accordingly, 2nd Army Headquarters intended to visit Vth Corps first after crossing the mountains.[62]

In the event, things turned out differently. Entering the mountains on 26 June, Ist and Guard Corps encountered no opposition, whereas Steinmetz on the left met and beat a small Austrian force and informed 2nd Army Headquarters of that fact in his evening report. The morning of the 27th found Frederick Wilhelm, Blumenthal, and the rest riding toward Vth Corps as planned when they were informed by the commander of 2nd Guard Corps, through whose headquarters they passed and who must have been in touch with Steinmetz, that Nachod had been occupied. Greatly relieved, the prince and his staff were just about to turn back to the center of their army when the sound of guns was heard from the southeast. Frederick Wilhelm at once sent out Verdy du Vernois to find out what was happening, but without waiting rode forward himself and got caught in a traffic jam where his horse was killed under him by a turning wagon. Now separated from most of his staff, though still accompanied by some of its members, the prince took up a commanding position and busied himself in siting some batteries to cover a retreat if one should become necessary. Meanwhile Verdy du Vernois, having collected Stosch and some other members of the staff, did the same at another point on the battlefield of Nachod—unnecessarily, as it turned out, because the moves he wanted carried out actually took place before he could make his influence felt. Later on that day, with the battle all but won and the staff (now reunited) inspecting troops, Verdy du Vernois happened to wander off on an errand and was able to detect an incipient Austrian counterattack that was just getting under way. He promptly took charge of whatever troops were within his reach, but was forestalled by the commander of 10th Division, who had also observed what was taking place.

Having spent the 27th, in Blumenthal's words, "as helpless spectators,"[63] 2nd Army staff rode back to rejoin the Guard at Kronow; no important messages were found to be waiting. A report was drafted and dispatched—reaching Moltke only on the morning of the 29th—and the staff had settled down for the night when a message from General Bonin's Ist Corps arrived to announce that it had met the Austrian 4th and 6th Corps at Trautenau and had been defeated by them. Still very much in the dark as to the extent of the defeat—Bonin had in fact retreated all the way back to Landeshut, whence he had come—Blumenthal prepared orders for the Guard to march to Bonin's aid on the next day.

At dawn on 28 June, a hot summer day, 2nd Army Headquarters rode slowly westward through the Eypel Pass in the wake of the Guard Corps. Unwilling to get too far away from Steinmetz on his left, Frederick Wilhelm halted and took up a central position at Kostelitz, where he hoped to be in touch with both of his wings;[64] the result was that he was unable to influence the operations of either. Sitting astride his horse and dispatching his staff officers to observe the Guard's combat against the Austrians at Soor, the prince was reduced, in his own words, to "smoking one nose warmer after another" while doing absolutely nothing.[65] His plight was worsened by the sound of a cannonade, coming from the direction of Steinmetz at Skalitz and amplified by freak weather conditions; it was the first hint he had received that a battle was taking place there also. With VIth Corps behind Steinmetz and totally out of touch, the Guard heavily engaged, and Ist Corps vanished into the mountains, it was all that Frederick Wilhelm could do to dispatch a single heavy cavalry brigade to Vth Corps's aid and hope for the best.[66] As it turned out, both Steinmetz and the Guard ended up by winning their separate fights without assistance from the prince, who throughout the day used his staff officers to keep in touch with developments but made no further decisions and sent out not a single order.

It was evening before 2nd Army Headquarters, thoroughly worn out by two long days in the saddle, rode forward to Eypel. Here they found waiting for them Major Burg, who had spent the day watching the Guard's operations; he informed them that Ist Corps had failed to participate in the combat at Soor. Now finally comprehending the extent of Ist Corps's defeat (or of its commander's cowardice, depending on one's point of view) during the previous day, Frederick Wilhelm at once sent orders for it to advance through the pass for the second time, and on the next morning took its commander aside "for a very serious conversation."[67] Meanwhile it was left to Blumenthal to plan the army's movements for the 29th, which consisted of the Guard advancing to Königinhof on the (upper) Elbe whereas Steinmetz with VIth Corps on his heels was to head for Gradlitz and thus reduce the gap separating him from the army's right wing.

Having won these three victories (at Nachod, Skalitz, and Soor), 2nd Army now supposed the Austrians too demoralized to offer further resistance; they proved wrong, however, for on the 29th two more engagements took place. One was fought by the Guard near Königinhof, the other by Steinmetz at Schweinschädel. The role of 2nd Army Headquarters, by this time reduced to a habit, consisted of listening to the sound of the cannonade coming from both directions at once. These combats also won, 2nd Army, like 1st Army in Bohemia, lost all trace of the enemy and decided to call a day of rest on the 30th. Throughout this period, moreover, 2nd Army had only a vague idea of what 1st Army was doing; there was scarcely any communication between the two armies and no possibility of cooperation.

Though the campaign in Moravia was thus marked by an almost unbroken string of victories, every single one of them was achieved by the corps on their own without either interference from or direction by Army Headquarters; and the same is true in regard to the one defeat suffered. In these combats the commander of 2nd Army took part, to the extent that he was informed at all, merely as a helpless spectator. Intelligence throughout the campaign was thoroughly bad, the very presence of Austrian forces being detected in most cases only when they were encountered in battle. Though kept informed of his corps' doings by means of his "eyes," the officers of his staff, Frederick Wilhelm's communications with his subordinates were mostly limited to post hoc messages coming in and sometimes crossing with marching directives coming out. Moltke's influence on the course of events was close to zero, dependent as he was on reports that took twenty-four or more hours to reach Berlin. All in all, and the use of the telegraph notwithstanding, the campaign thus confirmed the centuries-old experience that a force more than 30,000 men strong could only be commanded when concentrated in one block, and that, once dispersed, forces larger than this could not be commanded.

As 30 June dawned, in any case, that phase of the campaign in which the armies had been separated in space was already as good as over. With 1st Army at Gitschin and 2nd Army marching to catch up with its vanguard (the Guard) at Königinhof on the Elbe, the distance separating the two Prussian forces had shrunk to less than twenty-five miles, so that direct communications could be reestablished between them for the first time since 23 June—only to lead to a prompt misunderstanding concerning the date of 2nd Army's proposed arrival on the Elbe.[68] The enemy in west Germany having been defeated at Langensalza on 27 June, Moltke with his dozen or so staff officers was finally able to leave Berlin and take the field, with the king and hundreds of hangers-on trailing behind like so much useless ballast. The first period of the campaign, during which it had been commanded—to the extent that it had been commanded at all—by telegraph, was over; the second, to be conducted by more traditional means, was about to begin.

THE BATTLE OF KÖNIGGRÄTZ

On the morning of 30 June 1866, traveling by rail from Berlin to Reichenberg in Bohemia and stopping at Kohlfurt in order to send out a short telegram to 1st and 2nd Armies,[69] Moltke probably saw the situation as follows. After its victories of 27 and 28 June (news of the combats that had taken place on the 29th had not yet reached Moltke), 2nd Army was approaching the Elbe; the chief of staff wanted it to stay on the left (east) bank of the river and to bring up its right wing, consisting of Vth and VIth Corps. Last reported to be marching east for all it was worth with no enemy in sight, 1st Army was to continue its advance "without a pause" in the direction of Königgrätz—that is, a point on the Elbe lower than that at which 2nd Army was aiming. Of Benedek's whereabouts and plans Moltke knew no more than did his field commanders, but he apparently believed that the Austrians had crossed to the east bank of the Elbe and thus evacuated Bohemia.[70] Since he had left Berlin early in the morning, Moltke had not yet received news of the battle of Gitschin on the 29th, a state of affairs that was not unusual in this campaign.[71]

General Headquarters reached Reichenberg in the evening of 30 June and was given a highly colored account of the previous day's victory at Gitschin, which 2nd Army thought had been so decisive as to break the Austrians and to drive them back across the Elbe. Early in the morning Headquarters continued its journey to Schirow, a country house that had previously served as Frederick Charles's Headquarters and was therefore linked by telegraph both to 1st Army Headquarters at Gitschin and to Berlin. Arriving there around noon, Moltke found waiting for him a telegram from 2nd Army which announced that its Ist Corps had crossed the Elbe and that the remaining corps were scheduled to follow the next day.[72] Not one to get angry at subordinates, Moltke fired off a brief telegram to 2nd Army: "Yesterday's coded telegram [the one sent from Kohlfurt] ordered 2nd Army to remain on the left bank of the Elbe. Have you failed to receive this telegram, or do you have any particular reason for crossing the river with your entire force?" Apparently worried that there might be some factor at play of which he was unaware, Moltke supplemented this missive with another one to Blumenthal: "I am leaving for Gitschin tonight. 1st Army will rest tomorrow [this change of mind obviously resulted from the Austrians' sudden disappearance in front of both Armies] and possibly also on the day after that. A meeting with your officers desirable."[73]

At Königinhof, where 2nd Army Headquarters was now located, Blumenthal had in fact received Moltke's original telegram of 30 June on 1 July but had failed, because of some error in the encoding process, to grasp its meaning. Like Frederick Charles, he did not by this time have the foggiest idea of the Austrians' whereabouts; and like him, he believed 2nd Army's victories of the previous days to have driven the enemy across the Elbe, albeit in the opposite direction.[74] Each of the Prussian armies was thus exaggerating the significance of its own triumphs and, in the same breath, accusing the other of failing to discover the enemy on the bank of the Elbe farthest from itself, to which he had undoubtedly retreated. Now believing that the Austrians had gone "into the depths of Bohemia" and were to be found "at Kolin, Kuttenburg, etc.," Blumenthal proposed to cross the Elbe with his whole force (with 1st Army standing politely aside and leaving him room to do so) in order to pursue them there. Receiving Moltke's telegram at 0015 hours on 2 July to halt the crossing, he at once complied and informed General Headquarters by return wire. Later that morning, having received the chief of staff's second telegram calling for a meeting, he set off in a carriage with Verdy du Vernois to find Moltke at Gitschin.[75]

The staff conference—this can hardly be called a council of war, since the army commanders were not present—took place on the afternoon of 2 July in the king's presence, and found opinions divided. Given the enemy's disappearance neither Voights-Rhetz nor Moltke knew what to do next, whereas Blumenthal, by now in a thoroughly Napoleonic mood, proposed "to march straight on Vienna regardless of where the enemy might be."[76] His advice was rejected, and 2nd Army was again prohibited from crossing the Elbe. After a long discussion, it was decided to use the next day in order to rest the troops (this was to be the third consecutive day of rest granted to these lucky men), bring up Herwarth's forces from the rear so that they could draw level with 1st Army, and send out cavalry patrols to try and discover Benedek's whereabouts. The meeting then broke up, and the participants returned to their respective headquarters— the king and Moltke to houses commandeered for them at Gitschin, Voights-Rhetz to Kamenetz somewhat farther to the east, and Blumenthal in his carriage to Königinhof, where he arrived late that night.

Meanwhile, however, the information—or rather, the lack of it— on which the conferees had based their decision was already out of date. During the afternoon Frederick Charles, reacting to a report from a Colonel von Zychlinsky who had observed campfires on the heights overlooking the Bistritz Valley some five miles north of Sadowa on the night of 1–2 July, had sent out Major Unger of his staff to investigate. Taking along a lance corporal and sixteen uhlans, Unger directed himself to the height of Dub, which afforded a commanding view of the Bistritz Valley. On his way he encountered an Austrian patrol, took a couple of prisoners, and learned that there were at least four enemy corps concentrated in the area between the Bistritz and Königgrätz. As they rode on the news was confirmed by villagers whom they met on the way; they became involved in another skirmish, and Unger was able to observe the Austrians in their immensely strong positions at first hand. Returning to Kamenetz between six and seven o'clock in the evening, he at once proceeded to Frederick Charles's Headquarters and reported on what he had seen.[77]

With the enemy's presence confirmed, Frederick Charles now took another one of those independent, if somewhat misguided, decisions that marked the campaign from beginning to end.[78] Throwing his earlier caution to the wind, he and Voights-Rhetz between 1900 and 2100 hours worked out plans for an all-out frontal assault by 1st Army against the Austrian positions to start at 0700 hours the next day, while calling upon Herwarth's force to advance to Nechanitz and thus take the Austrians in their left (southern) flank. By 2130 hours all the plans were ready and orders had gone out to 1st Army's subordinate units; a messenger had also been dispatched to 2nd Army Headquarters, requesting its support in the coming battle. It was only now, three hours (at the very least) after being informed of the Austrian presence and *after* they had caused their divisions to leave for their starting positions, that Frederick Charles and his chief of staff decided that Moltke ought to be told. Arriving at Gitschin around 2200 hours, Voights-Rhetz went to find the king, discovered him already in bed (these were the days before electric lights), had him woken up, and made his report. After a short discussion—according to Voights-Rhetz's own account the king personally approved all of 1st Army's dispositions, thus confronting his principal adviser with a fait accompli—he went to see Moltke, who was likewise asleep. Waking up with a "God be praised" on his lips, the chief of staff leaped out of bed, put on a robe and a towel to cover his head, and sat down to discover what his subordinate had wrought. As the 1st Army troops were already well on their way by this time, there was nothing he could do but approve the plans presented to him; whether he was entirely happy with them—calling as they did for a frontal assault against formidable positions that was likely to result, at best, in an Austrian withdrawal—may well be doubted.[79]

Swallowing whatever anger he may have felt at 1st Army's display of independence, Moltke dictated an order calling upon Frederick Wilhelm to support 1st Army "by moving with all your forces against the right flank of the presumed enemy order of battle, attacking him at the earliest possible moment."[80] Two copies of this order were prepared, one going with the king's ADC, Finck von Finckenstein, who was to cover the twenty or so miles to Königinhof on horseback, and the other transmitted from Kamenetz to Reich-

135

enberg and from there, by telegraph, through Berlin and Libau to wherever 2nd Army had its nearest telegraph station at this time. The conference over, everybody went back to bed.

The scene of action now shifts back to 2nd Army Headquarters, where Blumenthal, returning at 0200 hours on 3 July, woke up Frederick Wilhelm and reported on the conference that had taken place at Gitschin. It must have been shortly after that time that the messenger sent by Frederick Charles arrived, carrying a request for assistance. Blumenthal, however, had just received his third explicit order not to cross the Elbe, and accordingly "rejected this in writing," adding that only Ist Corps and a few cavalry patrols would be able to come to Ist Army's support. Scarcely had this reply gone out than Finckenstein arrived, having ridden through the night; on his way he had alerted Ist Corps, but General Bonin—no doubt following the "serious conversation" he had had with Frederick Wilhelm four days previously—refused to budge without explicit orders from above. Having just declined a request by Ist Army, Blumenthal was understandably reluctant to comply with the fresh order now being presented to him; his hand was forced by Frederick Wilhelm, however, and orders went out to the corps at 0500 hours. By 0700 the first troops were on the move, 2nd Army Headquarters itself taking to horse at 0730 hours. Two to three hours, however, had already been lost by Bonin's reluctance to use his initiative where initiative was called for.[81]

While these events were taking place at 2nd Army, the troops of Ist Army were moving into their positions as planned. Marching with the vanguard of his 8th Division in the center, Frederick Charles and his staff had reached the heights of Dub by 0800 hours, surveyed the Austrian positions, and decided that since Benedek was obviously going to remain on the defensive it was up to him to start the battle at will. According to his own retroactive account, he felt like postponing the action; the troops were tired after a sleepless night—they had not yet had breakfast—and the crown prince could not be expected to reach the field before 1230 hours at the earliest. Frederick Charles therefore rode out to his right flank to reconnoiter, was prevented by the prevailing fog from seeing much, returned to Dub, and gave orders for the attack to start "slowly."[82]

It was 0800 hours when the king, accompanied by Moltke, Bismarck, Roon, and a large retinue, reached Dub and "at once gave the order for a full-scale attack across the Bistritz" against what was still considered to be a mere Austrian rearguard.[83] By this time the fog had lifted a little, and the party that was assembled at Dub—it was sufficiently conspicuous to attract Austrian cannon fire—now had a tolerably good view of their own center and right, though not of their left, where General Francesky's 7th Division fought the toughest action of the day in the Swiepwald and received not a single order during the entire time that it lasted.[84] Control was also lost over IInd Corps, whose commander, General von Schmidt, got his divisions mixed up with each other, misused them in a frightful way, failed to employ his artillery, and suffered unnecessarily high casualties in pointless attacks against the well-entrenched Austrians. Sometime during the morning, apparently on the king's initiative, General Headquarters moved forward from Dub to the lower heights of Roskos. The view from that point was not as good, with the result that several hours were to pass between the arrival of 2nd Army's leading units and the assembled commanders' awareness of the fact. Throughout this time Frederick Charles did little except receive the reports reaching him by messenger; in his own subsequent words, his principal task consisted of calming down "the long faces" around him, including (he says) Roon's.

It was now shortly after noon. The battle was going badly for the Prussians, and Royal Headquarters witnessed the spectacle of fleeing troops who were only stopped by the king in person, wielding his stick—or was it his scepter?—and swearing loudly. Moltke with Podbielski and Wartensleben had left Roskos, going forward to reconnoiter, but they saw little except a mighty bull that roamed along, undisturbed by the fury of battle all around.[85] It was in Moltke's absence that Frederick Charles, apparently still unable to comprehend Moltke's design of using 1st Army as an anvil against which the Austrians were to be crushed by 2nd Army acting as a hammer, ordered his reserve IIIrd Corps to join in the attack on the Austrian positions.[86] Returning to Roskos at 1130 hours, Moltke, realizing what a pointless waste of lives this was, came just in time to countermand the order. All eyes were now straining to discover a sign of 2nd Army. The prevailing mood was summed up by the king, who turned to his chief of staff and said, "Moltke, Moltke, we are losing the battle." Moltke, however, was not perturbed; he answered that not merely the battle but the campaign was as good as won and Vienna lying at the Prussian king's feet. Offered a case of cigars by Bismarck, he carefully picked out the best of the lot—thus wordlessly persuading the minister president that the situation could not be so bad after all.

Throughout this time, 2nd Army had been marching hell for leather to take part in the battle. Their leading forces, a detachment of the Guard commanded by Prince Kraft zu Hohenlohe Ingelfingen, had in fact reached the scene as early as 1200 hours, but owing to a strange topographical quirk they went unnoticed either by Moltke or by Benedek, who thought the shells passing high above his head were being fired by his own batteries. Around 1500 hours the presence on the battlefield of units belonging to 2nd Army was finally noticed at Roskos; Moltke now gave permission for IIIrd Corps to attack, and all control over it was at once lost. Like the commander of IInd Corps, Frederick Charles was to write later, General von Manstein was incapable of coming to terms with the independence suddenly thrust upon him after long days on the leash. His attack was a hopeless mess, and the general himself was to die in a lunatic asylum a few months later.[87]

Meanwhile, what of Herwarth's forces on the right? Colonel Doering, the head of the General Staff's Central Department, on this day was acting as an ordinary messenger. Having visited Ist Corps (2nd Army) during the night of 2–3 July, Doering returned to Gitschin early in the morning to find General Headquarters gone.[88] He followed it to Dub, rejoined Moltke, and was sent out at 1000 hours, in the company of Bronsart von Schellendorff, to find Herwarth at Nechanitz and order him to take the Austrians in their left flank so as to cut off a possible retreat to Pardubitz. Meeting Herwarth at Nechanitz as expected around noon, the two officers delivered their message but were persuaded by the general that he did not have sufficient cavalry to carry out the order. Riding back to Dub, Doering and Bronsart encountered "the entire cavalry corps" under Prince Albert coming up from the rear where Frederick Charles had kept it. They explained the situation to the prince and added that Herwarth did not have enough cavalry to carry out his assigned mission. Mistaking this explanation for an order from

General Headquarters, Albert went ahead and dispatched his 1st Cavalry Division to Herwarth's assistance—much to Frederick Charles's subsequent chagrin, and with the result that it arrived too late to take part in the battle at all.[89] Having sown this little piece of confusion Doering rode out to rejoin Frederick Charles, who had now moved his headquarters to Maslowed, farther forward; Bronsart stayed behind and rejoined Moltke at Roskos.

Though they were as yet hardly aware of the fact, the errors being committed by 1st Army no longer mattered at this time. Informed that his rear was being threatened by the Prussian Guard with Ist Corps following hard on its heels, Benedek at first refused to believe his ears and then proceeded to fight a brilliant rearguard action which, in the absence of one-half of the Prussian cavalry from the battlefield, enabled him to extricate 180,000 of his 210,000 troops. Meanwhile Frederick Charles at Maslowed had lost all idea of what was going on; he and his staff had just come under the fire of what were later revealed to be 2nd Army's batteries when a messenger from the Guard found them and explained that Chlum in Benedek's rear had fallen and that the battle consequently was as good as won. It now finally dawned on the staff of 1st Army that 2nd Army had played the role of Blücher at Waterloo, whereas they themselves had been reduced to the part of Wellington. The king, however, had not realized this even now. While 1st Army was in the midst of a cheering, hat-waving outburst of joy, a royal messenger arrived to say that unless 2nd Army arrived quickly the day would end as Jena had.[90] It took some time to convince this messenger, a General von Boyen, that General Headquarters back at Roskos had been out of touch with events and that the day's decision had already fallen.

Moving forward from Roskos around 1600 hours in order to join his victorious troops, King Wilhelm was caught in the mass of columns trying to cross the Bistritz, exposed himself recklessly to the Austrian batteries still firing from the heights above, and got separated from Moltke. The latter, prevented by the general confusion from organizing a pursuit, had not yet realized that what he had encountered and beaten was no mere rearguard but the entire Austrian Army. It was only on the following day, when it became possible to survey the battlefield and identify the Austrian formations that had been present, that the magnitude of the victory was realized.

To call Königgrätz a masterpiece of command, as many historians have, is thus slightly misleading. The battle was an unforeseen one, fought as a last-minute improvisation against an enemy whose whereabouts had not previously been discovered for forty-eight hours even though he was only a few miles away. The chief of staff had no part in planning it, and it may indeed have been fought somewhat against his will. The commanding general of 1st Army refused to comprehend his own role as an anvil even when it was explained to him in so many words by Moltke; he launched pointless, premature attacks which he was then unable to control. The outflanking movement that Moltke had planned to take place on the Austrian left never materialized, and the arrival of 2nd Army was delayed by a string of misunderstandings until it was almost too late. Furthermore, as Moltke wrote in his post mortem on 25 July, "we should make no bones about the fact that our worst error consisted in the inability of senior headquarters to make its influence felt on its subordinates. As soon as the divisions or brigades came near the enemy all direction from above often came to an end. Mutual cooperation among the arms was a rare phenomenon, and usually we only witnessed individual battalions, or even companies, belonging to entirely different regiments, which on their own initiative carried out the most wonderful deeds of war." The main reason behind this sad state of affairs, Moltke continued, were "the entirely arbitrary deviations from the fixed *ordre de bataille,* with the result that control became impossible to exercise."[91] Faced with a different adversary from the one just defeated, the army might find that these shortcomings could lead to "serious dangers." From a commander who had just gained a triumph of this kind, these were sober words indeed—proof, if any were needed, that there was more to the Prussian command system than pure mechanical efficiency.

CONCLUSIONS: THE TRIUMPH OF METHOD

The Prussian command system was as different from the Napoleonic one as it is possible to imagine. Whereas the one operated as a private institution (the emperor's Cabinet) addressing private individuals ("my cousin") about private matters ("my affairs"), the other was fully and completely militarized for the first time.

Whereas one worked through a large span of control and a central reserve, the other would have nothing of either. Whereas one was all brilliant improvisation and ad hoc measures without previous training to speak of, the other operated methodically on the basis of the most painstaking preparation in peacetime. Whereas frenetic overactivity dominated the one, calm prevailed in the other—this in turn being partly a result of the fact that, to speak with Marshall McLuhan, the "cool" medium of written staffwork was substituted for the "hot" one of hastily dictated orders. To sum up these differences in a phrase, the one was based on command from the front, the other on management from the rear. Nevertheless—and despite the differences between them—both systems were among the most successful of all time, a fact that in itself should suffice to serve warning against hasty generalizations.

I start, then, with what the Prussian General Staff in Moltke's day was not. It was not, as many of its opponents have claimed, a soulless machine carrying out its chief's orders with blind efficiency. The efforts of some of its own heads notwithstanding, it was not a body of men so carefully dressed (a metaphor from the world of the circus is the only one appropriate here) as to be capable of divining their commander's intentions from afar, without failure, and consequently of always making the right decisions in carrying them out. The technology at its disposal, although fully up to date, was certainly no better than that employed by its opponents and, being wire-bound, was if anything less useful in a mobile campaign waged in enemy territory. Seen from the point of view of modern organization theory, the staff as it existed in 1866 was not even a terribly well-constructed affair; once it took to the field its operation was based on no fixed division of labor, and the separation between staff and line duties was not strict.

The last-mentioned point, which by modern standards might be considered a serious weakness, was in fact one of the staff's greatest strengths. The point at which overspecialization would no longer allow most staff officers to step into each other's shoes at a moment's notice, or indeed carry out almost any task that might come to hand, had not yet been reached; nor, as Moltke's repeated requests for confirmation of the arrival of his orders and his references to "yesterday's coded telegram" show, had paperwork yet been carried to automatic excesses. Together, these factors made it possible to keep open that network of informal communication which is vital to the smooth functioning of any organization and which may easily be chocked off, but not replaced, by an excess of specialization and red tape. As described by Verdy du Vernois in his works on the campaigns of 1866 and 1870, Headquarters—first at army level, then of the entire Prussian-German forces—was not so much a formal structure in which each member had his well-entrenched niche and sphere of responsibility as an informal gathering of friends, meeting regularly once a day and taking their meals together whenever possible. Though the staff was better organized—and its internal information-transmission system more comprehensive—than anything previously attempted, access to each and every officer on the staff was quite easy, regardless of rank. Nor were there many secretaries, formal languages, standard operating procedures, or closed vans to channel and obstruct the free flow of ideas. Among the staff officers of each field army Moltke had trusted friends who could be relied upon to supplement the official reports with private correspondence; whereas the officers themselves, far from spending their day writing (or, as was to become the case in a later age, dialing) behind their desks, were mostly found riding, alone or in twos, all over the theater of operations. Observing events at first hand and with a practiced eye, they took action where action was called for; went on reconnaissance missions, not infrequently at the risk of their lives; carried important messages; and served as telescopes for their commanders.

Regarding the staff officers' function as a directed telescope, a word of explanation is necessary. In 1866 the members of the General Staff, most of them captains and majors, were not yet so prestigious as to be nicknamed the "demigods." Consequently they were the object neither of the troops' contempt nor of their resentment or fear. The telescope, in other words, was powerful enough to make out those details that would ordinarily be beyond the commander's view, but not so powerful as to produce the administrative equivalent of Heisenberg's Uncertainty Law in physics, which says that subatomic particles can never be measured because the very attempt to measure them will cause them to change. Exercising supervision that is close enough, yet not so close as to act as a brake or, even worse, to create disturbances in the system—that, after all, is a cardinal principle of good management.

As compared to Berthier's earlier *état major général,* Moltke's *Generalstab* offered several important organizational advances. The officers who did the detailed staff work at all levels, and the orderlies who carried the messages, were now at long last fully militarized experts carefully selected and trained in peace, not civilians or a haphazard assembly of local inhabitants and subalterns chosen on the basis of their performance in the field or simply their momentary availability. As even a cursory survey of the various missives exchanged during the 1866 campaign shows, staff work was now routinely being carried out on the basis of established secretarial practices. This in turn made possible an instrument of command whose essential quality consisted not of any great genius or infallibility but of a quiet reliability and consistency—both inseparable from the devout Lutheranism of the age—that were superior to anything Napoleon could muster.

To make this reliability possible, a certain stability in organization was as necessary to the Prussian General Staff as it had been to the Roman centurions, who often spent their entire active lives in a single legion and moved slowly upward through the ladder of ranks with its sixty different positions. With the Prussian staff officers spending much of their careers in a single institution, serving long tours of duty in Berlin and on the staffs of major formations in small garrison towns, an organization came into being in which every officer knew all the others well and which was thoroughly "run in," *eingespielt,* to use a German term that has no exact equivalent in English. This stability, caused partly by a promotion system based mainly on seniority, cut down the amount of information that had to be processed within the organization and also helps explain the Prussian (and later, the German) Army's extraordinary ability to pick itself up and recover from defeats. With their livelihood and advancement quite secure for a long time into the future, moreover, junior commanders in particular had no mortal fear of committing mistakes, which is the first prerequisite for learning.

Though Moltke thus possessed the apparatus to keep himself informed and to make his influence felt, neither this fact nor the existence of a properly articulated organization could prevent subordinate commanders from committing the many blunders documented on these pages, or keep tactical command from becoming a hopeless mess.[92] The latter problem was particularly acute. The wars of 1861–1865 and 1866 were, we recall, the first in history fought by men lying flat on their stomachs rather than standing erect on their feet. With their units spread out over spaces larger than ever before and the troops themselves diving for cover instead of marching about in dense array, commanders from the level of battalion upward found themselves unable to exercise the control of old. At Königgrätz in 1866 this led to an extraordinary mixup among the attacking units; the same was to take place, in aggravated form, in the battles of Worth and Gravelotte in 1870. The result, in each case, was a reckless waste of lives that did not escape the notice of intelligent, if unmilitary, observers such as Bismarck.

To deal with the confusion of the battlefield, which by 1870 was turning into a habit, the Prussians adopted several measures. The first and most essential of these was purely mental, namely a willingness to recognize the problem and a determination to solve it. The second was the system of universal conscription and reserve service that gave the Prussians numerical superiority in many of their battles.[93] The third was a heavier reliance on the artillery arm, which, being less mobile than the infantry, was easier to control and proved as great a success in 1870–1871 as it had been a failure in 1866. The fourth was a decentralization of command proceeding from the top down, involving in particular a delegation of responsibility to company commanders (*Hauptleute,* a title that speaks for itself), who became the single most important link in the entire chain of command. The realization that a company is the largest unit that can be directly commanded by a single man under the conditions of dispersion and mobility characteristic of the modern battlefield led to the system of command that stood behind many of the German successes in both world wars, a system that, in a somewhat watered-down form, continues to operate in the present Bundeswehr.

The fifth, and in the present context most important, means employed to correct the deficiencies of tactical control was a superior system of strategic command. Faced with the numerous blunders committed by his subordinates, culminating in pointless frontal attacks against Austrian cannon in 1866 and against French chassepot rifles in 1870–1871, Moltke's response was not to tighten controls. Instead, the General Staff—together with the telegraph—was used to monitor the operations of the field armies, which were granted an unprecedented degree of independence. Independence, combined with constant, intelligent monitoring, made possible a new degree of flexibility. Indeed, so flexible were Moltke's plans that it proved possible to accommodate his subordinates' moves, and their blunders, to the point of ensuring that even a battle that was tactically lost—as actually happened at Königgrätz—would result in strategic victory. Battle, which Clausewitz had compared to cash payment in business transactions—the ultimate goal toward which, though it may take place but rarely, everything strives—thus lost part of its importance, and became more like a long-deferred check finally entered into one's account. To put it simply, the way to overcome the loss of tactical control did not consist in forcibly imposing order upon disorder, as Moltke's own memorandum of 25 July 1866 had suggested. Instead, tactical command was decentralized, and a system of war was adopted that made strategy more, and tactics less, important.

Thus, though it is quite true that the most detailed preparations alone made possible those breathtaking mobilizations of 1866 and 1870, the true essence of the Prussian command system was not to try to foresee every move in war as if it were a railway timetable. On the contrary, the new means—among which the magnificent collections of maps, now freely available down to division level,[94] must be counted—were used in order to balance independence with control and thus create true flexibility. To Moltke, strategy was always "a system of expedients,"[95] and he always insisted that planning should go only as far as the first encounter with the enemy. To believe that every move in the campaign of 1866, or for that matter the campaign of 1870, was calculated in advance would be a gross error. At the very best, as Moltke himself put it, there may have been in existence a simple plan of operations sensibly carried out, but even this is doubtful.

In all this, technology—the telegraph—played a vital role: it alone made possible the smooth mobilization and deployment of the armies, and it permitted some degree of control over forces 200 miles apart. The telegraph's importance should not, however, be exaggerated. During the period of mobilization its role was larger than during actual hostilities, and the nearer the enemy the smaller the role it played. Technically it was far from perfect, and even the technical potentialities that did exist were not utilized to the full, as is shown by the thorough reorganization of the entire telegraph service that was carried out on Moltke's orders immediately after hostilities were over.[96] The capacity of the lines was limited, coding procedures were slow and elaborate, and transmission consequently uncertain to the point that no calculation could be made in advance about when even the most important messages would arrive. Throughout the campaign the telegraph had to be supplemented either by written messages traveling by rail between General Headquarters and the armies or by mounted orderlies connecting the latter with their subordinate corps and divisions. Furthermore, the telegraph created new vulnerabilities, as is shown by the Austrians tapping the lines of 2nd Army (and both sides doing it during the American Civil War). That things worked out as they did is proof not so much of any great technical brilliance or sophistication on the Prussian side as of the fact that the *limitations* of the telegraph were thoroughly understood and acted upon. It was Moltke himself who wrote that "no commander is less fortunate than he who operates with a telegraph wire stuck into his back."[97]

In what ways did Moltke's command system resemble Napoleon's? Moltke, like Napoleon but to a greater extent, knew full well that the flow of information to and from the units would never be sufficiently detailed, or arrive sufficiently fast, to allow control by a commander sitting at his headquarters in the rear, the invention of the telegraph notwithstanding. Like Napoleon, his method of dealing with the resulting uncertainty consisted not of imposing new and stricter controls but of reducing the amount of information needed to perform at any given level—that is, of building strong, independent forces, each containing a proper balance of the three arms and each possessed of its own organs of command, capable of operating, or at any rate holding out, independently for a limited period of time. Like Napoleon, he was a great decentralizer—though in Moltke's case the process of decentralization went even further in that it was not merely the details of execution that were delegated but, to the extent that subordinates were allowed real insight into his plans (even if they did not always benefit therefrom), the process of planning also. Both Napoleon and Moltke employed "directed telescopes" in order to monitor their independently operating forces and keep them in check, but Moltke went further: he virtually relinquished the tactical control that Napoleon had tried to exercise in many of his battles. Yet for all this, Moltke, like Napoleon but without his outbursts of rage, was not one to tolerate subordinates going off on their own private errands; his directives to Frederick Charles and to Blumenthal in 1866, and his summary dismissal of the insubordinate Steinmetz in 1870, are sufficient proof of this fact.

Like the eighteenth-century quartermaster staff in which it originated, the Prussian General Staff of 1866 is perhaps best understood as an organ in transition. It stood on the threshold of the old and the new, and somehow contrived to combine the advantages of both without falling victim to their weaknesses. Its organization was superior to that of any of its predecessors, yet still unburdened by excessive rigidity and specialization. It placed heavy reliance on careful planning and preparation but was not misled into believing that this planning and this preparation could be extended beyond the reach of the railheads and into the battlefield. It made use of the best that contemporary technology had to offer but did not allow itself to become the slave of that technology (which would happen to other staffs in subsequent periods). As Schlieffen was to put it in his inimitable style, "Viel leisten—wenig hervortreten—mehr sein als scheinen."[98]

5

THE TIMETABLE WAR

BETWEEN 1871 and 1914 a vast revolution swept over Europe and permanently altered the face of the Continent. Everywhere factories were erected, towns grew, and millions of peasants streamed from the countryside into the cities; at the turn of the century, what had for millennia been essentially agricultural societies had been metamorphosed into fully industrialized ones. To illustrate this development with a few figures only, industrial output (measured in terms of value) increased 155 percent in Austria-Hungary, 70 percent in France, 200 percent in Germany, 100 percent in Italy, 330 percent in Russia, and 900 percent in Sweden; even Britain, the only country that had been truly industrialized in 1870, registered a 60 percent increase.[1] The growth in the production of some key commodities was larger still. Mining for coal and lignite, for example, rose from 205 to 669 tons annually, and the output of pig iron rose from 11,035 to 38,550 thousand tons. Similar figures from other fields, such as the production of electricity and the length of railway track, could easily be adduced.

THE MODERN ALEXANDER

As national economies expanded, so did armies; their growth more than kept pace with the rise in population. In 1870 only one in seventy-four Frenchmen and one in thirty-four Germans were trained and available for the conduct of war; by 1914 these figures had risen

148

to one in ten and one in thirteen respectively. In that year the following reserves of trained manpower were organized in units and could be sent into the field, either immediately or following mobilization: France 3,200,000, Germany 2,730,000, Russia 3,900,000, and Austria-Hungary 2,300,000.[2] Armies numbering millions, in other words, had ceased being mere chroniclers' tales for the first time since Xerxes.

To cope with the immense problems of management and administration arising from the new size of armies, most countries by the turn of the century had adopted a General Staff system adapted from the Prussian model—the most important exceptions, Britain and the United States, being also the ones whose armed forces were far smaller than the rest.[3] More often than not, however, the new staffs captured the structure of the original but not its spirit, the spirit of a small, homogeneous, and comparatively informal organization whose members, while specialists, were not locked in their specialties. The most important medium through which the new gospel was spread, Bronsart von Schellendorff's *Generalstabsdienst,* was, as the title implies, a technical treatise dealing with organizations and procedure.[4] It paid scant attention to the network of informal communications that had been the real strength of the staff in Moltke's day, much less to the ethical and even religious ideals serving as the basis for that calm confidence without which the victories of 1866 and 1870 would have been inconceivable. Living in a scientific age (these were the years when the first industrial research laboratories were being established in Germany and the United States), men tried to discover the "secret" of the Prussian General Staff in the system of competitive examinations, the careful training, the articulated organization, the meticulous reporting system—that is, in every field that could be clearly defined in paragraphs and organization charts. The new approach did not spare the Great German General Staff—as it was now known—itself; expanding to 135 officers in 1871 and to 239 in 1888 (of whom 197 were Prussians, 25 Bavarians, 10 Saxons, and 7 Württembergians),[5] and adding one department after another to its structure, the staff was no longer the homogeneous gathering of friends that it had been. Training and professionalism improved, it is true, but only at the cost of a certain narrow-mindedness that seems to have disturbed Moltke, himself widely traveled and possessed of a well-rounded general education, during his final years. Out of the prestige of victory arrogance was born: in the years after 1871, subject to the adulation of half the world, the members of the General Staff came to be thought of, and thought of themselves, as demigods.

The scientific spirit of the age, which believed with Lord Kelvin that physics had already reached the limits of its development, also affected command in another way. War itself, long regarded as the province of art, now came to be thought of as a science, and consequently as subject to systematic study and analysis in the same way that physics or chemistry is. Clausewitz's warning concerning the incalculable moral forces governing war was often overlooked, and his discussion of the correct use of numbers in time and space was regarded as the key to his doctrine.[6] The belief in the scientific nature of war led to the establishment of war colleges in every leading country; to the proliferation of military journals; and to the vast numbers of officially published military histories whose bulky tomes, such as the five volumes by Alombert and Colin on the 1805 Austerlitz campaign, still provide modern researchers with inexhaustible troves of facts. It was a great period for the so-called principles of war, lists of which were drawn up and elaborated in many a leading book. It was also a time when a chief of staff, the German Alfred von Schlieffen, could in all seriousness charge his Historical Department with the task of discovering (or, rather, of confirming his own discovery of) "the philosopher's stone," the ultimate key to victory in all places and at all times.

Contributing further to the scientific cast of mind was the fact that most armies now consisted mainly of reservists—civilians who had to be called up to the colors in time of war, given training with their equipment, formed into units, and dispatched to their deployment areas. To prepare for carrying through this process rapidly and smoothly became the most important single task facing every General Staff in peacetime, entailing a vast and constantly refined organization in which every one of myriad little cogs—thousands upon thousands of trains, hundreds of thousands of telegrams—had to be integrated with clockwork precision. To perfect the process meant freeing it from possible enemy interference, which was achieved by having the troops detrain well behind the frontiers; deployment thus became simply an engineering feat. From this it was only a short step to the belief that war itself could be engineered by timetable and schedule. The Schlieffen Plan, envisaging the destruction of France in precisely forty-two days of preplanned maneuvering, epitomized this attitude.

Another contributing factor to what might be called "the engineering approach to war" was the extraordinary role played by the railroads. Having given proof of their military usefulness in 1866–1870, the railways turned into the principal means of strategic transport employed by every country, and the length of track in Europe was accordingly tripled between 1871 and 1914. Railways, however, are by nature an inflexible instrument; their use cannot be improvised—or so people, following the great Moltke, thought[7]— and their effectiveness is conditional on adherence to strict timetables kept under rigid centralized control. Since the Railway Department, owing to the role that it played in mobilization and deployment, had become the most important branch of every General Staff, its mentality came to govern the planning of war as a whole. The climax of this inflexibility in planning was reached on 1 August 1914. Asked by his imperial master to put German mobilization into reverse and deploy against Russia rather than against France, the chief of the General Staff, Helmut von Moltke the younger, threw up his hands in despair and swore that such a thing was impossible. As he later wrote, the very idea of such an improvisation being contemplated was sufficient to break his faith in the Kaiser for good.[8]

Finally, the routine of peace itself—a peace lasting almost two generations—may have contributed to the feeling that war had at long last been reduced to a science in which everything could be foreseen and calculated. When maneuvers, carefully laid out on specially designed exercising grounds so as to minimize damage to property, must substitute for the real thing; when war games are held with all participants gathered in a comfortable room, around a map or model of terrain; when the existing communications network, undisturbed by the enemy or by one's own troops (as was to happen again in 1914), can be freely used; when every exercise is followed by a thorough discussion, and each officer evaluated on his ability to keep everything in perfect order—under such conditions it is almost inevitable that the real nature of war as the most confused and confusing of all human activities will be lost sight of, and command come to be regarded mainly as the regular unfolding of carefully laid plans.[9]

Thus—to draw the threads of the argument together—the size of armies and the rise of the General Staff, the need for mobilization and the dependence on railways, and the effects of a prolonged peace all led to a belief in the feasibility of planning and control as means for attaining certainty in war; Moltke's dictum—that strategy was merely a system of expedients—was neglected or forgotten. To make possible this planning and this control, commanders in 1914 had at their disposal an array of technical devices that went beyond their predecessors' wildest dreams. As enumerated by Theodor von Bernhardi, chief of the German General Staff's Historical Department, in 1912, these included balloons, dirigibles, and "flying machines" for reconnaissance and artillery observation; motorcars and motorcycles for the transmission of messages and the maintenance of liaison; radio for communicating with major formations up to 130 or so miles away (the equipment of the day was still too cumbersome to be operated by headquarters below army level); buzzers, telephones, and various optical signaling devices for use "with the troops"; and a technically improved telegraph system whose employment was now supposed to reach down from Army to Corps and Divisional Headquarters and even below.[10] The extent of the change that had taken place may be gauged from the fact that, in Germany alone, the 1,000 telegraph stations of 1870 had multiplied to 637,000 in 1911, plus a telephone network of half a million subscribers. Even these figures understate the extent of the progress made in those years, moreover, for new technologies now made possible the transmission of two telegrams over the same wire, or the use of a single wire for both telephone and telegraph simultaneously.[11] To operate the new equipment, specialist units were being established, it being already obvious that they could not be improvised on the spur of the moment.[12]

Whether even these new technical means would really suffice to control the new million-strong armies, spread as they were over fronts hundreds of miles long, was the subject of some debate before 1914. Among the doubters were Bernhardi himself, who served warning against the belief in prior planning, and General von Schlichting, the onetime commander of the Prussian Guard who insisted that command by remote control was impossible and was finally dismissed for his views.[13] Most observers, however, reaffirmed the belief in positive control. Indeed, to renounce it would have entailed a return to much smaller armies—a step as inconceivable to a generation that quoted Clausewitz to justify its belief in the superiority of numbers as disarmament is to a subsequent one claiming to base its hope for peace on nuclear deterrence. In justification of their faith they could point to the 1904 German campaign against the Hereros in South East Africa, where radio was used for the first time to maintain communications between widely separated forces in the bush; and to the Russo-Japanese War of 1905 in which extensive use of telegraph and telephone made it possible, in the words of one German observer, for the Japanese field marshal Oyama to stay at headquarters far in the rear and "command operations with the aid of a map by cool mathematical calculations."[14] Schlieffen himself, though he had occasional reservations about the infallibility of his plans and the feasibility of controlling the forces needed to carry them out,[15] summed up the prevailing opinion in a passage that reads not unlike science fiction:

No Napoleon, surrounded by a glittering suite, will make his appearance on a height overlooking the battlefield. Not even the best telescope will enable him to distinguish much. His palfrey will form too easy a mark for the fire of countless batteries. The warlord will be located farther in the rear, in a house with spacious offices, where wire and wireless, telephone, and signaling equipment are available. Hordes of lorries and motor vehicles, fitted out for the longest journeys, there await their marching orders. There, seated on a comfortable chair, in front of a large desk, the Modern Alexander will have the entire battlefield under his eyes on a map. From there he telephones inspiring words, receives the reports of army and corps commanders, captive balloons, and dirigibles, which all along the front watch the enemy's movements and register his positions.[16]

Moltke the younger, who succeeded Schlieffen on 1 January 1906, did not quite agree with this picture;[17] nor was he encouraged by the results of an exercise which he held and which had shown the maintenance of communications between General Headquarters and the rapidly advancing armies to be problematic.[18] Nevertheless, when war broke out in 1914 the chief of staff, possibly because he was already a sick man, followed his predecessor's advice and did not advance his headquarters farther than Luxembourg.[19] From there, 150 miles from his decisive right wing, he tried to direct operations.

In the event, the reliance placed by the German Army upon modern means of communication to make the realization of its plans possible proved to be mistaken. In the absence of a properly organized corps of motor vehicles and dispatch riders, General Headquarters proved too desk-bound and soon lost touch with events at the front.[20] The permanent telegraph lines available to each German Army Headquarters could only be constructed at the rate of five miles a day, not enough to follow the rapidly advancing corps, which accordingly had to make do with hastily laid field wire of reduced reliability and transmission capacity. German signal doctrine, which made subordinate units responsible for establishing and maintaining communications to the rear instead of having the lines pushed forward from the top down, proved wrong and wasteful in men and material. Desirous of preventing the local population from wiring back news as to their own movements, the advancing troops themselves frequently cut cables and destroyed equipment.[21] Radio, the only link between General Headquarters and its right-wing armies (as well as among the armies themselves) during most of the campaign, functioned surprisingly well from a technical point of view; however, requiring elaborate coding and decoding procedures, it was too slow a means to permit effective command over eight (seven in the west, one in the east) field armies. It was, moreover, subject to jamming by a transmitter mounted on top of the Eiffel Tower in Paris.

The cumulative effect of these failings on the conduct of operations proved to be close to catastrophic. Instead of coolly directing the campaign from his desk, Moltke found himself passively awaiting messages that never arrived. Some of the armies remained out of touch for days on end,[22] and on 30 August General Headquarters was reduced to basing a crucially important decision on intercepted radio messages passing between subordinate headquarters.[23] Deprived of a firm directing hand from above, the commanders of 3rd, 4th, and 5th Armies in the German center followed their instincts and attacked the French in their front, instead of holding back and allowing 1st and 2nd Armies to scoop them up. Unable to control 1st Army on the extreme right wing, General Headquarters placed it under the command of 2nd Army to its left and thus allowed the latter's commander to direct its movements according to his own, rather than the campaign's, overall needs. The ensuing confusion was such that a bemused Moltke had to send a mere lieutenant colonel, Hentsch, on two successive fact-finding missions across his entire front in order to discover what the real situation was. The outcome of those missions is too well known to require a detailed account here. On 9 September 1914, the years of planning and preparation were reduced to one junior officer's decision, made in consultation with 1st and 2nd Army Headquarters (or with such parts of them as were within reach) but with no reference to General Headquarters, to have the German right wing retreat to the river Aisne. With that, and through no real tactical defeat, the outcome of the Marne campaign—and quite possibly that of the entire world war —was decided against the Germans.[24]

Similar mishaps, which took place to some extent within every army in 1914 (one need only think of the Russians at Tannenberg sending their radio messages in clear), could lead to one of two opposing conclusions. The first was that, in the future, planning would have to take greater cognizance of the technical limitations imposed by the existing communications equipment and that, consequently, only those operations should be undertaken that could be properly controlled. The other possible lesson was that, in the absence of reliable mobile means of communication, future operations should be planned so as to render superfluous the continuous exercise of positive controls from the top. Both approaches were tried by different belligerents, at different times during the war, and with rather different results, thus providing an object lesson as to what can, and cannot, be done by two different command systems operating on the basis of the same technology.

DISASTER AT THE SOMME

To the contending armies in 1914, the first few months of the war were a period of great confusion. Everywhere vast hordes advanced and clashed, overturning peacetime plans and becoming so disorganized that seven decades of historical scholarship have not quite succeeded in firmly placing responsibility for such major battles as Tannenberg and the Marne. In the west, the initial campaigns of movement were followed by the race to the sea; scraping up available formations from all possible and impossible directions, the General Staffs on both sides soon found their forces hopelessly tangled. It was in early November, when the first trenches made their appearance and warfare ground to a muddy halt, that this disorganization reached its peak. Clearly, it was time to stop and take stock.

From this point on, aided by the forced immobility of the trenches, order was slowly restored from chaos. On both sides divisions, old and new, were assigned measured sections of the front. The divisions were reorganized into corps, the corps into armies. A vast agglomeration of headquarters located at varying distances behind the front, linked by an even vaster network of semipermanent telegraph and telephone wires, was gradually constructed and took over direction of the war. All this required inordinate numbers of men and equipment; between 1914 and the end of the war the signal service of the German Army, for example, grew thirtyfold, from 6,000 to 190,000 men.

Placed in comfortable country houses—selected for the office space and ease of communications that they offered, but invariably out of artillery range and sometimes dozens of miles behind the front—staff officers down to corps level tended to fall into a bureaucratic routine and lose touch with the troops in the slimy holes. As the war went on and its dimensions grew, the task of day-to-day management gained in importance to the point where it often overshadowed the military side of things. General Charteris, for a long time Haig's chief of intelligence, described the atmosphere in his diary for 7 April 1916:

I am greatly struck by the fact that none of our visitors, even those with whom we have constant communications, have ever realized until they come here what an enormous organization the army in the field has grown into. Each one knows the particular department he has been concerned with. No one seems to have had much thought of the other parts of the organization. Here at GHQ, in our own little town away back from the front line trenches, there are few visible signs of war. We might almost be in England. Nearly every one of the ramifications of civil law and life has its counterpart in the administration departments. Food supply, road and rail transport, law and order, engineering, medical work, the Church, education, postal service, even agriculture, and for a population bigger than any single unit of control (except London) in England . . . Add to that, the purely military side of the concern . . .

The amazing thing is that with the exception of the transportation and the postal services, every particular part of the organization is controlled by regular soldiers . . . It all runs with extraordinary smoothness . . . Each department is under its own head, and all the heads take their orders from one man only—the Chief. He does not see any of the heads of these great departments more than once a day, and then very rarely for more than half an hour at a time. Some he does not see more than once a week . . . The work goes on continuously; office hours are far longer than of any civilian office in peace-time. There are few, if any, officers who do not work a fourteen hour day, and who are not to be found at work far into the night.

Then, apart from these great administrative departments, there is the General Staff Operations, which has charge of all the fighting, and my own department of Intelligence. The Operations section are supposed to do only the thinking and the planning, and not to concern themselves with detail, but as everything they have to plan for depends upon administration they have to know all that goes on . . .

All the work in all the departments is systematized now into a routine. Most of it is done in office. One of the great difficulties of everyone at GHQ is to get away from the office often and long enough to get in close touch with the front. Few can ever get much farther forward than the HQ of Armies . . .

Forward at Army Headquarters, one is nearer the fighting, but even they are now mostly in towns or villages several miles behind the front line. Farther forward still are Corps Headquarters, where there is generally plenty of evidence of war . . . but even Corps Headquarters are now pretty big organizations and are almost always in a village. In front of the Corps Headquarters the Divisions are mostly in farmhouses, but well in the fighting line. One can almost always get one's car up to them. But that is about the limit, and visits forward of them consequently take up a good deal of time. We all manage, anyhow, to see something of a division headquarters, but it is only when there is some particular object, more than simply looking around, that one can give up the time to go beyond them. I have not even seen a Brigade Headquarters in the front line for the last month.[25]

Although Charteris goes on to praise the fact that there are "no committees to confuse and delay" and that "all the formal letters and notes of peace-time have disappeared," officers, desks, and paperwork had in fact proliferated. To operate, a single British field army required a daily average load of 10,000 telegrams, 20,000 telephone calls, and 5,000 messages forwarded by the Military Dispatch Service.[26] As these figures show, 85 percent of all traffic went by wire, which is immobile, vulnerable to shellfire, and tends to become even more immobile if it is protected (that is, buried).[27] The effects of this fundamental immobility on the process of command has been well described by that great unconventional soldier, "Boney" Fuller:

As the general became more and more bound to his office, and, consequently, divorced from his men, he relied for contact not upon the personal factor, but upon the mechanical telegraph and telephone. They could establish contact, but they could accomplish this only by dragging subordinate commanders out of the firing line, or more often persuading them not to go into it, so that they might be at the beck and call of their superiors. In the World War nothing was more dreadful to witness than a chain of men starting with a battalion commander and ending with an army commander, sitting in telephone boxes, improvised or actual, talking, talking, in place of leading, leading.[28]

Since wireless was, owing to poor reliability and mutual interference by the primitive sets in use, of limited utility in trench warfare, effective command often ended where the wire did.[29] In an attempt to prevent this from happening, General Headquarters sometimes fell into the trap of constricting operations in such a way as to make them controllable by wire. It was this approach that led directly to the battle of the Somme.

Looking back upon the "Big Push" from the perspective of six decades and comparing the small gains with the terrible cost, it is easy to lose sight of the fact that the battle was, considering its size, one of the most thoroughly organized in history. Originating in a suggestion of the French commander in chief, General Joffre, in December 1915, the offensive was postponed time after time in order to allow preparations to be completed and roads, railway spurs, hospitals, base camps, water pumping stations, supply dumps, and transport parks to be constructed. When it finally "went over the top," there were available 400,000 men, 100,000 horses, 18 divisions, 1,537 guns (including 467 heavy ones), and almost three million artillery shells, the last figure exceeding the number fired at Borodino (1812) by a factor of fifty to one.[30] Also available were eight large and eleven small mines packed with explosives, all ready to turn a fourteen-mile section of German front into mincemeat. The training, assembly, and final deployment of this force over a period of four months had been a true masterpiece of scientific management; no detail (except the need for secrecy) had been overlooked, not even the supply of coffins for the dead. As the British Official History remarks, the final preparations proceeded with a clockwork precision that was made possible only by meticulous staff work, excellent communications, and centralized control. Every unit reached its starting position on time. Paths through the British wire entanglements had been made and clearly marked. All equipment, from maps to messkits, was ready to go—at 66 pounds per man there was, if anything, too much of it.

The thoroughness with which these preparations were made was exceeded, if possible, by the planning of the battle itself. One of the curious aspects of trench warfare is that it lent itself to quantitative analysis: so and so many raids per battalion per month, so and so many yards of front per man, gun, or horse.[31] Building on the manuals that eighteen months' experience had made available, claiming that the new "Kitchener Armies" were too green to do anything but follow rigidly prescribed orders (most divisions at this time in fact contained both regulars and volunteer battalions),[32] and quite possibly giving way to the natural bent of his own one-track mind, Haig had his chief of staff, General Kiggel, issue an order for the attack consisting of thirty-two sections on fifty-seven pages, excluding appendices on "the use of gas," "bridging preparations," and "divisional preparations."[33] The offensive was to open with a week-long bombardment of the German line, including both the garrison and its fortified strongholds and the approach roads leading to those strongholds. The second part of the artillery preparation was to consist of a barrage, a word that was new to the English language in 1916 and had been borrowed from the French. The barrage meant a curtain of exploding shells preceding the infantry attack and precisely coordinated with it, so as to allow the defenders no time between the moment that the shelling ceased and the arrival of the first waves of attacking troops.

In the absence of a reliable portable wireless, the coordination of infantry attacks with artillery support presented a difficult problem to which no really satisfactory solution was discovered by any belligerent in World War I. The method adopted by the British at the Somme was, nevertheless, extreme in its rigidity: based upon calculations concerning the number of shells that were needed to "destroy" a yard of trench, each group and battery was allotted its own "lane" running perpendicular to the front and was to concentrate its fire in that lane alone, ignoring whatever took place to the left and to the right. Firing was to proceed by strict schedule, the time to be spent on each successive target having been calculated to the minute in such a way as to allow for a slow, steady, uniform advance by the infantry following close behind. Though Forward Artillery Observers did accompany the infantry, their usefulness was limited by the fact that changes in the firing tables could be authorized only by Corps Headquarters, whose location, on the average, was five to ten miles behind the front.[34] Under such conditions, changes and re-bombardments, even when ordered, were likely to come at the wrong time and at the wrong place. The system also worked the other way around, however; deprived of all control over their own schedules and put in harness, artillery commanders came to regard their batteries simply as machines for the production of fire. They operated blindly, without a thought for anything but the mechanical sequence of loading, aiming, and firing.[35]

It is interesting—in view of the above—to note that the starting time of 0730 hours had originally been suggested by the French, in order to enable the Forward Artillery Observers to watch the fall of shot. The British had wanted to start at an earlier hour; but when they changed their minds and accepted the French proposal, the rigidity of their artillery organization still prevented them from making use of the opportunity thus presented.

The plan for the infantry attack was similar to that of the artillery. The theoretical limit for the depth of the advance was set by the range of the guns, say an average of six thousand yards from the gun line and five thousand from the front trenches; in practice, however, fire was only effective if it fell within sight of a Forward Artillery Observer who, supposedly communicating by telephone, could correct the deflection and elevation of his battery's guns. Assuming the artillery observer's vision to be limited to a thousand yards, and his distance from the leading infantry forces to be a thousand yards also, the most extreme range at which the fall of shot could be observed was four thousand yards in front of his forces' trenches, which happened to be almost exactly the maximum distance of the objectives to be reached by any British infantry units on the first day of the Somme. These objectives were thus determined by engineering considerations and not by what was known of the enemy, who, for all the role that he played in the planning process, might as well have been on the moon. The result was that the German second position was not included in the first day's objectives on more than half of the entire fifteen-mile front and remained intact, which ensured the failure of the attack before it ever got under way.[36]

The objectives having been laid down, tactics were made to follow suit. What the British High Command feared most, given the experience of every war since at least 1866, was the kind of battlefield confusion that would make effective command from above impossible. To prevent this, each corps, division, regiment, and battalion was assigned a patch of front of standard length across which it was to advance, slowly and deliberately so as to avoid disturbing the troops' alignment, toward prescribed objectives to be reached within a prescribed period of time. Having reached those objectives—a mile to two and a half miles away, though most involved a walk of one and a half to two miles—the troops, regardless of the strength of the opposition facing them, were to halt, consolidate, reestablish communications, and wait for the second wave to catch up, the guns to be pushed forward, and the entire process to start afresh, in machinelike fashion. Confusion, in a word, was to be banished from the battlefield; that this could only be done at the cost of constricting tactics to the point that the battle would be lost before it ever started nobody seems to have considered.

With their units' orders going into such detail, there was no need for commanding officers from battalion upward to accompany their men, and indeed for them to do so would merely have put them beyond their superiors' reach. They were, accordingly, forbidden to go forward—a prohibition that, to their credit, many of them chose to ignore.[37] Even when officers did accompany their men, however, they were explicitly prevented from using their initiative, since "no further advance [was] to be made until all preparations have been made for entering upon the next phase of operations."[38]

To complete this picture of the British command system at the Somme, a word concerning the communications network forward of Divisional Headquarters is necessary. As has been noted above, wireless did not work well under conditions of trench warfare, and was in any case too bulky to be carried forward under battlefield conditions. To make up for its absence a variety of devices were employed, including homing pigeons (useful only for one-way communication by the leading troops to the rear, and always of doubtful reliability), messenger dogs (much beloved by the Germans also), runners, flags, lamps, colored rockets and boards with which to indicate the position of the troops to observers and to friendly aircraft, and klaxon-equipped aircraft to make at least some communication between pilots and infantry possible. That none of these would really solve the problem of command in offensive warfare could be, and was, foreseen; the conclusions that the British High Command drew from this fact proved wrong, however. Battlefield conditions having allegedly rendered intelligent cooperation between superior and subordinate commanders (and among subordinate commanders) impossible, the British hoped to make it superfluous by loading the individual infantryman with vast amounts of equipment and food (this represented the British method for making him independent for a limited period of time) and prescribing a slavish adherence to predetermined plans. Haig's own personality, the supposedly inadequate training of his troops (which nevertheless did not prevent him from demanding from them paradelike precision in moving under fire), the nature of trench warfare, and possibly also some peculiarities of the British "national character" contributed to this solution; in it lay the seeds of disaster.

The finest military machine ever assembled by the British Empire swung into action, following a ten-day preliminary bombardment, on 1 July 1916, a broiling hot day with good visibility after a foggy start. To observe the progress of the attack, Haig early in the morning left his permanent headquarters at Montreuil, forty-five miles behind the front, and went forward as far as the Château de Beauquesne, fourteen miles behind the front, from where it was possible to hear the guns firing. By entrusting the offensive to a single field army—General Rawlinson's 4th—Haig had in any case robbed the plan of whatever flexibility it might have possessed and, incidentally, neutralized himself in his capacity as commander in chief. At about nine o'clock, having observed for a while, he returned to Montreuil, had breakfast, and settled down to wait.

Modeling his behavior on that of the commander in chief, Rawlinson too spent the first hour of the attack at an advanced command post. In his case it consisted of a high point near Albert, only four miles behind the front, from where it was actually possible to see the shells bursting over the German lines. Here the general lingered until about 0730 hours, when the detonation of the mines signaled the beginning of the infantry attack. He then motored back to Querrieux, had breakfast, and settled down to wait for the reports of his five corps commanders to reach him over the direct telephone lines connecting Army Headquarters to each of them. Averaging five miles behind the front, the corps commanders had little idea of what was happening, however, and even the situation of divisional commanders in their fortified command posts close behind the gun line was little better. Brigade commanders were somewhat better informed; best of all (among those who did not take part in the initial attack) was the position of those battalion commanders, one or two per brigade, who had been left behind in order to lead the second wave and who were therefore able to watch their comrades in front being scythed down by the German machineguns' fire. These anxious men rang up their brigade commanders, who in turn rang up the divisional commanders; some divisional commanders may even have telephoned their corps commanders. Proceeding in such a manner, and in the absence of a directed telescope wielded by General Headquarters—whose officers did not normally penetrate farther forward than Divisional Headquarters[39]—it was inevitable that, from somewhere along the line, an officer more stubborn (or with a greater willingness to shoulder responsibility) than the average should send back the reply: carry out your orders, stick to the plans.

The plans were indeed being carried out with a vengeance. Displaying that discipline for which they are famous, the British battalions attacked in four to eight waves a hundred yards apart, marched slowly and almost shoulder to shoulder and, forbidden to break into a run or take cover, lost 60,000 men in a single day (20,000 dead). By nightfall many battalions numbered barely a hundred survivors, clinging to the foremost German trenches that they had captured or hiding in shell holes. Not the least curious aspect of it all was the fact that superior headquarters failed to realize the magnitude of the defeat either on this or on the following days; there is nothing in either Haig's or Rawlinson's diary to indicate that they had an inkling of having at their hands one of the worst catastrophes to befall any army in the entire history of war. On the evening of 1 July, while Haig wrote in his diary that "few of the VIIIth Corps [apparently had] left their trenches," that corps had already taken 13,-000 casualties and had ceased to exist as a fighting force. Not exceptional callousness (though a dose of that may have been inevitable and indeed indispensable to a general commanding under the peculiarly futile conditions of World War I) but rather the wirebound communications system was responsible for this fact, since it collapsed once the trenches had been left behind. Its shortcomings should have been realized in good time, however, and the system of sending regular information from the bottom up should have been supplemented by its active pursuit from the top down. That this was not attempted even by corps commanders must be attributed to the habits inculcated by telephonitis and trench warfare and probably constituted the worst single error in command committed during the Somme offensive.[40]

Of all Rawlinson's forces, the most successful by far were the 18th and 30th Divisions on the extreme right wing. Owing partly to French support, the artillery barrage on this sector of the front had been more successful than elsewhere; part of the German trenches had been leveled, their defenders killed or stunned. The two divisions accordingly reached their objectives—on either side of Montauban Abbey—between 1300 and 1400 hours and found themselves, much to their surprise, looking out over open country. The commanding general of XIIth Corps, Congreve, actually telephoned General Headquarters requesting permission to carry on; however, the success had happened at what, from the Plan's point of view, was the wrong place, and in any case the day's schedule had been met. Permission for the advance to continue was refused.[41]

The details of the struggle that went on at the Somme for five months after the opening move need not concern us here. The battle quickly degenerated into a slogging match and, to the extent that it succeeded in wearing down the German Army to a point from which it never quite recovered, may even be considered a British "victory." To the endless series of local attacks and counterattacks that succeeded the big push of 1 July, there were, however, a few interesting exceptions. The first of these took place in the morning of 10 July when 114th Brigade, 38th Division, launched an attack on Mametz Wood and succeeded in reaching its objectives with hardly any loss. Two battalions actually asked permission to go on, reporting that resistance had all but ceased, but Division Headquarters considered it "impossible to alter the artillery programme" and the opportunity was allowed to pass. Confirming Fuller's account of the way things were done, the brigade commander on this occasion was forbidden by his superiors to leave his headquarters—with the result that he found himself with nothing to do, all communications with the troops having been lost.[42]

The second instance deserving a mention is even more illuminating, demonstrating as it does that the requirement for control had been exaggerated by higher headquarters and that British troops, comparatively inexperienced as they were, were capable of operating without it and of achieving good results. On 10 July 1916, Rawlinson—by now aware of the magnitude of his losses—concluded that the only way to carry the German second line was to approach it under cover of darkness in order to neutralize the German machineguns' fire. Haig, as might be expected from so meticulous a mind, at once objected that control could not be exercised at night, but a meeting of corps and divisional commanders held on the next day found them in strong support for the idea. Following a three-day preliminary bombardment Rawlinson's infantry did in fact attack at 0325 hours on 14 July, and within two and a half hours had attained its objective on a front three and a half miles long on both sides of Longueval and for what were, by World War I standards, fairly light casualties: 9,194 men wounded or killed. Yet when the commanding general of 3rd Division, Haldane, applied for permission to use a brigade that he still had in reserve for the task of pursuit, it was explicitly forbidden. As the Official History comments, "it was in the highest degree unfortunate that, at a moment when fresh troops were at hand to maintain the impetus of the advance, such a delay . . . should have been imposed by higher authority. Responsibility might well have been delegated to the division commander . . . who [was] in the best position to know what could, and could not, be done."[43]

It is not the task of this book to pass judgment on Haig as a military commander, and in any case a comprehensive discussion is better postponed to the end of the chapter. The characteristics of the British command system at the Somme are worth summing up, however, since they represent, in as extreme a form as can be found, a school of thought that has had adherents from Plato onward.[44] Under this system, carefully laid plans rigorously and undeviatingly carried out are regarded as the one way to overcome the inevitable confusion of the battlefield. Not only is strict centralization required in order to prevent any *faux pas* by subordinates, but operations must be staggered so as to allow for the reestablishment of proper order and control at the end of each phase. Planning and obedience—twin sides of the same coin—are regarded as the key to victory; any opportunism, or any mutual cooperation not explicitly provided for, is discouraged if not prohibited, it being assumed that the commander in chief alone is in possession of all the facts and therefore able to introduce whatever changes in the plan may be required. To prevent waste and secure coordination, rigid adherence to plans is prescribed; yet, as the above case study shows, such adherence in the end is conducive to generating waste and hindering coordination. Haig himself, positioned at his headquarters where he hoped to have all the facts at the end of a telephone wire, ended up by having none at all, and, as his diary shows, was one of the worst-informed men on the Somme. Given the vacuum thus created, and since nobody except the commander in chief was authorized to make use of his own initiative, the plan took on a life of its own. While men were being mowed down by the thousands,[45] the staff, immersed in their routine, found nothing better to do than to serve warning concerning the effect of verdigris on vermorel sprayers or the need to keep pets out of the trenches.[46]

The British command system at the Somme may in part be explained, though scarcely excused, as arising naturally from the circumstances of trench warfare and the technology of the time. Their vision obstructed by countless craters and the fountains of earth sent up by thousands of shells and millions of bullets, commanders in the rear had an impossible task in keeping in touch with their men in front without a reliable portable wireless. Very difficult, too, was the wielding of a "directed telescope," though it must be added that the British, possibly acting on a telephone-dependent habit, did not even try. Since this was a war of machines that relied for their functioning on an incessant, well-coordinated stream of ammunition and spare parts, a considerable degree of centralization was absolutely indispensable in the preparatory stage and, not unnaturally (centralization is a highly contagious disease), tended to extend itself to the actual battle also. It is possible to carry centralization too far, however; instead of dividing the offensive between two or more armies and thus creating flexibility at the top to offset the rigidity at the bottom, Haig compounded the problem by entrusting the attack to 4th Army alone (though 5th—Reserve—Army did play a small diversionary role). The division of 4th Army into five corps did not do much to correct the situation; under the plans of General Headquarters each of them was to march straight ahead, and instances of formations coming to each other's aid are, accordingly, not recorded on the Somme.

Although some parts of the command system were thus dictated by the dominant technological and tactical factors of the age, others were not. If they had gone with their men, battalion and brigade commanders would have lost touch with their superiors and to that extent been rendered ineffective; by forbidding them to do so, however, General Headquarters made them even more ineffective and at the same time deprived the troops of whatever on-the-spot direction that their commanders might have been able to provide. Channeling the advance into parallel lines, each perpendicular to the front and strictly separated from its neighbors on either side, was meant to enable higher headquarters to maintain an overall picture of the situation; in the event, however, not even this was achieved, and any possible opportunities for mutual support were lost. Lost, too, and for the same reason, were any opportunities that presented themselves for exploiting local victory and continuing the advance. The correction of fire by Forward Artillery Observers was meant to secure accuracy, but with fire control centralized in the hands of

Corps Headquarters this aim would have been impossible to attain even if adequate communications had existed. Technological facts of life, in other words, determined only some aspects of the British command system at the Somme. The rest may be put down to various factors, including the peacetime structure of the army as a total institution that strove to regulate every detail in the lives of the long-time professionals who were part of it, and possibly also the way that Haig's own one-track mind worked.

That the British reaction to the technological circumstances governing trench warfare in World War I was not the only possible one is demonstrated by the command system employed by the Germans during their 1918 offensives. Though the signals technology with which both sides worked was remarkably similar, they used it to devise very different solutions to the problem of command. It is with the German solution, then, that the next section must deal.

THE EMPEROR'S BATTLE

Measuring military achievement, even under the repetitive and easily quantifiable conditions of World War I, is always a questionable undertaking. Nevertheless, it would surely be difficult to find an offensive as unsuccessful as the one at the Somme in 1916, producing so many casualties for so little tactical gain; whereas the German offensive of March 1918 was, by those very standards, the most spectacularly successful of all attacks launched on the western front during the whole of World War I.[47] Within a mere four days, the Germans recaptured ground that the British had fought over for four months—and did so, moreover, in the face of defenses considerably stronger than those they themselves had been able to muster at the Somme twenty-one months before.[48] Their success was due partly to the introduction of new weapons—flame throwers, submachine guns—and partly to new tactics, known as infiltration; also, and above all, to a new method of command made possible by, and necessary to, those weapons and those tactics.

Like the British and the French, the Germans were taken by surprise by the outbreak of trench warfare on the western front in the autumn of 1914; like them, they responded by building up a carefully constructed network of headquarters and communications that, as time passed and the front remained stationary, tended to harden and take on permanence. German signaling equipment was, by and large, very similar to that employed by their opponents, and the consequences of its use were, accordingly, also similar.[49] Located as far to the rear as their Allied counterparts (with whom, it is said, they sometimes arrived at a tacit agreement not to allow each other's peace to be disturbed by shelling),[50] German staffs too fell victim to telephonitis, a tendency by higher headquarters to interfere in every small detail simply because it was so easily done. And a growing mountain of paperwork appeared, endless forms and correspondence that allegedly had to be processed by the troops if Germany's limited resources were to be efficiently husbanded. It was known as *der Papierkrieg*, the paper war.[51]

But the German organization never became quite as rigid as its British counterpart. Helping to prevent such an outcome was the army's social structure in peacetime: the army consisted of conscripts who expected to serve for two years and get out, not of long-time regulars spending half a lifetime there. Besides, there was the tradition of Scharnhorst and Gneisenau, who, following the defeat at Jena and the discrediting of the old Prussian automatism, had laid the foundations for a command system based on free, intelligent cooperation between the commander and the members of his staff. Moltke's wars in 1866 and 1870–71 had shown that system at its best; and although such cooperation at the highest level was made more difficult in the years immediately preceding 1914 by the expansion of the staff (and possibly also by Schlieffen's influence), the idea by that time had percolated further down, taking root at the echelons most crucial to the functioning of any army: the battalion, the company, and the platoon, and even the NCO-commanded squad, which now made its debut as an independent tactical unit.

With the experience of Königgrätz and any number of battles in the Franco-Prussian War to guide them, the Germans came to regard confusion as the normal state of the battlefield, and the remedy was sought not in any strict regimentation on the British model but in further decentralization and the lowering of decision thresholds. At a time when German industry was based on authoritarianism—mitigated, sometimes, by paternalism—the army went its own way and sought to extend the spirit of free cooperation from the highest levels, for which it had originally been intended, to the lower ones. In 1906, accordingly, the Regulations read: "Combat demands thinking, independent leaders and troops, capable of independent action." The idea was taken a step further in the 1908 Regulations, the key sentence of which was to appear in every subsequent edition right down to 1945: "From the youngest soldier upward, the total *independent* commitment of all physical and mental forces is to be demanded. Only thus can the full power of the troops be brought to bear."[52]

Building on these principles, the German Army in the spring of 1915—at the time when the British launched the first of their unsuccessful offensives at Neuve Chapelle—was already experimenting with a less rigid system of command. On the eve of the Gorlice-Tarnow breakthrough, the "General Instructions" of 11th Army, issued by General von Mackensen and his chief of staff, von Seeckt, read as follows: "The attack, if it is to succeed, must be pushed forward at a rapid pace . . . Thus the Army cannot assign the attacking corps and divisions definite objectives for each day, lest by fixing them the possibility of further progress may be obstructed." The instructions went on: "Any portion of the attacking troops which is successful in pushing on will expose itself to the danger of envelopment. Thus the troops which least deserve it may meet with disaster as a result of their own rapid advance. Consideration of this possibility makes it necessary for the Army to fix certain lines, which should be reached by the force as a whole, and if possible simultaneously. *Any progress beyond these lines will be thankfully welcomed by the Army and made use of.*"[53] Recognizing that the offensive could not be closely controlled from above, von Seeckt was thus laying down minimum objectives, not maximum ones as did Haig and Kiggel at the Somme.

The method of command adopted by 11th Army in the east was, admittedly, favored by several factors. The Germans were facing a second-rate opponent. A breakthrough in these large, sparsely populated spaces was never as difficult to achieve as in France. There was no dense network of railroads over which the defender could retreat while simultaneously denying its use to the attacker. Nevertheless, the Germans soon demonstrated that the same principles were also applicable to the defensive fighting on the western front.

There the timing of counterattacks, to take place as soon as one's own trenches had been occupied by the enemy and before he could get organized for defense, was of vital importance. An *Oberste Heeresleitung* circular issued early in 1916 accordingly read:

As a matter of experience, the division in the front line had best keep control of its own interference [i.e., reserved for counterattack] troops; that division knows the progress of the battle and the terrain, and has the greatest stake in holding on to its fighting zone. Only in this way [can] we assure unity in battle action. For the same reason [that is, the need to save time by dispensing with the reference to higher headquarters] it is advisable to have the headquarters of the division in the front line and the interference division at one and the same command post ... Rank of the commanders must not be allowed to interfere ... [Rather than await the call of the front line division] the commander of the interference troops had better orient himself with his own means at hand concerning the situation, and *independently* order the general counterattack. Army Headquarters ordered, and not without justification: *"It is strictly forbidden to delay local counterattacks while permission of the next higher headquarters is requested."* That is indeed very correct; such a question merely shows that the commander is lacking in decision and energy, and in waiting for an answer so much time is lost that the shock would come too late. This holds good equally for small and large engagements.[54]

The Germans, then, recognized that accurate timing is vital in the counterattack, and were prepared to buy it, even at the expense of possible confusion by lowering decision thresholds. This helps account for the German Army's remarkable capacity for reorganization and recuperation, which has been the subject of much comment in both world wars; indeed, the principle served it well in the series of counterattacks that stopped the British infantry at the Somme in 1916 and, a still greater achievement, their tanks at Cambrai in 1917.

To make sure that overall coordination would not be lost in spite of the greater independence granted low-level echelons, it was necessary once again to resort to a "directed telescope," consisting of practiced, trusted observers engaged in the active pursuit of information from the top down to cut across and supplement that coming from the bottom up. As Kuhl describes it:

When I was chief of the General Staff of an army every officer at head-quarters, not merely the general staff officers but the adjutants, ordnance, and signal officers as well, was assigned a section of the front. Each one was to visit the foremost line once a week and keep himself carefully informed of developments in his section. While going on these visits they were handed questionnaires reminding them of the most important problems to be investigated: the state of the trenches, supply, clothing, etc. . . . Later, when I was chief of staff of an Army Group with four armies under its command, such visits were no longer possible to carry out on a routine basis. Every time a large-scale operation broke out I sent a member of my staff there in order to gain an immediate impression of the local situation, the strength of the [enemy] attack, and the situation of the troops.[55]

The twin elements of the German command system—the greater independence granted to subordinate leaders and the employment of general staff officers as the commander's "eyes"—thus complemented each other. The second was made necessary by the first; the first was in turn kept within bounds by the second. It was further assisted by the fact that German units up to corps level were built up on a regional basis, so that staff officers visiting their assigned sections of the front would often encounter personal friends to whom it was possible to talk informally, thus again cutting across the normal reporting system.

In 1918, faced with the need to get in a smashing blow and end the war before the Americans could bring their full weight to bear, it became Ludendorff's task to mold these principles into a form that would permit the attainment of the goal that had eluded all commanders on both sides since 1914, a breakthrough in the west.[56] A man of brutal, driving energy, Ludendorff's approach to the problem was very different from that of his predecessors. Whereas they had relied on strategic considerations to select the site of their would-be breakthrough (in the case of the British on the Somme, this happened to be the strongest part of the entire German line in the west), Ludendorff started from the assumption that tactics were more important than strategy: it was a question above all of launching an offensive at a point where a tactical breakthrough was possible, not where a strategic one was desirable.[57] This inversion of normal planning procedure served the Germans well in that it made possible a most careful study of tactical problems; on the other hand, it also carried the danger that the blow, even if successful, would be somewhat pointless.

The part of the front between Lens and La Fère on both sides of St. Quentin, representing the extreme right flank of the British-held sector of the line, having been selected after considerable argument between Ludendorff and his aides, preparations got under way in December of 1917 and proceeded throughout the winter. Like the British preparations in 1916, but with far greater emphasis on secrecy, they consisted of building roads, railway spurs, airfields, depots, hospitals, and communication networks; of amassing men, horses, guns, and supplies; and of thorough training that was meant, in the words of the basic directive issued on 1 January 1918, to rid men, commanders, and staffs of the habits inculcated by four years of trench warfare and instill into them a new offensive spirit.[58] Unlike the British at the Somme, the German General Staff did not fall into the trap of regarding the entire army as a homogeneous lot; well aware that his forces were now, judged by peacetime standards, little better than a disordered militia, Ludendorff had the best troops of each division pulled out and gathered into specially organized, specially trained storm-troop detachments whose purpose was to spearhead the attack. Insofar as it was necessary to bring up troops (all those under thirty-five years of age) all the way from the eastern front, the organizational effort involved was, if anything, even larger than that preceding the Somme in 1916; as had happened then, the German planning and preparations were completely successful.

In 1916 at the Somme, the British had confined each of their attacking corps to a lane running perpendicular to the front; the corps were thus unable to offer mutual support. The Germans in 1918 partly solved this problem by attacking diagonally across the front and by dividing the forty-seven assault divisions between three armies (from right to left, 17th, 2nd, and 18th, commanded by von Below, von der Marwitz, and von Hutier respectively), which provided a much greater measure of flexibility at the top.[59] At the end of January, moreover, 18th Army to the German left was transferred from Army Group, Bavarian Crown Prince, to Army Group, Imperial Crown Prince, so that the offensive was now divided between two Army Groups. Reasons connected with dynastic prestige may have had something to do with this decision; Ludendorff, however, justified it on the grounds that he wanted to exercise personal command rather than relinquish it to subordinates, as Haig had on the Somme. In judging the arrangements he made, it must be kept in mind that the positions of the two men were not analogous; Haig was merely the commander in chief of an expeditionary force, though a large one, whereas Ludendorff in 1918 was the virtual dictator of a great power engaged in a world war.

Whatever the merits of this top-level organization, the tactical principles governing the German offensive were as different from the British ones as it is possible to imagine. Their revolutionary nature is perhaps best explained by a direct quotation from the training directive of 1 January 1918 entitled "The Attack in the War of Position":

3. The attack ... demands STRICT COMMAND, CAREFUL AND THOROUGH PREPARATION, AND THE COOPERATION OF ALL ARMS within the fighting units and with the neighboring units, and also a clear grasp of the objectives to be reached. On the other hand, every attack offers the OPPORTUNITY FOR FREE ACTIVITY AND DECISIVE ACTION at all levels down to the individual soldier ...

4. CLOSE LIAISON BETWEEN ALL ARMS AND ALL COMMANDERS, from the front to the rear and from the rear to the front, and laterally, is indispensable ... Only such liaison enables the High Command to take the necessary measures in time.

5. The objective of the attack is to penetrate as deeply as possible into the enemy positions aiming, at the very least, at the gun line which must be reached on the first day ... The first break in is comparatively easy to achieve. The difficulty consists in bringing up reinforcements at the correct time and place. The opponent, taken by surprise, must not be allowed to recover his balance. His countermeasures must be overturned by the offensive's rapid progress. EVERYTHING DEPENDS ON A RAPID ADVANCE, CARRIED OUT BY THE LEADING TROOPS IN THE CERTAINTY THAT FLANK AND REAR PROTECTION, AS WELL AS FIRE SUPPORT, WILL BE TAKEN CARE OF FROM BEHIND.

The danger lest the offensive will spend itself is great. The dead point must be overcome by the energy of the commanders, located far in front, and by the stream of fresh reinforcements from the rear.

THE MOST CRUCIAL FACTOR IS NOT THE NUMBER OF TROOPS BUT THE FIREPOWER OF THE ARTILLERY AND THE INFANTRY. FORCES THAT ARE TOO NUMEROUS MAY OBSTRUCT EACH OTHER AND COMPLICATE THE SUP-

PLY PROBLEM. EVERYTHING DEPENDS ON RAPID, INDEPENDENT ACTION BY ALL HEADQUARTERS WITHIN THE FRAMEWORK OF THE WHOLE, AND ALSO ON THE ABILITY OF THE ARTILLERY AND AMMUNITION SUPPLY TO KEEP UP.[60]

Elaborating on these principles, the directive goes on to say that, in the attack as in the defense, the division is the basic unit of organization, since it alone possesses all the staffs and technical means to ensure a properly integrated cooperation of all arms. Separate arms' chains of command, bypassing the division and leading directly to corps headquarters, were to be avoided. The planning was to be as detailed as possible but not so detailed as to rob subordinate commanders of elbow room. The troops should be assigned precise objectives during the initial stages of the advance but not subjected to unnecessary limitations once those objectives were attained. Commanders up to division level should follow their troops forward and keep the necessary signal units and equipment close at hand; where staffs were too large to do this, forward command posts should be established, or else headquarters from division level upward were to employ lookouts, runners, and airborne observers to watch the progress of the battle and report on it independently from the troops themselves. "The greater the mobility of the attack," the directive went on, "the farther forward is the proper place of senior commanders, often on horseback."

Though the troops were instructed to report—using colored rockets—every time certain objectives were reached, lines crossed, shifts in enemy artillery fire detected, and so on, senior headquarters were warned not to place too much reliance on those reports. Instead, they were to use their own means—the directed telescope once again—in order to gain a picture of events in their own units and neighboring ones. Liaison officers were to be detached by the artillery to the infantry and by the infantry to the artillery; it was quite clear, however, that interarm cooperation during the later stages of the attack would not be practical unless chains of command were decentralized. This meant that some of the artillery and mortar batteries would not take part in the barrage but would be kept limbered up and ready to move; attached to the leading infantry regiments and following closely behind their advance, these batteries were to offer direct fire support wherever and whenever called upon to do so by battalion and even company commanders. Machine guns, too, hitherto considered primarily a defensive weapon, were to accompany the leading troops, as were detachments carrying flamethrowers, a new weapon in 1918. The result would be integrated teams of all arms, capable of dealing with obstacles on their own and thus to some extent independent of communication with, and support from, senior headquarters far in the rear.

To combat the obstacles in their way was not, however, the main task of the leading troops. Reaching the enemy positions at the same moment as the last shell of the barrage, they were supposed to bypass surviving centers of resistance ("The lateral clearing of the trenches can only be recommended in the smallest of attacks," the directive read) and leave behind detachments to deal with them if necessary, but never to allow the momentum of the advance to be spent or contact with the retreating opponent to be lost. No provisions were made for maintaining the cohesion of the attack, and commanders were explicitly warned not to allow local checks and even reverses to delay the offensive as a whole. With reliance placed on momentum and improvisation from below rather than on planning and control from above, the advance was bound to be chaotic. The Germans sought to counter the chaos by having senior commanders operate far forward and by preparing for the establishment of a telephone communications network immediately in the infantry's wake. Commanders, nevertheless, were warned not to place too much reliance on this network, and to use blinkers, pigeons, and runners instead.

One problem to which no complete answer was found was the coordination of the infantry's advance with that of the creeping barrage. The shortcomings of a preplanned artillery firing schedule were well understood; in the absence of a portable wireless system, however, the best solution under most circumstances still remained precisely such a schedule, with fire progressing in orderly leaps from one target to another. Yet the artillery was explicitly warned against impeding the infantry's progress, and communication between the two arms was to some extent secured by extensive reliance on colored rockets to signify that predetermined lines had been reached and crossed. Another measure adopted by the Germans to overcome this problem was to train the infantry to follow right on the heels of their own exploding shells, a solution that demanded good morale and a certain degree of ruthlessness and inevitably led to some casualties, but would, in Ludendorff's words, save losses in the end.

The tactical details having been settled in this manner, the offensive's strategic objectives were laid down in a directive issued over Hindenburg's signature on 10 March:

1. The Michael attack will take place on March 21st. Break in into the first hostile positions at 0940 hours.

2. The first great tactical objective of Army Group Crown Prince Rupprecht [on the right wing] will be to cut off the British in the Cambrai salient and gain, north of the junction of the Omignon stream with the Somme, the line Croisilles-Bapaume-Péronne-mouth of the Omignon. Should the progress of the right wing [17th Army] be very good, it will be carried further, beyond Croisilles. The subsequent task of this Army Group will be to push forward in the direction of Arras-Albert, to hold the Somme near Péronne securely with the left wing, and with the main weight of the attack on the right wing to upset the balance of the British front on the [German] 6th Army's front as well as on the front of the attack, and thus free further German forces from position warfare for the advance.

3. Army Group German Crown Prince [on the left] will first gain the line of the Somme south of the Omignon stream, and the Crozat Canal. The 18th Army will also be prepared to extend its right wing as far as Péronne. This Army Group will study the question of 18th Army being reinforced by divisions from 7th, 1st, and 3rd Armies [farther to the left] . . .

The German offensive was not conceived as a frontal attack, then, but rather as an attempt to cut across the British rear with the right wing, using the center (2nd Army) and the left (18th Army) first in subsidiary attacks and for holding off the French to the south, then to reinforce the breakthrough on the right. With this sequence in mind, and convinced that the success of the attack would be determined, in the words of the directive of 1 January, "by the weight of machines, not of men," 18th Army was allocated twice as many guns per mile of front, but only 50 percent more men, than was 17th Army.[61]

177

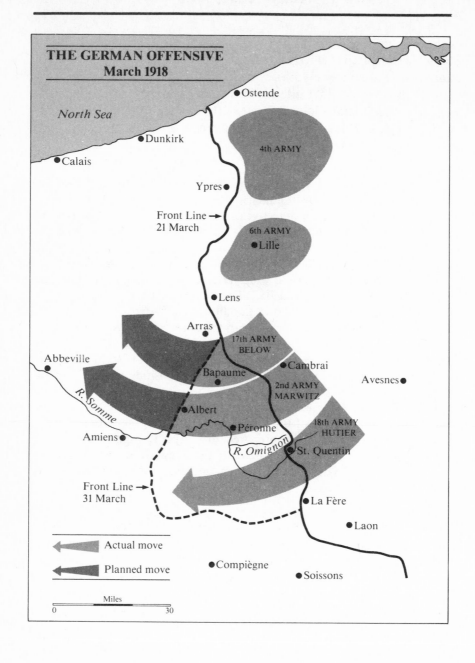

THE GERMAN OFFENSIVE
March 1918

North Sea

Ostende

Dunkirk

Calais

4th ARMY

Ypres

Front Line
21 March

6th ARMY
Lille

Lens

Arras

17th ARMY
BELOW

Abbeville

Cambrai

Avesnes

Bapaume

2nd ARMY
MARWITZ

R. Somme

Albert

Amiens

Péronne

18th ARMY
HUTIER

R. Omignon

St. Quentin

Front Line
31 March

La Fère

Laon

Actual move

Planned move

Compiègne

Soissons

Miles

0   30

At exactly 0540 hours on 21 March 1918, a wet and foggy day, 6,608 German guns all along the forty-mile front opened a bombardment whose precision and intensity had never before been seen.[62] Opening fire without prior registration in order to maintain surprise to the last possible moment, shifting methodically from target to target according to a predetermined schedule, the German guns alternated between high explosive and gas so as first to demolish the British strongholds, then catch the stunned survivors as they emerged from the remains of their dugouts. After exactly four hours and fifty minutes the bombardment abruptly reached its climax with a smashing rain of explosive shell directed against the first British line. This lasted for five minutes and then changed, without a pause, into a creeping barrage closely followed by the leading storm detachments. Finding most of the British positions smashed to bits and bypassing the rest, the German infantry made rapid progress and took only half an hour to break through the enemy's first line, an unheard-of achievement by World War I standards. By 1400 hours the British had everywhere been pushed back to their main battle zone and, in the case of 5th Army on their right, were already clinging desperately to its rear edge. With their telephone network demolished by the bombardment and runners unable to get through owing to the presence of German infiltration parties, the cohesion of the British forces began to break down; unlike their opponents, they had neither been organized for independent action nor been trained for it.

Meanwhile, far in the rear, at their Avesnes headquarters, Ludendorff and his staff had nothing to do but sit at their desks and wait. Their agonies were further exacerbated by the presence of the Kaiser who, as in 1914, lost his head at the announcement of the first successes and was already raising the hurrahs of victory. By noon on the 21st the morning fog had lifted and given way to sun; this facilitated the work of the German observation balloons, five per division, which followed closely behind the attack. Nevertheless, a look at the diary of Crown Prince Rupprecht of Bavaria for the 21st and the following days shows how little information headquarters really had. An occasional progress report got through, supplemented here and there by a report from a pilot indicating that a British column had been seen retreating.[63] From this and other sources[64] it is clear that the breakdown in communications was quite as bad as it had been on the Somme in 1916, and that General Headquarters was unable to form a clear picture of events; unlike the British, however, the Germans had expected this to happen and organized accordingly. The attack was thus able to make good progress in spite of the breakdown of control from above, and indeed made use of that very confusion in order to further accelerate its pace.

By the evening of the 21st, nevertheless, enough information had got through to Avesnes to make possible at least some tentative conclusions. Contrary to what the Germans had expected, the fighting in front of 17th Army and the right wing of 2nd Army had been brutal and costly in casualties, yet neither army succeeded in getting beyond the British battle zone or pinching out the strategic Cambrai salient on which they converged from two directions. Contrary to plans, too, Hutier's comparatively weak force on the left wing had advanced farther than any other force, cutting through the opposing British 5th Army (General Gouch) with such ease that 17th Army actually believed it had caught the enemy in the midst of a retreat. Thus Ludendorff was presented with a choice between opportunism and tenacity of purpose; he could reinforce his right wing in the hope of belatedly carrying out his original plan, or he could shift reserves to his left in order to exploit the extraordinary and unexpected success of Hutier's 18th Army. On the evening of 21 March he opted for the first of these alternatives, thus disregarding his own tactical principle of always taking the enemy in the flank. Three reserve divisions were assigned to the Bavarian Crown Prince's Army Group, and all three armies were ordered to continue the advance as planned on the next day.

On 22 March, another foggy day, the pattern of success was repeated. Ludendorff in his memoirs notes considerable gains by 18th and 2nd Armies—the latter in particular was doing rather better at this stage—and little if any by 17th Army whose right wing (IXth Corps) was stuck fast in front of the strongly fortified town of Arras.[65] In his orders for the continuation of the offensive, issued on the morning of the 23rd, Ludendorff nevertheless stuck to his guns; three more reserve divisions were assigned to Army Group Bavarian Crown Prince, and the continuation of the attack by all three armies was ordered. Ludendorff, then, was displaying little of the opportunism that he demanded of his subordinates. Instead of halting 18th Army and using it as a pivot on which the remaining forces further to the south could turn, and sending his reserves into those parts of the front where the attack had been most successful, he continued to hammer straight ahead in what had by this time turned into divergent directions. Later in the day, talking to his deputy Wetzel, the quartermaster general even mentioned the possibility of 6th and 4th Armies farther to the north joining in the offensive, thus going in for another frontal blow against the British and failing to make use of whatever successes there were still to be won by 18th Army.

The next two days, to judge by the diary of a staff officer serving on the extreme right wing of the German offensive, appeared to justify Ludendorff's decision.[66] Things now went better for 17th and 2nd Armies, the bulk of whose forces were said to be making "fantastic progress," though the situation in front of Arras remained stationary. Ludendorff, however, still would not deviate from his original plan of smashing and unhinging the British front rather than driving a wedge between them and the French, as Hutier's unexpected success now allowed him to do. On the morning of 25 March he ordered the attack by 6th Army to start on the 28th, thus reducing the role of 18th Army to that of a mere flank- and rearguard against the French who, following a meeting between Haig and Petain on the 24th, were now beginning to come up in force from the south.

By the time the new attack could get under way, in any case, the advance had already spent itself. Drunk with fatigue—the Germans, unlike the British, did not relieve their leading divisions by allowing a second wave to pass through them, it being assumed that such a procedure would cause the attack to lose momentum and coherence—and unable to resist the temptation of looting the rich British stores that were now falling into their hands, the attacking troops were slipping out of control and were no longer responding to orders. As Ludendorff saw the situation, "17th Army was already exhausted; it had lost too heavily on the [unsuccessful days of] 21 and 22 March, apparently because it had fought in too dense a formation. 2nd Army was fresher but was already complaining of the old shell holes. It could get no further than Albert . . . 18th

Army was still full of fight and confidence"—but Ludendorff for some reason ordered it to refrain from crossing the line Noyon-Roye on 29 March. With that, the offensive was substantially at an end.

Ludendorff's exact reasoning during these days has never been explained and, given the state of the sources, probably never will be. Nevertheless, an explanation should probably be sought neither in strategic nor in psychological terms, but rather in those of the twin factors that helped shape World War I, the railway and the telegraph. Reliance on the railway made it difficult to move forces laterally behind the front, especially when they were already closely deployed behind it, as in this case. Reliance on the telegraph, which was dependent on wire, made it difficult to control armies once they were attacking in the field, especially a field as devastated by warfare—this was the scene of the "scorched earth" policy during the 1917 German retreat to the Siegfried Line—as the one over which the attack took place. In the defense, and on a smaller scale during the attack also, it was possible to overcome these difficulties in part by relying on the stationary communications network of trench warfare or by allowing subordinate commanders far-reaching freedom of action. Corps and divisions, however, let alone armies, could not be thrown about in the same way that storm detachments were, and attempts to do so would merely lead to the kind of traffic jam that had all but halted the flow of supplies to the German 1st Army during its simultaneous combats on the Marne and the Ourq in September 1914.[67] In other words, technical factors beyond Ludendorff's control may have prevented him from changing the attack's center of gravity even as it was under way; admittedly, however, this must remain an unproven hypothesis.

In the event, the success of the 1918 offensive stood in direct proportion to the consistency with which the new principles of command, as explained in the directive of 1 January, were carried out. It made better progress at 18th Army, which had the famous Colonel Bruchmüller to plan the artillery bombardment and the details of interarm cooperation, than at 17th Army on the right wing which, according to Ludendorff's own account, tried to fight by the old system of close control until compelled to mend its ways by heavy casualties. From what evidence has survived it certainly does not seem that Ludendorff's own control over the battle was in any way too close; if anything, the armies were allowed too much freedom, since at one point (23 March) they were all found advancing in divergent directions with no attempt being made to echelon them behind each other and coordinate their blows, as should and possibly could have been done. Ludendorff, moreover, erred in using his reserves in accordance with the original plan rather than at the point where enemy resistance was at its weakest; given the state of the art, however, this may have been to some extent inevitable.

While the overall strategic direction of the German campaign thus left something to be desired in failing to provide the required flexibility, on the tactical level it was an immense—and, as the next few months showed, repeatable—triumph that must be regarded as the direct precursor of the spectacularly successful Blitzkrieg techniques employed early in World War II.[68] This triumph was served by a technology virtually identical to that employed by Haig at the Somme, yet it was achieved by means of a command system as different from the British one as it is possible to imagine. Where the British had—no doubt, partly owing to the relatively sketchy training of their troops—feared disorder above all things, the Germans accepted it as inevitable and sought to circumvent the problem by putting a heavy emphasis on independent action by subordinate commanders and even by individual men. Where the one attack advanced in carefully dressed lines toward objectives straight ahead, the men forbidden to look left or right, the other was given no prearranged tactical objectives beyond the initial ones and flowed forward in small, loose groups, maintaining neither alignment nor formation and expected to cooperate with, but not depend on, their neighbors on both sides.[69] Whereas British commanders from battalion upward were explicitly forbidden to leave their command posts for fear that telephone contact between them and their superiors would be lost, German ones were instructed to position themselves as far forward as possible, thus keeping in touch with the front even at the expense of the rear and maintaining, if nothing else, the ability to exercise their motivating functions. Where British divisions did not possess the freedom to use their reserves without permission from corps, German divisions fought their own battles with corps serving merely as holding headquarters. Where British organization was centralized to the point that cooperation between the artillery and the infantry was possible only at corps level, virtually all of the German artillery was commanded from divisional headquarters and some of it was put at the disposal of regimental commanders who were thus able to call upon, and receive, direct fire support. Though technological circumstances made it inevitable that the German bombardment and barrage should be almost as rigidly planned and executed as their British counterparts, the shortcomings of these methods were recognized and some provision for combatting targets of opportunity made.[70]

As compared with the British command system at the Somme, the German one thus placed reliance on lower decision thresholds and fewer controls, combined with self-contained units and (it cannot be emphasized too often) at least the attempt to wield a directed telescope of superior effectiveness. The case in favor of the German system is made all but unanswerable by the fact that it worked for the British, too, in the few cases where it was applied, and this in spite of the allegedly inferior training of the troops. On the other hand, those German forces (17th Army) that did not fully carry out the directive of 1 January paid the penalty in blood and merely spent themselves in front of the British defenses in spite of the relatively much greater weight, in men and machines, allotted them. A case as apparently foolproof as this seems to beg for further discussion, and this will be provided by the next section.

CONCLUSIONS: MACHINE-AGE WARFARE

The war of 1914–1918, to return to the theme that opened this chapter, was the first in history to be waged mainly by machines rather than by men. To put it in a different way, the traditional balance between animate and inanimate implements that had governed the conduct of war since the dawn of history was upset, and a new one took its place after the crisis years of 1914 and 1915 during which critical shortages of ammunition made their appearance in every army. The extent of the change is perhaps best illustrated by means of a few figures taken from the field of logistics. Whereas the German Army in 1870–71 had fired only 199 rounds per artillery barrel during its five-month campaign against France, the 1,000 rounds per barrel that the same army had in reserve in 1914 only lasted it five or six weeks, expenditure sometimes rising to 400–500 per day in

1918. In 1870–71 over nine-tenths of all supplies consumed by the German army consisted of food and fodder, whereas by 1916 two-thirds of all supplies required by a British division consisted of am-munition (especially artillery and explosives), engineering materials (concrete, steel girders, wire, the poles needed for setting up the wire, duckboards, sandbags), and equipment of all kinds. Thus the requirements of armies, per man and per horse, had risen almost threefold, and even this understates the size of the burden placed on the rear services. Traditionally food and fodder had been gathered on the spot, either directly by the army or by means of contractors, a procedure that was rendered all but impossible by the stationary nature of trench warfare. Instead, everything—fodder included—had to be brought up from the rear, with the result that horse feed became the most bulky single commodity to be shipped from Britain to France during the entire world war.

Men, to quote Patton, can eat their belts, and horses in war have often been fed nothing at all until they dropped. Machines, how-ever, cannot be mismanaged without ceasing to function, completely and much more quickly than either horses or men. The infantry can always go another mile, or so many of its commanders seem to be-lieve. A cannon without ammunition is a useless hulk of metal, how-ever, and the lack of a spare part can turn a machine gun from a death-dealing contrivance of unrivaled excellence into a mere un-wieldy encumbrance. Unlike food and fodder, which can be foraged and to some extent stretched, the supplies required to keep machines going do not grow on trees. With a few unimportant exceptions (the use of captured arms, for example, which becomes more difficult as weapons training grows more complicated and as the arms them-selves are manufactured to smaller tolerances so that they cannot take just any kind of ammunition and spare parts),[71] they must be brought up from the rear, usually by means of more machines that add their own requirements to the pile. All this, needless to say, cannot be achieved without careful planning and coordination from the top. Without a firm directing hand providing for the uninter-rupted flow of supplies, replacements, and reinforcements a ma-chine-age army will cease to function within a matter of days in the same way as an automobile factory deprived of its supply of parts. Insofar as such an army consists of more specialized parts and to that extent is more dependent on mutual cooperation, its disintegration may possibly be more rapid and more complete than that of a preindustrial force.

World War I armies, then, were far more dependent on their rear services than their predecessors had been; the conduct of war had reached back from the battlefield into the factory and into the office. Unless extreme care were taken to prevent this from happening, the methods of the office and of the factory would come back to dominate the battlefield. Starting with the strategic railways, in the management of which they had first been introduced by the Prussians in 1866–1870, and gradually creeping forward until they reached the foremost trenches in 1914–1918, these methods were absolutely indispensable if the armies of a million men with their countless machines were to deploy or even to exist. It was these methods that enabled preparations for such large-scale offensives as we have described to be successfully completed; yet to extend them even further into the battlefield was to invite the kind of bloody disaster that overtook the British at the Somme. There were two basic reasons for this, and each is best discussed separately.

First, the network of communications that is vital to the functioning of modern management was absent from World War I battlefields. With optical means as unreliable and as limited in capacity as they had always been, messengers unable to get through the storm of steel, and newly laid wire communications constantly being demolished by the intensity of the artillery bombardment, the battles of World War I simply did not permit the kind of close control that was necessary, indeed vital, to allow preparations for them to be completed. To put it differently, Haig's system of command represented an attempt to turn battle itself into an industrial type of operation, but he did not possess the communications system that alone makes industrial production possible. In view of the disparity between effectiveness of the communications system in the hands of the defender and in those of the attacker, and quite regardless of the defensive power of modern weapons that so many critics have commented upon, his failure can hardly be considered surprising.

The second, and in my opinion even more important, factor working against the extension of industrial controls to the battlefield is the nature of war itself. Although modern works on military matters are as fond of comparing command with management as their predecessors were of comparing war with science, management and command are by no means identical. Quite apart from the problem of motivation, the difference between them consists precisely in the greater uncertainty governing war, the most confused and confusing of all human activities. The essence of war, to quote Clausewitz once again, is a confrontation with the enemy's independent will. That will is constrained by, but not absolutely subject to, the means at his disposal. Coming on top of the normal environmental uncertainty governing all human affairs, this fact renders war difficult if not impossible to calculate. To fail to make allowance for this is to doom one's efforts to failure before they even get under way—unless, that is, one's own material superiority (quantitative or qualitative) is so great as to turn war itself into a massacre.[72]

Neither of these two problems—the second, by definition—was at all new to World War I, but their importance was enhanced by the absence of compensating factors like those that helped the elder Moltke achieve his great victories. In World War I on the Western Front neither side possessed an overwhelming numerical superiority overall (when that superiority was finally created by the Americans joining in, it decided the war), and whatever local superiority could be attained was quickly offset by railway transports moving, undisturbed by enemy interference, behind the front. Artillery, which Moltke had used in 1870 to offset his inability to control the infantry, was now at least as effective in the defense as on the offense. Strategy, used to correct tactical deficiencies and even defeats in 1866–1870, did not and perhaps could not exist in the same form on the Western Front of 1914–1918. Had Moltke not been able to use strategy in 1866, where would the battle of Königgrätz have ended? On the far side of the (lower) Elbe, perhaps, where the Prussian chief of staff planned to resume the struggle in case of defeat.

Given these problems—compounded, one can only speculate, by the fact that most British medium-level officers were ex-civilians and thus trained in the methods of the office and the factory—there were but two ways to overcome the confusion that had prevailed on every battlefield since at least the American Civil War. The first consisted of forcibly imposing order upon disorder, that is, of a return to Frederick II's system of the automatically fighting army—a system that, in the face of vastly improved defensive firepower, proved even less successful in 1916 than it had in 1756–1763 or, for that matter, in 1806. The alternative was to extend Moltke's principle of free cooperation at the highest level downward, place greater responsibility on the shoulders of commanders down the line, and take disorder in stride as inevitable and even, insofar as it affected the enemy as well, desirable. As happened in Napoleon's day, that army proved superior which had recognized the *limitations* of the technical means at its disposal and, rather than allow those limitations to shape and confine its methods of waging war, had found a way to go around them, even to make use of them. If this solution did not lead to victory in the end (though it came quite close to achieving that goal), the reason was that it was not completely understood by all the German armies, and because new technological and logistical factors made it more difficult to apply at the highest level than was the case either previously or afterward. To the extent that it was now the lowest, rather than the highest, levels which were reformed, command had thus come full circle since Napoleon set up the corps organization around 1800. Nevertheless, it was in the principles initiated by him, put on a firm organizational and doctrinal basis by Moltke, and extended down the chain of command by Ludendorff, that the secret of success had to be sought.

6

MASTERS OF
MOBILE WARFARE

DURING the twenty-year armistice that followed World War I, another technological revolution transformed the art of war and permanently changed the face of battle. In 1914, it was almost possible to grasp the relative warmaking potentials of most countries simply by glancing at a diagram depicting annual coal and steel production. Such a chart would have revealed that Belgium produced 24.8 and 2.3 million tons of coal and steel respectively, Russia 30.2 and 4.2, France 39.9 and 4.1, Britain 275.4 and 6.9, Germany 247.5 and 16.2, and the United States 483.8 and 25.1.[1] Twenty-five years later the importance of these figures, although still great, had been overshadowed by another and more modern set: the number of automobiles made, the quantity of aluminum (for aircraft) extracted, and the quantity and quality of the electronic products assembled. This book being concerned above all with command on land, I shall leave the question of aluminum alone except to note that by 1939 Germany had turned into the world's largest producer of it. The problems raised by motor vehicles and electronics, however, and their effects on warfare, cannot be dismissed so easily.

"THE FUSTEST WITH THE MOSTEST"

In 1914 the seven German field armies that invaded France and Belgium had 500 motor trucks among them, or approximately one per 3,000 men. In 1939 a single German armored division had

189

15,000 men and over 3,000 motor vehicles, of which 14 percent or so were Armored Fighting Vehicles (AFV, or *Kampfkraftwagen*) and the rest were soft-skinned, mainly road-bound cars, trucks, and motorcycles. In 1918 the British never mustered more than 48 tanks for any single operation of war;[2] twenty-five years later the Germans at Kursk employed 1,500. In 1944, at Normandy, the Allies by the end of June had landed 452,460 men and 70,190 motor vehicles, a ratio of 6.4 to 1.[3] As is often the case, the list of figures could be extended almost indefinitely. To do so without inquiring into their meaning, however, would produce little.

Strategically, the rise of the gasoline-powered motor vehicle meant that armies were now released from the tyranny exercised over them by the railways since the days of Moltke and Grant. The result was a tremendous gain not so much in the linear speed or in the number of ton-miles that could be lifted (for both of which purposes the railways, so long as they are free from air interdiction, have retained their superiority to the present day) as in the flexibility it provided. The increase in operational mobility was also remarkable, an armored or motorized division being easily capable of covering the distance in a hour which had taken Napoleon's troops a day to march.[4] Speed and flexibility—kept within bounds, it is true, by the vastly increased logistic tail that was now required to cater to the needs of thousands of motor vehicles superimposed upon all the other demands of war—being the main advantage of the new implements, victory would go to the side which would know best how to exploit these qualities. War, which in 1914–1918 had been reduced largely to a question of the mostest, once again came to incorporate the fustest as well. In the conduct of a Blitzkrieg offensive, or for that matter of a mobile defense of the kind mounted by the Germans in 1943–1945 and by the Israelis on the Golan Heights in 1973, it was a question above all of making such flexible use of one's resources as to outnumber the enemy at any given point. The rise of the motor vehicle once again made it possible for the decisive margin of superiority to be provided by speed rather than by sheer mass. Seen from this point of view, armored warfare has more in common with the campaigns of Napoleon than with those of Moltke or Haig, and hence the methods employed to command it are, unsurprisingly, also similar.

Napoleon, it will be remembered, was able to revolutionize war by employing organizational and procedural means in order to overcome and transcend the limits imposed by the technology of the time. This implied, in the first place, the establishment of independent strategic units and a corresponding delegation of authority to the corps commanders; the institution of a—given the state of the technology of the time, none too reliable—two-way information and coordination system within the army, to direct which it was necessary to have Berthier's General Staff; and, finally, a directed telescope to check on the operation of that information system and to keep the independence granted to the corps within bounds. Like Napoleon, but in charge of forces whose mobility was far superior and which consequently spread over much larger spaces, the World War II panzer leader was forced to decentralize the chain of command and rely on intelligent initiative at every rank, beginning with the lowest,[5] in order to seize every fleeting opportunity and exploit it to the hilt.[6] Like him, the armored commander was compelled to institute some means to counterbalance this decentralization and prevent it from degenerating into sheer chaos, which Montgomery for example did by establishing his "Phantom" system of liaison officers who used car and aircraft to visit every part of the theater of operations and report back directly to headquarters. Finally, like Napoleon, the armored commander required a two-way communications system to maintain contact with his highly mobile forces—and it was at this point that he was fortunate to have at hand a new technology, radio.

Grown robust, simple to operate, and portable during the interwar years, with technical improvements increasing the spectrum of frequencies that could be employed and thus partly eliminating the mutual interference that had been one of the key obstacles facing its utilization in trench warfare, radio by 1939 had become suitable for tactical as well as strategic use; for communication between vehicles on the move[7] as well as among stationary headquarters; and for combined air–land operations (the inability of aircraft to communicate with their own bases while on sortie, to report reconnaissance findings directly to headquarters, and to converse with the ground forces below was a major constraint on their effectiveness in World War I) as well as for purely land-bound ones.

Technical quality as such is not the crucial variant that determines the effectiveness of radio-based command systems, a fact that is conclusively proved by the astonishing German victories of 1939–1942 over opponents whose communications technology was, by and large, very similar to their own. As important as the quality of the equipment in use is its quantity (in turn dependent on price and ease of manufacture), which determines whether it will be made available to subordinate commanders (even, in the case of motorized formations, to individual vehicles) or merely to higher headquarters. Nor is the distribution of identical sets to all sufficient; what counts is a carefully considered master plan that will assign the various pieces of apparatus, each possessing its own performance characteristics, in accordance with the needs of each commander and headquarters. Thorough training and well-considered operating procedures are indispensable if one is to end up with a well-integrated network rather than a babylon of mutually interfering voices. (It will not do, for instance, to have each station call whomever and wherever it likes, at any length and using any kind of terminology.) Even when all these requirements are met and the signal services properly organized, it is as vital to familiarize the rest of the troops with them as it is to make the communicators aware of the needs and problems of the troops at large. Finally, the limitations of radio—including the vital questions of security, overloads, mutual interference, jamming, and under many conditions limited range and reliability—must be thoroughly mastered and countered before, rather than during, actual hostilities.[8]

Although Fuller and Liddell Hart are widely given credit for the invention of armored warfare, there is very little in their writings to indicate that they paid close attention to these problems; the same, with less justification, is true for many subsequent studies of the Blitzkrieg.[9] Thus the credit for recognizing the importance of the question, for the first successful attempts at its solution, and for the first brilliant demonstration of how armored command ought to operate belongs essentially to two men: Heinz Guderian—himself, not accidentally, an ex-signals officer who entered World War I as a lieutenant in charge of a wireless station—and General Fritz Fellgiebel, commanding officer, Signals Service, German Wehrmacht during most of the Nazi era. Between them these men developed the principles of radio-based command that, in somewhat modified and technically infinitely more complex form, are still very much in use today.[10]

Radio, which for the first time in history came close to making reliable, instantaneous two-way communication between mobile forces possible, regardless of the relative positions and speed of the forces and regardless also of the weather, time of day, and terrain, revolutionized command in another way too. As earlier chapters have shown, one way to understand the history of command since the Middle Ages is to see in it the story of growing specialization and immobilization. Starting off as fighting men better sired, better armed, or simply stronger than the rest, commanders from the fifteenth century on began to do less fighting and more commanding, a process that gradually caused them to relinquish their previous place in their armies' front ranks and take up fixed positions in the rear. As the size of military forces increased and the weapons at their disposal grew more powerful, the distance separating commander from front tended to increase to the point that Ludendorff in 1918, a mere thirty miles behind the front, was closer to the fighting line than were most World War I commanders in chief. Radio, by making communication between any two points possible, reversed this trend; once again, as in the days of Gustavus or Marlborough, commanders could be found far forward. Accompanied by a small forward headquarters, they were mounted on a tank or AFV distinguished from the rest only by the forest of antennae decorating it; the fluid nature of modern motorized warfare, and the ubiquitous threat from low-flying fighter bombers, now for the first time in over a century made commanders almost as vulnerable as their troops, with the result that they took good care to remain as inconspicuous as possible. To see for oneself, something that Haig and Moltke had only been able to do—if at all—by leaving headquarters and thus temporarily relinquishing overall control, now again became the essence of a commander's job; with the not unexpected result that the instrument for doing so, a hefty pair of binoculars slung over one's chest, was elevated into a status symbol that no commander could afford to be without.

The critical importance of command in armored warfare cannot be exaggerated and is equaled only by the lack of systematic attention paid to it by most military historians. This is nowhere more evident than in the series of brilliant campaigns that marked World War II—Rundstedt's Army Group A in 1940, Guderian's Panzergruppe 2 in 1941, Rommel's Afrika Korps in 1941–1943, Manstein's Army Group Don early in 1943, and Patton's Third U.S. Army in 1944. Apart from the last named, these campaigns were waged against equal or superior numbers and decided as much by the sheer brilliance with which formations were handled as by any other factor. Since all of them are now four decades old, however, I have chosen as a case study a different military organization of more recent years: the Israelis in 1967 and 1973.[11]

A SYSTEM OF EXPEDIENTS

Though much has been written about the command system of the Israel Defense Forces (IDF),[12] the best short summary may perhaps be found in a lecture given by the then chief of staff, General Mordechai Gur, early in 1978:

A proper command system might be compared to a ballistic missile. The missile is accelerated by its fuel. It is supposed to reach a remote objective, and that objective only, with great precision, while being subject to many forces, both external and internal, during flight. A good missile will reach its objectives while overcoming those forces—the weather, wind, etc. It is built on the assumption that unforeseen forces will affect its flight; and it must be able to identify and overcome those forces during that flight. Occasionally, however, the forces affecting the missile's flight are too strong for it to overcome on its own. It is for this purpose that a controlling mechanism is needed, able to follow the missile in its flight and correct its course when necessary, but without causing the missile to stop. The missile receives these corrections and continues on course toward its target. Few missiles reach their objective with absolute precision, and some do not reach it at all. Only when the missile is far off course, however, is its self-destruct mechanism activated. The decision to destruct should not be made by reason of minor or temporary deviations, but only in case the missile is clearly not about to reach its target . . .

A proper command system should be able to set itself goals, and then strive to attain those goals in spite of the clear realization that things will go wrong, but also in the confidence that, when they do go wrong, the system will be able to overcome the obstacles. Such a system might operate in two different ways. The first is to plan everything in detail, then start going. The second is to lay down general objectives only and to start going at once. The system then gains momentum, and the details are filled in even as progress is being made. The IDF normally takes the second of these ways. It is like a smart bomb being released on the basis of general data, without the target even being seen. Later, after a few miles, the bomb identifies the target and is locked on it. From this point it flies on accurately until the objective is reached . . .

Can an army be constructed in this way without missing too many of its objectives? The answer is that doctrine, research and development, and organization cannot, as experience has shown, be built on the basis of detailed plans. Guidelines must be laid down and the system put into gear. However, this is only possible when the bureaucratic machine is reasonably lean and fast in operation, and on condition that the information passed by it is correct and accurate. Without fast and accurate feedback, it would have been impossible for the IDF to exist, much less to respond to the changing times . . .

A proper command system, then, consists of a combination of thorough, even pedestrian, preparation with freedom that is granted to the imagination and to individual daring. Its operation is based on three principles, namely (a) a clear definition of the objectives to be attained; (b) thorough planning; and (c) a proper order of priorities. This third condition implies the recognition that, whatever one's priorities are, some things are going to suffer neglect. One's list of priorities should be subject to constant reexamination. The danger of adhering to a single idea, and even worse, to a predetermined plan, must be avoided. Discipline and teamwork must be combined with improvisation. Controls, both external and internal, must be in continuous operation.

All three conditions must appear self-contradicting; but in reality it is the balance between them that determines the IDF's unique character . . .

Innovation during execution itself; discipline; and improvisation—these are the three basic elements that make up the IDF's command system, even if the latter two sometimes contradict each other.[13]

One note that should be added is that the balance among planning, discipline, and improvisation may change not only from one army to the next but also within one and the same force over time. This is well illustrated by the development of the IDF itself. As constituted during Israel's 1948–49 war of independence, the IDF was a fairly

large force by regional standards but suffered acutely from a shortage of equipment, above all heavy weapons.[14] The balance between
human and material resources being what it was, a heavy premium
had to be put on compensating factors of a spiritual nature: individual daring (*heaza*), maintenance of aim (*dvekut bamatara*), improvisation (*iltur*), and resourcefulness (*tushia*), all of which still remain
key elements of the fighting doctrine that the IDF systematically in-
culcates into, and demands of, troops and commanders at every
level. Contributing factors to this emphasis on independence and
initiative were the acute shortage of signaling equipment, which was
responsible for several major incidents during the 1956 Sinai campaign, and the fact that the IDF, being a small force, could not afford the reserves which would have enabled General Headquarters
to influence the battle.[15]

Going to war in 1956, the IDF's entire command system was tailored to operate within these constraints. As Dayan put it in his
diary:

We shall organize separate forces for each of the main military objectives,
and it will be the task of each force to get there in one continuous battle,
one long break, to fight and push on, fight and push on, until the objective is gained . . . [This system] also suits the character of our army and of
our officers. To the commander of an Israeli unit I can point on a map to
the Suez Canal and say: "There's your target and this is your axis of advance. Don't signal me during the fighting for more men, arms, or vehicles. All that we could allocate you've already got, and there isn't any
more. Keep signaling your advances. You must reach Suez in forty-eight
hours." I can give this kind of orders to commanders of our units because
I know they are ready to assume such tasks and are capable of carrying
them out.

Since the units "must stick to 'maintenance of aim' and continue to
advance until their objective is gained, they must be . . . self contained, carrying with them all they will need to reach their final target, and not be dependent on outside supplies." The need for the
greatest possible independence to be granted to, and demanded of,
each separate force was also emphasized by Dayan during several
meetings with his staff.[16]

The results of such a command system were, perhaps, predictable.

Having effectively neutralized himself by his system of mission-style orders and the lack of a central reserve, Dayan was left with little to do. He accordingly spent the campaign flying and motoring all over the Sinai, accompanied only by a radio truck and sometimes running into the midst of still undefeated enemy troops. From time to time he would turn up at some brigade headquarters (though a divisional organization did exist on paper, brigades were the largest operational units employed by the IDF in this campaign) and order an attack or change the axis of advance. For the most part, however, the brigade commanders acted as if General Headquarters did not exist, which to most intents and purposes was precisely the case.

Given wide latitude in regard to the way in which they were to carry out their missions, some of the brigades were successful, others less so, others too much so. Perfectly successful, in spite of technical hitches bordering on incompetence (the entire brigade, it turned out, did not have a single wrench for replacing flat tires), was the advance of the then Lieutenant Colonel Sharon's paratroopers past and through several fortified Egyptian positions to link up with the battalion dropped at the Parker Memorial, almost 120 miles from the frontier, within thirty-six hours of the beginning of the campaign. Less than successful was the attempt by 10th brigade to capture Um Katef, for which failure Dayan relieved its commander on the spot.[17] Too successful was the unauthorized advance of 7th Armored Brigade, which not only upset the entire plan drawn up by HQ but also changed the campaign's character from an advance by (more or less) motorized infantry into a highly effective, if technically primitive, Blitzkrieg based on tanks. Too successful, too, was Sharon's determination to enter the Mitla Pass, another unauthorized move for which his men paid a heavy price in blood.[18] Furthermore, as Dayan notes—though naturally without pointing to himself as the main culprit—the heavy emphasis on improvisation and the absence of a strong controlling hand meant that "our capacity for misadventure is limitless," including several cases in which Israeli units fired at each other or were strafed by Israeli aircraft. Granted "a huge measure of independence" (Dayan again), the brigade commanders failed to coordinate their movements; on one occasion, an entire brigade stood by with folded arms while two others were fighting to capture Abu Agheila. Nevertheless, against an Egyptian Army whose plans were based on the elimination of any need for mutual support and coordination even at the level of the individual soldier, Dayan's system of "organized chaos"—as colloquial Hebrew puts it—was effective enough.[19]

The campaign over, its lessons were studied by a committee headed by Dayan's second in command and successor as chief of staff, General Laskov.[20] The most important lesson to emerge was the recognition that in the future the IDF's main striking force would have to consist of the armored brigades which, though partly acting against orders, had played such a crucial role in the Sinai campaign. On the other hand, the day of paratroopers and motorized infantry fighting independently appeared to be largely over. Second, a general tightening of control was required in order to eliminate technical hitches of the kind that had almost brought Sharon's advances to a halt, secure better coordination between air and ground and between the ground forces themselves, and prevent further misadventures.

Between 1956 and 1967, aided by a fairly constant and relatively massive influx of new equipment and guided by such professionally expert soldiers as Laskov, Tzur, and Rabin, the IDF improved its technical services and communications system out of all recognition by imposing strict discipline and controls.[21] But this reorganization was not allowed to impinge on operational doctrine, which—now that armor had become the dominant arm—put an even heavier emphasis on speed and on independent action at every level as a means for achieving speed. As General Rabin, at that time serving as deputy chief of staff, summed it up in 1960, "commanders and headquarters [of armored forces] must be able to gather intelligence, process it, prepare orders, and issue them *while on the move.*"[22] It would not do to wait for detailed planning to be completed before starting a move; such a delay was harmful and should not be tolerated. Instead, "commanders of armored forces should operate according to a method which defines objectives, targets and timetables, lays down demarcation lines between the units, and determines the general method of conducting the battle. An armored commander should be so trained as to make him as little dependent on his superior as possible in deciding how to act." The job of superior headquarters did not consist of confirming the plan of its subordinate units in every detail; rather, it was to exercise "constant pressure" for greater speed, provided only that speed was combined with order and effectiveness. Moreover, even had the IDF possessed the world's most advanced communications gear, which was far from being the case in the 1960s, gaps and moments of uncertainty would always appear. Hence, in the words of another officer who was to rise to the position of chief of staff, "when in doubt—attack."[23]

Came June 1967 and the Israeli Army gave a dazzling demonstration of what a command system based on a proper balance in General Gur's trio—planning, discipline, and organization—could do. In that war the bulk of Israel's forces—three division-sized task forces of varying composition, each tailored to the mission it was supposed to perform, plus an independent brigade (Reshef Force) in the north, a total of nine brigades—was concentrated against the Egyptian Army. Commanding this front was General Yashayahu Gavish, whose Rear Headquarters (responsible for rear zone administration, logistics, traffic control, evacuation, and so on) was located in the Negev Desert at Nir Yitzhak under the command of his chief of staff. The commanding general himself spent most of his time either "accompanying" units down to brigade level—by which, according to his own definition, he meant staying at that unit's headquarters and observing developments at first hand—or else helicoptering from one unit to another; again, in his own words, "there is no alternative to looking into a subordinate's eyes, listening to his tone of voice."[24] Other sources of information at his disposal included the usual reporting system; a radio network linking him with the three divisional commanders, which also served to link those commanders with each other;[25] a signals staff, whose task was to listen in to the divisional communications networks, working around the clock and reporting to Gavish in writing; messages passed from the rear, that is, from General Headquarters in Tel Aviv, linked to Gavish by "private" radiotelephone circuit; and the results of air reconnaissance forwarded by the Air Force and processed by Rear Headquarters. Gavish did not depend on these sources exclusively, however; not only did he spend some time personally listening in to the radio networks of subordinate units (on one occasion, Gavish says, he was thereby able to correct an "entirely false" impression of the battle being formed at Brigadier Gonen's headquarters) but he also had a directed telescope in the form of elements of his staff, mounted on half-tracks, following in the wake of the two northernmost divisions and constantly reporting on developments.[26] With most of his staff occupied in this way, Gavish himself flew around in two helicopters, accompanied solely by his intelligence officer, a few members of the Operations Department, and the deputy signals officer, who together made up Forward Headquarters, Southern Command.

Of the four days that the campaign lasted, only the first was planned in any detail; the rest was pure improvisation. Since there was no provision for coordinated action by forces larger than one division, the task of Southern Command consisted mainly of assigning axes of advance, laying down boundaries, and allocating air sorties among its three divisions.[27] Detailed tactical planning was left to the division commanders, each of whom went about his task in a way dictated by the job at hand as well as his own character and training. On one extreme—this was General Sharon's division in the south—planning for the night battle of Abu Agheila was precise and detailed, requiring unfailing coordination and excellent control that were in turn made possible by outstanding advance intelligence and by the fact that the fortified Egyptian positions, extensive as they were, nevertheless stood on their own and were easily isolated from outside intervention. In the north, however, the need for deception (the Egyptian High Command was to be misled into thinking that the Israeli offensive would proceed from south to north, as it had in 1956, instead of the other way around) prevented equally good intelligence from being gathered by air and land reconnaissance. The result was that the presence of an entire Palestinian brigade was left undetected and that the battle, which could not be planned in advance, ran out of control and was fought mainly by individual brigadiers, with entire battalions getting lost in the dunes.[28] Under such circumstances "maintenance of aim" became the overriding consideration; as long as subordinate commanders stuck to the objectives assigned to them they were encouraged, indeed pushed, to act without waiting for orders and follow what appeared at that moment to be the line of weakest resistance.

Since Gavish's plans did not provide for combined operations by forces larger than one division (except to the extent that units from one division, Yaffe's, at one point opened the way in front of Tal's advance on Bir Lachfan), the command decisions made by Gavish himself were relatively few and far between.[29] The first of these was made around noon on 5 June, the first day of the campaign, when he asked and received permission to throw in Reshef Force ahead of schedule. Another decision had to be made a few hours later when it was a question of delaying Sharon's planned night attack on Abu Agheila until the following morning so that the Air Force, whose success had surpassed all expectations, could take part in the battle; Sharon, however, claimed he could take Abu Agheila on his own, and events proved him right. The most important single command decision was made shortly after noon on the second day of the campaign, 6 June. With his initial objectives attained, and informed by General Headquarters that the Egyptians were "collapsing" (the Israeli radio interception service, which during this campaign was functioning admirably, must have intercepted the order to retreat issued by the Egyptian commander in chief, Fieldmarshal Amer), Gavish was faced with the question of whether to engage in a straightforward pursuit or whether to go for the more daring plan of going around (in reality, through) the retreating Egyptians in order to reach and block the eastern entrances to the Gidi and Mitla passes, the enemy's sole routes of escape. After consulting with the members of his Forward Headquarters from approximately 1400 to 1630 hours on the 6th, Gavish decided on the latter option. The divisional commanders were then summoned for a meeting. The situation was explained to them and they were issued their orders. All this, Gavish says, took only a very short time.

Apart from Reshef Force, which had been earmarked for occupying the Gaza Strip and could not therefore be used elsewhere, Southern Command in 1967 had no reserves. It did, however, to some extent make up for this lack by assigning the five armored brigades under its command to whatever division needed them most at the moment. In doing this it was assisted by the fact that the divisions were really task forces and not yet standardized, as was to become the case during subsequent years. This method of relying on "internal" reserves is sound enough as long as the higher commander's authority is undisputed, and provided it is not employed too frequently; otherwise its use will lead to chaos.

The commanding general, Southern Front, recalls that in 1967

"command, control, and communications were well nigh perfect."
This statement is certainly borne out by the outcome of the campaign. Given the confused nature of mobile warfare, it was to be expected that not even such excellence could prevent some errors.
Among those should be counted the paratroopers of Brigadier
Eytan (chief of staff, 1978–1983) being taken by surprise in the
dunes of Raffah and fighting a confused battle with no assistance
from the divisional commander, Tal; an episode in which some of
General Yaffeh's battalions came within an inch of opening fire on
each other; and another, on 7 June, when air strikes ordered by
General Gavish against Bir Lachfan came within minutes of being
carried out when an armored brigade under Gonen reported that it
had occupied the place.[30] More seriously, an order that Dayan had
issued for stopping short of the Suez Canal was not received, or else
disregarded, by one of Sharon's brigadiers, Dani Matt, whose paratroopers reached the waterline before General Headquarters in Tel
Aviv realized what was taking place.[31] The tendency, already evident in 1956, for the "noble steeds" (Dayan's phrase) to run out of
control and overshoot their mark thus persisted, and so did the excessive self-confidence of which it was a symptom.

On the whole, however, the excellence of the Israeli command
system in 1967 cannot be seriously disputed. The nature of armored
warfare being what it is, a large measure of independence had to be
granted to subordinate commanders, a need that was recognized at
all levels beginning with General Headquarters in Tel Aviv. From
Gavish downward, commanders on the Egyptian Front positioned
themselves far forward, making decisions on the spot and relying on
oral orders, written ones being drawn up subsequently for the
records of the next highest headquarters. The span of control—two
or three brigades per division, three divisions to the Front—was
fairly small, but owing to the limited size of the IDF as a whole did
not cause too large a gap to open between commanders and subordinates. The distribution of authority was sufficiently clear, and the
chain of command sufficiently firm, to make possible the use of an
internal reserve, and Southern Command took good care not to
abuse this means in its hand by too frequent use. Command from
the front, the constant monitoring of radio networks, and the
directed telescope present in the form of Headquarters Detachments

following behind two of the three divisions—the latter an innovation for which Gavish deserves the credit—were all used as a check on the independence granted to, and demanded of, subordinate commanders. Planning varied between two extremes, as exemplified by Generals Sharon and Tal, and was well adapted to circumstances. In no case did it go beyond the first day of the campaign, thus keeping in line with Moltke's dictum that plans should only go as far as the first clash with the enemy. Once the role of planning was at an end the training of Israeli commanders ensured that expedients should not be lacking at any level, beginning with the tanks that reached the Mitla Pass without fuel and in tow and ending with Gavish's deservedly celebrated decision to pass his forces through the enemy in order to block his retreat. The command system that made the success of 1967 possible is thus best understood in terms of a series of balances. By definition, however, such balances are delicate and difficult to maintain; and the next few years were to see them disturbed.

1973 : PLANNING AND PREPARATIONS

Between 1967 and 1973, aided by a massive influx of American arms and equipment, the traditional character of the IDF as a military force rich in manpower but poor in hardware was transformed.[32] To quote a few figures only, the IDF in 1967 had 1,145 men per combat aircraft and 343 per tank; six years later both figures had been cut approximately in half and now stood at 614 and 176 respectively.[33] (By way of comparison, the 1980 figures for the German Bundeswehr—said to be the best-equipped force in NATO—were 900 and 143.)[34] Possibly as a result of this sudden expansion, maintenance standards deteriorated; the reserves that went to war on Yom Kippur 1973 no longer found the Emergency Depots in as good an order as in 1967.

The new balance between men and equipment, coupled with the sheer size of the forces and some of the lessons of the 1967 war—including in particular the impression made by the outstanding victories of a few armored brigades—led to changes in organization. After much argument, a standardized divisional organization re-

placed the task forces of 1967, thus making the use of internal reserves more difficult and to this extent reducing the ability of higher
(corps) headquarters to influence the battle. The balance between
armor and infantry, already tilting toward the former from 1956 on,
was upset further as subordinate units—platoons, companies, and
battalions—were trimmed down (and the latter deprived of their organic infantry components) in favor of a wider span of control at
brigade and division headquarters.[35] These changes, as well as the
general neglect of infantry, including mechanized infantry, made
subordinate units up to brigade level less self-contained and less
able to deal with a variety of threats. As a result, two-way communications, from the bottom up and from the top down, became more
important than they had been.

The geographical expansion caused by the 1967 war, during
which Israel occupied territory three times its own size, also led to
further changes. Before 1967 the IDF, with the exception of its
training installations, had been an almost completely mobile field
force whose presumed theaters of operations were sufficiently close
to the mobilization centers—in some cases, less than a dozen
miles—to make almost instantaneous deployment possible. With
the distance between Tel Aviv and the front tripled and quadrupled,
however, it became necessary to construct, in the Sinai Desert as
well as on the Golan Heights, vast complexes of training areas,
camps, depots, maintenance facilities, and headquarters, all linked
to each other by a constantly expanding network of signal services.
A sudden predilection for fortification—paradoxically, it had never
been considered either necessary or possible along the pre-1967 borders, which had been far more difficult to defend—did its share to
transform the IDF from a mobile into a comparatively static force.
Not surprisingly, the commanders of this force too gradually became accustomed to exercising at least a large part of their functions
from permanent, well-equipped headquarters.

On 6 October 1973, taken by surprise by the Egyptian offensive,
the forces available to the commanding officer, Southern Front
(Shmuel Gonen), were as follows. A single low-quality infantry brigade was holding the partly dismantled Bar Lev fortifications along
the Suez Canal.[36] Behind it was an armored division, made up of
conscripts, stationed some fifty miles to the rear. The plan of de-

fense, code-named "Dovecot" and rehearsed many times, was based on the assumption that there would be sufficient warning time to enable the tanks to drive forward and take up positions in and between the sixteen strongholds forming the line, where they were to hold out, supported by the Air Force, until the reserves arrived. This was to take forty-eight hours; at that time a counterattack toward the canal would take place, culminating in a crossing. Preparations for it—equipment and designated crossing places—had been made in advance.

In the event, sufficient warning *was* received to enable the plan to be carried out; however, around noon on 6 October, Gonen—possibly acting on instructions from above—refused permission for the commander of the Armored Division, Sinai, to move his forces forward, saying that war was not yet certain and that such a move would unnecessarily provoke the Egyptians.[37] When permission to advance the division to the canal was finally granted, it was based on the assumption that the Egyptian offensive would open at 1800 hours, not at 1400 as it actually did. Consequently General Mandler's tanks, racing forward, were met on their way (which, since it led to the strongholds, had been pre-identified by the Egyptians) by a hail of anti-tank missiles. By nightfall on the 7th two-thirds of their number had been lost.

The forward movement of Mandler's armored division was not the only thing that went wrong on 6–7 October. The Bar Lev strongholds, which were supposed to act as the eyes of Southern Command and report on enemy strength and movements, proved too few and far between to handle this task, the more so since the Egyptian offensive initially bypassed many of them and left the garrisons isolated in the rear. Air reconnaissance, which should have filled the gap, proved ineffective in the face of massive missile defenses and was also hampered by urgent calls for air support at the Golan Heights. Consequently, the picture of the situation formed at General Gonen's main headquarters at Refidim, fifty miles to the rear, was a confused one right from the beginning.[38]

Late on the afternoon of 6 October, in an effort to gain a better understanding of what was happening, Mandler's chief of staff, Brigadier Pino, took a helicopter (significantly, this is the sole recorded personal reconnaissance of the entire front made by any se-

nior Israeli commander during the first days of the war in the Sinai)
and made a hazardous flight along the canal. He brought back
"what he [Pino] believed to be the first clear picture of the situation," but this did not prevent Gonen from getting lost again. At
0100 hours on 7 October, having in the meantime moved to his
Forward Headquarters at Um Hasheiba and thus having cut the
distance that separated him from the canal by half, Gonen apparently believed that his forces had returned to the canal almost
along its entire length. Totally misreading the situation of Mandler's
brigades, which by morning on the 7th had already been reduced to
half, Gonen saw no need to make use of the chief of staff's authorization, granted him on the evening of the 6th, to evacuate those of
the strongholds which were not playing a vital role in the defense.[39]

By 1100 hours on 7 October, Mandler's brigades—or what was
left of them—had been permitted by their commander to withdraw
to the so-called Artillery Road, running some six miles east of the
canal and parallel to it.[40] In retrospect, the basic dilemma facing the
Israelis in the Sinai—whether to link up with the strongholds or
concentrate on fighting the Egyptian forces that had penetrated in-
land—was already clear; whether Gonen realized this at the time
can no longer be established, however, and in any case he now had
fresh cause to feed his optimism: the reserves were mobilizing faster
than expected and some of them were already reaching the front. By
0800 hours on the 7th the two senior reserve commanders, Generals
Adan and Sharon, had reached their divisions' respective deployment areas along the Lateral Road, twenty or so miles east of the
canal, and so had the leading detachments of their forces. Gonen—
who during his previous career had served under both Adan and
Sharon—now proceeded to divide the front, assigning the northern
sector to Adan, the central one to Sharon, and the southern one to
Mandler. Each of the three divisions was to take over the remnants
of one of the three regular brigades, thus initiating the first of a great
many confusing reassignments that were to take place during the
next few days. In addition, operating to Adan's right and forming
the northernmost part of the Israeli line, there was to be another
brigade under Brigadier Magen.

Thus Gonen, and also Sharon (who as soon as he arrived at his
headquarters proposed a counterattack, aimed at linking up with

the strongholds in his sector, to take place that very evening),[41] were comparatively serene, but a very different picture was being formed back at General Headquarters in Tel Aviv. Returning from a Cabinet meeting at 1100 hours on the 7th, General Elazar was told by his deputy, General Tal, that "all our strongpoints along the Bar Lev Line have been surrounded. The Egyptians are holding a strip of territory which, at places, is ten miles wide."[42] How this estimate was formed, and by whom, can no longer be established; however, it stood in clear contradiction to the fact that Gonen's advance forces were at this stage still holding the Artillery Road along its entire length.

Defense Minister Dayan, returning from a morning visit to the Golan Heights,[43] picked up this version of the situation and then flew to Gonen's headquarters, where he arrived at 1140 hours. According to the most reliable of several accounts,[44] he opened the meeting with the words "This is war. Withdraw to the high ground" and then proceeded to draw a line on a map east of Refidim through Mounts Maara and Malek right down to Abu Rudeis on the Gulf of Suez. "Leave the [Bar Lev] fortifications, let whomever can evacuate. The wounded will have to remain prisoners." According to Herzog, Gonen agreed that the fortifications had to be evacuated, but he did not see any urgent reason to retreat thirty miles. Instead, he decided to deploy his main forces on the Lateral Road and to leave only advance units to hold the Artillery Road. Dayan did not dispute this decision; before returning to Tel Aviv, he dropped the enigmatic comment that his words were to be interpreted as "ministerial advice."

The minister of defense having left, Gonen at 1206 hours established contact with his divisional commanders and ordered them to deploy with their main forces on the Lateral Road, keeping only "small, mobile forces" forward on the Artillery Road, six miles east of the canal, "to report and delay the enemy advance." He also decided—belatedly, as it turned out—to use Elazar's authorization of the previous evening, and radioed permission for the men of the surviving strongholds to try and break out if they so desired.[45] At 1310 hours Gonen reported these moves to Elazar and, according to the latter's biographer, also mentioned a counterattack that he planned to launch as soon as the first hundred of Sharon's tanks—

his division's T/O consisted of approximately two hundred—reached the Lateral Road. At this, it is said, Elazar grew very angry; he rejected the idea, almost shouting at Gonen. Before counterattacking, the chief of staff said, it was necessary to have sufficient forces at hand. Meanwhile Gonen was to fight a delaying battle by the book and yield no ground unless forced to.[46]

In the early hours of the afternoon of 7 October, a gap was thus opening up between the views of Southern Command and those of General Headquarters—a fact of which at least Elazar, possibly recalling a 1972 exercise in which Gonen had dissipated his forces in premature counterattacks, was painfully aware. Elazar's misgivings concerning Gonen were confirmed at 1350, when Sharon called him—thus typically going over the head of his direct superior—to complain that Gonen was about to dissipate his, Sharon's, forces. Now apparently concluding that Gonen required a tight leash, Elazar told Sharon that he would visit Southern Front that afternoon. He then called Gonen again, telling him: "Let Arik [Sharon] stay concentrated, but if you need tanks for reinforcements—take them. That's how we hold on until the evening, supported by the Air Force." In any case, he did not "intend to counterattack with one division only. When we counterattack, we shall use larger forces." Elazar also said that the counterattack should be delayed to allow the Israeli forces to organize, and to permit the Egyptians to attack first and get their heads broken; this idea, according to his own postwar account, he was to carry around during the next few days until the Egyptians actually attacked on 14 October.[47]

It was now 1425 hours. Dayan, who according to his memoirs "could recall no moment in the past when I had felt such anxiety"[48] (others were later to claim that he had turned defeatist, depressing everybody's morale by using the words "destruction of the Third House of Israel"), entered Elazar's office. He told the chief of staff that the attempts to link up with the strongholds would have to cease and that he, Dayan, was going to propose to the Cabinet a deep withdrawal. As Elazar later explained it to his biographer, he did agree that the strongholds were as good as lost, but "unlike Dayan, I was thinking of a counterattack. He [Dayan] was determined on a new defensive line in the rear, whereas I did not think a voluntary withdrawal in front of the Egyptians was necessary."[49]

On his visits to both the northern and southern fronts, Dayan had been accompanied by General Zeevi, the former commanding general, Central Front, facing Jordan. Zeevi had been appointed "aide to the chief of staff" on 6 October, four days after doffing his uniform and retiring from the army. After Dayan left, Zeevi explained to Elazar that the situation on both fronts was actually worse than Tel Aviv realized. Reports from Gonen in particular were too rosy, there being in fact no question of launching a counterattack in the Sinai even on Tuesday, 9 October. He, Zeevi, was not quite as pessimistic as Dayan—"but you here are too optimistic," he said.[50]

At this point a word is necessary on the physical surroundings—always an important factor in command—of Elazar. Since noon on 6 October he and his staff had been working in the so-called Pit, an underground headquarters complex below the General Staff building in Tel Aviv, where they had spent the first sleepless night of the war. Here the usual to-do prevailed—staff officers going in and out, telephones jangling, radios crackling—and was aggravated by overcrowding and cigarette smoke (Elazar himself was a heavy smoker). Elazar, moreover, was surrounded by a galaxy of generals, the heroes of 1967; although for the most part they were out of uniform, they had dropped in to lend a hand. Unable or unwilling to drive away these men, among whom were several of his own former superiors, Elazar had to put up with—at the least count—three former chiefs of staff (Generals Yadin, Tzur, and Rabin) as well as Generals Zeevi and Yariv, the former head of Military Intelligence. Each of these men naturally felt the need to justify his presence by making remarks or going on missions. As Napoleon once wrote to the National Assembly, one bad general is preferable to two good ones. A cardinal problem of the Israeli command system in 1973 was precisely that it was afflicted by a phalanx of supposedly excellent generals.

His conversation with Zeevi over, Elazar explained to those present that the IDF could not afford to risk more than one division in an early counterattack. He then called Gonen once more—the chief of staff on this day seems to have felt positively obliged to talk to Southern Command constantly—and, after speaking to him, turned back to Zeevi and said: "You say that we at General Headquarters are too optimistic, but listen to this. Gonen wants to take Sharon tonight and attack the Egyptians at Deversoir [just north of the Great Bitter Lake], beat them, travel 30 miles to the south—fighting all the way, at night—attack Suez, and wave a bridgehead with 250 tanks in it."[51] In response, Elazar once again categorically refused permission for Gonen to attack that evening.

Elazar was still discussing the plans for the next day when a message from the prime minister arrived. Dayan, it turned out, had gone directly from General Headquarters to see the prime minister, reported on the situation as he saw it, and offered to resign. Horrified by the pessimism suddenly evinced by the national idol, Mrs. Meir at first refused to credit her ears, then summoned the chief of staff to join the discussion.[52] Apparently reaching her office around 1600 hours, Elazar offered a less pessimistic estimate of the situation than had Dayan, then went on to explain the three alternative courses open to the IDF in the south. The first was to launch a limited counterattack by a single division, staying on the east bank of the canal; the second, to accept Dayan's proposal and retreat; the third, to accept Gonen's idea for a counterattack by two divisions at the earliest possible moment, culminating in a crossing. Since he felt the third course was too risky, Elazar argued in favor of the first—that is, a limited attack by 200 to 300 tanks on the morning of 8 October, a move that might clear the east bank if it succeeded and would not be disastrous even if it failed. He then asked permission to go to Southern Command and decide on the spot. Dayan seconded the proposal, and the meeting came to an end.[53]

At 1630 hours Elazar returned to General Headquarters. Here he was handed a message from General Peled, commander of the Air Force, indicating that seven out of fourteen Egyptian bridges had been knocked out since attacks on them had started two hours previously and that the remainder would be knocked out by nightfall. Having told Peled "to come and get a kiss," Elazar, surrounded by the excitement of those present (among them Zeevi, who suddenly felt that now everything was possible) informed the prime minister. He then called Gonen and told him to summon the three divisional commanders for a meeting at Southern Command Headquarters. Before setting out himself Elazar explained the three courses open to the IDF to his staff, repeated his own preference for the first one, and told them it had received the Cabinet's (in truth, the prime minister's) blessing.[54] On 8 October, too, another counterattack was to take place on the Golan Heights—this being a clear departure from the IDF's doctrine, which had always considered it impossible to mount two major thrusts against two opponents simultaneously.

Early in the evening of 7 October Adan flew to Um Hasheiba. There he met General Mandler but not Sharon; Sharon waited in vain for a helicopter from Southern Command to pick him up and later expressed his belief that "somebody did not want me there."[55] Entering Gonen's headquarters, Adan recalls, "I had to force my way through scores of male and female soldiers crowded in the bunker's corridors . . . I saw the familiar faces of friends and colleagues but also noticed many outsiders and reporters. The war room was jammed with staff officers and visitors. The place was a mess; you could barely find your own feet. Looking at maps and listening to transceivers, I tried to follow reports from our forces along the front, but in vain. So deafening was the noise in the room and so distorted the sound from the radio that it was impossible to understand anything . . . I could not help thinking that it had to be impossible to work out any coherent plan amidst such disorder."[56]

Since General Elazar had not arrived—his insistence on planning the counterattack in person had already cost a few hours, and was to cost a few more before the conference adjourned at 2200 hours and thus made it necessary to carry out the actual preparation during the small hours of the night—the discussion started without him. Gonen, Adan, Mandler, and Gonen's chief of staff, Brigadier Ben Ari, discussed the Egyptians' whereabouts, the fate of the strongholds, and a possible Israeli counterattack. At 1845 hours Elazar arrived, accompanied by the manager of his office, a Lieutenant Colonel Shalev who took notes of the meeting, and by former chief of staff Yitzhak Rabin. At 1920 hours the conference opened; since Gonen's war room was jammed with people it took place in the general's private quarters, a room three yards square where there was hardly enough room to sit.

Opening the formal conference, Gonen described the situation. The enemy, with "five infantry divisions and perhaps hundreds of tanks," were crossing all along the canal, "seeking to move east." Though concentrations of tanks had been identified at three places, the Egyptian "main effort" had still not been discovered, more than twenty-four hours after the beginning of the war. His plan called for a nighttime counterattack by Adan's and Sharon's divisions, each operating in his own sector and using Egyptian bridges to cross the canal. Having crossed, Sharon was to turn north and link up with Adan.[57]

General Mandler was the next to speak; he too favored a two-division counterattack on the 8th but wanted it to be launched by his own and Sharon's divisions so that the crossings, if there were to be any, would take place only in the central and southern sectors of the canal. Less optimistic than either of his colleagues, Adan said that any attempt to link up with the strongholds (this question must have been mentioned by the others too) was bound to fail; the remaining ones were to be evacuated immediately. On the 8th there would take place "a limited counterattack . . . aimed only at taking the initiative from the Egyptians and halting their westward advance, destroying that part of the Egyptian armored forces which had thrust deep into our territory, no longer protected by the ramparts near the canal." Ben Ari, the last to speak, agreed with Adan.

After a good deal of discussion Elazar summed up. The chief of staff had made up his mind in favor of a limited counterattack before leaving Tel Aviv, and he accordingly rejected Gonen's and Mandler's plans as too ambitious. There was to take place on the next day "a limited, graduated counterattack from Qantara to the south" by Adan's division, with Sharon standing in reserve. Adan's move was to start in the morning. He was to stay two miles away from the canal, "swarming with [Egyptian] infantry equipped with anti-tank weapons." If Adan required aid he would get it from Sharon, who was ordered to stand ready for the purpose; otherwise Sharon would start an attack of his own, also proceeding from north to south, after Adan's offensive came to an end around noon. Permission for Sharon to move out of reserve Elazar explicitly kept for himself. "As many as possible" of the strongholds were to be "rescued," but only by way of exploiting success if there should be any. An eventual crossing was subjected to the same condition, and again Elazar reserved permission to himself.[58]

It was now around 2100 hours. The conference had lasted over two hours, proof enough that it was less tidy than this summary

212

would suggest. Lacking reconnaissance units in contact with the enemy,[59] the Israeli commanders had no clear idea of the Egyptians' whereabouts; hence the plan was based on guesswork concerning the place they should have been had they been operating according to "Soviet Doctrine," which as a matter of fact they were not.[60] It was thought that the Egyptians had reached a line seven to eight miles east of the canal, instead of the actual three to four.[61] How Adan could hope to defeat the Egyptians without ever coming to grips with their main force, consisting of infantry, has never been explained. (The Israelis constantly counted tanks, both their own and the enemy's, in the mistaken belief that this was the most important factor, exaggerating those in their own hands and minimizing those of the Egyptians.)[62] Nor is it clear how Adan expected to rescue any of the troops still remaining in the strongholds without coming within two miles of the canal. Some ambiguity also remained, it would appear, concerning the direction of Sharon's attack. Elazar had wanted him to advance from Tassa southward, but Gonen on the following day was to make him disengage altogether and send him far to the south to a point opposite the Mitla Pass so that Sharon's division would launch its offensive from there. Finally, given the fact that Elazar had only "three divisions between here and Tel Aviv" (including the three badly worn regular brigades), his plan for a graduated attack, risking little, was logical— assuming, that is, that an offensive on 8 October was indeed imperative, and that it was impossible to wait for more Israeli forces to arrive or for the Egyptians to take the offensive and, in Elazar's words, "break their heads."

The conference over, Elazar reported to Dayan by phone and left. Accompanied by Adan, he met Sharon, who had just arrived and was entering the bunker. Sharon repeated his earlier idea about linking up with the strongholds that night; Elazar did not absolutely refuse, but referred him to Gonen instead. With Adan, Sharon entered Gonen's room, and the conference was resumed. Sharon explained his position to Gonen, who did not turn him down flat but only said there was at that time no plan for linking up with the strongholds. Developments during the night might lead to a change of plan, however, and Gonen did not object to Sharon preparing a plan for reaching the strongholds in his sector. Southern Command,

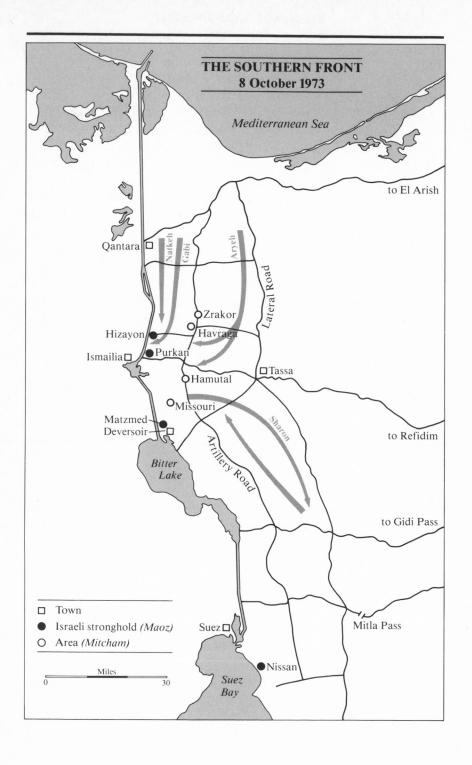

THE SOUTHERN FRONT
8 October 1973

Mediterranean Sea

to El Arish

Qantara

Natkeh

Gabi

Aryeh

Lateral Road

Zrakor

Havraga

Hizayon

Purkan

Ismailia

Hamutal

Tassa

Missouri

Sharon

Matzmed
Deversoir

to Refidim

Bitter Lake

Artillery Road

to Gidi Pass

☐ Town

● Israeli stronghold *(Maoz)*

○ Area *(Mitcham)*

Miles

0   30

Suez

Mitla Pass

● Nissan

Suez Bay

Gonen said, would examine the situation toward dawn and make its decision.[63]

Back at General Headquarters Elazar first met with his deputy, General Tal, and the chief of Military Intelligence, General Zeira, who listened to his plan. A larger meeting with the members of the General Staff followed at 0035 hours, and again Elazar explained his plan. When Dayan dropped in at 0100 hours, and suggested a crossing north of Qantara, the chief of staff responded that the country was unsuitable; he, Elazar, was going to cross—if at all—only by way of exploiting success, and then not in the north but way to the south, at the culminating point of Adan's offensive. Sharon, too, might cross eventually, but only if his attack was unexpectedly successful. Dayan having left, Elazar went to bed. It is typical of what passed for Israeli staff work that no written record was kept of any of these conferences. Nor did Elazar issue written orders for the attack he had masterminded. He did, however, ask to be waked up when a copy of Gonen's orders arrived, so that he would be able to talk to him in person.[64]

Back at Um Hasheiba, according to Adan, Gonen went to bed at 0100 hours.[65] He was waked half an hour later, signed the written orders prepared by his staff, and was back asleep by 0205. By 0245 the orders, made out in overlay forms and consisting of a map accompanied by a brief text, were being flown to Tel Aviv. According to Adan, the purpose of the attack was defined as "mopping up the zone between the Artillery Road and the Canal water line; destruction of the enemy forces in that area while extricating forces from the strongpoints and pulling back stuck tanks; and readiness for a crossing to the other side of the Canal." Whether this really constituted a radical departure from the previous evening's summing up, as Adan claims, is questionable; Elazar, at any rate, did not think so when he approved Gonen's plan at 0535 hours.[66] At 0605 Elazar talked to Gonen over the phone connecting their headquarters; though he was informed of the intention to cross by using an Egyptian bridge, he again approved his subordinate's plan. He did, it is true, warn Gonen against coming too close to the water line; that the two things were in direct conflict does not seem to have entered his head—which, by this time, was probably muddled from lack of sleep.[67]

Since Adan never saw Gonen's written orders until after the war, Elazar's approval did not matter; for all the role that writing played on 8 October the officers involved might as well have been illiterate. At 0345 hours, having been waked up once again and told of the worsening situation of some strongholds in Adan's sector, Gonen tried to call him but failed. He therefore talked instead to Brigadier Magen—Adan's deputy, in charge of a semi-independent force holding the northernmost sector of the canal—saying that Adan's attack should not proceed as far south as originally planned; rather, he was to go only as far as stronghold Purkan, opposite Ismailia, before seizing an Egyptian bridge and making a crossing. Should Adan fail to find a bridge at Purkan, Gonen added, he was to carry out his original mission and proceed as far south as stronghold Matzmed. The crossing, again using an Egyptian bridge, was to take place at that point.

Informed by Magen that Adan's brigade commanders had already been given their orders (which they had—at 0130 hours) and could not redeploy at a moment's notice, Gonen appeared to reconsider; at 0413 hours he radioed a "correction" and told Magen to have Adan cancel the crossing operation at Purkan, go straight for Matzmed instead, and cross there. Gonen wanted Magen to inform the brigadiers of this change over the radio, but the latter rightly pointed out the confusion that such a procedure might generate. Thereupon Gonen said: "Okay, [Adan] should get organized in his present location. I shall assign the link up operation to [Sharon]. He will link up with the strongholds and return and only then will [Adan] proceed southward and cross the canal at Matzmed."[68]

This incredible exchange being at an end—by now, none of the commanders involved could have had much of an idea as to who was to attack what, and in which order—Gonen, though not without some difficulty (radio communications throughout this day were thoroughly bad, partly because their constant and lengthy use by the various headquarters led to mutual interference, and partly because the Egyptians were jamming them), established direct contact with Adan. Asked whether he could "move [from north to south] to strongholds Hizayon, Purkan, and Matzmed and link up with their garrisons while proceeding on [his] mission" and then prepare for a crossing at Matzmed, Adan replied that the answer depended on developments during the morning. Gonen then raised the idea, already discussed with Magen, of having Sharon approach the strongholds first, and ended by saying that "you [Adan] must be prepared for both possibilities."

Even this additional piece of confusion introduced by Gonen was not the end of the matter. At 0432 hours the commander, Southern Front, contacted Sharon and told him to drive south, where he was to cross the canal near stronghold Nissan, opposite Suez City. This, then, was a clear departure from Elazar's plan, and one that can be explained only in reference to Gonen's own proposal of the previous day.

Even when one disregards the strategic and operational problems confronting the Israeli offensive—whether an attack at such an early date, launched by such disorganized forces, was necessary at all; whether it could or should have taken place simultaneously with an attack on the Golan Heights; whether it should have been graduated rather than concentrated; and whether a move across the Egyptian front was really preferable to a breakthrough at any one point[69]—the planning procedures themselves were wrong from beginning to end. Whether the chief of staff should have planned the offensive in person, rather than leaving what was after all only a limited move aimed at regaining the initiative to the discretion of the commanding general, Southern Front, is questionable; that he could have done so without putting down a single word in writing is incredible. Although Elazar's insistence on reviewing Gonen's plans before they were carried out was sound, his failure to notice the changes allegedly introduced into it is strange, to say the least, pointing either to his own inattention and fatigue or to the fact that the conclusions arrived at during the general's conference of 7 October were sufficiently ambiguous to allow various different interpretations. That Gonen and Adan each understood the plan in his own way is certain, and it may well be supposed that the bedlam prevailing both at Southern Command and at General Headquarters contributed to this outcome. The chain of command was thoroughly unsound; not only was Gonen made to carry out a plan that was diametrically opposed to his own, but he was to do so while in charge of two subordinates who had both been his own superiors and one of whom (Sharon) was constantly bypassing him and talking directly to the

217

chief of staff. Since Gonen proved unable to enforce his authority, Elazar's insistence on personally laying down the main lines of the offensive is understandable, though this was done at the cost of weakening Gonen's position still further. Even less comprehensible than any of these—unless it was caused by an absolute shortage of troops, which should have doomed the counteroffensive in the planning stages—was the inability of the Israelis to keep themselves informed of the enemy's whereabouts, on which the entire idea behind the plan was hinged. Had such errors been committed during an exercise at any staff college, those responsible would have failed the course. As it was, however, the Israelis proceeded to compound them by putting the plans into practice.

1973 : THE COUNTERATTACK

In the morning of 8 October, following his difficulties in communicating with Gonen, Adan selected as his command post a hill codenamed Zrakor about six miles east of the canal. From there he had tolerable communications with Gonen but, as it turned out, an inadequate view of the territory in which his division was to operate. His 162th division consisted of Colonel Gabi's 460th brigade with two reorganized tank battalions,[70] the same ones that had fought on 6–7 October and had been defeated; Colonel Natkeh's 212th reserve brigade with three more tank battalions, which had already suffered some loss to an Egyptian ambush that caught them on their way to the front; and Colonel Aryeh's 500th brigade, which, though consisting of three fresh tank battalions, was still some way in the rear. Adan's mechanized infantry brigade under Colonel Fedaleh was still too far from the front to take part in the battle, as was his divisional artillery; in the event, all that the Israelis had available for the great counteroffensive of 8 October were four artillery barrels. The air situation was little better. Shortly after dawn, the Egyptian positions were attacked by a few planes which Gonen, for some reason, insisted on directing with his own observers rather than Adan's. After that, nothing.[71]

At 0753 hours Adan issued the final orders for the attack. Since Natkeh was already engaged, fighting Egyptian armor near Qantara, and Aryeh's brigade was still twenty miles to the rear, the divisional offensive was carried out by a mere two tank battalions under Gabi. Gabi was told "to plan to link up with Hizayon and Purkan strongholds, but to do so only upon a specific order."[72] The movement started at 0800 hours, and six minutes later Gonen contacted Adan by radio and reminded him not to come close to the waterline.[73] Driving south parallel to the canal and some five miles to the east of it—the large distance being apparently the result of a map-reading error[74]—Gabi's brigade encountered hardly any resistance and by 0900 hours had reached a line opposite Hizayon, the northernmost of the strongholds in Adan's sector. Once there, Gabi redeployed in preparation for the linkup, as ordered. As he was doing so his battalions came under observation by Sharon, who had taken up a position on an overlooking hill known as Havraga, and who was thus in a better position to know what was going on than was Adan himself. The northernmost of Sharon's battalions was also watching.[75]

At 0900 hours Natkeh informed Adan that he was doing well near Qantara and had destroyed a number of Egyptian tanks. Adan thereupon told him to prepare for a move southward to Matzmed, but "to move there only on my order."[76] At 0922 Gonen contacted Adan and this time pressed for crossings at both Hizayon and Matzmed.[77] At 0938 hours the commanding general, Southern Front, was back on the air—the radio operators were certainly not left unemployed on this day—and repeated his request for a crossing to take place at Hizayon; when Adan said he needed air support to carry out this mission, it was promised him.[78] Even this, however, was not to be Gonen's final word. At 0955 hours he asked Adan to extend his attack farther south than originally planned, as far as Missouri and the Chinese Farm areas, and was told by Adan that the division would try to do so "if it's very important."[79]

At 1000 hours, Natkeh was enjoying a lull in front of Qantara, having previously done quite well. Gabi's two battalions were deployed opposite Hizayon, coming under Egyptian artillery fire which, on this and other days of the war, was assisted in finding its targets by the loose wireless discipline maintained in the IDF. Aryeh's brigade at this time was driving comfortably along the Lateral Road, almost twenty miles to the rear, and had likewise reached a line level with Hizayon without, naturally enough, encountering a single Egyptian soldier. In response to Gonen's request—in all these exchanges, given Gonen's position, there could be no question of orders—to extend his attack southward, Adan decided to entrust this new mission to Aryeh's brigade, but he detached one battalion that was to come to Gabi's aid. This was the first of many confusing reassignments to take place on that day.[80]

A mere ten minutes after his last conversation with Gonen, Adan was contacted by Ben Ari—it was now 1005 hours—who had a startling piece of news: "There are some slight indications that the enemy has begun to collapse, so it's very important, very important, to rush at maximum speed with all your forces along your entire axis from the north, from Qantara, to down below, to make contact and destroy. Otherwise they're liable to get away!"[81] Instructed to bring down Natkeh from Qantara and launch an attack on Hizayon, Adan, according to his own subsequent account, tried to argue, but, knowing that Southern Command possessed (or should have possessed) intelligence sources other than his own, decided to comply. This involved bringing down Natkeh from Qantara—but since Magen in the north said he could not assume responsibility for the sector thus evacuated, only two battalions actually took part in the move.

Although the reasons behind the sudden wave of optimism at Southern Command have never been explained, an educated guess can be made. As has been remarked, Israeli tactical intelligence barely functioned during the first days of the war: there were few if any attempts at ground reconnaissance, and the Air Force was all but unable to carry out low-level photographic missions over the canal.[82] Consequently Gonen was reduced to listening in to his subordinates' radio networks, and it was there that the misunderstanding originated. In particular, Natkeh's brigade had been doing well against the Egyptians from 0800 to 1000 hours; its commander exaggerated his successes, however, and Gonen was misled.[83] Gabi's brigade likewise gave a somewhat partisan account of the "battles" it fought against the handful of Egyptian troops encountered, and indeed nobody listening in to any of Adan's networks would have thought something had gone seriously wrong until midafternoon.[84] It is also possible, as one account has it, that a conversation between Ben Ari and Adan was misunderstood, and consequently misrepresented, by an anonymous NCO who was monitoring the network at

Southern Command. When Adan asked Ben Ari, in one of their many conversations during the morning, about the exact location of the Egyptian bridge he was to seize in the Hizayon area, that NCO somehow got the impression that the crossing had already taken place. As we shall presently see, the welcome news spread like wildfire, and soon everybody "knew" of the Egyptian collapse.[85]

None of the above, nevertheless, would have sufficed to mislead Gonen had he not been more than ready to believe any scrap of favorable news. Like a great many other Israelis, Gonen early in the war found it difficult to adjust to a situation in which Egyptian forces were actually making a stand—in front of those invincible tanks of his, what is more—and fighting. As the language he and Elazar used proves—there was talk of "waving" the Egyptians across the canal, of "going to" the strongholds (as if this did not involve fighting one's way right through the enemy forces), and of "changing the entire situation" by putting a company of tanks across the canal—the Israelis by and large adhered to Dayan's so-called bird theory, according to which Arab forces, like birds, would always scatter after hearing a few bangs. It is that theory, after all, which alone can explain the counterattack of 8 October: launched by a single disorganized and decimated tank division, without prior reconnaissance and on the basis of a few hours' hurried preparation in the middle of the night, with neither air nor artillery support.

Convinced that the offensive was making headway, Gonen at 0955 hours called General Headquarters to report progress and request permission to cross, as agreed. Elazar was away at a Cabinet meeting; told—by way of his assistant, General Zeevi—that Adan's forces were approaching Hizayon and that there was an Egyptian bridge waiting to be used nearby, he did not explicitly approve a crossing.[86] Zeevi misunderstood, however, and told Gonen to go ahead. Gonen did so, and at 0957 hours ordered Adan to cross at Hizayon. A mere eighteen minutes later Gonen again called Zeevi, and this time asked permission to cross not merely at Hizayon but at several other points further south as well, his plan being apparently to "wave" a number of shallow footholds on the other side so as to prevent the Egyptians from destroying their own bridges—yet another sign of the overconfidence that reigned on that day. Elazar still hesitated; Gonen, he told Zeevi, had better make sure that the areas selected were free of enemy forces and that the Israeli forces on the far side would be strong enough to resist being cut off. Turning back to the assembled government ministers, Elazar went on explaining his plan. He emphasized the need to stay away from the canal, and added that, according to the latest reports, a linkup with Hizayon had already been achieved. That this involved a contradiction Elazar inexplicably failed to see; or perhaps his failure is made only too explicable by the fact that he was trying to report to the Cabinet and, at the same time, direct an offensive approximately two hundred miles away.[87]

A few minutes passed, and Zeevi called Elazar for the third time. On this occasion he was answered by Lieutenant Colonel Shalev, the manager of Elazar's office who had accompanied the general to the Cabinet meeting. Gonen, Zeevi explained, only asked permission for "optional crossings"; so far he had ordered but one crossing to take place at Hizayon. When Shalev retorted, correctly, that Elazar had not yet permitted a crossing to take place at *any* point, Zeevi said that such permission had been given during the first conversation and that the question now was whether Gonen was to be granted "an option" for crossing at additional points. Even as he was talking to Shalev, Zeevi was handed a message that said a crossing had taken place—the speed with which welcome news spread on this day borders on the incredible. This new information, together with Gonen's request, was transmitted to Elazar in writing; and the chief of staff, evidently acting on the assumption that the conditions he had stipulated did in fact exist, gave his approval.

Elazar was destined to be interrupted twice more before the Cabinet meeting came to an end. Shortly after the conversation reported in the preceding paragraph, the unfortunate chief of staff was handed another (fourth) message from Southern Command: now they were asking his approval for moving Sharon south to the Gidi Pass in preparation for his division's attack against the Egyptian Third Army. Elazar gave his approval—by 1040 hours, Gonen had been so informed—and it was transmitted to Sharon. He was still talking to the Cabinet when a fifth message arrived. Elazar took a glance at it, then turned to the ministers and said, "To judge from the nagging from below, they already have a bridgehead on the far side."[88] Nagging aplenty there was, indeed; but for this the chief of staff, who on this occasion had insisted on personally approving

222

company-sized moves that were taking place a couple of hundred miles away, was himself to blame.

Having left the Cabinet room, Elazar twice—at 1100 and 1125 hours[89]—spoke to Gonen. The latter advocated his original scheme of the previous day, that is, of moving Sharon to the south, not merely to the Gidi but as far as the Mitla, and having his division's attack start from that point and proceed from east to west. Himself misled by the optimistic reports of the brigades,[90] Gonen succeeded in persuading the chief of staff to fall in with his scheme, despite Elazar's misgivings that Sharon would be unable to launch his attack before the onset of darkness. Turning to his staff, Elazar said, "Since this is a marginal thing, let him do as he likes"—marginal things evidently being all Elazar was prepared to leave to his principal subordinate in the south.[91]

With that exchange Elazar, according to his own account, "was through with today's battle." Feeling well satisfied, he set out to visit Northern Command at Mount Cna'an (neither he nor any other senior officer, according to General Eytan, visited the Golan Heights proper before Wednesday, the 10th) and thus left his subordinates free to commit even more errors. Having been told by Gonen that the enemy were "collapsing," Adan shortly after 1000 hours came under pressure from Ben Ari to cross here, there, everywhere. At the same time he was to proceed beyond his original objective as far south as the Missouri area in order to launch an attack there as well.[92] Adan asked for a battalion of Sharon's division to help him carry out this mission, and, after some discussion, it was promised him.

Around 1100 hours, Adan's division was deployed as follows. Natkeh, with two battalions, had finally disengaged at Qantara and was on his way south, staying out of range of the Egyptian anti-tank weapons as agreed and consequently meeting with little opposition. Aryeh, with the two battalions left him, was moving west from the Lateral Road to a point known as Hamutal, previously held by one of Sharon's battalions with whose tanks—now on their way east prior to their planned move to the Mitla—he met on the way, causing congestion and bottlenecks. Between the two, Gabi's brigade, reinforced in the rear by Aryeh's third battalion (Lieutenant Colonel Eliashiv) was still deployed opposite Hizayon, taking Egyptian artillery fire and vainly waiting for air and artillery support to start its attack on the stronghold. At 1100 hours one of Gabi's battalions (Lieutenant Colonel Amir) had run out of fuel and ammunition and withdrew after receiving permission to do so. Left on its own, the other battalion—commanded by Lieutenant Colonel Adini—found its radio equipment malfunctioning and was unable to communicate with brigade headquarters. Listening in to the Southern Command network, Adini heard something about a canal crossing being ordered; he also watched a few Israeli aircraft dropping bombs on the Egyptian positions ahead. In the belief this was the air support they had been expecting for the last two hours, the battalion charged. They drove forward a mile and a half and got within half a mile of the waterline before being halted by a hail of anti-tank fire. Adini himself was wounded and evacuated; by the time order had been restored and a retreat ordered, eighteen of the battalion's twenty-five tanks were out of action.[93]

Still watching from his hill at Zrakor, his communications a mess, Adan by his own admission had no idea of what was happening—a confession made all the more damaging by the fact that Sharon from his vantage point at Havraga had a better view of Gabi's progress than did the divisional commander himself. Gonen called to find out how things were going, and Sharon told him that Gabi's forward battalion (Adini's) was under heavy artillery fire and making no progress. However, Sharon could still see many of Gabi's tanks deployed in the rear, these being presumably Amir's and Eliashiv's battalions.[94] Under these circumstances, with Adan out of the picture and Sharon reporting that things were going well, there was no reason why Gonen should reconsider his order for Sharon to extricate his troops in preparation for their southward move, nor why Sharon himself should surrender any of his battalions to Adan. Repeatedly pressed by his subordinates to let them come to Gabi's aid—at one point Gabi himself broke into Sharon's network and demanded such aid—Sharon refused in no uncertain terms, with the result that his subordinates were still wondering what was happening even as they started their journey to the Mitla.[95]

Adan at Zrakor was unaware of Adini's attack, though he did manage to pick up enough fragmentary reports to learn, at 1140 hours, that his central brigade was in trouble. To his right the divisional commander could already see the dust thrown up by Natkeh's tanks as they approached; they would reinforce Gabi and all would be well. In preparation for launching his second and presumably decisive attack against Hizayon, Adan ordered Natkeh to meet Gabi for "updating on the terrain and the enemy"—this procedure being tantamount to admitting that he, the divisional commander, had scant idea about either. He fixed a dividing line between Gabi and Natkeh and then waited for the second attack to go in, meanwhile busying himself with his left (southern) flank where Sharon's withdrawal had left a gap that only Aryeh's brigade could fill. Instead of standing by to support his division's attack as ordered, Adan was later to complain, Sharon evacuated the positions he was holding without arranging to have them occupied by other troops, thus leaving Adan's southern flank exposed.[96]

Having waited in vain for air support—which, Adan says, Southern Command kept promising throughout the morning—the battalions now assembled in a rough semicircle four or so miles around Hizayon started their attack at about 1330 hours. On the left Aryeh's two battalions were halted almost at once; his forces could not advance toward Hamutal and Hizayon simultaneously, the brigade commander radioed Adan, and in any case they had to deal with a fresh group of Egyptian tanks that had just crossed the Firdan bridge and were making their way south. In the center, Eliashiv's battalion—assigned to Gabi from Aryeh's brigade—likewise failed to advance, apparently because it was waiting for air and artillery support that never materialized.[97] Of the five battalions that were available, more or less, only Natkeh's two actually moved forward; and of those one—Lieutenant Colonel Natan's—was halted almost immediately by Egyptian fire. Natkeh himself, accompanying his other battalion (Lieutenant Colonel Assaf Yagouri), continued the movement; as his forward headquarters drew Egyptian fire, however, he found himself "fighting for his life," and contact between him and Yagouri was lost.[98] According to one account, Adan contacted Natkeh to ask how he was doing. Natkeh did not know; he thought Yagouri might have crossed the canal, and promised to find out and report back.[99] At the time this exchange took place, soon after 1430 hours, Yagouri's battalion had been as good as wiped out and its commander was a prisoner of the Egyptians.

By this time, according to his own admission, Adan had lost all control over events. Isolated at Zrakor, his communications mal-

225

functioning because of Egyptian jamming and the interference from Southern Command's intermediate stations (not to mention his own attempts to update himself by breaking into his subordinates' networks), the general learned of Yagouri's failure before he had even issued orders for the attack to begin. He was still wondering how it could have happened when a new crisis arose. Aryeh's brigade, at long last arriving near Hamutal, was driving into what they thought was unoccupied terrain (it had previously been evacuated by Sharon's forces) when they suddenly came under fire from "thousands of Egyptian infantry, supported by many tanks." Adan was just about to order him to withdraw when his own command post was located by the Egyptian listening service and made the target of an artillery barrage. Leaving some of his staff to evacuate the casualties, the general himself moved forward to Havraga, which had previously afforded Sharon such a fine view of the battle, and summoned Natkeh and Gabi to meet him there. No sooner had they arrived and the conference started—three stocky men, as Adan notes, all with broad shoulders—than an Egyptian counterattack got under way, and the brigadiers were urgently called back by their deputies.

This last attempt to regain control over the division having failed, Adan spent the rest of the afternoon as a spectator, helplessly listening in as his subordinates first panicked, then gradually recovered their nerve and started lighting bonfires by shooting up Egyptian tanks. Behind him Gonen was equally helpless; the commanding general, Southern Front, had realized something was wrong and halted Sharon's southward drive at 1445 hours, but proved unable to make his headstrong subordinate come to Adan's support.[100] In the end only one of Sharon's units, of company size, took part in the battle raging around Hamutal and was forced to retreat after losing three of its eight tanks. And so the day came to an end, with Adan's forces reduced to little more than half their previous strength and abandoning their positions. It was the worst defeat in the IDF's history.

CONCLUSIONS: REVERSE OPTIONAL CONTROL

Pronouncing judgment over historical events is something never to be lightly undertaken, especially when, as in this case, the events are still quite recent and controversial. Of the participants, many are still alive and well; their memoirs, speeches, and interviews with journalists, not to mention the war diaries (which some say have been forged), together constitute an embarrassing wealth of material. Here an attempt will be made to understand the defeat by looking at the command setup itself, the planning of the offensive, and the way the offensive was actually carried out.

Enough has already been said about the command setup to make a long repetition unnecessary. Gonen, it will be recalled, was new to his job, a junior major general (Hebrew *Aluf*) who had seen service under two of his three principal subordinates, all of whom also carried the rank of *Aluf*. Against this background, he not unnaturally found it difficult to issue orders; at best he could forbid this or that wild scheme, but, as Adan's memoirs show, Gonen's positive authority was limited to repeated "requests" that a plan be changed or a unit transferred from one division to another. Although situations in which junior officers must command their seniors are probably inevitable in any army—particularly so in the IDF, where retired generals were given divisional commands—Gonen's position was made even more difficult by the fact that the chief of staff clearly had little confidence in him. Under such circumstances the commanding general, Southern Front, was doomed to failure, apart from any errors he might commit, and leaving aside also the question of whether his command was an example of the Peter Principle, as the government-appointed Agranat Investigation Committee was to claim after the war.[101]

If the command setup was bad, the way the offensive was planned was worse. With no reconnaissance units in touch with the enemy (significantly, it was the reconnaissance troop attached to Sharon's division, not any technological device, which later in the war discovered the gap between Second and Third Egyptian Armies that allowed the Israeli canal-crossing to take place), the Israelis were forced to trust their intuition in regard to the enemy's whereabouts—even though their entire plan hinged on exact knowledge of the Egyptian anti-tank positions. While imposing his own scheme on Gonen, Elazar nevertheless left the detailed planning to him; and then proceeded to compound the error by failing to note whatever discrepancies there may have been between the plans presented to him on the morning of the 8th and his own instructions of the previous day. Gonen in turn twice attempted to change the plan after it had already been transmitted to the division and even brigade commanders, and although he later returned to the original version his frequent changes of mind generated confusion. To this extent, the criticism to which he was subjected after the war appears fully justified.

Not even all of these errors, however, need have led to the offensive's failure had not Elazar insisted on commanding it by means of what one may call, for lack of a better term, "reverse optional control." Following the June 1967 war, at a time when the Israeli Army was still basking in its supposed invincibility, much was written of the new system of command it had allegedly invented and perfected, called "optional control." Optional control was designed to allow maximum independence to subordinate commanders while giving superior headquarters the option of interfering at any time, particularly when it was a question of changing the axis of advance or avoiding excessive casualties. Somewhat resembling Moltke's system of *Weisungen,* but applied at a much lower level in the military hierarchy, it demanded excellent junior commanders and, even more important, mutual trust between them and their superiors.

In 1973 the quality of Israel's junior officer corps was still very high, possibly even better than it had been in 1967;[102] mutual trust, however, was lacking at Southern Command because of very bad personal relations among the senior commanders.[103] For this reason, and also because Elazar totally lacked any kind of directed telescope for gathering information independently, his method on 8 October was exactly the opposite of optional control. Instead of giving subordinates a free rein and intervening only in case of need, his distrust of Gonen led him to reserve approval of the most important moves to himself. Gonen, in turn, was thereby compelled to restrict Adan and Sharon in a similar way, and so right down the line. Since each officer was expected to keep in touch with his superior, he selected his own position in such a way that he would be able to do so at all times, even if this meant that he would not be available for his subordinate. It was this system of reverse optional control, in many ways more reminiscent of the British at the Somme than of modern armored warfare as practiced by the Israelis themselves, that was at the root of the problems.

228

Consider the way the Israeli chain of command actually operated on 8 October. At the bottom was Natkeh, who at 1430 hours was in touch with Adan, his immediate superior, but totally unable either to see or to hear his own subordinate, Yagouri, whom he was supposedly accompanying in combat. Adan in turn was at Zrakor, a position specifically selected for the advantages that it offered in regard to communications with Gonen, but which did not afford nearly as good a view of his own forces as did Havraga, where Sharon was stationed. It was from Zrakor that he heard of Adini's attack after it had taken place. Gonen throughout the day remained at his Um Hasheiba command post, not because he was a coward—none of these men were—but presumably because, given the difficulties in communicating, it was the only place from which reliable contact with General Headquarters could be maintained. At the top of the hierarchy, Elazar found himself reporting to his own direct superiors—the Cabinet—at the very time that he was supposed to be making the decisions he had reserved for himself: the orders for Adan to cross the canal and for Sharon to launch his division's attack. The fact that he was actually at the Cabinet when these decisions had to be made meant that another link, in the form of Zeevi or Shalev (and at one point, both), had to be interposed between him and Gonen. Even omitting Yagouri, whose ill-starred attack took place later, it is thus clear that the offensive was commanded by a divisional commander who did not know what was going on reporting to a front commander who knew even less, who in turn reported to a chief of staff who knew less than either. Under the system of reverse optional control, however, it was the man who knew the least who made the crucial decisions. This he did, on the basis of one telephone call that came in every fifteen minutes[104] and interrupted other business, on a little piece of paper, after hardly any thought, working through either one or two intermediaries, and in regard to events that were taking place a couple of hundred miles away.

Forced by Elazar's command system—or by distrust of Gonen, which amounts to the same thing—to remain at places from which they could communicate with their superiors at all times, each of these men was compelled to rely on his subordinates' reports for information. Partly owing to communication difficulties and partly because the overconfident Israeli field commanders exaggerated the slight clashes they had had with the Egyptians into major victories, many of these reports were misleading. In the absence of a directed telescope, there was no way to correct the impression thus being conveyed. The result was that the system of reverse optional control backfired. Instead of certainty being created by means of supervision from the top downward, uncertainty spread from the bottom up.

An important point to be noted in this context is the fact that the Israeli failure was not primarily due to technological inadequacy. Having enjoyed six years in which to turn the Sinai into a fortress, the IDF in 1973 had a communications system that was technically about as good as it could be. It was certainly much superior to the one employed in 1967, and may indeed have been too good insofar as it enabled Elazar to proceed as he did. Yet more advanced technology of the kind now being introduced into many armies around the world—not least the Israeli one—might, assuming it can be made to work reliably and without interference from other systems, have solved some of the problems encountered. For example, a Position and Azimuth Determination System might have spared Gabi his map-reading errors, though it would hardly have aided him in carrying out the absurd mission that required him to destroy the Egyptians while staying out of range. A Position Location and Reporting System would have enabled Adan and Gonen to locate their subordinate units at any moment regardless of their relative positions, and thus spared them any doubts in regard to who had crossed the canal and where. Various sensors linked to computers and television screens, and positioned so as to overlook the battlefield or else suspended above it, might have eliminated at least part of the uncertainty concerning the whereabouts of the Egyptian positions.[105] Finally, improved technology and much improved wireless discipline together might have given Israeli commanders a true capability for communicating between any two points, a capability that some of them at any rate did not have in 1973. In the absence of such a capability, and given the system of reverse optional control, they were not able to use their own eyes.

Each of these technical devices would potentially represent an important step forward, but none of them could in itself have corrected the major deficiencies of the Israeli command setup in 1973. These deficiencies, to repeat, included the overconfidence generated by victory; a mistaken doctrine that regarded tanks as all-important and then proceeded to attribute similar views to the enemy; a faulty command organization; a lack of mutual trust among the senior commanders involved; incomprehensible staff procedures; and the absence of a directed telescope to supplement the flow of information from below by an active quest for it from the top. Without exception, these deficiencies were organizational in nature, and thus it was possible to change course by sending a former chief of staff, General Bar Lev, to take over from Gonen on Wednesday, 10 October. From that point command by reverse optional control from Tel Aviv came to an end. Though one of the divisional commanders—Sharon—continued to behave in a headstrong, not to say insubordinate, manner, sufficient cohesion was achieved to enable a complicated water-crossing operation to be successfully planned and carried out.

It cannot be the purpose of this book to inveigh against the introduction of more and more sophisticated electronic wizardry into command systems—and given the direction in which the world is moving, any attempt to do so would in any case constitute a call in the wilderness. The last four chapters ought to have made it quite clear, however, that any given technology has very strict limits. Often the critical factor is less the type of hardware available than the way it is put to use. Specifically, since a decisive technological advantage is a fairly rare and always temporary phenomenon, victory often depends not so much on having superior technology at hand as on understanding the limits of any given technology, and on finding a way of going around those limitations. Furthermore, as the Israelis discovered during the 1973 and 1982 wars, dependence on technology inevitably creates vulnerabilities that an intelligent enemy will not be slow to exploit. The opportunities for doing so, moreover, increase rather than diminish with the complexity of the technology in use.[106] Finally, it is quite possible to have too much technology, even to the point of turning it into its own worst enemy, as the following chapter will seek to demonstrate.

7

THE HELICOPTER AND THE COMPUTER

IN THIS CHAPTER the analysis will abandon large-scale conventional warfare and move to counterinsurgency. The case selected is that of the United States in Vietnam between 1965 and 1968: that is, the so-called forward stage of strategy, when the hope for a clear-cut military victory had not yet died and before the desire to get out became the overriding consideration that eclipsed all military operations.

Until the advent of nuclear weapons in 1945, and since then also in conflicts where no superpower countries are involved, there existed no limits, in principle, to the amount of force that could usefully be brought to bear in war. Provided it had sufficient forces at its disposal, each side could set its aim as high as its fancy took it—and sometimes, as in the case of Hitler's invasion of the Soviet Union or the Allied demand for "total surrender," this amounted to little short of annihilation. Under such conditions Clausewitz's dictum about war being the instrument of politics was almost deprived of meaning, since the former was inflated to the point where there was little left to the latter to do.

Conditions, however, have changed since 1945. Never again after Hiroshima could even the maddest of dictators trust to purely military means in order to gain absolute victory, since to do so was tantamount to suicide. Consequently politics, which had been edged into a corner by the evolution of modern "total" war between 1914 and 1945, emerged with a vengeance and has assumed a greater role

232

than ever in governing armed conflict. Vietnam was selected as a case study here precisely because that war illustrates this point. That is, it was not a purely military conflict but rather one in which the impact of politics was felt at every stage, which means, of course, that an analysis of the way command operated cannot be limited to looking at the field or the jungle but instead must extend to decision-making systems at the top—in other words, to Washington, D.C., where the war was begun and, ultimately, lost.

Vietnam is also interesting from another point of view. In a world increasingly dominated by weapons too powerful to use, large-scale sustained conventional warfare as practiced through the ages appears to be running short of space. It is becoming more and more difficult to imagine future conflicts in which thousands of tanks will slash over hundreds of miles, as Hitler's did in 1940–1942 and Patton's in 1944. Living in the shadow of nuclear weapons, men are increasingly turning to forms of conflict to which those weapons are irrelevant—that is, insurgency and counterinsurgency above all. This development may be disliked by some who still hanker after the time-honored games with their clear outcomes; it leaves us with no escape from considering Vietnam, however, since that still remains the largest and best-documented counterinsurgency campaign yet waged.

Analyzing command as exercised in Vietnam is not without its problems, and these are best exposed at the outset. Unlike the previous campaigns discussed, deliberately selected because they were brief, the war in Vietnam as here investigated lasted over a period of some three years. Unlike other campaigns, too, it did not consist of a single operation of war but rather of an endless series of repetitive acts, many of which were so standardized as to acquire collective names such as "Eagle Flight," "Bushmaster," and "Search and Destroy." The study of command in such a war properly calls for quantitative data, but in spite of the fact that Vietnam was the most analyzed war in history not much evidence of this kind is available for the field in which we are interested. Nor is this absence of data altogether accidental; Vietnam, like the October 1973 war, still belongs to contemporary affairs and not to history, and good works based on official records rather than on impressions are only beginning to come out.

Finally, a warning. In all scientific research, accuracy in assessing

233

the effect of any single factor depends on success in neutralizing the effects of all others, and the same is true for history. An investigation of the way command operates in war surely is not without justification, but only so long as the presence of numerous other factors that give war its shape is constantly kept in mind. Whatever the conclusions of this chapter, they should not mislead the reader into thinking that it was errors in command, whether at the top or at the field level, which alone caused the war in Vietnam to be lost. To an extent greater than for any other campaign studied in this book, and precisely because it was a guerrilla war faced by counterinsurgency methods, Vietnam saw economic, social, and cultural factors impinging on command at almost all levels. This of course is not to say that no errors were committed in the field of command proper, nor even that avoidance of these errors could not have led to a more successful outcome for the United States. It does mean, however, that things must be seen in a correct perspective, which is as true of history as it is of command.

THE AGE OF COMPLEXITY

During the twenty years after 1945, another great series of technological advances swept over the armed forces of the world and left them more complex than ever before. Those two decades saw the introduction of jet aircraft and of helicopters; the application of electronics and automation to fire control, communications, electronic countermeasures, and logistics; the advent of medical electronics, simulators, and meteorological radar; and the appearance on the battlefield of the first guided weapons for anti-tank or anti-aircraft use. Thus, not only did numerous new types of weapons and equipment enter the inventory, but each successive generation tended to be several times as complex as the one it replaced and required many more different spare parts. The growing managerial and logistic burden that ensued is perhaps best expressed in terms of cost: in 1965 a main battle tank or fighter bomber, for instance, was between ten and twenty times as expensive as its World War II predecessor.[1]

The growing complexity of the armed forces was making itself felt in the field of personnel as well. Toward the end of World War II the 9,700,000 men enlisted in the U.S. Services were divided into 1,407 different Military Occupation Specialties (MOS's), the average number trained in each MOS being thus 6,894.[2] When the forces contracted during the immediate postwar years the number of MOS's also declined, reaching a nadir in 1952, but then started growing again. By 1963 the number of enlisted men in all four services was approximately 2,225,000, in 1,559 MOS's, so that the average number of men in each MOS was down to 1,427—and even this figure misrepresents the true situation because many of the 1963 MOS's, especially those connected with the rapidly growing field of electronic gear maintenance and operation, were really agglomerations of several different specialties. Furthermore, the distribution of personnel among the various MOS's had changed. In 1945, fifty MOS's associated with ground combat accounted for 25 percent of all enlisted personnel, but eighteen years later the same fifty MOS's constituted only 14 percent of all enlisted personnel. The proportion of large, homogeneous outfits consisting of men in comparatively few MOS's therefore declined, that of units incorporating specialists in many different trades rose. Consequently, a calculation that would put the complexity, relative to size, of the 1963 armed forces at 6,894 divided by 1,559, or four and a half times that of their 1945 predecessors, would probably err on the side of caution.[3]

A cause as well as an effect of complexity, specialization means that in order to carry out any given task the cooperation of more and more personnel belonging to different trades is required. As the number of specialties grows, the amount of information needed to coordinate their performance grows not arithmetically but geometrically, everybody (or groups of every kind) having to be coordinated with everybody else. Individual members of the organization are responsible to, and therefore in communication with, both their direct superior and with the person in charge of their own branch or specialty, creating even more of a demand for information. Though exact figures would be almost impossible to come by and more or less meaningless even if available, it is suggested as a rough and ready guide that, unit by unit, the amount of information needed to control the U.S. Forces in 1963 was perhaps twenty times (4.5 × 4.5) larger than in the case of their 1945 predecessors.

The number of specialties as such is one factor governing the amount of information needed to control any given organization while performing any given mission. At least as important, however, is the structure of the organization; the greater its stability, the better acquainted individual members are with each other, and the stronger their mutual trust, the smaller the demand for regulations, standard operating procedures, orders, and reports, and, conversely, the easier the percolation of required information among men and units. For millennia military planners have recognized this fact and used every means at their disposal to encourage the cohesion of the units, even at the expense of overall administrative flexibility.[4]

The U.S. forces in Vietnam were the acme of instability.[5] Not only did the system of rotating personnel in and out of the country annually and in groups of four prevent anybody from getting thoroughly acquainted with anybody else, but company and battalion commanders held their posts for an average of less than six months, and the situation at brigade and division level was hardly any better.[6] Excessive specialization also worked against the stability of the forces as a whole, since it meant that, to carry out any one mission, endless task forces had to be created and then dissolved as soon as that mission was over. Since no one could ever take anyone else for granted, cooperation among the men inside any given unit, and between units, was always very difficult to achieve, and could be had only on the basis of an inordinate flow of information.

The obverse side of specialization is, inevitably, centralization. The more specialized the members and units of any given organization, the less capable any of them separately is of making independent decisions that may affect the whole, and the greater the need for overall direction from the top. Furthermore, an organization with a high decision threshold—that is, one in which only senior officials are authorized to make decisions of any importance—will require a larger and more continuous information flow than one in which that threshold is low. It so happened that, during the two decades after 1945, several factors came together and caused the American armed forces to undergo an unprecedented process of centralization. In the first place, there was the revolutionary explosion of electronic communications and automatic data processing equipment, which made effective worldwide command and control from Washington a practical technological proposition. Second, there was the preoccupation during the 1950s with the need for fail-proof positive control systems to prevent an accidental outbreak of nuclear war, a preoccupation that led first to the establishment of the World Wide Military Command and Control System (WWMCCS) in 1962 and then to its progressive extension from the Strategic Air Command, for which it had originally been designed, down to the conventional forces. New administrative techniques, such as cost-benefit analysis with its inherent emphasis on the pooling of resources and the careful meshing of each part with every other, further contributed to the trend toward central management, as did the appearance on the market of the data processing hardware needed to make it possible.

Presented with such opportunities for asserting centralized control, decisionmakers in Washington were not slow in seizing them. Within eighteen months of entering office as secretary of defense, Robert McNamara had put into operation the Defense Intelligence Agency (DIA) to replace the separate Service intelligence organizations, the Defense Supply Agency (DSA) to oversee procurement of all equipment used by more than one service, and the Defense Communications Agency (DCA) to take over the Pentagon's central communications facilities. Furthermore, the Office of Defense Research and Engineering (ODRE) was expanded and assigned the task of supervising all Pentagon-sponsored research programs.[7] The temptation that all these developments represented for decision making by remote control proved irresistible; between 1946 and 1975 the president was involved in 73 percent of two hundred crises that took place all over the world, even though legal requirements for his intervention existed in only 22 percent of them.[8] Such highly publicized events as the 1962 Cuban Missile Crisis, during which President Kennedy personally supervised the location of each U.S. Navy vessel involved in the blockade, further reinforced the tendency toward greater and greater centralization.[9]

Complexity and specialization, organizational instability and centralization—these factors, to draw the threads of the argument together, caused an inordinate increase in the amount of information needed to make any given kind of decision at any given level, or, which comes to the same thing, to enable any given unit within the Services to carry out any given mission. To cope with all this infor-

237

Table 2. The strength and equipment of regiment-sized forces, 1943–1971

	1943: Regiment	1971: Brigade	Change (%)
Personnel	3,135	2,553	− 19
Weapons			
Rifles	2,725	2,119	− 22
Machine guns	74	129	+ 74
Anti-tank weapons	153	396	+159
Radio sets	81	539	+565
Vehicles	205	415	+102

SOURCE: Z. B. Bradford and F. J. Brown, *The U.S. Army in Transition* (Beverly Hills, Cal., 1973), p. 138.

mation, signals and communication services inside the Forces were of course expanded many times over, the extent of the change being perhaps best illustrated by the data in Table 2. The number of radio sets rose from one set for every 38.6 men in 1943 to one set for 4.5 men in 1971, an 857 percent increase that far exceeded the figure for any other kind of equipment. The increase made it possible to multiply the number of communication channels to each divisional headquarters fourfold, from eight in Korea to thirty-two in Vietnam.[10] Multichannel VHF service was now extended to units as far down as artillery batteries, and such outfits as 1st Infantry Division were provided with thirty-five sole user circuits terminating in the operations room over and above the normal complement of signaling equipment.[11] Owing to technical progress that had taken place since 1945, moreover, even these figures underestimate the resulting increase in information-transmission capacity. By the time the war in Vietnam was fought, transistors had replaced vacuum tubes in most forms of electronic equipment, which greatly improved reliability and portability. Specially designed VHF radio sets, such as the AN/PRC-25 and AN/VRC-12, provided excellent short-range communications even under difficult jungle conditions. The Integrated Wide Band Communications System (IWBCS) constructed in Vietnam between 1966 and 1968 at a cost of $500 million employed the new technique of topographic scatter to do away with the old cable network in providing voice, teleprinter,[12] and data relay services from one end of the country to the other; it also incorporated the first fully automated telephone system ever deployed in a theater of war. To bridge the Pacific to Guam, the Philippines, Honolulu, San Francisco, and Washington, every available technical device was utilized, from submarine cable to relay by satellite—the latter being likewise a first.

This improvement in the quality and flexibility of communications was not achieved without paying a price in terms of the logistic overheads carried and the number of personnel needed to install, operate, and maintain the new equipment. By 1963 the number of MOS's connected with these tasks was around 400, over one-quarter of the total number in the Forces,[13] and growing. Inside Vietnam the 1st Signals Brigade of the Strategic Communications Command, responsible for providing signals support to the Military Assistance Command, Vietnam (MACV), was a force larger than a division whose 23,000 troops constituted fully 5 percent of all U.S. troops in the country.[14] Within the divisions themselves some 20 percent of all personnel consisted of radio telephone operators, this figure being divided about equally between those whose sole MOS this was and those who carried it out in addition to their other duties. An estimated one-third of all major items of equipment brought into the country consisted of electronic communications gear, and over half a million different kinds of spare parts for this gear had to be stored. The 1st Signals Brigade had to establish 150 facilities throughout South Vietnam in order to maintain the equipment; indeed, so complex were organization and equipment that divisional signals battalion commanders spent 90 percent of their time simply running their own outfits. To put it briefly, the communications establishment made possible by the revolution in technology, and necessary in order to deal with the consequences of specialization and complexity, had itself turned into a major source of both specialization and complexity. The cure was part of the disease.

Communications systems alone, however numerous and sophisticated, could give only a partial answer to the problems created by the military-technical revolution. What was needed, it was felt, were entirely new techniques for analyzing and understanding war, techniques that would take its complexity into account and come up with precise, quantitative answers to replace the qualitative judgments of old. As it happened, such techniques did appear to present themselves in the early 1960s in the form of systems analysis. Originating in the models long employed by businessmen and economists to forecast and coordinate production runs, systems analysis was brought to the Pentagon by Robert McNamara in an effort to provide a more rational basis for top-level decision making. As practiced by the Office of Systems Analysis (OSA) and the so-called whiz kids—most of them professional economists drawn from universities and think-tanks—the technique is said to have been distinguished by (a) an attempt to clearly define the parameters of each separate problem as part of a larger problem and containing smaller ones, so that a chain of implications was created in which the nation's overall security problems were theoretically linked to the length of the skirts to be worn by female Pentagon employees; (b) an effort at making the underlying assumptions explicit, so as to present a number of alternative solutions based on those assumptions; and (c) the employment of quantitative means where quantification was possible.[15] The results, though seldom very sophisticated mathematically, owed much to statistical evidence and were often expressed in terms of equations, which is one reason why systems analysis acquired a bad reputation among those unable or unwilling to understand.

Those who regard systems analysis as inherently the wrong tool with which to approach problems of war probably go too far, but the technique is like all others in that it does have limitations.[16] First, since it consists essentially of an attempt to model and quantify, systems analysis lends itself better to financial and technological problems than to operational ones, where the enemy's independent will is not entirely governed by the means at his disposal; to air and naval warfare than to ground operations; to small-scale, relatively simple operations than to larger, more complex ones; and to a purely military war than to one in which social and political factors count for everything.[17] Second, an approach whose favorite device is number-crunching may be tempted to exclude those moral and spiritual factors which, though all-important in war, cannot be quantified easily (if at all). Moreover, there exists a difference between counting and understanding, a fact that was nowhere more obvious than in Vietnam, with its pseudo-scientific but frequently meaningless—as well as wildly inaccurate—counts of "enemy" bodies and "pacified" villages. By failing to penetrate into the nature of things—something that requires in-depth knowledge of local conditions—and counting them instead, quantitative methods of analysis stand in danger of resulting in a substitute for, rather than a form of, understanding.

The role that systems analysis in general, and the office responsible for it in particular, played in Vietnam has often been exaggerated. Neither was a product of the war; both had first been instituted to help review and shape the defense program (including above all its financial side) at a time when Vietnam was still very much a sideshow. The whiz kids' hand was most evident in the financial planning of the war; in top-level decision making as to the number and type of units to be sent to Vietnam; and in the development of logistic plans that attempted to forecast attrition rates and future production requirements of aircraft. The influence of the Office of Systems Analysis on the conduct of the war inside Vietnam was thus quite limited, though it did circulate an unofficial monthly known as the Southeast Asia Analysis Report that was widely read by Washington decision makers.[18] Furthermore, apart from the occasional visits by members of the staff to the "field," the OSA at no time possessed independent information sources of its own and had to be content with collating and interpreting the MACV-assembled statistics. As Alain Enthoven, its head, points out, the ability of his office to act as a directed telescope in the hands of the president and secretary of defense was thereby strictly limited, and the staff did not possess the specialized military skills that would be vital in playing such a role. Since not even General Westmoreland has claimed that the office (or the secretary to which it was subordinate) tried to dictate his moves inside Vietnam in any detail, many of the charges often brought against it may safely be dismissed. Yet the systems approach, and the types of data it called for, did help create the information pathologies that characterized the war in Vietnam and made no small contribution to its outcome. It is to those pathologies, their nature and their symptoms, that the next section is devoted.

HOW MUCH IS ENOUGH?

If complexity is one standard by which to judge whether any given armed force is up to date, the organization through which the

United States attempted to run the war in Vietnam certainly came up to the mark. At the top stood the secretary of defense, the only man besides the president with any kind of overall authority over the war but to whom (as to the president) it was only one issue among a great many, and not always the most important one. Subordinate only to president and secretary of defense were the National Security Council (NSC) and the Joint Chiefs of Staff (JCS). The NSC, headed by McGeorge Bundy and Walt Rostow, played a major role in the decision-making process that led to the American involvement in Vietnam but had less influence after 1965; the JCS worked to protect the interests of the Services under them and acted as a conduit through which first General Harkins, and then General Westmoreland, submitted their endlessly expanding requests for manpower and resources. The theater commander, if there was one, was Admiral Ole Sharp, who, as commander in chief, Pacific (CINCPAC), had his headquarters in Hawaii, some three thousand miles from Vietnam. He was the direct superior of Westmoreland's MACV and also commanded the Seventh Fleet and the B-52 bomber squadrons of the Strategic Air Command stationed in Guam and Thailand. Together with the Joint Chiefs of Staff, CINCPAC was responsible for waging the air war against North Vietnam, but their plans for doing so were subject to very tight supervision by the secretary of defense and his assistants and, acting on their advice, the president himself.

Inside Vietnam, General Westmoreland was in command of all American forces. He had no authority, however, over units and installations in, or forays into, the neighboring countries of Thailand, Laos, and Cambodia. While this problem could be solved up to a point by conducting clandestine operations and by setting up periodic meetings with the U.S. ambassadors to those countries, political reasons prevented Westmoreland from gaining any authority at all over the South Vietnamese and Korean forces and allowed him only limited authority over the much smaller Australian and New Zealand ones. The civilian side of the American presence in South Vietnam (the Civil Operations and Revolutionary Development Support, or CORDS, headed by Robert Komer) was outside his jurisdiction, and cooperation with it had to be coordinated by the U.S. embassy. Also not subject to his orders were any number of information and intelligence agencies, all with a finger in the Vietnam war and many of them run from Washington.[19]

Appearances notwithstanding, Westmoreland's control over even his own forces was not as complete as it might have been. He had no authority over the Strategic Air Command and Seventh Fleet units participating in the war in South Vietnam. Himself an Army general, he had Air Force as well as Navy and Marine units under his command. Relations with the Marines in particular were always problematic; not only were they reluctant to get far away from their cherished beaches (which does much to explain their preference for an enclave strategy and pacification at the expense of search-and-destroy missions), but they also refused to allow MACV free use of their organic air component.[20] In issuing his orders to them Westmoreland had to tread carefully while looking back to Marine Corps Headquarters in Washington, whose intervention he wanted to avoid as much as possible. His control over them remained much more limited than over Air Force and Navy (riverine patrol) units; their willingness to cooperate with the Army has generally been awarded high marks.[21]

The inappropriateness of the American command structure for dealing with Vietnam has been the subject of frequent commentary, most critics concentrating either on the absence of a single overall coordinator or on the problematic nature of Westmoreland's relations with the South Vietnamese and with parts of his own forces.[22] What I am concerned with here, however, is not any alternative organization that might have been established but the effect that complexity itself had on the way in which the command process operated. The MACV itself, it has been noted, was an extraordinarily complex organization. A pamphlet two hundred pages thick was needed to outline the MACV's several dozen components and the hundreds upon hundreds of missions, relationships, and functions that those components possessed between them. The MACV, moreover, being but one (if by far the most powerful) of numerous American agencies involved in running the Vietnam war, there resulted an insatiable demand for coordination and information that, as we shall presently see, not even the world's most advanced military signals communications network was ultimately able to cope with. The diffusion and frequent uncertainty of lines of authority led to a tendency, typical for Vietnam, to couch even straightforward military orders in terms of "requests."

The way in which things were handled at the top is well illustrated by a passage from *The Pentagon Papers:* "The JCS were actually insisting [at what time is not clear—M.v.C.] upon the achievement of a noncommunist South Vietnam and their military aim accorded with that view. They were holding to the basic strategic concept written in JCMS 702-66, a month earlier, one which had elicited so little reaction from either McNamara or his staff. No doubt the resistance of the JCS was heavily influenced by the COMUS-MACV-CINCPAC reaction to the draft NSAM . . ."[23] And so on, and so on. The president, Sec/Def, OSA, CINCPAC, COMUS-MACV, and countless other agencies mentioned in the thousands of pages kept producing and circulating memoranda for comment and action. A torrent of paper flooded decision makers at all levels; little of it was read in its entirety, much less implemented.[24] Himself up to his neck in paperwork, Westmoreland kept a split-second schedule and seldom spent more than "many minutes" in the company of any one person.[25] The excess of paperwork that went on was recognized even at the time; claiming that the forces in Vietnam were requisitioning "far too much office stationery," the JCS at one point issued a directive limiting to senior officers the right to ask for more.[26] A solution was thus sought, typically enough, in terms of even greater centralization.

If complexity was one reason behind the inordinate amounts of information needed to run the Vietnam war, centralization was another. Again, there has been a tendency by part of the literature to exaggerate this problem; though command of fire bases from the White House was theoretically possible, there is no indication that it was ever attempted in practice. Centralization, however, was much in evidence in two important aspects of the war. The first, the air war against North Vietnam, was run by McNamara and his assistants from Washington on the basis of information and target lists supplied by the DIA, JCS, and CINCPAC. The command system that resulted has to be seen to be believed; directives emanating from the Office of the Secretary of Defense (OSD) specified the targets to be struck, the weather conditions under which the mission might or might not be carried out, and even the minimal level of training that individual pilots had to possess. Since performance was judged statistically, in terms of cost-benefit calculations and the efficient use of resources, there was a strong incentive for the men actually in the field to ignore the local tactical situation.[27] Furthermore, the outcome was a vast information flow that had to be sent all the way from the carriers to CINCPAC and the Joint Chiefs of Staff and McNamara's desk and back again.

Another field in which centralization reigned supreme, helping create a huge demand for information that could not subsequently be satisfied, was the logistic system servicing the American forces in Vietnam. This was originally due to a deliberate decision; in his haste to get as many American combat units into the country within the shortest possible time, Westmoreland in 1965 took the risk of stripping away their organic logistic support.[28] The relatively static nature of the war, and cost-benefit considerations that favored the centralization and pooling of resources, subsequently prevented that support from being restored. Supplies and maintenance were provided instead by specialized Logistic Command Centers that gradually spread throughout South Vietnam and operated on a territorial basis. The system was dependent on constant, detailed communications between the Logistic Command Centers and the outfits in the field and, furthermore, on the former's ability to develop and maintain a statistical model of the latter's requirements, clearly an impossible task in view of the endless movements of units of many different types from one tactical area to another. The inability to forecast demand in turn increased the requirement for supplies still further, often making it necessary to requisition specific items from sources located on the far side of the Pacific. As it turned out, the necessary amount of information simply could not be handled by the requisitioning system, computerized and unprecedentedly sophisticated though it might be. Instead of using information to finetune the relationship between supply and demand, units were forced to send back men (the stationary Logistic Command Centers, with no permanent ties to any single outfits, insisted that the field come to the rear instead of vice versa) to walk over acres of stores and depots as far away as Okinawa and pick up whatever was needed. When the necessary items were located, they often turned out to consist of equipment which the headquarters in charge insisted it did not have.[29] In the future, wrote General Heiser of the 1st Logistic Command, it would be necessary to resort to a less centralized system and restore service units to their parent outfits, thus doing away with much of the requirement for information though at the expense of creating some slack resources.[30]

Specific examples of high-level authorities being called upon to decide very minor matters are, given the structure of the command system, easy to come by; two will suffice here. One is an argument between the JCS and the OSA in July 1967 over whether the forces in Vietnam were to be reinforced by two C-141 cargo aircraft, a decision that finally had to be made by McNamara in person. In October of the same year, with half a million American troops already stationed in and around Vietnam, President Johnson had to be called upon to decide whether or not to send in an additional three battalions.[31] Every such decision involved a blizzard of draft action memoranda literally flurrying about. Each had to be justified in detail by Westmoreland's MACV in Saigon, then passed back for comment and review through successive headquarters all the way back to Washington. As Northcote Parkinson once wrote, such methods, when combined with the uncanny ability of modern means of communications to reach into every nook and cranny, tend to concentrate all power in a single man—and he, through overwork, clearly out of his head.

It will never be possible to document adequately the amount of information needed to wage the war in Vietnam, but a few examples will illustrate the size of the flow. The intelligence component of MACV (the Combined Intelligence Center, headed by General McChristian and serving the South Vietnamese as well as the U.S. forces) alone received three million pages of enemy documents per month, of which some 10 percent proved to be of "intelligence value" and were accordingly translated. At the beginning of 1967, well over half a ton of reports coming in from this source alone were being printed every day, with "every indication of greater volume in the future."[32] Already in 1965, with the American troop buildup limited to one-third of its eventual size, the Army Strategic Communications Facility at Phu Lam was processing some eight thousand messages coming into, or going out of, South Vietnam every day. The flow increased still further, however, so that a second message center had to be established at Na Trang in November. By the end of 1966 both centers together were processing half a million messages per month,[33] a figure that went on to double itself within the next year—and all this was exclusive of a monthly load of five million punched computer cards.

Many factors, including some inherent in modern warfare and others specific to the time and place, contributed to this insatiable demand for information, a demand that in the end the communications and data processing systems were unable to meet. This inability is most readily documented in the field of enemy intelligence; such intelligence is, in Patton's words, "like eggs, the fresher the better." The U.S. forces in Vietnam depended on many different sources of intelligence, from the eyes of scouts riding vehicles at the head of columns and the interrogation of peasants in the field to the most up-to-date high-frequency and infrared detection devices operated by the Air Force. Some of these means were put into the hands of troops down to battalion and even company level. Others, particularly those that were complicated or expensive to operate, were concentrated under the auspices of higher headquarters or even different Services. The more centralized the operation of any single means, of course, the greater its dependence on a reliable and rapid communication device for the timely gathering of the intelligence and for its processing and dissemination back to the troops. The inability of the system to cope with the demand for timely information is shown in Figure 2. Under conditions as difficult as those in Vietnam, and against an enemy as elusive as the Viet Cong/North Vietnamese Army, the chronic inability of the system to transmit information in time meant that even some of the intelligence sources in the hands of formations as far down as divisions were all but useless.[34]

A second indication that, during the war in Vietnam, a gap opened between the demand for information and the ability of the communications system to transmit it may be found in the distribution of messages among the various categories of precedence. In 1944–1945, only about one-third of all messages processed by First U.S. Army Signals Headquarters in France and Germany were placed in either of the top categories.[35] In Vietnam, however, the proportion of traffic classified as either "Immediate" or "Flash"

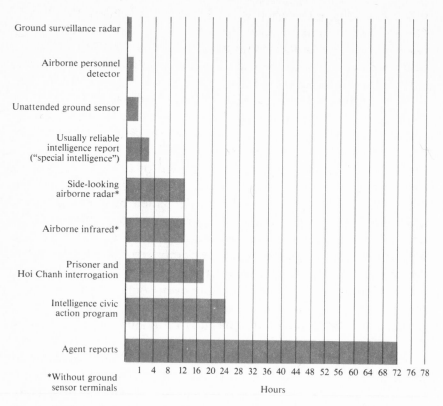

Figure 2. The timeliness of intelligence reports (average hours elapsed from event to receipt of report)

sometimes exceeded one-half of the total, creating bottlenecks, indicating that messages placed in the lowest categories were regarded by the troops as standing scant chance of getting through on time if at all, and incidentally compelling the Joint Chiefs of Staff to institute a new "Superflash" category so as to ensure that their own messages would in fact get through.[36] As General von Harlingen, commanding officer of the 1st Signals Brigade, put it in his final debriefing report, attempting to get all messages through in time led inevitably to a definite slowdown in the traffic, which could and did cause bottlenecks and even the loss of messages altogether.

If the proliferation of top-priority traffic was one sign of information pathology, the excessive use of high-secrecy messages constituted another.[37] The vast number of copies of orders and reports that were stamped "Top Secret," thus requiring special facilities for transmission, is said to have been typical of the war in Vietnam.[38] One reason for this may have been the chronic inability of the American troops to make out good Vietnamese from bad; another was the system of rapidly rotating personnel in and out of the country, leading to a situation in which neither men nor commanders could get to know or trust each other thoroughly. The price to be paid for excessive secrecy is frequent slowdowns in the traffic because of overloading of the specialized equipment needed. Like so much else discussed in this chapter, secrecy is best understood as both symptom and cause of information pathology.[39]

Another sign of information pathology in Vietnam, already noted, was the proliferation of sole user circuits ("hot lines") at every level, a typical divisional operations room containing no fewer than thirty-five such lines. Such lines represent the attempts of those in authority to overcome a blocked information system and to make sure that messages coming to them, or emanating from them, will get through, even if resources therefore stand idle some of the time and are denied to everybody else. While such methods are inevitable in any large organization, the price to be paid for decreasing overloads on the reserved lines is increasing them on all the rest.

That all these factors together—specialization, instability, centralization, complexity, and the resulting information pathologies—did in fact cause a serious slowdown of the command process can readily be proved from the extraordinarily long periods that were often required to plan, prepare, and mount operations. Thus, in the fall of 1967, the operations "Cedar Falls" and "Junction City" each employed somewhat more than two divisions, and each required some four months from decision to action. A plan for cutting off the Ho Chi Minh Trail by invading Laos took six months to develop,[40] and another for the relief of Khe San from another base a mere thirty miles away took two months.[41] The most notorious instance of slowness in planning, however, is provided by the history of the abortive raid on the prisoner-of-war camp at Son Tay in 1970:

9 May 1970   1127th Intelligence Unit discovers existence of POW camps at Ap Lo and Son Tay.

25 May	Deputy Director for Plans and Policy (Brigadier General Allen) arranged briefing with Special Assistant for Counterinsurgency and Special Activities (SASCA), Brigadier General Blackburn. Allen plan discussed.
25 May	Air Force request for POW rescue mission forwarded to Chairman, Joint Chiefs of Staff.
26 May	SASCA requests intelligence data from DIA.
27 May	Mission requirement presented to Director of Operations, Joint Chiefs of Staff, by SASCA; recommendation for operation to Chairman, JCS.
29 May	Admiral Moorer, chairman to be, JCS, briefed on projected mission by SASCA.
1 June	Review of rescue mission alternatives with Director of Operations, JCS, and Director, DIA. Feasibility Study Group established (25 planners).
2 June	Chairman, JCS, briefed by SASCA.
5 June	JCS briefed on mission recommendation by SASCA; in-depth feasibility study ordered.
8 June	Deputy Chiefs of Staff for Operations (DCSOPS) briefed.
9 June	CIA, Special Assistant for Southeast Asia Matters, asked to join feasibility group.
10 July	Rescue mission recommendation discussed at JCS meeting; SASCA Final Recommendation approved by JCS.
13 July	Colonel Simons appointed to lead operation.
14 July	U.S. prisoners moved from Son Tay.
15 July	Brigadier General Manors (USAF) appointed commander of operation by JCS; Eglin Air Force Base designed as training site for mission. Recruitment of volunteers and specialists at Fort Bragg commences.
8 August	Commencement of five days' detailed planning by deputies' security section organized.
10–14 August	Planning Group convened by SASCA.
9 September	Commencement of training for mission.
28 September	Air Force and Army teams rehearse joint assault.
6 October	Completion of training.
8 October	National Security Adviser Henry Kissinger briefed on operation.
10 October	Original deployment date for assault set, subsequently postponed.
18 November	President Nixon briefed by Chairman, JCS.

21 November   Mission launch; success is total, except that the camp is found empty.[42]

As it happened, the prisoners were taken away, and Son Tay evacuated, on the very day that the American units earmarked for the mission started training after four months of planning. Against an enemy as elusive as the Viet Cong/North Vietnamese Army, such long lead times were simply not good enough; to put it in different words, the combination of organizational complexity with modern communications resulted in decision cycles longer than those of the enemy, who was far less sophisticated on either count. Lest it be thought that such lead times are somehow inherent in the complexity of present-day warfare, compare the three weeks that the Germans in 1941 took to plan and carry out a combined assault by two divisions—including paratroopers and both airborne and seaborne forces—against the island of Crete; or, an even better example, the speed with which the Israelis moved from the moment that the Air Force plane was hijacked to Entebbe in 1976 to the rescue mission one week later.[43]

THE MISDIRECTED TELESCOPE

So far, the analysis in this chapter has concentrated on the quantity of information that was needed to command the U.S. forces in Vietnam. However, the kind of information employed by the Americans in order to manage the Vietnam conflict is also worth investigating. It is in this field that we can hope to find the causes of some of the characteristic ways command operated in this strange war.

In general, each period may be said to possess its own favorite instruments for looking at, and making sense of, the external world. To employ a simple analogy, so long as God was believed to rule mankind directly, insanity had to be regarded as his special handiwork and was accordingly treated by means of prayer and exorcism. Once the seventeenth-century scientific revolution had dethroned God in favor of the Newtonian clockwork universe, mechanical causes such as a blow on the head took His place as an explanation for lunacy, the cure being sought, appropriately enough, in other mechanical devices, such as cold baths or centrifuges for whirling the patients about. Freud's employment of dreams, hypnosis, and free association as lenses through which to investigate mental phenomena led directly to his discovery of the unconscious as the root of madness and to attempts to manipulate it. In turn, the invention of unprecedentedly sensitive measuring instruments made possible the present-day preoccupation with the body's biochemistry and electronics, causing the unconscious to be put on the back burner; instead, the very same phenomena—depression, for example, or schizophrenia—are now treated with electric shocks and drugs.

With strategy, as with lunacy, each place and period has sought to understand it by using its own favorite instruments. As Clausewitz noted—and, from our special point of view, not surprising—prior to the eighteenth century, writings on strategy in the sense that he himself made classical were almost entirely absent.[44] The earliest attempts to formulate strategic doctrines were derived from siege warfare and therefore relied on geometry as a tool for understanding, the result being treatises that read like extensions of Euclid. There followed internal and external lines, numerical superiority, moral force, and outflanking movements, each in its time regarded as the master key through which wars were won. The frustration of siege warfare in 1914–1918 gave birth to the indirect approach, which, as is often the case, was then projected back through history. Subsequently, the shifting balance between men and technology led to the present view, which all too often regards war simply as the outgrowth of the machines with which it is waged.[45]

The favorite lens through which the American defense establishment chose to understand, plan, and wage the war in Vietnam consisted of statistics. As already noted, the selection of systems analysis as the method for making high-level decisions about budgets and the structure of military forces carried with it a penchant for quantification that was subsequently expanded into other fields also. Two of the most important decisionmakers, McNamara and Westmoreland, both of whom at one time or another had been associated with the Harvard Business School, appear to have loved statistics for their own sake and surrounded themselves with men whose predilections were similar. At a time when computers were still very new and very exciting, it was sometimes thought that their use in problem-solving in itself constituted a superior method of analysis.

The trend toward statistics was probably enhanced by the very size of the information flow needed to run the war in Vietnam, leading to a situation in which messages could not be read but had to be counted instead.

Although some of the drive toward statistics thus came from factors inside the command system itself, it is undeniable that Vietnam, a guerrilla war without fronts, was difficult to grasp except by statistical means. Arrows or colored patches on a map, even the act of fighting itself, meant comparatively little in a war whose ultimate objective was the allegiance of a people and the building of a nation. Progress toward either being difficult to determine, indirect means had to be substituted: the percentage of the population in "pacified" areas as measured by the Hamlet Evaluation System (HES), the number of miles of road or waterway opened to traffic, the country's economic activity as measured in tons of rice brought to the urban markets. The enemy situation in its turn was measured by the number of incidents and the body count,[46] and the performance of friendly troops was put in terms of kill ratios. The figures had to be analyzed in a thousand ways, a task for which computers were often used.

Some of the disadvantages of the system, including in particular the often notorious inaccuracy of data, have been the subject of frequent comment,[47] but others are less well understood and must be briefly discussed here. Statistics, even when accurate, can never substitute for in-depth knowledge of an environment, a knowledge that the Americans in Vietnam were almost entirely without.[48] The lack of it tends to convert genuine political and military problems into bogus technical ones. Though the reams of figures in a computer printout may appear impressively comprehensive and accurate, their meaning is often ambiguous: for example, a drop in the incident rate may signify (among several other things) either that the enemy is being defeated or that friendly forces are less than successful in locating him and bringing him to battle.[49] Since the patterns that form the objective of statistical analysis only become visible at fairly high levels in the hierarchy (further down, the figures are by definition meaningless), reliance on such analysis is itself a contribution toward centralization and the information pathologies of which centralization can be a cause. Statistics may have been the only way to handle the flood of incoming messages—running, at the Pentagon level, into the hundreds of thousands per day—but in the process, statistics reduced the contents of those messages to the lowest common denominator. Finally, statistics constitute one of the most abstract forms of information known to man; although they can possibly present a good picture of a whole phenomenon, the relevance of any given set of figures to this or that particular event at this or that particular place may well be next to zero.

Thus, following analyses based on vast amounts of data, the MACV in Saigon or the Office of Systems Analysis back in Washington might produce tables to show (these are actual examples) that combat activity peaked in 1968 and 1972; that the heaviest fighting always took place in the first half of the year, a somewhat unsurprising fact since this also happens to be the dry season; that there were, year by year, so many attacks (large, small, or other), so many cases of harassment, terrorism, sabotage, propaganda, and anti-aircraft fire; that Viet Cong strategy, as analyzed by these methods, "called for constant small harassment punctuated by a few high points of activity"; that such and such a percentage of all villages in this or that district had been "pacified"; and that so and so many fighter bomber sorties had been flown in such and such a period.[50] Given the nature of the data and of the methods used for analyzing them, it is thus not surprising that, in the words of one of OSA's advocates, "perhaps the most dramatic" finding of the Office of Systems Analysis was that the United States was not winning the war of attrition and that the addition of more troops would not solve the problem. The conclusion that no more troops should or could be sent, incidentally, had already been arrived at by McNamara, reasoning independently along entirely different lines.[51]

What effect did all this have on the actual command system in Vietnam? Based on post-action reports, statistics of the kind discussed above did not constitute enemy intelligence, in the true sense of the word. Gathering the information on which they were based was a heavy and, in the case of body count, hazardous burden on the troops, to whose specific requirements its relevance was often doubtful. Constantly subjected to pressure for more and more data of this kind, the troops not unnaturally responded by feeling that it did not matter what one reported so long as it looked good in the Efficiency Reports. The result, to borrow Jeremy Bentham's cruel phrase about natural rights, was "nonsense on stilts." Clogged with data whose accuracy and relevance were both open to question, the military reporting system lost much of its value and had to be supplemented, and in part replaced, by other forms of information-gathering.

The peculiar role played by helicopters in commanding the war in Vietnam has been the subject of frequent and interesting comment;[52] few of those who noted the phenomenon have attempted, however, to look for its causes or to relate it to the general way in which the command system operated. As one observer has written, the helicopter tended to exaggerate two of the fundamental traits of the American national character, impatience and aggressiveness[53]— possibly a pertinent remark, but not really an explanation. Other factors that help account for the extraordinary role that helicopters played in command must include the new machine's glamorous image and the prestige associated with having such a thing at one's beck and call; the tendency to use them in order to accumulate flying hours, leading toward air medals and eventual promotion; and the fact that the helicopter does indeed provide a fast and flexible means for getting commanders from one place to another and for obtaining an overall view of the battlefield.[54] It is this last factor that has led to the adoption of the helicopter as a tool of command in every modern army. In the difficult, often roadless Vietnamese terrain, such speed and flexibility made the helicopter particularly attractive.

Under the conditions peculiar to the war in Vietnam, major units seldom had more than one of their subordinate outfits engage the enemy at any one time. Ordinarily this should have permitted each commander to control a larger number of subordinates, thus leading to decentralization and a flattening of the hierarchical structure; instead, it led to a very different phenomenon. A hapless company commander engaged in a firefight on the ground was subjected to direct observation by the battalion commander circling above, who was in turn supervised by the brigade commander circling a thousand or so feet higher up, who in his turn was monitored by the division commander in the next highest chopper, who might even be so unlucky as to have his own performance watched by the Field

Force (corps) commander. With each of these commanders asking the men on the ground to tune in to his frequency and explain the situation, a heavy demand for information was generated that could and did interfere with the troops' ability to operate effectively. Yet what were the medium-level and senior commanders to do? As the discussion so far has shown, the normal channels of military reporting in Vietnam were often flooded with inaccurate, irrelevant information that could not be transmitted and processed on time. To get through at all, uncommonly powerful directed telescopes had to be employed by commanders from General Westmoreland—who insisted on his right to make unannounced visits to all levels[55]—downward. That the telescopes in question were frequently so powerful as almost to paralyze the action they were supposed to monitor is, in view of the circumstances, scarcely surprising.

The other phenomenon associated with command in Vietnam that can be explained only with reference to the inadequacy of the ordinary military reporting system is the enormous role played by the media, especially television. Once again, it is essential not to lose perspective; other factors, including the openness of American society and a growing tendency on the part of the public to discount official statements as mendacious, were of course involved. Nevertheless, the importance of the media as a source of information for decisionmakers in Washington and even, to some extent, for the MACV in Saigon is best understood as deriving in part from the media's ability to cut through the military information system itself.

The media as they operated in Vietnam had much in common with some aspects of the command system. Both journalists and commanders often spent only a short time in the country and on the job, and both were thereby prevented from acquiring a thorough knowledge of the environment. Both spent much of their time flitting into and out of places where dramatic events took place, sometimes even sharing the same helicopters.[56] Unlike commanders, however, newsmen enjoyed an advantage in that they did not have to deal with statistics and were therefore able to transmit a direct image of events. Nor did the information they sent up have to be summarized afresh by every intermediate headquarters, the result being often considerable time s vings. Journalists in general, and television in particular, mostly dealt with the specific rather than with the general, and to this extent were often able to present a more accurate picture than the one compiled from a mass of statistical reports. Often operated by men with little understanding for either the country or the war, and subject to no supervision but their own, the media acted as an undirected telescope that could and did focus attention on individual events to the detriment of the picture as a whole. Their strong point—their ability to cut through the normal information channels—thus also constituted a weakness.

Possibly the best example of the way that the media, acting as an undirected telescope, influenced the war in Vietnam is afforded by the 1968 Tet offensive. At a time when the 90 percent of South Vietnam not visited by newsmen saw 85 percent of all American maneuver battalions deployed and 80 percent of all U.S. casualties (it was in the unreported area that My Lai took place on 16 March 1968), the media made it appear as if the war was being fought solely in Saigon, Hue, and Khe San.[57] So powerful was the ability to focus the attention even of senior decisionmakers that General Westmoreland came to live in his operations room while the "siege" of the Marine base at Khe San lasted. In Washington the "symbolic" and "historic" value attributed to Khe San first caused President Johnson to extract a written pledge from the Joint Chiefs of Staff that it would not be allowed to fall, then to have a model of the base constructed in the White House basement around which he and his advisers spent their time. Whether in fact General Giap ever intended to overrun the base remains unknown; that the U.S. media were able to focus attention on the siege—and thus away from the coming Tet offensive—appears certain, regardless of whether it was planned in this way by the North Vietnamese.

The way that the helicopter, the media, and the tactical field radio functioned is perhaps best understood as an attempt to overcome the shortcomings of the military reporting system as it operated in Vietnam. Owing to a variety of circumstances favoring its use, the helicopter was turned into such a powerful directed telescope that it distorted the operation of the system it was supposed to help monitor and was even capable of bringing it to a halt. The media moved wildly out of control, concentrating on events selected mainly for the drama that they would bring to newspaper headlines and television screens, and thus helped pull the entire war out of focus. Field radio was used as a rapid and effective means of communications, regardless of security. Probably none of this, to repeat, would have happened had not the normal channels of military information been deficient to begin with.

CONCLUSIONS: THE PATHOLOGY OF INFORMATION

The U.S. forces deployed in Vietnam were among the most complex in history. Not only was top-level organization diffuse and chaotic to the point that nobody and everybody was in charge, but an entire regular command structure designed for conventional warfare was transplanted into a guerrilla environment for which it was not suitable. Extreme specialization of personnel and of units, coupled with adherence to the traditional triangular chain of command, meant that headquarters was piled upon headquarters and that coordination between them could only be achieved, if at all, by means of inordinate information flows.[58] A tendency toward centralization, the pooling of resources, and the running of the war by remote control—especially evident in the field of logistics and in the air war against North Vietnam—further augmented the demand for information. Though the signals network that the U.S. Army established in South Vietnam was the most extensive, expensive, and sophisticated in history, it proved in the end incapable of dealing with this "bottomless pit," as General Abrams once put it.[59]

Although the most obvious military result of the information pathologies produced by complexity and centralization was the long lead time often needed to prepare and launch an operation in Vietnam, others made themselves manifest in the roles played by the helicopter and the media and in the way that field radio was used. Confronted with a military information network that was impossibly complex and in the end often unable to cope, decisionmakers not unnaturally responded by attempting to cut through by any and every means that presented themselves. Commanding officers in Vietnam relied on the helicopter; officials in Washington depended on the media to supplement the frequently highly abstract, imprecise, and slow-to-arrive information percolating through normal military and defense establishment channels; and the troops chatted over their radio sets.

To guard against a misunderstanding at this point, I must stress that there is nothing inherently wrong in the use of extracurricular sources of information; their employment may, in fact, be a prerequisite for the creation of a functioning command system. When the regular channels are blocked or distorted by disease, however, the effort to cure that disease by drugs that are too powerful, or insufficiently specific, or insecure, is not likely to succeed.

Thus, in the end, the effort to minimize the cost-benefit ratio by the coordinated action of thousands of little cogs, all to be interconnected and fine-tuned to the performance of their missions in the hands of a supreme management team, backfired. Instead of resources being economized, hundreds of thousands of tons of ordnance were dropped or fired away in return for few if any enemy casualties.[60] Instead of the war being fought surgically and selectively against a highly elusive enemy while sparing the population, entire districts were flattened so that they could be saved. Instead of all data being available to top-level decisionmakers, they often ended up with a form of knowledge that was too diffuse and abstract for use. Instead of the helicopter's extraordinary capabilities being used to improve the command process, they often ended up by obstructing its operation. Designed to produce accuracy and certainty, the pressure exercised from the top for more and more quantitative information ended up by producing inaccuracy and uncertainty. Instead of being sure of what they were doing, the Americans by measuring output—often the only thing that could be measured with any accuracy—ended up doing what they could be sure of.

Undoubtedly, some of the factors responsible for this mess are inherent in the nature of modern war. Others were specific to the time and place, while others still—including in particular excessive specialization, centralization, and instability in the organization of the forces—could conceivably have been avoided by a better understanding of what the war was all about.[61] The real point of the story, however, is that while up-to-date technical means of communication and data processing are absolutely vital to the conduct of modern war in all its forms, they will not in themselves suffice for the creation of a functioning command system, and that they may, if understanding and proper usage are not achieved, constitute part of the disease they are supposed to cure. The outlay involved in the

American command system in Vietnam was enormous, but this very outlay involved a heavy additional logistic burden and in the end collapsed under its own weight. The men who designed the system and tried to run it were as bright a group of managers as has been produced by the defense establishment of any country at any time, yet their attempts to achieve cost-effectiveness led to one of the least cost-effective wars known to history. The technical ability of the command systems in their various forms to make their influence felt at the lowest levels was unprecedented, but this very ability probably did as much to distort the process of command as to assist in its work. To study command as it operated in Vietnam is, indeed, almost enough to make one despair of human reason; we have seen the future, and it does not work.

8

CONCLUSION: REFLECTIONS ON COMMAND

PROBABLY the most important point to emerge from these case studies is that command cannot be understood in isolation. The available data processing technology and the nature of the armaments in use; tactics and strategy; organizational structure and manpower systems; training, discipline, and what one might call the ethos of war; the political construction of states and the social makeup of armies—all these things and many more impinge on command in war and are in turn affected by it.

Command being so intimately bound up with numerous other factors that shape war, the pronunciation of one or more "master principles" that should govern its structure and the way it operates is impossible. No single communications or data processing technology, no single system of organization, no single procedure or method, is in itself sufficient to guarantee the successful or even adequate conduct of command in war. In the past, command systems radically different from each other have led to equally good results. Conversely, the success of a given command system at any one time and place constitutes no guarantee of its success in others, even where technological and other circumstances are not fundamentally different. It has been shown quite possible for a command system to be more successful at one level than at another (indeed, for success in command at one level to cancel out failure on another, deliberately or otherwise), or in one phase of operations than in the next. To paraphrase Frederick the Great's remark about command-

261

ers, the ideal command system, like Plato's Republic, exists only in heaven.

More specifically, the command system suitable for the direction of a static defense may not—indeed, most probably will not—allow the conduct of a rapid offensive by mobile forces over large spaces. The principles governing command in, say, a conscript army or a militia may lose some of their effectiveness when applied to a regular force where training, discipline, and the relationship between officers and enlisted men are all quite different. The fundamentals of command in conventional war may require modification, even inversion, in a counterinsurgency environment where purely military factors are less important than psychological and political ones. It is possible for the command system appropriate to the logistic aspects of any given armed conflict not to be relevant to its operational ones, and for the very principles that enabled preparations for an undertaking to be successfully completed to obstruct its execution at a later stage. Finally, in the shadow of nuclear escalation an entirely different approach may well be necessary, one whose cardinal aim is not merely to ensure successful performance at the hour of need, but also, and perhaps even more important, to prevent that hour of need from arising at all.

Command systems, in the sense employed throughout this study, consist of organizations, procedures, and technical means; command itself is a process that goes on (or is supposed to go on) within the system. To capture the actual operation of that process in any but the most fragmentary and impressionistic way, quantitative data concerning the size, direction, and type of the information flow inside the system are required, yet I know of no historical command system for which data that would make a statistical analysis possible are available. Furthermore, even if such data were available, it is more than probable that they would have failed to capture many of what one suspects are precisely the most important aspects of command. The informal, and sometimes tacit, communication that goes on inside an organization; its vital, but ultimately undefinable, ability to distinguish between relevant and irrelevant information fed to it; the mental processes that, often unknown even to himself, do take place inside a commander's head; the tone of voice with which a report is delivered, or an order issued; the look on a man's face, the glimmer in his eye, when handed this or that message—none of these would be recorded.

The term "system," one of the buzzwords of the present age, is appropriate to the technological environment in which we live, but the fact is that all systems that are not purely mechanical (a self-regulating steam engine, for example) consist at least partially of people, and that those people are by no means entirely identical with, or solely the product of, the system. It is thus likely that the operation of the very same set of structures, procedures, and technical means by a different group of people will alter its character radically.

Finally, given the close and mutual interdependence of all factors, the term "command system" is itself in one sense a misnomer. When the dichotomy between the "directing" brain and the "directed" body is set up, the fact that there is not a single member in any armed force at any time or place who has not performed some of the functions of command for at least part of the time is deliberately ignored. Conversely, command systems as soon as they exceed a certain very limited size themselves come to consist of men who must be commanded, a task that is often far from trivial. No commander has ever planned or communicated all of the time, no private—however lowly—ever spent all his time obeying orders. Establishing a separate category called "command system," separated from all other components that make up an armed force, is no doubt an indispensable step toward understanding. Unless extreme care is taken, however, that very step will introduce an element of distortion and thus risk defeating its own purpose.

To generalize on the nature and functioning of command is, in view of the above, an act of considerable temerity. It is an act that must be undertaken here, but not before the boundaries within which this study has moved are once again clearly defined. I am dealing with command as a process that makes use of information in order to coordinate people and things toward the accomplishment of their missions. The problem of motivation (which affects command to the extent that more motivation may make it possible to have less command, and vice versa), and also the fact that individual people differ in ways that must and do affect command, are excluded. The study deals mainly with conventional war on land—or perhaps one should say, the conventional aspects of war on land—

and does not attempt to come to grips either with the problem of nonmilitary factors as they affect warfare or with the shadow cast by nuclear weapons. Its concern is the forces in the field, not their mobilization, administration, and equipment at base. Though other factors have intruded from time to time, active operations against a hostile military force have been the main concern throughout. An attempt has been made to stick to the intermediate level of operations—that is, the one between the lowly (though supremely important) problems of minor tactics, represented for example by command over a four-man tank crew, and the rarefied upper spheres in which politics, economics, and military affairs become inseparable. Little or no attention has been paid to psychological questions, such as the way in which, given the biological properties of brain and sensory organs, information should effectively be presented to individual persons within the command system.

The ring, then, has been formed; the ropes within which the wrestlers must move, tightened. As has been our method from the beginning, the first wrestler will be made to represent the challenge with which warfare confronts demand, and the second the ways in which command systems have tried to meet this challenge.

THE QUEST FOR CERTAINTY

From Plato to NATO, the history of command in war consists essentially of an endless quest for certainty—certainty about the state and intentions of the enemy's forces; certainty about the manifold factors that together constitute the environment in which the war is fought, from the weather and the terrain to radioactivity and the presence of chemical warfare agents; and, last but definitely not least, certainty about the state, intentions, and activities of one's own forces. As the Greek commander-historian Polybius put it twenty-three hundred years ago: "Every deliberate act in war requires a fixed time for its commencement, and a fixed period, and an appointed place, and also requires secrecy, definite signals, proper persons through whom and with whom to act, and the proper means. It is evident that the commander who is happy in the choice of each and all of these will not meet with failure; but the neglect of any one of them will ruin the whole design. So true it is that nature makes a single trivial error sufficient to cause failure in a design, but correctness in every detail barely enough for success."[1] To make certain of each and every one of a vast multitude of details, then, each of which must be coordinated with all others in order to achieve optimum results—that is the ultimate purpose of any command system. It was in an attempt to achieve this goal, however remote and theoretical, that history saw the development of command systems and the search for improved organizations, technical means, and procedures.

Certainty itself is best understood as the product of two factors, the amount of information available for decision making and the nature of the task to be performed. An invisible hand, much like that which, according to Adam Smith, regulates the balance between supply and demand, determines the relationship between the two. Everything else being equal, a larger and more complex task will demand more information to carry it out. Conversely, when information is insufficient (or when it is not available on time, or when it is superabundant, or when it is wrong, all of which can be expressed in quantitative terms), a fall in the level of performance will automatically ensue. The history of command can thus be understood in terms of a race between the demand for information and the ability of command systems to meet it. That race is eternal; it takes place within every military (and, indeed, nonmilitary) organization, at all levels and at all times.

In view of the tremendous developments in command systems that have been documented here, reaching from a chieftain's head to the modern general staff giving employment to thousands of highly trained experts, and from a piece of bark to the digital computer, can it be said that the race is being won? The answer, in spite of much fashionable talk and some recent writings on automated and electronic battlefields, in which everything that exists can be seen and everything that can be seen can be hit, appears to me to be an unqualified no. Taken as a whole, present-day military forces, for all the imposing array of electronic gadgetry at their disposal, give no evidence whatsoever of being one whit more capable of dealing with the information needed for the command process than were their predecessors a century or even a millennium ago. Though modern technical means undoubtedly enable present-day command systems

265

to transmit and process more information faster than ever before, regardless of distance, movement, or weather, their ability to approach certainty has not improved to any marked extent. Nor, given the fact that this goal has proved elusive through every one of the many revolutions in organization, technology, and procedure that have taken place in the past, does there appear to be much hope of achieving it in the foreseeable future. Clausewitz's dictum that "a great part of the information obtained in war is contradictory, a still greater part is false, and by far the greatest part is uncertain" remains as true today as it was when first written down, against the background of incomparably simpler circumstances, a hundred and fifty years ago.[2] To believe that the wars of the future, thanks to some extraordinary technological advances yet to take place in such fields as computers or remotely controlled sensors, will be less opaque and therefore more subject to rational calculations than their predecessors is, accordingly, sheer delusion.

Why are present-day command systems unable, for all their sophistication, consistently to produce greater certainty than their predecessors? The first reason is the nature of war. As Clausewitz also points out, war brings to the fore some of the most powerful emotions known to man, including fear, anger, vindictiveness, and hatred. Consequently, and even disregarding the manifold ways in which the human mind distorts information in the very act of processing it, the quest for certainty cannot be expected to proceed rationally all or even most of the time.[3]

Second, war consists of two independent wills confronting each other—where there is but one will there can be no war, only a massacre. Though each of the contending opponents is to some extent bound by the nature of the means at his disposal and the environment in which he operates, neither those means nor that environment is ever so constrictive as to preclude considerable freedom of action. With each side free and, presumably, willing to double-cross the other to the utmost of his ability, the progress of the struggle between them is largely unforeseeable. Consequently, the attainment of certainty is, a priori, impossible.

Even more important than these considerations—which after all will retain their validity only as long as man remains man and war, war—are the logical obstacles facing the quest for certainty. In order to attain certainty, one must first of all have all the relevant information. The more the available information, however, the longer the time needed to process it, and the greater the danger of failing to distinguish between the relevant and the irrelevant, the important and the unimportant, the reliable and the unreliable, the true and the false.[4] There would appear to be no way out of this self-defeating dilemma except what Napoleon calls "a superior understanding"—one based, to be sure, on training and practice, but ultimately relying no less on intuitive judgment than on rational calculation.

It is scarcely surprising that the quest for certainty, given the practical and logical obstacles in its way, has been costly in every sense of the term. Until about 1800 the cost was kept within limits by the fact that information, especially long-distance information, was so scarce that it could be handled by a single man. From that time onward, however, the amount of information processing made necessary by the growing complexity of armies, and made possible by the increasingly sophisticated communications instruments at their disposal, grew by leaps and bounds. To cope with the flood of information, staff was piled upon staff, procedure upon procedure, machine upon machine. With each stage in the growth of staffs, the problem of coordinating the staff's parts with each other, and the staff as a whole with the forces, was compounded. With each new well-defined procedure or formal language, the gain in reliability and precision was offset by a decline in the informal communications, redundancy, and flexibility that are indispensable for the generation of ideas. With the addition of each machine, procedures had to be more strictly defined in order to make automation possible, while the expense of research, development, operation, and maintenance soared. The process, relatively slow at first, gained momentum after 1870 and especially after 1945. During the four decades that have passed since then, the percentage of "command personnel" within a typical Western army has risen fivefold.[5] The growth in the cost of command systems, relative to that of the forces as a whole, has been greater still, even to the point of raising the question whether, assuming the trend continues for another generation, anything will remain of the latter at all. The quest for certainty, in other words, will logically end only when there is nothing left to be certain about.

267

In sum, then, neither the numerous organizational changes that have taken place since 500 B.C., nor the technical advances that were introduced after about 1850, have significantly altered or even reduced the quintessential problem facing any command system, that of dealing with uncertainty. Though such advances, from the semaphore to the observation balloon, have often misled contemporaries into thinking the problem would be solved or at least diminished, in the end those hopes were invariably disappointed.

THE ESSENCE OF COMMAND

The best system of command, to caricature Clausewitz's famous dictum on strategy, is always to have a genius in charge, first in general and then at the decisive point. However excellent in principle, this advice is less than useful in practice, the problem consisting precisely in the inability of military (and nonmilitary) institutions to achieve certainty either in producing a steady supply of geniuses or in identifying the decisive points into which, once available, they should be put.

Uncertainty being the central fact that all command systems have to cope with, the role of uncertainty in determining the structure of command should be—and in most cases is—decisive.[6] In general, the more important the human element as opposed to the technical element in any given situation, and the more important the enemy's action in shaping that situation, the greater the uncertainty involved. The various ways in which these factors interact help account for the endless diversity to be found among both historical and present-day command systems; it explains, for example, why function-oriented (logistical) command systems are often more centralized and mechanized than output-oriented (operational) ones, and why the command system that makes possible the successful completion of preparations for a military enterprise may be inadequate or even positively harmful once that undertaking is under way. It is vital, in other words, for the structure and modus operandi of any command system to be adapted to the measure of uncertainty involved in the performance of the task at hand.

The nature of the task is not the only determinant of the amount of information required for its performance; equally important is the structure of the organization itself. The more numerous and differentiated the departments into which an organization is divided, the larger the number of command echelons superimposed upon each other, the higher the decision thresholds, and the more specialized its individual members, then the greater the amount of information processing that has to go on inside the organization. Uncertainty, in other words, is not dependent solely on the nature of the task to be performed; it may equally well be a function of a change in the organization itself.

Confronted with a task, and having less information available than is needed to perform that task, an organization may react in either of two ways. One is to increase its information-processing capacity, the other to design the organization, and indeed the task itself, in such a way as to enable it to operate on the basis of less information. These approaches are exhaustive; no others are conceivable. A failure to adopt one or the other will automatically result in a drop in the level of performance.

Conversely, if an improvement in performance is sought, the same two approaches are open. An improvement in performance being by definition associated with a greater demand for information, it is possible either to enhance the organization's capacity for information processing or to restructure the organization in such a way as to enable it to operate with a reduced capacity. The former approach will lead to the multiplication of communication channels (vertical, horizontal, or both) and to an increase in the size and complexity of the central directing organ; the latter, either to a drastic simplification of the organization so as to enable it to operate with less information (the Greek phalanx, and Frederick the Great's robots) or else to the division of the task into various parts and to the establishment of forces capable of dealing with each of these parts separately on a semi-independent basis. It is a central theme of this book that, through every change that has taken place and given any one level of technological development, the first two of these approaches are inadequate and stand in danger of becoming self-defeating, and that, the likelihood of further change notwithstanding, the third one will probably remain superior to them in virtually every case.

Taking the superiority of the third method as proven from the

269

time of Cynoscephalae on (in 197 B.C., an unnamed Roman military tribune took ten maniples and attacked King Philip's phalanx in the rear, breaking the power of the Macedonian monarchy), what are the implications for the organization of command systems and the way they operate? Attempting to generalize from the historical experience studied here, I suggest that there are five such implications, all interacting with each other: (a) the need for decision thresholds to be fixed as far down the hierarchy as possible, and for freedom of action at the bottom of the military structure; (b) the need for an organization that will make such low-decision thresholds possible by providing self-contained units at a fairly low level; (c) the need for a regular reporting and information-transmission system working both from the top down and from the bottom up; (d) the need for the active search of information by headquarters in order to supplement the information routinely sent to it by the units at its command; and (e) the need to maintain an informal, as well as a formal, network of communications inside the organization.

The fact that, historically speaking, those armies have been most successful which did not turn their troops into automatons, did not attempt to control everything from the top, and allowed subordinate commanders considerable latitude has been abundantly demonstrated. The Roman centurions and military tribunes; Napoleon's marshals; Moltke's army commanders; Ludendorff's storm detachments; Gavish's divisional commanders in 1967—all these are examples, each within its own stage of technological development, of the way things were done in some of the most successful military forces ever. The realization that certainty is the product of time as well as of information, and the consequent willingness to do with less of the latter in order to save the former; the postulation by higher headquarters of minimum, rather than maximum, objectives; the freedom granted junior commanders to select their own way to the objective in accordance with the situation on the spot, thus cutting down on the amount of data processing required; and the willingness of superior headquarters to refrain from ordering about their subordinates' subordinates—all these are indispensable elements of what the Germans, following the tradition of Scharnhorst and Moltke, call *Auftragstaktik,* or mission-oriented command system. Behind them all, there must be the realization that a certain amount of confusion and waste are, owing to the great uncertainty involved, inevitable in war; and that such confusion is not inconsistent with, and may indeed be a prerequisite for, results.

It is not enough, however, simply to allow subordinate commanders wide latitude and then demand that they fill it with their initiative; to do so they must first be properly trained and then provided with the right organizational means. The Roman maniple and cohort, like the Napoleonic *corps d'armée* and Ludendorff's storm detachments in 1918, were cohesive, self-contained organizations, both tactically and in regard to their command systems. This cohesion—often obtained by carefully selecting men and commanders and then allowing them to serve together for comparatively long periods of time, even at the expense of overall flexibility—and this self-containment have the effect of reducing the need for communications and information processing both inside the units themselves and between them and higher headquarters; they also ensure that errors, when made, will be limited in scope. Furthermore, the self-containment of subordinate units helps simplify planning by reducing the time and effort that have to be spent on overall coordination. If exercising central control over limited resources is one way of maximizing cost-effectiveness, distributing those resources among subordinate units may, by virtue of eliminating much of the need for planning, coordination, and internal communication, be another. Since disruptions in the communications process, and consequently uncertainty, are inherent in war, I would suggest that distributing the resources may often be the more effective way to maximize cost-effectiveness.

To enable superior headquarters to retain control over subordinate ones, a regular system for transmitting information from the top down, from the bottom up, and laterally among the subordinate units is indispensable and must naturally become more complex as the state of the art advances. Situation reports and checklists, forms and information copies, are therefore inevitable; to prevent them from causing more harm than good, however, several precautions must be taken. First, it is vital that veracity should be given equal place with "results" as a criterion by which reports are evaluated, or else the mutual trust on which any military organization is ultimately based will quickly be destroyed. Second, the number and extent of the routine reports demanded from subordinate headquarters should be limited to the indispensable minimum and be framed in such a way as to appear relevant to those headquarters' own needs. Units that must fill in endless reports on matters that are none of their concern will, presumably, very soon come to feel that the contents of those reports do not really matter; and the same thing will happen if superior headquarters, through neglect or oversight, does not properly utilize those reports and keeps badgering subordinates for information already sent.

Next, an indispensable prerequisite for all of the above is that information be actively sought by the top using its own independent means, not merely demanded of the bottom as a matter of routine. By setting out to look for the information that it needs at the time it is needed, instead of making subordinates report on everything all of the time, headquarters may well save enormous amounts of work and time, both for itself and for the units it controls. At the same time, by cutting through the repeated summarizing of information on its way from the bottom up, the directed telescope will help assure both immediacy and veracity. In the absence of such a telescope superior headquarters stands in danger of becoming a prisoner of its own reporting system; without it, too, no means will be available to counteract the natural tendency of any decentralized organization to degenerate into a set of semi-independent units where decision making becomes a bargaining process.

To enable the directed telescope to carry out its proper function, care must be taken to design it in such a way as neither to intimidate subordinate commanders nor to become an object of their contempt. The selection of the personnel and of the technical means employed; the frequency of the inspections and the manner in which they are conducted; the organizational relationship of the telescope to the organism it is supposed to watch—all these must be so designed as not to result in a curtailment of subordinates' initiative, or in their resentment, or in sugar-coating. Where a single telescope cannot answer all these demands it may be necessary to employ two different ones, each directed at a different part of the organization or of its activities. Object lessons in the wielding of such telescopes are provided by Napoleon, Moltke, Patton, and Gavish; Wellington and Montgomery (the so-called Phantom system) could be added. What is likely to happen in the absence of telescopes is well illustrated by the fate of Haig's armies on the Somme; and the use of too powerful a telescope—too powerful, no doubt, in part because the regular information system was deficient to begin with—is demonstrated by Westmoreland in Vietnam.

Finally, in order to prevent the entire system from seizing like an overheated engine, it is vital that the formal communication system be supplemented by an informal one that acts, so to speak, as lubricating oil. In any large organization, the virtues of formal communications systems—standardization, brevity, and precision—cannot be denied; those very virtues, however, also make such systems more subject to interruption and less flexible as a vehicle for original ideas than their unchanneled, redundant, and imprecise informal counterparts.[7] As several examples in this study have sought to demonstrate, the danger that formal communications reduce command, and indeed thought itself, to trivia is a real one indeed. It must be guarded against by a design that deliberately leaves room for face-to-face, unstructured interaction among people who know each other well enough in order *not* to limit their exchanges entirely to the line of business. To make such exchanges possible, again, a certain stability and homogeneity in organizational structure are vital. Such homogeneity and such stability must be paid for, it is true, in the form of a loss of overall flexibility. When carried beyond a certain point, they may lead to inbreeding, degeneration, and groupthink. Nevertheless, such exchanges represent the best way both of cutting down the total amount of communications that has to take place and of improving the quality of that communication.

Thus, it is suggested here that some current ideas concerning the ways to protect future headquarters against destruction by precision-guided munitions homing on their electronic emissions are wrong;[8] and that the proposed solution, namely dispersion and mobility achieved through having each officer sit in his own van and use modern technology to communicate with the others, is not only prohibitively expensive but will lead to a host of demoralized, out-of-touch people exchanging vast amounts of data about nothing at all. Far better, instead, to study the Israeli solution, which consists of putting all the key officers into a single vehicle, thus permitting face-to-face interaction. The saving thus effected is said to be enor-

273

mous. Israeli tactical headquarters at brigade level are no larger than those of U.S. companies, with the added bonus that they are inconspicuous, leave a smaller electronic signature, and are to this extent better protected also.[9]

Returning now to the two basic ways of coping with uncertainty, centralization and decentralization, it must be noted that they are not so much opposed to each other as perversely interlocking. In war, given any one state of technological development, to raise decision thresholds and reduce the initiative and self-containment of subordinate units is to limit the latter's ability to cope on their own and thus increase the immediate risk with which they are faced; in other words, greater certainty at the top (more reserves, superior control) is only bought at the expense of less certainty at the bottom. Conversely, the high level of performance both of the Roman legion and of the Grande Armée, of Moltke's armies and Ludendorff's storm detachments, was ultimately possible thanks to a readiness at higher headquarters to accept more uncertainty while simultaneously reducing it at lower ones. Properly understood, the two ways of coping with uncertainty do not therefore consist of a diminution as opposed to acceptance, but rather of a different distribution of uncertainty among the various ranks of the hierarchy. Under the first method the security of the parts is supposed to be assured by the certainty of the whole; under the second, it is the other way around.

A point to be noted is that these remarks seem to apply to all periods studied in this book and therefore appear to be independent of any specific stage of technological development. Nor, it is suggested, will their relevance be reduced in the future. So long as command systems remain imperfect—and imperfect they must remain until there is nothing left to command—both ways of coping with uncertainty will remain open to commanders at all levels. If twenty-five centuries of historical experience are any guide, the second way will be superior to the first.

To make the same point differently, the most important conclusion of this study may be that there does not exist, nor has there existed, a technological determinism that governs the method to be selected for coping with uncertainty. At various periods in history, and in the face of any one set of requirements arising from the art of war as exercised in those periods, different military organizations, though making use of the same general communications and data processing technology, have approached the problem from radically different angles and with radically different results. There was nothing in the nature of any single technology, whether based on the *signum* or on the telephone, the messenger or the computer, to dictate which of the two solutions should be adopted.

Far from determining the essence of command, then, communications and information processing technology merely constitutes one part of the general environment in which command operates.[10] To allow that part to dictate the structure and functioning of command systems, as is sometimes done, is not merely to become the slave of technology but also to lose sight of what command is all about. Furthermore, since any technology is by definition subject to limitations, historical advances in command have often resulted less from any technological superiority that one side had over the other than from the ability to recognize those limitations and to discover ways—improvements in training, doctrine, and organization—of going around them. Instead of confining one's actions to what available technology can do, the point of the exercise is precisely to understand what it cannot do and then proceed to do it nevertheless. This, after all, is in accordance with the doctrine of Lao Tzu, who long ago said:

> Once grasp the great form without a form
> and you will roam where you will
> with no evil to fear,
> calm, peaceful, at ease.
> The hub of a wheel turns upon the axle.
> In a jar, it is the hole that holds water.
> So advantage is had
> from whatever there is;
> but usefulness rises
> from whatever is not.

NOTES

All translations are mine, except in cases where an English-language edition of a work originally published in another language is available (as indicated in the notes). Translations from Hebrew, however, are mine in every case; English versions of Hebrew publications have been cited in the notes for the convenience of the reader.

1. INTRODUCTION: ON COMMAND

1. Here understood as the sum total of organization, technical means, and procedures at the disposal of the commander.

2. According to the data in T. N. Dupuy, *The Evolution of Weapons and of Warfare* (Indianapolis, 1980), p. 312, the number of square meters per man has grown by a factor of 400 since Napoleon and of 1.45 since the Second World War.

3. See for example R. Haasler and H. Goebel, "Das Unbehagen am technologischen Fortschritt in den Streitkräften," *Wehrwissenschaftliche Rundschau,* February 1981, pp. 36–41.

4. See for example H. Dickinson, "Survivability—Key Ingredient for Command and Control," *Military Review,* November 1981, pp. 19–25.

5. See J. A. Welch, "Some Random Thoughts on C^3," in C. P. Tsokos and R. M. Thrall, eds., *Decision Information* (New York, 1979), pp. 343–344.

6. It can be mathematically shown that, even in the case of an organization with as few as 300 variables, it will take six billion years for a computer weighing as much as the earth, every atom of which carries a

"bit" of information, to work out all possible combinations. See S. Beer, *Brain of the Firm* (New York, 1972). It is suggested, however, that working out which of these combinations "make sense" may take even longer.

7. On the concepts of "noise" and "information" and the relationship between them, see the pathbreaking study by R. Wohlstetter, *Pearl Harbor: Warning and Decision* (Stanford, Cal., 1962), especially chaps. 1 and 2.

8. See for example H. Wust and L. F. Himburg, *Das militärische Führungssystem* (Frankfurt am Main, 1974), p. 19, and R. Zeller, *Plannungs- und Führungssystem* (Regensburg, 1978), p. 8.

9. This is hardly the place to enlarge on the (imperfectly understood) workings of the human mind, but a few commonsense words on this question are necessary. Disregarding the problems of cognition—whether a zebra is a black animal with white stripes or vice versa—the solution to which depends on one's will, it may be said that in order to classify and arrange (that is, "understand") information reaching us we rely on a mental matrix consisting of concepts and the relationships between them. "Understanding" means arranging the information in accordance with the matrix, while information that cannot be so fitted appears "illogical." The matrix in each person's mind is partly his own alone, partly shared with other people. Its origins are partly biological, partly psychological, partly the outcome of training and education, and partly the result of practical experience. The connection between the matrix and the actual world is always problematic. Some of its parts are likely to be true, others false. When more than, say, 50 percent are false we classify the person as deranged. Since the external world changes, the matrix must also change; this takes time, however, and some parts of the matrix are apt to be more up to date than others. No foolproof way exists to ensure that one's matrix corresponds to reality, but knowing it may not is at any rate a good starting point. Mental flexibility consists of the ability and willingness to change one's matrix when necessary.

10. R. A. Beaumont, "Command Method: A Gap in the Historiography," *Naval War College Review,* Winter 1979, pp. 61–73.

11. See D. Showalter, "A Modest Plea for Drums and Trumpets," *Military Affairs,* February 1975, pp. 71–73.

12. *In Laws and Outlaws* (London, 1962), p. 99. This may be the best work on management ever written.

13. Quoted in E. Kessel, *Moltke* (Stuttgart, 1957), p. 515.

14. See on this problem M. van Creveld, *Fighting Power: German and U.S. Army Performance, 1939–1945* (Westport, Ct., 1982), especially chap. 12, section c.

2. THE STONE AGE OF COMMAND

1. *Diary of the Sinai Campaign* (London, 1966), p. 66.

2. As late as the War of the Austrian Succession (1740–1748) the French commander in chief, Maurice de Saxe, was invariably depicted in full armor.

3. Not accidentally, the first definition of the term "strategy," in English and in anything like its Clausewitzan sense, is found in 1825: "The art of bringing one's forces as rapidly as possible to the decisive point." *Oxford English Dictionary,* vol. 10.

4. For a good description of the way these things were done see Fredericus Rex, *Werke,* ed. G. B. Holz, vol. 4, *Militärische Schriften* (Berlin, 1913), chaps. 2 and 6.

5. For a good discussion of this problem see J. R. Alban, "Spies and Spying in the Fourteenth Century," in C. T. Allmand, ed., *War, Literature and Politics in the Middle Ages* (Liverpool, 1976), pp. 73–101. For a discussion of operational intelligence in the ancient world see D. W. Engels, "Alexander's Intelligence System," *Classical Quarterly,* 54, 1980, pp. 327–340.

6. See the Book of Esther 3:13; 8:10; and 8:14. Also Herodotus, *The Histories,* viii.98, and Xenophon, *Cyropaedia,* viii.6.17. For a modern account see H. C. Brauer, "Die Entwicklung des Nachrichtenverkehrs," diss., Nuremberg, 1957, p. 56 ff.

7. See the description in Procopius, *Anecdota,* chap. 30. Ancient relay systems are discussed in great detail by G. Riepl, *Das Nachrichtenwesen des Altertum* (Hildesheim, 1913; rprt. 1972), chaps. 1–3.

8. A. M. Ramsay, "The Speed of the Roman Imperial Post," *Journal of Roman Studies* 15 (1929), pp. 60–74.

9. There are numerous references to fire signals in Herodotus, Aeschylus, Sophocles, Thucydides, Polybius, Pausanias, and Diodorus Siculus, among others. Roman references are, for one reason or another, much rarer but some can be found in Livius and Osian. See H. Fischl, *Fernsprech- und Meldwesen im Altertum* (Schweinfurt, 1904), pp. 19–30.

10. For attempts to improve the information-carrying capacity of optical telegraphs see Polybius, *The Histories,* x.44. The system here suggested is unlikely to have been used in practice, however, since calculations based on the time it would have taken to transmit messages, and the capacity of the human eye to distinguish between closely grouped objects, show its operation to have been very cumbersome. Without the aid of a telescope, distances between stations would have to be kept small, which is presumably why the first successful system was only built at the time of the French Revolution.

11. See G. Webster, *The Roman Imperial Army* (London, 1969), pp. 246–248, for a short but useful summary of the evidence concerning military optical signaling systems. On their employment see above all E. N. Luttwak, *The Grand Strategy of the Roman Empire* (Baltimore, Md., 1978), especially p. 55 ff.

12. Vegetius, *Epitoma Rei Militaris,* iii.5.

13. *Militärische Schriften,* chap. 14.

14. See W. K. Pritchett, *Ancient Greek Military Practices* (Berkeley, 1971), pp. 127–133. Far from this being standard operating procedure, the use of mounted scouts had to be explicitly recommended to Xenophon's ideal general in *Cyropaedia,* vi.3 ff.

15. An example of the way things were done is provided by Alexander's scouts, who first reported sighting Persian horsemen in the distance two days before the battle of Gaugamela. Alexander personally rode forward some eleven miles and captured a few prisoners, and from them he learned that the Persian main force was another six miles away. The total of seventeen miles is on the large side; many armies were detected at considerably shorter range, sometimes as little as 600–800 yards. See Xenophon, *Hellenica,* 4.2, and Arrian, *Anabasis,* iii.8. Cavalry patrols also served as Caesar's normal method of obtaining enemy intelligence; *De Bello Gallico,* i.15.1, iv.11.6, and viii.3.1.

16. An important exception is formed by the Roman legion, on which more below. Units larger than three thousand men, sometimes as many as ten thousand, are attested to in the Persian, Chinese, and Mongolian armies. The sources for all of these are rather scant, however, and with the exception of the Mongolian ones there is no indication that any of them were permanent.

17. On countless occasions throughout history, armies made up of various contingents met before embarking on a campaign or at any rate before giving battle—for example, Anthony linking up with Caesar before Dyrrhachium, Marlborough with Prince Eugene before Blenheim. Far from disproving my point, however, these instances reinforce it. Armies only approached the enemy when united in one block, even when they were made up of various contingents coming from different directions.

18. W. W. Tarn, *Hellenistic Military and Naval Developments* (New York, 1968), pp. 39–40.

19. See C. Oman, *A History of the Art of War in the Middle Ages* (London, 1937), vol. I, p. 273 ff.

20. On the logistics of an army without mechanical transport see G. Perjes, "Army Provisioning, Logistics and Strategy in the Second Half of the 17th Century," *Acta Historica Academiae Scientarium Hungaricae,*

16, 1970, pp. 1–51; D. W. Engels, *Alexander the Great and the Logistics of the Macedonian Army* (Berkeley, 1978), chap. 1; and M. van Creveld, *Supplying War: Logistics from Wallenstein to Patton* (Cambridge, 1977), chap. 1.

21. This was the way Gustavus, for example, operated in Germany in 1631, and Marlborough in 1704.

22. See W. Erfurt, *Der Vernichtungssieg, eine Studie über das Zusammenwirken getrennter Heeresteile* (Berlin, 1938), pp. 2–9.

23. Very little has been written on the history of military maps and the constraints they imposed on operations, and my own research has failed to bring up much of significance. The Romans (according to Sallust, Caesar, Varro, Juvenal, and Lucian, among others) did have them, though the only one that has come down to our hands—the so-called *Tabula Peutingeriana*—is really an itinerary for getting from one place to the next and lacks precisely the two-dimensional quality that is vital for the conduct of strategy. The people of the Middle Ages were mostly uninterested in maps except for the purpose of schematically representing the world. Although place maps, on the one hand, and representations of the world, on the other, have always existed, everything in between remained problematic until about 1500, when the first proper two-dimensional map showing roads and distances was made in Italy; even then it remained a rare exception for another 150 years. It was only toward the end of the seventeenth century that real progress began to be made by basing maps on triangulation, but even so good ones remained a collector's item, much sought after by royal cabinets. Eighteenth-century maps, though well able to show the location of towns and natural obstacles, still had no contour lines and could not therefore show the configuration of terrain so important in tactics. Even in 1740–1748 Frederick II had to resort to captured Austrian maps to overrun Silesia. See *Paulys Real Encyclopädie der Klassischen Altertumwissenschaft* (Stuttgart, 1957), "Karten"; L. Bagrow and R. A. Skelton, *Meister der Kartographie* (Berlin, 1973), pp. 30–118; O. Albrecht, "Kurze Geschichte des militärischen Karten- und Vermessungswesens bis zum Anfang des ersten Weltkrieges," *Fachdienstliche Mitteilungen des … Militärgeographischen Dienst,* 1970, pp. 3–7; and R. V. Tooley, *Maps and Map Making* (London, 1952).

24. The importance of astronomy in the training of commanders is well brought out by Polybius, *The Histories,* ix.8.14–16. Even Napoleon early in the nineteenth century often prefaced his orders with the words *au point du jour* (at the beginning of the day) rather than naming a specific hour for a march or a battle to start.

25. Frederick II recommended that armies march in five or so col-

umns with the outer ones separated by about a Prussian mile (four English miles). *Militärische Schriften,* chap. 18.

26. *On War,* trans. J. J. Graham (London, 1962), vol I, pp. 266–267, and vol. II, p. 32.

27. In some cases—for instance, Poitiers in A.D. 1356—battles also happened by accident when commanders had lost all trace of each other and blundered about blindly. See H. J. Hewitt, *The Black Prince's Expedition of 1355-1357* (Manchester, 1958), pp. 108–109.

28. At Illerda, 49 B.C.; see B. H. Liddell Hart, *Strategy* (New York, 1967), pp. 54–55.

29. F. E. Adcock, *The Greek and Macedonian Art of War* (Berkeley, 1957), p. 82.

30. Clausewitz, *On War,* vol. II, p. 32.

31. See on these meanings D. D. Irvine, "The Origins of Capital Staffs," *Journal of Modern History,* 10, 1938, p. 162 ff.

32. By far the best analysis of the system is H. Reinhardt, "Grosse und Zusammenstellung der Kommandobehörden des deutschen Feldheers im II. Weltkriege," U.S. Army Historical Division Study P 139 (n.p., n.d.).

33. For what little is known about pre-Greek staff organizations see J. D. Hittle, *The Military Staff: Its History and Development* (Harrisburg, Pa., 1961), pp. 10–16.

34. *Lac. Pol.* 13.7. The "peers" apparently included the polemarchs, an unknown number of senior officers who were given a combination of *lochoi,* the largest permanent units, as occasion might demand, and three full citizens (*Spartiates*) appointed to wait on them.

35. The task of heralds in both ancient and medieval armies was to serve as channels of communication between the opposing armies, for which purpose they were granted diplomatic immunity that was sometimes abused.

36. Greek armies seldom numbered more than ten to fifteen thousand men. Their campaigns lasted anything between three and sixty days. In friendly territory, and in that of neutral states, methods of supply included markets where the troops could buy provisions out of their pay or subsistence money; in enemy country, supplies were obtained by plunder. See Pritchett, *Ancient Greek Military Practices,* pp. 29–49.

37. Arrian, *Anabasis,* ii.25.1–5. Numerous councils of war, sometimes including only the ten "generals" and sometimes a hundred "captains" as well, are described in the *Anabasis.*

38. J. K. Anderson, *Military Theory and Practice in the Age of Xenophon* (Berkeley, 1970), pp. 66–67.

39. Arrian, *Anabasis,* v.24.6; Athenaios, *Deipnosophists,* x.343b. The

diary is said to have been an innovation instituted by Alexander's father, Philip, after a Persian model.

40. Arrian, *Anabasis,* vii.4–5.

41. For Syria see B. Bar Kochva, *The Seleucid Army* (London, 1976), chap. 4; for Egypt, J. Lesquier, *Les Institutions Militaires de l'Egypte sous les Lagides* (Paris, 1911), pp. 99–103.

42. See W. W. Tarn, *Alexander the Great* (London, 1936), vol. I, pp. 12–13, and vol. II, p. 39.

43. On Parmenion see Engels, *Alexander,* p. 55. If I read the sources correctly, Eumenes the secretary was himself one of these commanders, which demonstrates how unspecialized even such an official could be.

44. See Plutarch, *Alexander* xli.2–5; xlii; liv.3; and lx.1.

45. See R. O. Fink, *Roman Military Records on Papyrus* (n.p., 1971), passim. For records kept in Rome during imperial times see R. Watson, *The Roman Soldier* (New York, 1969), p. 87, and Watson's "Documentation in the Roman Army," in H. Temporini, ed., *Aufstieg und Niedergang der Römischen Welt* (Berlin, 1974), vol. II, part I, pp. 493–507.

46. *Bellum Africanum,* 1–11. Significantly, sealed orders are again mentioned in a similar context by Frontinus, *Strategamata,* i.1. Since a ship's captain might expect to lose touch with his commander in chief owing to storms or faulty navigation or something of that kind, the use of written orders in such a context is logical.

47. R. W. Davies, "The Daily Life of the Roman Soldier," in Temporini, ed., *Aufstieg und Niedergang,* vol II, part I, pp. 301–308.

48. Appianus, *Roman History,* viii.2.66.

49. Onasander, *The General,* iii.1–3.

50. According to one modern historian Roman councils of war shared no power with the commander. They were called by him as he saw fit in order to tender advice, which was not, however, binding. Other functions included the issuing of instructions and "sounding out" the army. See J. Kromayer and G. Veith, *Heereswesen und Kriegführung der Griechen und Römer* (Munich, 1928), p. 459.

51. Cicero, *Ad Atticum,* viii.12, B 1; *Bellum Civile,* i.15.4–6; i.34.1; i.38.1. Also J. Harmand, *L'Armée et le Soldat à Rome de 107 à 50 avant notre ère* (Paris, 1967), pp. 355–356.

52. Harmand, *L'Armée,* p. 198 ff. Service at headquarters must have substituted for study at a staff college, the earliest of which was opened only in the second half of the eighteenth century.

53. *Ad Atticum,* vi.18.1. Pompey too sent private letters home in 49 B.C.; ibid., viii.12, A, B, C, and D.

54. *de Bello Gallico,* ii.1.1; iii.9.1; iv.34; v.25.5.

55. It might be argued that Roman consuls embodied the govern-

ment in their own person (they had *imperium*) and therefore did not have to correspond with the capital except to ask for reinforcements and so on. In imperial times, the *cursus publicus* made it possible to exercise considerably tighter control; nevertheless, large-scale offensive warfare usually required the emperor's presence, as demonstrated by the campaigns of Traianus in Dacia and Mesopotamia and of Marcus Aurelius in Germany. On Roman staff work in imperial times see F. Millar, "Emperors, Frontiers and Foreign Relations, 31 B.C. to A.D. 378," *Britannia*, 13, 1982, pp. 1–23.

56. Plutarch, *Sertorius*, iii.2; Dio Dassius, *Roman History*, xxix.98.1; ibid., xxxvi.3.2–3.

57. Plutarch, *Crassus*, xxi.1–5; xxii.1–6; and xxix.2–3.

58. See the *Bellum Hispanicum*, passim. In this war, incidentally, Pompeius stationed lookouts along the Spanish coast to report on a possible landing by Caesar.

59. *Ad Familiares*, ii.17, 3. On this occasion the *praesidia* had to be withdrawn to avoid being overrun by the enemy, implying some kind of frontier guard.

60. The *speculatores* are mentioned in *de Bello Gallico*, ii.11.2 and as spying out the enemy camp. They must have been specialists, for one does not entrust such a task to the intelligence of any common soldier.

61. *Bellum Hispanicum*, xiii.

62. *de Bello Gallico*, i.12.2; i.21.1 and 4; i.41.5; iii.2.1.

63. Ibid., i.50.4; ii.16.1; ii.17.2. Frontinus, *Strategamata*, in his chapter on spies, always refers to them as belonging to the commander in chief and never mentions anybody coming between him and them.

64. On the organization of supply in Caesar's army see A. Labisch, *Frumentum Commeatesque, die Nahrungsmittelversorgung der Heere Caesars* (Meissenheim am Glan, 1975).

65. See T. F. Tout, *Chapters in the Administrative History of Medieval England* (Manchester, 1937), vol. II, section vi, p. 131 ff.

66. E. Boutaric, *Institutions militaires de la France avant les armées permanents* (Paris, 1863), p. 267 ff.

67. See A. E. Prince, "The Payment of Army Wages in Edward III's Reign," *English Historical Review*, April 1944, pp. 137–160.

68. On the way it was done see G. Basta, *Il Governo della Cavalleria Leggiera* (Frankfurt am Main, 1612), and L. Melzo, *Regole militare sopra il governo de servitio particolare della cavalleria* (Antwerp, 1612).

69. For Maurice see J. Wijn, *Het Krijgswezen in den Tijd van Prins Maurits* (Utrecht, 1934), pp. 32–36, 371–375; for Gustavus Adolphus, Hittle, *The Military Staff*, p. 41; for Wallenstein, V. Loewe, *Die Organisa-*

tion und Verwaltung der Wallensteinischen Heere (Freiburg i B, 1895), pp. 29–30; and for Cromwell, C. H. Firth, *Cromwell's Army* (London, 1962), pp. 57–63.

70. *Oxford English Dictionary,* vol. 8.

71. Paris, 1775.

72. *Militärische Schriften,* chap. 18. See also W. Goerlitz, *Der deutsche Generalstab* (Frankfurt am Main, 1950), pp. 17–19.

73. *Oxford English Dictionary,* vol. 10.

74. Graf von Schmettau, Jr., *Lebensgeschichte des Grafen von Schmettau* (Berlin, 1806), pp. 344–346.

75. On Cadogan see D. Chandler, *The Art of War in the Age of Marlborough* (London, 1976), passim.

76. "J'ai ici une grande machine à gouverner," he once wrote hypocritically to his brother Henry, "et je suis seul. Je tremble quand j'y pense." (I have a large machine to run here, and I am alone. I tremble when I think of it.) On Frederick's command system see G.L.W., "Der grosse König im Grossen Krieg," *Allgemeine Militär-Zeitung,* 1870, nos. 7 and 8, pp. 49–51, 57–59.

77. C. H. P. von Westphalen, *Geschichte der Feldzüge des Herzogs Ferdinand von Braunschweig-Lüneburg* (Berlin, 1959), especially vol. I, pp. 134–137. For examples of the kind of work entrusted by Ferdinand to his secretary see ibid., vol. II, pp. 186–189.

78. P. Bourcet, *Memoires Historiques sur la Guerre que les Francois ont Soutenue en Allemagne depuis 1757 j'usqua en 1762* (Paris, 1797), especially vol. I, pp. 106–115.

79. Compare Bourcet's enumeration of a quartermaster general's duties, above, with the very much more restricted one in Westphalen, *Geschichte der Feldzüge des Herzogs Ferdinand,* vol. II, pp. 200–201.

80. Before Pultave, for example, the Swedish infantry colonels are found copying down the king's *ordre de bataille;* C. H. von Berenhorst, *Betrachtungen über die Kriegskunst* (Osnabrück, 1978), p. 39.

81. See an example in Frederick's *Militärische Schriften,* chap. 17.

82. Westphalen, *Geschichte der Feldzüge des Herzogs Ferdinand,* vol. I, p. 409.

83. The first staff college was founded by Bourcet at Grenoble in 1764 but closed soon thereafter. Immediately after the Seven Years War Frederick II also founded his Académie des Nobles, but this was allowed to languish by his successors until refounded as the Kriegsakademie in 1807.

84. This was P. Thiebault's *Manual des Adjutants Généraux et des Adjoints Employés dans les Etats Majors . . . des Armées* (Paris, 1806).

85. For a few examples of such letters see C. G. Cruickshank, *Elizabeth's Army* (Oxford, 1966), p. 55 ff.

86. Some recent works on the administration of armies in the early modern period include A. Corvisier, *Armies and Societies in Europe, 1494–1789* (Bloomington, Ind., 1979); G. Parker, *The Army of Flanders and the Spanish Road, 1567–1659* (London, 1972); and I. A. A. Thompson, *War and Government in Habsburg Spain, 1560–1620* (London, 1976).

87. A. von Schlieffen, "Der Feldherr," *Gesammelte Schriften* (Berlin, 1913), vol. I, p. 5.

88. See Thucydides, *The Peloponnesian War,* vi.66.3–4. According to A. W. Gomme, *A Historical Commentary on Thucydides* (Oxford, 1970), vol. IV, p. 103, the elaborate subdivision of the Spartan army is itself sufficient to explain its superiority over other Greek forces.

89. Standards, as distinct from improvised signs (a coat upon a pole used to show that this or that detachment had reached a predetermined position, often behind the enemy or on his flank), are only once mentioned by Greek sources (Arrian, *Anabasis,* vii.14.10). The papyri, it is true, do mention something called *semeiophoroi,* but graphic representations prove that the phalanx, unlike the legion, did not carry them and their true nature remains unknown. See Kromayer-Veith, *Heereswesen,* pp. 132–133.

90. Unlike the Romans, the Greeks used only two instruments for giving acoustical signals, the trumpet and the horn. So small was the number of signals that surprises could sometimes be achieved by reversing their usual meanings. (See Diodorus, *Deipnosophists,* xiv.52.1–5, and Xenophon, *Anabasis,* iv.2.14.) The lack of variation testifies to the simplicity of command functions and, by implication, of tactics.

91. A good description of a commander entering battle, if only an imaginary one, is provided by Xenophon, *Cyropaedia,* iii.57–60.

92. The great outflanking battles were Mantinea I (418 B.C.) and Nemea and Coronea (both 394 B.C.). See Thucydides, *The Peloponnesian War,* v.70–71; Xenophon, *Hellenica,* iv.2.13 ff; and ibid., iv.3.15 ff. For the tactical changes brought about by these battles see F. E. Adcock, *The Greek and Macedonian Art of War* (Berkeley, 1957), p. 84.

93. For this battle see above all Plutarch, *Pelopides,* xxiii. Since the Thebans on this occasion attacked in a highly unusual echelon formation, Epaminondas probably ordered each successive unit to advance when it saw its neighbor to the left so and so many yards ahead. With that his command function was at an end, however, since the only attempt to maneuver during the battle was carried out by the losers trying to sidestep the Theban onslaught.

94. How the phalanx in the center was commanded is not clear from

the surviving sources. Alexander seems to have divided it between the army's two wings, and his successors may have done the same. An overall "phalanx commander" is never mentioned; had he existed, he might have been too powerful a figure for the ruler's comfort. Hellenistic sources are in any case little interested in the phalanx, since the decision invariably fell with the cavalry on the wings.

95. Eumenes at Parataikene (317 B.C.); Diodorus, *Deipnosophists,* xix.27–30. On all these Hellenistic battles see J. Kromayer, *Antike Schlachtfelder* (Berlin, 1931), pp. 391–446.

96. So Antiochus III at Raphia (217 B.C.) and Magnesia (190 B.C.); also Philip V of Macedonia, this time leading a phalanx rather than cavalry, at Cynoscephalae in 197 B.C.

97. Arrian, *Anabasis,* ii.11. A very good analysis of this battle is to be found in J. F. C. Fuller, *The Generalship of Alexander the Great* (London, 1958), pp. 163–180.

98. For the battle of Gabiene see Diodorus, *Deipnosophists,* xix.40–43.

99. For the battle of Raphia see E. Galili, "Raphia, 217 B.C., Revisited," *Scripta Classica Israelica,* 3, 1976–77, pp. 52–126. Galili correctly emphasizes the difficulty that the commanders on both sides must have experienced in controlling their vast forces.

100. The question as to just what unit served what purpose in what period and which of them were provided with standards is debated. See A. von Domaszewski, *Aufsätze zur römischen Heeresgeschichte* (Darmstadt, 1972), chap. 1, and Webster, *The Roman Imperial Army,* pp. 134–141.

101. So important were the standards that many military moves took their names from them, such as *signa tellere* (to march out of camp), *signa movere* (to march away), and *signa constituere* (to halt).

102. On the way (it is thought) that standards and bugles were combined, see Kromayer-Veith, *Heereswesen,* pp. 518–519.

103. H. Delbrück, *Geschichte der Kriegskunst im Rahmen der Politischen Geschichte* (Berlin, 1921), vol. I, pp. 276–277, 438.

104. Normally, psychologists tell us, a person's span of control is limited to about seven objects or actions; see the classic paper by G. A. Miller, "The Magical Number Seven," *Psychological Review,* 63, 1956, pp. 81–96. I suggest, however, that confusion and stress during battle will reduce the maximum number that can be controlled to three or four.

105. Tacitus, *Annales,* i.64.8.

106. It is possible that the military tribunes, of whom there were six (later, twelve) in each legion, served as high-powered messengers in the hands of the legion commander, for their number does not correspond with any kind of unit. This, however, is uncertain.

107. Kromayer-Veith, *Heereswesen,* p. 318.

108. See his role at Zama from Polybius, *The Histories,* xv.13.7.

109. Ibid., x.1–5.

110. *de Bello Gallico,* ii.22.

111. *Bellum Africanum,* 12–18.

112. Philo of Byzantium, *Poliocertica,* v.4.28, and v.68–69. In the fourth century A.D. Ammianus Marcelinus in his *Historiae,* xix.7, explicalls such behavior highly unusual.

113. See Beha ed Din, *Life of Saladin,* in C. W. Wilson, ed., *Palestine Pilgrims' Texts Society* (London, 1897), vol. 11, pp. 282–283, for a description of the towerlike structure that marked King Richard the Lionheart's carriage during the battle of Arsouf in 1191.

114. Numerous examples of such contingents are brought by F. Lot, *L'Art militaire au Moyen Age en Europe et dans le Proche Orient* (Paris, 1946).

115. *Vita Dagoberti,* chap. 30, quoted in Oman, *The Art of War.*

116. This is the interpretation of O. Heermann, *Die Gefechtsführung abendländischer Heere im Orient in der Epoche des ersten Kreuzzugs* (Marburg, 1897), pp. 112–117. R. C. Smail, *Crusading Warfare, 1097–1193* (London, 1976), p. 171, considers Heermann's interpretation too complicated but concedes that Prince Bohemond was in effective control of his forces and commanded the reserves. For a list of battles in which the commander in chief acted this way see J. F. Verbruggen, *The Art of Warfare in Western Europe during the Middle Ages* (Amsterdam, 1977), vol. I, pp. 198–199.

117. One of the most complex of all medieval battles, Hastings saw William the Conqueror carry out, at the crudest interpretation, twelve different tactical moves. He also fought in person, had three horses killed under him, and personally killed at least one Saxon nobleman. How it was all done we have no idea—unless one assumes that he spent most of his time hacking about him in the melee and that the apparent complexity of the battle is merely due to post hoc reconstruction.

118. The identity of these messengers is unknown. Medieval armies had their heralds, but these were noncombatants forming part of an international guild who were used to communicate between hostile armies. At Agincourt the heralds of both sides spent the battle together watching it from the top of a nearby hill.

119. For Crecy and Poitiers see Oman, *The Art of War,* vol. II, pp. 136 ff and 170 ff. At Poitiers the Black Prince fed in one unit of bowmen after another before advancing and personally taking King Jean of France prisoner. The role of King Philip at Crecy is made sufficiently clear by the

fact that he had a horse killed under him and was lightly wounded in the neck by an arrow.

120. Edward III at Crecy did not do so, it is true, but solely because he wanted his son to gain his spurs; Froissart, *Chronicles* (London, 1968), p. 82.

121. On these battles see G. R. L. Fletcher, *Gustavus Adolphus and the Thirty Years War* (New York, 1963), pp. 186 ff and 283 ff.

122. See R. S. Quimby, *The Background of Napoleonic Warfare* (New York, 1957), pp. 9–10.

123. As late as the middle of the seventeenth century the commander's "entourage" only consisted of "supernumerary officers, comrades, adjutant generals well known to the army." See T. M. Barker, *The Military Intellectual and Battle: Raimondo Montecuccoli and the Thirty Years War* (Albany, N.Y., 1975).

124. F. W. von Zanthier, *Versuch über die Märsche der Armeen, die Lager, Schlachten und die Operations-Plan* (Dresden, 1778), p. 19.

125. One reason why the duke could move about so successfully, it must be added, was the fact that his tactics—first creating a diversion on a flank, then breaking through in the center—were stereotyped. Consequently they lost their effectiveness and the French were able to counter them at Malplaquet in 1709.

126. On this battle see R. Savary, *His Britannic Majesty's Army in Germany during the Seven Years War* (Oxford, 1966), p. 75 ff.

127. See his own description in *Militärische Schriften,* chap. 25.

128. The history of the term *coup d'oeil* is significant since it exemplifies the way things developed. Frederick II defines it as the ability of a commander to judge the number of troops that may fit into a given piece of terrain or else to grasp the military advantages that terrain may offer. To Clausewitz, it is the ability to discern where the decisive stroke might take place. The term fell into disuse mostly after 1850, implying that the commanders were no longer able to see much with their own eyes.

3. THE REVOLUTION IN STRATEGY

1. Eighteenth-century armies were regularly preceded by laborers, bridgelayers, carpenters, and so on, whose task it was to prepare the roads for the armies' advance.

2. It was for this reason among others that most European wars before 1800 took place in southern Germany, northern Italy, and the Low Countries. Perjes, "Army Provisioning," p. 4.

3. The Latin *consul, praetor, dictator, dux* (= duke, doge, duke), and *imperator* and the Germanic *Kunig, Jarl* (= earl, "brave") are all titles of military origin that still figure in our political vocabulary.

4. See van Creveld, *Supplying War,* pp. 56–57.

5. During the 1813 campaign in Saxony, for example, the emperor received daily dispatches from Paris, usually arriving within about one hundred hours of being sent, as well as equally frequent letters from agents in Amsterdam, Erfurt, Mainz, Milan, Munich, Strasbourg, Stuttgart, and Würzburg. Messages arrived from the empress, the grand chancellor, the minister of police, and the commanders of depots and training camps throughout the empire. All movements across the Rhine in both directions were monitored and reported to Napoleon on a daily basis. See A. J. F. Fain, *Manuscrit de Mil Huit Cent Treize* (Paris, 1824), vol. II, pp. 47–52, and H. Giehrl, *Der Feldherr Napoleon als Organisator* (Berlin, 1911), pp. 66–67.

6. In 1809 Napoleon possessed a hand-drawn set of 1:100,000 maps covering the whole of Europe west of Russia, a considerable achievement if it is remembered that the Germans themselves only had one of 1:200,-000 covering Germany after 1870.

7. This density an early nineteenth-century Russian quartermaster general put at ninety people per square mile. Cäncrin, *Uber die Militärökonomie im Frieden und Krieg* (St. Petersburg, 1821), p. 311.

8. The relationship between supply and mobility in the years before and after 1800 was, nevertheless, not as simple as this single-sentence summary suggests. See van Creveld, *Supplying War,* chaps. 1, 2.

9. M. de Saxe, *Reveries on the Art of War* (Harrisburg, Pa., 1947), pp. 36–37.

10. Clausewitz, *On War,* vol. II, p. 38.

11. When operating along parallel roads each corps was told to forage on only one side of its route; when following each other on a single road they were supposed to forage on different sides of it. See Napoleon's order to Murat, 21.9.1805, *Correspondance de Napoléon Premier* (Paris, 1863), vol. XI, no. 9249.

12. This constitutes a description of the actual operations of Davoût's IIIrd Corps in the 1805 Austerlitz campaign.

13. The Chappe telegraph was an optical system consisting of a series of towers with mounted movable beams on top. The stations, six to ten miles apart, were each manned by two officials, one working the beams and another watching through a telescope. The system could transmit messages at up to two hundred miles a day, but its reliability—owing to the low redundancy of the signal language used and also to the weather—was poor and its immobility in space made it unsuitable for the

transmission of operational, as opposed to strategic, messages. Nevertheless, by 1815 there were four lines reaching between Paris and Ostend, Brest, Rome, and Munich with a branch to Mainz, and optical systems constructed on similar principles continued to be built until the 1830s. See Giehrl, *Der Feldherr Napoleon,* pp. 66–67.

14. Napoleon's main problem of command in Spain was that the king, his brother, was militarily incompetent and could not be counted on to exercise effective command. On the other hand, none of the marshals would defer to each other, so the emperor was obliged to try and command by remote control. See J. L., "Méthodes de Commandment de Napoléon pendant les Guerres d'Espagne," *Revue Historique,* 44, 1911, pp. 458–483, and 45, 1912, pp. 57–90, 235–263, 450–453.

15. Las Casas, *Mémorial de Sainte Hélène* (Paris, 1869), vol. II, p. 18.

16. M. Bourienne, *Memoirs of Napoleon Bonaparte* (London, n.d.), p. 154.

17. Quoted in Vaché, *Napoléon en Campagne* (Paris, 1900), p. 4.

18. "He knows everything, he does everything, he can do anything." Sieyes quoted in D. Chandler, *The Campaigns of Napoleon* (London, 1963), p. 262.

19. Las Casas, *Mémorial,* vol. VI, p. 359.

20. "Activity, activity, speed, my best wishes to you." Napoleon, *Correspondance,* vol. XI, no. 9386.

21. After Duroc's death in 1813—he was killed by a cannonball while standing on a hill at the emperor's side—Caulaincourt performed both their functions.

22. On the Black Cabinet see Giehrl, *Der Feldherr Napoleon,* p. 52 ff. Supervised by Fouché, the Cabinet during the empire's heyday employed over a hundred men and opened several thousand letters a day, including all the mail of Allied officers.

23. See for example Berthier's order to General Zanoschek, March 1808, in Napoleon, *Correspondance,* vol. XIV, no. 12130.

24. *Précis de l'Art de la Guerre* (Osnabrück, 1973, reprint of the 1855 edition), vol. II, pp. 181–182.

25. Quoted in J. L. Lewal, *Tactique des Ravitaillements* (Paris, 1881), p. 29.

26. A. de Philip, *Etude sur le Service d'Etat Major pendant les Guerres du Premier Empire* (Paris, 1900), p. 5 ff.

27. The divisions were: 1st Adjutant General—general staff archives, collections of laws, discipline, organization, inspections, control, troop movements, councils of war, prisoners, situation reports; 2nd Adjutant General—army diary, armaments, artillery, pioneers, camps, subsistence, hospitals, gendarmerie, command of places; 3rd Adjutant General—re-

connaissance, plans, marches, communications, postal services, employment of guides; 4th Adjutant General—establishment of general headquarters, its police units, cantonments, caserns.

28. Quoted in de Philip, *Etude sur le Service d'Etat Major,* p. 24.

29. By far the best description of Berthier's headquarters, as opposed to Napoleon's, is K. Vitzthum von Eckstädt, *Die Hauptquartiere im Herbstfeldzug 1813 auf den deutschen Kriegsschauplätze* (Berlin, 1910), pp. 79–88.

30. "Sender of the emperor's orders." Ibid., p. 79.

31. On Daru see R. Tournes, "Le GQC de Napoleon Ier," *Revue de Paris,* May 1921, p. 137 ff; also H. Nanteuil, *Daru et l'Administration Militaire sous la Revolution et l'Empire* (Paris, 1966).

32. See for example Napoleon to Murat, 14.12.1806, in Napoleon, *Correspondance,* vol. XIV, no. 11464; Giehrl, *Der Feldherr Napoleon,* p. 27 ff., and de Philip, *Etude sur le Service d'Etat Major,* pp. 62–64.

33. Chandler, *The Campaigns of Napoleon,* p. 1034 ff.

34. See P. C. Alombert and J. Colin, *La Campagne de 1805 en Allemagne* (Paris, 1902), vol. 1, documents "Annexes et Cartes," pp. 53–56. The figures here given only include the units' "general" staffs and not their administrative sections and various special commanders.

35. De Philip, *Etude sur le service de l'Etat General,* pp. 45–50.

36. See Giehrl, *Der Feldherr Napoleon,* pp. 5–6.

37. Napoleon, *Correspondance,* vol. XIII, no. 10854, 21.9.1806. Just why Napoleon wanted the area reconnoitered in such detail is not entirely clear, since by the time Bertrand was sent out he must already have known that the Grande Armée would move into Saxony by way of the Thuringian Forest.

38. Ibid., vol. XXV, no. 20190, 28.6.1813.

39. Ibid., vol. XIII, no. 10804, 17.9.1806.

40. Ibid., vol. XIII, no. 10743, 5.9.1806. Napoleon did not always work in such splendid isolation, however. Occasionally he engaged Berthier in written, if largely rhetorical, games of question and answer by the way of contingency planning. See for example ibid., vol. XVIII, no. 14795, 30.3.1809.

41. Ibid., vol. XIII, no. 10744.

42. *Unpublished Correspondence of Napoleon I,* ed. E. Picard and L. Tuetey (Duffield, N.Y., 1913), no. 625.

43. Napoleon, *Correspondance,* vol. XIII, nos. 10746 and 10747.

44. Ibid., no. 10756.

45. Ibid., nos. 10759 and 10761.

46. Ibid., nos. 10764, 10765, and 10766.

47. Ibid., no. 10768.

48. Ibid., no. 10773. Incidentally, by arranging for Berthier to act independently upon the arrival of information from the French ambassador in Dresden it was possible to save several days.

49. Ibid., no. 10804.

50. Ibid., nos. 10800 and 10803.

51. Ibid., no. 10817.

52. Ibid., no. 10821.

53. *Unpublished Correspondence,* ed. Picard and Tuetey, nos. 659 and 664.

54. Napoleon, *Correspondance,* 10818. According to these orders the final deployment was to take place between 2 and 4 October. Possibly the danger of a rapid Prussian movement westward also accounts for Bertrand's mission mentioned above.

55. Murat's reports are printed in H. Bonnal, *La Manoeuvre de Jena* (Paris, 1904), p. 193. Each marshal had his own light cavalry, as well as an espionage system the reports of which he was supposed to communicate directly to the emperor.

56. Reports printed in Bonnal, *La Manoeuvre de Jena,* pp. 191–200.

57. Napoleon, *Correspondance,* vol. XIII, no. 10920.

58. Ibid., no. 10941.

59. Ibid., no. 10961.

60. Bonnal, *La Manoeuvre de Jena,* p. 300.

61. Napoleon, *Correspondance,* vol. XIII, no. 10979.

62. Ibid., no. 10977.

63. Ibid., no. 10980.

64. Napoleon's orders are printed in *Correspondance,* vol. XIII, nos. 10981, 10982, and 10984; Berthier's, in Vaché, *Napoléon en Campagne,* pp. 45–46.

65. Napoleon, *Correspondance,* vol. XIII, no. 10994.

66. Ibid., no. 11000.

67. This, of course, does not mean that these were the only reasons why the emperor disliked wars of attrition.

68. The letter to Ney is printed in Napoleon, *Correspondance,* vol. XIII, no. 11003; those to the remaining marshals are printed in Vaché, *Napoléon en Campagne,* pp. 172–174.

69. P. de Ségur, *Un Aide de Camp de Napoléon, 1800–1812* (Paris, 1873), vol. I, p. 313.

70. The Order of the Day is printed in Napoleon, *Correspondance,* vol. XIII, 11004.

71. Some early twentieth-century worshippers of Napoleon, notably Vaché and Bonnal, ascribed every fault in Napoleon's orders to Berthier's editing. Regardless of the fact that this would have been proof of re-

markable incompetence by the chief of staff (and by his master in retaining him for so long), this is made unlikely, in the present case, by the consideration that Berthier would hardly have dared alter an order as important as this one. Rather, the order must have been dictated and sent out verbatim without revision.

72. See M. P. Foucart, *Campagne de Prusse* (Paris, 1887), vol. I, p. 625. This is a report by Victor, Lannes's chief of staff.

73. Ségur, *Memoir,* vol. I, p. 313.

74. The Fifth Bulletin, Napoleon, *Correspondance,* vol. XIII, no. 11009. Like many stories contained in the Bulletins, this one may be apocryphal.

75. Quoted in A. Vagts, *A History of Militarism* (Toronto, 1959), p. 270.

76. Saxe, *Reveries,* pp. 211–215.

77. Quimby, *Background,* chap. 13.

78. A. Wavell, *Soldiers and Soldiering* (London, 1953), pp. 47, 52–53.

79. This was Bernadotte's own subsequent excuse; Vaché, *Napoléon en Campagne,* p. 201.

80. See D. Riesman, "The Oral and Written Traditions," in E. Carpenter and M. McLuhan, eds., *Explorations in Communication* (Boston, 1960), p. 110.

81. Napoleon, *Correspondance,* vol. XIII, no. 10992. In this letter to the empress Napoleon describes himself as traveling between twenty and twenty-five leagues a day.

4. RAILROADS, RIFLES, AND WIRES

1. See for example the November 1981 issue of the *Military Review,* in which eight articles are concerned solely with the technology of command whereas one (by Major Dennis H. Long, U.S. Army) explains why this should not be so.

2. During the Civil War the two sides between them laid fifteen thousand miles of wire and employed one thousand operators. See M. T. Thurbon, "The Origins of Electronic Warfare," *Journal of the Royal United Services Institute,* September 1977, p. 61.

3. Figures and quotations from M. Jähns, *Geschichte der Kriegswissenschaften* (Berlin, 1899), pp. 2865–67.

4. In 1814, with his armies reduced in size, Napoleon reasserted his control brilliantly, only to lose it again when he had 120,000 men at Waterloo.

5. H. von Moltke, *Militärische Werke* (Berlin, 1892–1912), vol. II, part 2, pp. 173–176.

6. See van Creveld, *Supplying War*, p. 81.

7. See the famous memorandum of 16.9.1865 in *Militärische Werke*, vol. II, part 2, pp. 253–257. Contrary to the claims of most historians, this memorandum did not lay the theoretical foundations of the strategy of external lines, since it dealt solely with logistics and their effect on the order of march.

8. In 1866 every military expert, including Moltke's own collaborators, criticized the Prussian deployment. Friedrich Engels even went so far as to say that it was only explicable on the ground that the king of Prussia, unlike the emperor of Austria, commanded in person, royal commanders being notoriously feeble-minded.

9. For a good example of the kind of work involved see W. Gröner, *Lebenserinnerungen* (Göttingen, 1957), pp. 70–71.

10. The number of troops per mile went down from twenty thousand in 1815 to twelve thousand in 1866; B. H. Liddell Hart, "The Ratio of Forces to Space," in *Deterrent or Defence* (London, 1960), p. 98. Dupuy, *The Evolution of Weapons*, p. 312, says that the space occupied per man went up by 25 percent.

11. For the Austrian mobile field telegraph see *Allgemeine Militärische Zeitschrift*, 1855, nos. 73 and 74, p. 573.

12. Ibid., 1855, nos. 27–28, p. 210.

13. Ibid., 1859, nos. 39/40, 41/42, pp. 337 and 355.

14. T. Fix, *Militair-Telegraphie* (Leipzig, 1869), pp. 54–58.

15. The only exception, the battle of Königgrätz itself, was presented to Moltke as a fait accompli by the commanding officer, 1st Army.

16. *Oesterreichische Militärische Zeitschrift*, vol. II, 1861, no. 2, pp. 150–154. This is an anonymous review of a book, *Über den Einfluss der Eisenbahnen und Telegraphen auf die Kriegsoperationen* by one L. von M.

17. On the origins of the German General Staff see Irvine, "The Origins of Capital Staffs"; P. Bronsart von Schellendorff, *Der Dienst des Generalstabes*, 3rd ed. (Berlin, 1893), pp. 111–117; and the more anecdotal account in Goerlitz, *The German General Staff*, chap. 1.

18. Military history remained the second most important subject on the curriculum of the Kriegsakademie (after tactics) right down to 1945. The German General Staff was also unique in that several of its heads, from Scharnhorst through Moltke to Schlieffen, were themselves distinguished military historians.

19. See H. von Boehm, *Generalstabsgeschäfte: Ein Handbuch für Offiziere aller Waffen* (Potsdam, 1862), p. 9.

20. K. Greenfield, *The Organization of Ground Combat Troops* (Washington, D.C., 1947), p. 361.

21. B. Overbeck, *Das königliche Preussische Kriegsheer* (Berlin, 1862).

22. K. von Blumenthal, *Tagebücher* (Stuttgart, 1902), entry for 6 July 1866.

23. See T. Krieg, *Wilhelm von Doering, ein Lebens- und Charakterbild* (Berlin, 1898).

24. It was Wartensleben who, when delivering a message during the battle of Königgrätz, was greeted with the words "But who is this General Moltke?" See H. von Wartensleben, *Erinnerungen,* Berlin, 1897, pp. 35–36; and also D. Showalter, "The Retaming of Bellona: Prussia and the Institutionalization of the Napoleonic Legacy, 1815–1876," *Military Affairs,* April 1980, p. 63, n. 27.

25. See the description (pertaining to the 1870 campaign) in J. von Verdy du Vernois, *Im Grossen Hauptquartier 1870/71* (Berlin, 1895), pp. 16–19.

26. O. von Lettow-Vorbeck, *Geschichte des Krieges von 1866 in Deutschland* (Berlin, 1899), vol. II, p. 94.

27. See Boehm, *Generalstabsgeschäfte,* pp. 262–266. There was a Ist Department responsible for "all strategic, tactical and topographical matters"; a IInd Department that dealt with organization, equipment, and armaments; and a IIIrd Department responsible for political matters.

28. J. von Verdy du Vernois, *Im Hauptquartier der Zweiten Armee, 1866* (Berlin, 1900), p. 41; Bronsart von Schellendorff, *Der Dienst der Generalstabes,* pp. 215–216.

29. 2nd Army consisted of Ist, Vth, and VIth Corps; 1st Army consisted of a Cavalry Corps, IInd Corps, IIIrd Corps, and 7th and 8th Divisions (responsible to 1st Army directly with no intermediate corps headquarters); and the Army of the Elbe consisted of three divisions.

30. Even a writer as critical of the German General Staff as J. Wheeler-Bennett in *The Nemesis of Power* (New York, 1967) admits its "phenomenal capacity," "genius," and "brilliance" on the first page of his introduction. For a modern view of these qualities see T. N. Dupuy, *A Genius for War* (London, 1977), chap. 17, significantly entitled "The Institution of Excellence."

31. That nothing should have been published on the operations of the Nachrichtenbureau at the time is only natural, and the documentary material has been destroyed by fire in World War II. To judge from the fact that the bureau was able to trace the Austrian deployment by rail but lost all track of their movements after the railheads had been left behind, it may be possible to surmise that it had agents stationed near strategic

junctions all over the Habsburg Empire. These agents presumably either reported to the Prussian military attaché in Vienna—which would have been possible until the declaration of war in mid-June—or else, and more likely, used the telegraph to pass coded messages by way of Switzerland. See Krieg, *Wilhelm von Doering,* pp. 148–152, which describes the Nachrichtenbureau as an improvised organization set up for the purposes of the campaign.

32. Kessel, *Moltke,* pp. 292–293, 445–447.

33. Moltke, *Militärische Werke,* vol. I, part 2, no. 79.

34. This letter is quoted in W. Foerster, ed., *Friedrich Karl von Preussen: Denkwürdigkeiten aus seinem Leben* (Stuttgart, 1910), vol. II, p. 67.

35. On these arguments, which make entertaining reading, see ibid., p. 30 (Frederick Wilhelm explaining that "it is always a bad thing to fix the meeting point [of separate armies] in a place where the enemy is standing"; Krieg, *Wilhelm Doering,* pp. 154–157; Kessel, *Moltke,* pp. 453–454; and T. von Bernhardi, *Tagebuchblätter* (Leipzig, 1897), vol. 6, pp. 7, 240, 280, 309–310, and vol. 7, pp. 253–258.

36. Moltke, *Militärische Werke,* vol. I, part 2, no. 135.

37. While one telegraphic message forbade 2nd Army from making any major move without permission, the written one that followed explained: "Don't let my previous cable make you believe that it is my intention to limit the army's operations in the face of the enemy, by directives from above. All my efforts are designed to prevent this. However, the general decisions whether an army must act on the offensive or stand on the defensive or must retreat, can only be made by His Majesty so as to coordinate all movements." Ibid., nos. 88 and 89.

38. Ibid., no. 95

39. Lettow-Vorbeck, *Geschichte des Krieges von 1866,* vol. II, p. 56.

40. Headquarters of 1st Army was at Muskau until 13 June, then moved to Görlitz; 2nd Army Headquarters was at Fürstenstein until 13 June, when it moved to Neisse.

41. Moltke, *Militärische Werke,* vol. I, part 2, nos. 107 and 108.

42. Ibid., no. 21.

43. Ibid., no. 126, and editor's note on p. 230.

44. Ibid., no. 129.

45. Foerster, *Friedrich Karl von Preussen,* pp. 40–41.

46. Ibid., p. 38; see also K. von Voights-Rhetz, *Briefe aus den Kriegsjahren 1866 und 1870/71* (Berlin, 1906), p. 39.

47. E. von Francesky, *Denkwürdigkeiten* (Bielefeld, 1901), p. 297.

48. Moltke, *Militärische Werke,* vol. I, part 2, no. 140.

49. See Bucholtz, "Uber die Tätigkeit der Feldtelegraphen in den

jüngsten Kriegen," *Militär-Wochenblatt,* 1880, no. 41, pp. 742–747; Merling, *Die Telegraphentechnik in der Praxis* (n.p., 1879), p. 469; and Moltke's own order of 25 July 1866 in *Militärische Werke,* vol. II, part 2, pp. 142–143.

50. Calculation based on Foerster, *Friedrich Karl von Preussen,* pp. 54 and 55, and Moltke, *Militärische Werke,* vol. II, part 1, nos. 140, 142, 144.

51. See Lettow-Vorbeck, *Geschichte des Krieges von 1866,* p. 383.

52. Foerster, *Friedrich Karl von Preussen,* p. 36.

53. For this episode see G. A. Craig, *The Battle of Königgrätz* (London, 1965), p. 65 ff.

54. According to his biographer, Frederick Charles had recognized the Austrian intention to fight at Jung Bunzlau "from the Austrian preparations (emplacements etc.)" and from the reports of a "Prussian coming from Münchengrätz and Jung Bunzlau [he could hardly have passed the two places in that order] who had seen them "crammed with troops." Foerster, *Friedrich Karl von Preussen,* p. 48.

55. Ibid., p. 53.

56. Ibid. On 30 June 1866 Voights-Rhetz, to save face, was still reporting to his wife that the Austrians had retreated first to Jung Bunzlau and then to Gitschin. Voights-Rhetz, *Briefe,* p. 7.

57. Already on the 29th a telegraph line between Reichenberg and Münchengrätz was in existence, but it was unreliable and most messages were transmitted by orderly. See Foerster, *Friedrich Karl von Preussen,* p. 59, n. 1.

58. Moltke, *Militärische Werke,* vol. I, part 2, nos. 142, 143, 144.

59. Ibid., no. 145.

60. Foerster, *Friedrich Karl von Preussen,* pp. 56–57.

61. Ibid., pp. 61 and 62.

62. Verdy du Vernois, *Im Hauptquartier der Zweiten Armee,* p. 65 ff; also Blumenthal, *Tagebücher,* entries for 20, 22, 23, and 25 June 1866.

63. Blumenthal, *Tagebücher,* p. 93.

64. Verdy du Vernois, *Im Hauptquartier der Zweiten Armee,* p. 97.

65. E. Kraft von Hohenlohe Ingelfingen, *Aus Meinem Leben, 1848–1871* (Berlin, 1897), vol. III, p. 246.

66. Verdy du Vernois, *Im Hauptquartier der Zweiten Armee,* p. 98.

67. Ibid., p. 108.

68. Foerster, *Friedrich Karl von Preussen,* pp. 59, 61.

69. Moltke, *Militärische Werke,* vol. I, part 2, no. 146.

70. Lettow-Vorbeck, *Geschichte des Krieges von 1866,* vol. II, p. 369.

71. Moltke, *Militärische Werke,* vol. I, part 2, no. 147, and editor's note on p. 240.

72. Unsure of the reasons behind 2nd Army's move, Moltke asked Stülpnagel (significantly bypassing Voights-Rhetz) whether he had received any news that might explain what was going on, but received a negative answer. A direct telegraph wire between the two armies, Stülpnagel added, did not exist. Lettow-Vorbeck, *Geschichte des Krieges von 1866,* vol. II, pp. 385–386.

73. Moltke, *Militärische Werke,* vol. I, part 2, nos. 148 and 149.

74. Lettow-Vorbeck, *Geschichte des Krieges von 1866,* vol. II, p. 386.

75. Their journey is described in Verdy du Vernois, *Im Hauptquartier der Zweiten Armee,* p. 127.

76. Blumenthal, *Tagebücher,* entry for 6 July 1866.

77. For this entire episode see the spirited account in T. Fontane, *Der deutsche Krieg von 1866* (Berlin, 1871), pp. 457–459.

78. Writing post facto Voights-Rhetz claimed credit for rediscovering the Austrian Army, saying that "our outposts" had watched the Austrians move laterally along the far bank of the Bistritz "from 0800 hours in the morning to 1500 hours in the afternoon." From this, the chief of staff, 1st Army, says, "I calculated a strength of 35,000 men [there were in fact almost 200,000] with parks and cavalry . . . Benedek had to be there, for he had been seen at Gitschin [he had in fact been at Josephstadt on the 29th]. From these elements I could deduce that the Austrians were planning to make another stand in front of the Elbe, and had to assume they would assemble all available forces to escape defeat. This was what happened." Voights-Rhetz, *Briefe,* p. 7. The 1st Army chief of staff may have been mistaken; or else he was writing with history in mind.

79. Schlieffen, *Gesammelte Schriften,* vol. I, p. 132.

80. Moltke, *Militärische Werke,* vol. I, part 2, no. 152. According to a letter in Voights-Rhetz, *Briefe,* pp. 13–15, written with the intention of ridiculing Moltke, it was he himself and Wartensleben who drafted the order while Moltke talked to the king.

81. See Blumenthal, *Tagebücher,* entry for 6 July 1866.

82. For this account of Frederick Charles at Königgrätz see Foerster, *Friedrich Karl von Preussen,* pp. 76–79.

83. Wartensleben, *Erinnerungen,* p. 31.

84. Francesky, *Denkwürdigkeiten,* pp. 360–363.

85. Kessel, *Moltke,* p. 479.

86. H. Friedjung, *Der Kampf um die Vorherrschaft in Deutschland 1859 bis 1866* (Stuttgart, 1898), vol. II, p. 58.

87. Foerster, *Friedrich Karl von Preussen,* pp. 104–106. It thus turns out that, of nine Prussian corps in 1866, two were without commanders and two (IIIrd and Vth) were commanded by madmen.

88. Krieg, *Doering,* pp. 183–185.

89. Foerster, *Friedrich Karl von Preussen,* p. 107.

90. M. von Poschinger, *Kaiser Friedrich in neuer quellenmässiger Darstellung* (Berlin, n.d.), vol II, p. 24. This, of course, was nonsense, since the worst that the Prussians faced at Königgrätz was a tactical check, whereas Jena had been strategically decided before it was fought.

91. Moltke, *Militärische Werke,* vol. I, part 2, pp. 75–76. The old French expression *ordre de bataille* appears in the original.

92. For this and the following paragraph see the brilliant analysis in G. F. R. Henderson, *The Science of War* (London, 1905), pp. 3–8, 118–121.

93. At Königgrätz, nevertheless, the number of men on both sides was roughly equal.

94. Verdy du Vernois, *Im Hauptquartier der Zweiten Armee,* p. 58. In the Grande Armée, by contrast, even the corps had often marched into the blue.

95. Moltke, *Militärische Werke,* vol. I, part 2, p. 293.

96. Stoffel, *Rapports Militaires, 1866–1870* (Paris, 1871), pp. 346–350.

97. Moltke, *Militärische Werke,* vol. IV, part 1, p. 42.

98. An approximate translation would be: "Work hard—make no waves—be more than you seem."

5. THE TIMETABLE WAR

1. See C. M. Cipolla, ed., *The Fontana Economic History of Europe* (London, 1973), vol. 4 (2), statistical appendix.

2. Figures from H. von Kuhl, *Der deutsche Generalstab in Vorbereitung und Durchführung der Weltkrieg* (Berlin, 1920), pp. 16, 53, 103.

3. Both countries, however, did set up General Staffs of their own in 1900–1905.

4. German editions: Berlin 1875–1876, 1884, 1905; English: London 1887–1880, 1893, 1895, 1905; French: Paris 1876; American: published by the Adjutant General's Office, Washington, D.C., 1899.

5. Goerlitz, *The German General Staff,* p. 96.

6. See J. Wallach, *Kriegstheorien, ihre Entwicklung im 19. und 20. Jahrhundert* (Frankfurt am Main, 1972), chap. 4. It is only fair to add, however, that the French General Staff, directed by Foch and Grandmaison, took the opposite tack and disregarded material in favor of moral factors.

7. "An error in the deployment, once made, can never subsequently be corrected." Moltke, *Militärische Werke,* vol. II, part 2, p. 291. By 1914

the network of lines covering Europe had become sufficiently dense to overturn this dictum, however, as proved by the moves of the French 6th Army on the Ourq and by the Germans at Tannenberg.

8. H. von Moltke, Jr., *Erinnerungen, Briefe, Dokumente* (Stuttgart, 1922), pp. 21–23. The Kaiser, who was no fool, retorted, "Your uncle would have given me a different answer."

9. On the effects of peace on the German Army see ibid., p. 339.

10. In *On War of Today* (New York, repr. 1972), pp. 163–178. In general, systematic analyses of the new communications technology and, even more, its effect on warfare were as rare then as they are today.

11. H. Thun, *Die Verkehr- und Nachrichtenmittel im Kriege* (Leipzig, 1911), pp. 172–173. The number of words that could be transmitted had grown from six hundred to two thousand per hour.

12. See C. M. Saltzman, "The Signal Corps in War," *Arms and the Man,* 49, 1909, unpaged, and E. D. Peek, "The Necessity and Use of Electrical Communications on the Battlefield," *Journal of the Military Service Institution of the U.S.,* 49, 1911, pp. 327–344.

13. S. Schlichting, ed., *Moltkes Vermächtniss* (Munich, 1901). This book argues in favor of decentralization.

14. Thun, *Die Verkehr- und Nachrichtenmittel,* pp. 184–185.

15. See Schlieffen's letter to his sister Marie, 13.11.1892, in E. Kessel, ed., *Graf Alfred Schlieffen—Briefe* (Göttingen, 1958), pp. 295–296; his speech in honor of the elder Moltke's hundredth birthday in Schlieffen, *Gesammelte Schriften,* vol. II, p. 439; and his summary of a 1904 wargame in his *Dienstschriften* (Berlin, 1937), vol. II, pp. 49–50.

16. "Der Krieg in der Gegenwart," *Gesammelte Schriften,* vol. I, pp. 15–16.

17. Moltke, Jr., *Erinnerungen,* pp. 292, 293.

18. Gröner, *Lebenserinnerungen,* p. 75.

19. According to Moltke's own subsequent account the choice of location was governed by the fact that "I could not take the Kaiser on a tour of France" (though of course this was just what his uncle had done in both 1866 and 1871). H. von Moltke, Jr., *Die deutsche Tragödie an der Marne* (Potsdam, 1934), p. 18.

20. Gröner, *Lebenserinnerungen,* pp. 167–168.

21. For the technical failures of German signals organization in 1914 see especially P. W. Evans, "Strategic Signal Communications . . . the Operations of the German Signal Corps during the March on Paris in 1914," *Signal Corps Bulletin,* 82, 1935, pp. 24–58.

22. Reichsarchiv edition, *Die Weltkrieg* (Berlin, 1921–), vol. I, p. 609; H. von Kuhl and A. von Bergmann, *Movements and Supply of the German*

First Army during August and September 1914 (Fort Leavenworth, Kans., 1935), passim.

23. W. Gröner, *Der Feldherr wider Willen* (Berlin, 1931), p. 130.

24. On the Hentsch mission see W. Müller-Löbnitz, *Die Sendung des Oberstleutnants Hentsch am 8-10 September 1914* (Berlin, 1922); also the remarkable account in K. Strong, *Men of Intelligence* (London, 1970), pp. 13–18.

25. J. Charteris, *At GHQ* (London, 1931), pp. 208–210.

26. Evans, "Strategic Signal Communications," p. 29. The Germans in 1917 had 332,000 miles of wire in the west, 220,000 in the east. The average monthly expenditure was 250 pounds of wire per mile of front. W. Balck, *Development of Tactics—World War* (Fort Leavenworth, 1922), pp. 133–134.

27. Preparing for the battle of the Somme, the British had every important wire forward of divisional headquarters buried six feet deep. In all, 7,000 miles were thus buried. See J. E. Edmonds, ed., *France and Belgium, 1916* (London, 1932), vol. I, p. 286.

28. In *Generalship: Its Diseases and Their Cure* (London, 1937), p. 61.

29. See D. L. Woods, *A History of Tactical Communications* (Orlando, Fla., 1945), pp. 225–226. The sets in use all depended on tall aerials, and were therefore dangerously conspicuous; to use modern jargon, they left a high signature. Before the introduction of three electrode vacuum tubes, moreover, the transmission of voice by wireless was impossible.

30. Borodino figure (60,000 rounds fired by the artillery of either side) from C. Duffy, *Borodino: Napoleon against Russia, 1812* (London, 1972), p. 140.

31. On these aspects of trench warfare see T. Ashworth, *Trench Warfare, 1914-1918* (New York, 1980), pp. 53, 84–85.

32. See J. Keegan, *The Face of Battle* (London, 1976), pp. 215–218.

33. On Haig see N. Dixon, *On the Psychology of Military Incompetence* (London, 1976), especially pp. 249–253. Haig was, by all accounts, well educated, rigid, unimaginative, and scrupulously clean, probably too clean to have visited any headquarters forward of divisional headquarters throughout the war.

34. On the artillery plans see Edmonds, *France and Belgium 1916,* vol. I, pp. 294, 296–297; and vol. II, 567; also M. Middlebrook, *The First Day on the Somme* (New York, 1972), p. 262.

35. "On the whole," wrote battery commander Neil Tyler in his diary for 1 July, "we had a very delightful day, with nothing to do except send numerous reports through to Head Quarters and observe the stupendous spectacle before us. There was nothing to do as regards controlling my

battery fire, as the barrage orders had all been produced beforehand." Quoted in Keegan, *The Face of Battle,* pp. 262–263.

36. Edmonds, *France and Belgium, 1916,* vol. I, appendices 8 and 10.

37. Middlebrook, *The First Day,* p. 144.

38. Rawlinson order, 4 June 1916, quoted in Edmonds, *France and Belgium, 1916,* vol. I, pp. 311–312.

39. Charteris, *At GHQ,* p. 144. In theory, aircraft should have acted as a directed telescope, and many of the pilots did in fact try to work in this capacity, displaying great bravery in flying as low as fifty feet over the ground in the face of small arms fire. In the absence of radiotelephone communication between them and the infantry, however, information could barely be transmitted and even identification was liable to remain uncertain. The planes of 1916, moreover, were not yet equipped with a radio link to base, so that any reports they might deliver were bound to be delayed.

40. On the morning of 1 July, 109th Brigade of Xth Corps won a great success; within an hour of leaving the trenches it had captured the German first line and was ready to carry on. Corps commander General Morland had no way of knowing this, however; not a single divisional commanding officer, deputy, or adjutant had gone forward with the second wave. See A. H. Farrar-Hockley, *The Somme* (Philadelphia, Pa., 1964), pp. 104, 111.

41. On these events see Edmonds, *France and Belgium, 1916,* vol. I, p. 337, and Middlebrook, *The First Day,* p. 163.

42. J. Marshall-Cornwall, *Haig as a Military Commander* (New York, 1971), pp. 196–197.

43. Edmonds, *France and Belgium, 1916,* vol. I, pp. 83–84.

44. *The Laws,* xii, 942A: "The great principle is that no one—should be without a commander; nor should the mind of any one be accustomed to do anything . . . of his own motion, but in war and in peace he should look to and follow his leader, even in the least things being under his guidance . . . there neither is nor ever will be a higher, or better, or more scientific principle than this for the attainment of salvation and victory in war."

45. By 6 August 1916 the British had suffered 120,000 casualties over and above the ordinary losses of trench warfare and were trying to keep the figure a secret: Kiggel to the army commanders, 6 August 1916, the Kiggel Papers, V/31/8, at the Liddell Hart Centre for Military Archives, King's College, London.

46. R. Graves, *Goodbye to All That* (London, 1957), p. 217.

47. It might be argued, nevertheless, that the Somme offensive ended

up by breaking the backbone of the old German Army, whereas the Germans in 1918 achieved only their own exhaustion.

48. For a comparison of the defenses on both sides on both occasions see C. Barnett, *The Swordbearers* (London, 1963), p. 297.

49. On German signaling equipment in 1916–1918 see M. Schwarte, ed., *Die Technik im Weltkrieg* (Berlin, 1920), p. 266.

50. Vagts, *A History of Militarism*, p. 395.

51. See Kuhl, *Der deutsche Generalstab*, pp. 198–199; also A. Praun, *Soldat in der Telegraphen- und Nachrichtentruppe* (Würzburg, 1965), p. 28.

52. Quoted in W. Schall, "Führungsgrundsätze in Armee und Industrie," *Wehrkunde*, 1964, pp. 8–10. All emphases in this and the following quotations are my own.

53. Quoted in Edmonds, *France and Belgium, 1916,* vol. I, p. 298. Compare this to a letter addressed to Kiggel by one of his staff officers in July 1916 in which it is suggested that only a slow, deliberate, step-by-step advance may lead to results and that even the maintenance of secrecy is, therefore, of no account. The Kiggel Papers, iv/3, Liddell Hart Centre for Military Archives, King's College, London.

54. Quoted in Balck, *Development of Tactics,* p. 162–163. I have chosen to quote the U.S. Army translation of 1922, though dated, rather than substitute one of my own. For the importance of "independence" and "initiative" by "all ranks" in defensive fighting, see also E. Ludendorff, *Urkunden der Obersten Heeresleitung* (Berlin, 1922), pp. 606–607. By contrast, Haig at the Somme complained of his troops having too much initiative.

55. Kuhl, *Der deutsche Generalstab,* pp. 201–202.

56. On the strategy of the German offensive see Barnett, *The Swordbearers,* pp. 280–292.

57. E. Ludendorff, *My War Memoirs* (London, n.d.), vol I, pp. 590–591.

58. Much information on the German preparations, particularly concerning the methods to maintain secrecy, is to be found in a collection of German documents translated by the British and thus saved from the fire that destroyed the Potsdam archives in 1945. These are now files PH3/54, PH 3/287, and Msg101/206 at the Bundesarchiv-Militärarchiv, Freiburg i B.

59. In the planning of the German offensive, Corps Headquarters were bypassed. Each division was told to prepare its own plan and report directly to Army Headquarters. Corps remained purely a holding echelon.

60. Printed in Ludendorff, *Urkunden,* pp. 642–645. All emphases are in the original.

61. The directives are quoted from Reichsarchiv ed., *Der Weltkrieg,* vol. XIV, appendix 38a. The figures come from the same source.

62. See the majestic description in Barnett, *The Swordbearers,* pp. 306–307.

63. Rupprecht, Crown Prince of Bavaria, *Mein Kriegstagebuch* (Munich, 1922), pp. 101–105.

64. J. Gies, *Crisis 1918: The Leading Actors, Strategies and Events in the German Gamble for Total Victory on the Western Front* (New York, 1974), p. 83.

65. Ludendorff, *My War Memoirs,* vol. II, pp. 598–599.

66. A. von Thaer, *Generalstabsdienst an der Front und in der O.H.L.* (Göttingen, 1958), p. 172, entry for 25 March 1918. This diary of the chief of staff of IXth Corps, 17th Army, with its extremely detailed editor's notes, is one of the few sources that allow the historian to follow events (though not to understand their significance, for which purpose Thaer was positioned at too low a level) on a day-to-day basis.

67. See van Creveld, *Supplying War,* p. 128.

68. The best account of these techniques, reading almost like a paraphrase of Ludendorff's 1918 directive, is still F. O. Miksche, *Blitzkrieg* (London, 1944).

69. For a worm's-eye view of how things worked in practice see the letter of storm trooper Nikolaus Schulenburg quoted in Gies, *Crisis 1918,* pp. 82–83.

70. For details see J. E. Gascouin, *L'Evolution de l'Artillerie pendant la Guerre Mondiale* (Paris, 1920), pp. 210–216.

71. In front of Acre in 1800 Napoleon kept himself supplied with ammunition by having enemy cannonball collected, paying five sous for every one brought in.

72. It may not be an unimportant fact that such situations were most common in the colonial wars immediately preceding World War I, and that the British had more experience in colonial warfare than did anyone else. As Hilaire Belloc put it nicely: "Whatever happens we have got / The Maxim Gun, and they have not." Quoted in J. Ellis, *The Social History of the Machine Gun* (London, 1973), p. 94, which also describes many massacres.

6. MASTERS OF MOBILE WARFARE

1. Coupled with a few demographic data, these figures could plausibly be interpreted to the effect that Russia would be unable to equip the vast armies it was about to raise; that France and Britain together were economically superior, but militarily about equal, to Germany alone; and that the United States had the potential to dwarf everybody else.

2. J. Wheldon, *Machine Age Armies* (London, 1968), p. 26.

3. R. G. Ruppenthal, *Logistical Support of the Armies* (Washington, D.C., 1953), vol. II, pp. 419 and 421.

4. Least affected of all was the speed of tactical movement, which even today hardly exceeds that of a man walking.

5. See the German Heeresdienstschrift 300, *Truppenführung* (Berlin, 1936), vol. I, paragraphs 10 and 13: "The emptiness of the battlefield demands independently thinking and acting warriors who exploit each situation in a considered, determined and bold way . . . from the youngest soldier upward, the independent commitment of all spiritual, intellectual, and physical faculties is demanded."

6. The best analysis of these questions, which can be faulted only on grounds of excessive brevity, is E. N. Luttwak, "The Strategy of the Tank," in *Strategy and Politics* (New Brunswick, N.J., 1980), especially pp. 299–302.

7. Without wireless, World War I tanks—their crews isolated in noisy steel boxes, and sometimes communicating with each other by means of hammer blows on the head—were totally deaf and almost entirely blind, a factor that does as much as anything to explain their relative ineffectiveness. To try and remedy these faults, Fuller says, senior Tank Corps officers regularly accompanied their men into battle; but they were the only officers who did, and the effect necessarily remained somewhat limited. See H. Blume, ed., *Die Führungstruppen der Wehrmacht* (Berlin, 1937), pp. 167–168.

8. For a good, though nontechnical, account of the problems associated with the use of radio for command purposes, see S. Bidwell, *Modern Warfare* (London, 1973), particularly pp. 79–89.

9. See for example C. Messenger, *The Art of Blitzkrieg* (London, 1976).

10. On the two men and their achievement see K. Macksey, *Guderian, Panzer General* (London, 1976), especially pp. 66–67. Macksey correctly emphasizes that the development of a command system and a proper radio-based signals service were as vital to the development of the Blitzkrieg as were the tanks themselves.

11. Before finally deciding to concentrate on the Israeli example I researched Patton's command system, with unsurprising results. Patton, to begin with, made sure that his principal aides met him, and each other, informally each morning to discuss the day's operations before proceeding to the larger and more formal staff conference of 3rd Army. In converting Colonel Fickett's Cavalry Group for closely following subordinate units and listening in to their radio networks (the so-called Household Cavalry), and by having his chief of staff arrange for each member of the staff to visit the front once a week with a list of predetermined questions to ask, Patton possessed a directed telescope of unrivaled excellence. This in turn enabled 3rd Army to demand, and receive, fewer reports than did the rival 1st Army, a fact that can be statistically proved from the records held at the National Archives. Moreover, statistical analysis can be employed to show that 3rd Army made less frequent use of top-priority communications than did other headquarters, which was both cause and effect of a less centralized method of command. Trusting his staff—who, following the formal and informal morning briefings, were thoroughly familiar with his ideas and, as important, confident of his support—Patton was able to get away from headquarters during most of the day, visiting subordinate units and raising morale by means that were as effective as they were unorthodox. As he himself summed it all up in his farewell speech to his staff, no other Allied commander at his level had so much free time at his disposal. See boxes RG-2046 and RG 94-10823, as well as the TUSA and FUSA After Action Reports, the National Archives, Suitland, Md.; Patton's own *War as I Knew It* (London, n.d.); O. W. Koch and R. G. Hays, *G-2: Intelligence for Patton* (Philadelphia, Pa., 1971); R. S. Allen, *Lucky Forward* (New York, 1947); C. R. Codman, *Drive* (Boston, 1957); H. H. Semmes, *Portrait of Patton* (New York, 1955); H. Essame, *Patton: A Study in Command* (New York, 1974); H. M. Cole, *The Lorraine Campaign* (Washington, D.C., 1950); and M. Blumenson, ed., *The Patton Papers* (Washington, D.C., 1961). Martin Blumenson also spent the best part of an afternoon sharing some of his ideas on Patton with me, for which I am grateful.

12. See E. N. Luttwak and D. Horowitz, *The Israeli Army* (London, 1975), pp. 53–59, 161–164; D. Horowitz, "Flexible Responsiveness and Military Strategy: The Case of the Israeli Army," *Policy Sciences,* vol. I, 1970, pp. 191–205; and R. Gissin, "Command, Control and Communications Technology: Changing Patterns of Leadership in Combat Organizations," Ph.D. diss., Syracuse University, 1979.

13. M. Gur, "The IDF—Continuity versus Innovation" (Hebrew), *Maarachot,* March 1978, pp. 4–6.

14. In November 1947 the nascent IDF was said to have possessed 49,000 men for whom, however, it only had 14–20,000 small arms, 200 machine guns, and 700 light and 200 medium mortars. Figures from T. N. Dupuy, *Elusive Victory: The Arab-Israeli Wars, 1947–1974* (New York, 1978), p. 8.

15. The most outstanding of these incidents was the decision of the commanding general, Southern Front, Assaf Simhoni, to throw 7th Armored Brigade into the battle twenty-four hours earlier than had been planned. Being out of touch—the radio equipment carried on his jeep had not the range to communicate with Simhoni—Dayan was unable to stop the move and learned of it only after it had taken place.

16. Dayan, *Diary,* pp. 39–40, 43, 60.

17. Ibid., pp. 112–115.

18. Ibid., pp. 97–99. Though unauthorized, Sharon's move may be defended on the ground that his brigade's position at the Parker Memorial was hopelessly exposed to a possible counterattack by Egyptian armor. See B. Amidror, "The Mitla: The Fire Trap" (Hebrew), *Haolam Hazeh,* 9.10.1974, pp. 16–17, 26.

19. As far as the Israelis could find out, the Egyptian plans for defending the Sinai were based on a thorough historical-geographic study of all possible axes of invasion, each of which was then carefully fortified. High-level headquarters assigned each man and each gun to a position and rehearsed the rapid manning of those positions. Once in position, the individual soldier was provided with sufficient water, food, and ammunition, as well as spare weapons, to hold out without either comrades or commanders—in other words, without command. In the event, Israeli attempts at deception notwithstanding, most of the fortified positions were occupied in good time. Once this had been done, command from above virtually came to an end and the Egyptian commanders, left with nothing to do, took to their heels. It was, one Israeli officer wrote, like playing chess against an opponent who was allowed to make but one move for every two of one's own. See M. Illan, "The Use of Surprise in the Sinai Campaign" (Hebrew), *Maarachot,* October 1966, pp. 23–27.

20. For a discussion of these lessons see Luttwak and Horowitz, *The Israeli Army,* pp. 149–152.

21. Ibid., pp. 190–191; also S. Teveth, *The Tanks of Tamuz* (London, 1969), chap. 9.

22. Y. Rabin, "After the Great Maneuvers" (Hebrew), *Maarachot,* Aug. 1960, pp. 6–9. The emphasis is Rabin's.

23. M. Gur, "The Experiences of Sinai" (Hebrew), *Maarachot,* Oct. 1966, pp. 17–22.

24. This and the following paragraph are based on my interview with General Gavish in Tel Aviv on 7 February 1982.

25. On the average, Gavish says, he spoke to each of the divisional commanders once every thirty minutes.

26. The staff sections followed Generals Tal and Yoffe, operating in the north and center respectively. General Sharon in the south did not have a directed telescope aimed at him, and in fact his role in the campaign was largely confined to the first twenty-four hours.

27. Apart from some rocket-carrying Fouga trainers assigned to him in order to assist General Tal's armored breakthrough on the first day, Southern Front had no organic air support. Each morning the Command was informed of the number of sorties it would be allocated during the day, though this might be changed later. It was then a question of distributing the sorties among the divisions. Coordination was achieved by means of a moving "bombing line" beyond which the Air Force was free to do as it pleased. Within the bombing line sorties had to be coordinated with the divisional commanders who would ask for strikes of type X at place Y. Detailed tactical coordination was in the hands of Forward Air Controllers attached to each division.

28. On the difference in the way that Sharon and Tal planned their battles see B. Amidror, "The Race for El Arish" (Hebrew), *Haolam Hazeh,* 18.12.1974, pp. 11, 26.

29. In 1967, Gavish remembers, interference by General Headquarters was minimal. Rabin and his deputy, General Bar Lev, each visited Southern Command once. They were briefed on the situation each time but made no on-the-spot decisions.

30. B. Amidror, "Gorodish's Error" (Hebrew), *Haolam Hazeh,* 26.2.1975, pp. 18–19.

31. A similar episode took place in the Jordan Valley, where an armored force crossed the river without waiting for permission and had to be recalled. See M. Dayan, *Story of My Life* (London, 1976), p. 370. In this and many of the following references, I was confronted with the problem that many of the translations of Hebrew books into English are bad to the point that the original meaning is lost. I therefore normally gave the English page number, but the translation is often my own.

32. Even as late as 1964 a surplus of manpower made a choice between selective service and a shorter period of conscription necessary. Though purely military considerations pointed to the former solution, the latter was chosen for social reasons.

33. The 1967 figures are from N. Safran, *From War to War* (New York, 1968), appendix B, pp. 441–444. The 1973 figures are from Inter-

national Institute for Strategic Studies, *The Military Balance, 1973–1974* (London, 1973), p. 30.

34. International Institute for Strategic Studies, *The Military Balance, 1981–1982,* pp. 30–31. If the *mobilized* strength of the Bundeswehr is taken as a basis for calculation, however, the figures drop to 2,160 and 343.

35. A. Adan, *On the Banks of the Suez* (n.p., 1980), p. 7.

36. The construction of the Bar Lev Line was opposed by Generals Tal and Sharon, both of whom argued that the Sinai was best defended by a combination of patrols in front and armored fists in the rear. When Elazar replaced Bar Lev as chief of staff in 1972, Sharon, now GOC South, implemented this policy by evacuating and sealing some of the strongholds. Gonen, taking over from Sharon in the summer of 1973, reversed the latter's policy and started reopening and remanning the fortifications. See A. Dolav, "The 8th of October of General Gonen" (Hebrew), *Maariv,* 7.2.1975, pp. 23, 27.

37. C. Herzog, *The War of Atonement* (London, 1977), p. 53.

38. See the Agranat Committee Report (Hebrew), printed in *Haaretz,* 30.1.1975; also Z. Schiff, *October Earthquake: Yom Kippur, 1973* (Tel Aviv, 1974), pp. 78–79.

39. Herzog, *The War of Atonement,* pp. 156–157.

40. For the story of those brigades see ibid., pp. 163–167.

41. Ibid., p. 182.

42. H. Bar Tov, *Dado: Forty-Eight Years and Twenty Days* (Tel Aviv, 1978), vol. II, p. 59. Since the English version of this book has been heavily abridged I have used the Hebrew one instead.

43. Dayan, *Story of My Life,* p. 500.

44. Herzog, *The War of Atonement,* pp. 182–183. On this meeting see also Schiff, *October Earthquake,* pp. 91–92, and Bar Tov, *Dado,* pp. 59–60. Dayan himself claims to remember only "drinking a great deal of black coffee" with Gonen.

45. Adan, *On the Banks of the Suez,* p. 61.

46. Bar Tov, *Dado,* vol. II, pp. 61–62.

47. Ibid., p. 62.

48. Dayan, *Story of My Life,* pp. 63–65.

49. Bar Tov, *Dado,* vol. II, pp. 63–65.

50. Ibid. While Bartov's account of this episode is confused, there can be no doubt that Elazar was less optimistic than his principal subordinates in the south and did not intend to allow them to attack before 8 October at the earliest.

51. Ibid., vol. II, p. 66.

52. G. Meir, *My Life* (London, 1975), pp. 360–361. Dayan's account of the meeting is in *Story of My Life,* pp. 500–501. See also Herzog, *The War of Atonement,* p. 183.

53. This account of the meeting is based on Bar Tov, *Dado,* vol. II, pp. 66–67.

54. Ibid., pp. 70–71. Schiff, *October Earthquake,* pp. 79–80, 90–91, has a rather confused account according to which the air strikes were ordered by Elazar in person around 1400 hours. If this is correct, then the mere two and a half hours from the time the orders were issued to the reported destruction of the bridges seems very brief, while GHQ's readiness to believe Peled's report shows how overconfident they really were.

55. Quoted in Dupuy, *Elusive Victory,* p. 413, footnote.

56. Adan, *On the Banks of the Suez,* p. 95.

57. Ibid., p. 60. Since the Soviet bridging equipment used by the Egyptians was designed to carry only the comparatively light Soviet tanks, not the much heavier American ones used by the Israelis, it is doubtful whether a crossing of the Egyptian bridges would have been practicable in any case.

58. This account of the meeting is based on Adan, *On the Banks of the Suez,* pp. 95–100; Bartov, *Dado,* vol. II, pp. 73–75; Dayan, *Story of My Life,* pp. 503–504; and Herzog, *The War of Atonement,* p. 184.

59. Adan, *On the Banks of the Suez,* p. 117.

60. A. Sella, "Soviet Training and Arab Performance," *Jerusalem Post Magazine,* 8.2.1974, pp. 6–7.

61. See on this the exceptionally interesting article by Lt. Col. Zeev, "The Entire System Was Creaking" (Hebrew), *Maarachot,* April 1979, pp. 6–11.

62. Bar Tov, *Dado,* vol. II, p. 78. Various estimates took into account as many as 900 Israeli tanks in the Sinai, against the actual 500 (many of which were still on their way), and 500 Egyptian ones instead of the actual 600.

63. Adan, *On the Banks of the Suez,* p. 100; Herzog, *The War of Atonement,* p. 184.

64. Bar Tov, *Dado,* vol. II, pp. 97–99.

65. Adan, *On the Banks of the Suez,* p. 107.

66. Bartov, *Dado,* vol. II, p. 87.

67. Adan, *On the Banks of the Suez,* p. 115.

68. Ibid., pp. 112–113. On this exchange see also the article by E. Tavor, "The Longest Day" (Hebrew), *Haolam Hazeh,* 11.12.1974, pp. 18–19, 22.

69. See B. Amidror, "A Foolish Plan" (Hebrew), *Haolam Hazeh,* 20.8.1975, pp. 14–15, and the same author's "Firing from the Hip" (Hebrew), *Haolam Hazeh,* 20.8.1975, pp. 8–9, 43–44.

70. An Israeli tank battalion consisted of twenty-four tanks, so that Adan had around two hundred tanks if those attached to his own and brigade headquarters are included.

71. Adan, *On the Banks of the Suez,* p. 119.

72. Ibid., p. 119.

73. Ibid., p. 120. Also A. Dolav, "The Eighth of October of General Gonen" (Hebrew), *Maariv,* 7.2.1975, pp. 23, 27. This is the only account in which Gonen speaks for himself.

74. Dolav, "The Eighth of October," p. 23.

75. B. Amidror, "The Fist Disintegrates" (Hebrew), *Haolam Hazeh,* 25.6.1975, pp. 32–33.

76. Adan, *On the Banks of the Suez,* p. 120.

77. Ibid., p. 121. Bar Tov, *Dado,* vol. II, p. 93, has a slightly different version according to which it was Ben Ari (not Gonen) who spoke to Adan and told him to link up with Hizayon first and then to proceed to Matzmed and cross there.

78. Dolav, "The Eighth of October," p. 23. According to Adan, *On the Banks of the Suez,* p. 121, Gonen actually said that he (Adan) was getting air support—an account that, if true, illustrates the extent of mutual incomprehension.

79. Adan, *On the Banks of the Suez,* p. 122.

80. Ibid.

81. Ibid., p. 123.

82. Z. Schiff, "Tactical Intelligence Difficulties in Disseminating Information" (Hebrew), *Haaretz,* 14.2.1975, p. 2.

83. Dolav, "The Eighth of October," p. 27; Amidror, "The Fist Disintegrates," p. 33.

84. Z. Sternhall, "Hamutal as an Example" (Hebrew), *Haaretz,* 2.2.1975, p. 2.

85. Tavor, "The Longest Day," p. 19. It must be added that Sharon's men, watching from Havraga, also thought things were going well; B. Kedar. *The Story of "Mahatz" Battalion* (Hebrew) (Tel Aviv, 1975), p. 19.

86. Adan, *On the Banks of the Suez,* p. 129.

87. The same factor may also explain why it was possible for Elazar to believe he could attack with a single weak division, cross at four or five points, and yet be strong enough to avoid being cut off at any one of them.

88. Bar Tov, *Dado,* vol. II, p. 97.

89. Ibid., pp. 98–99. Adan, *On the Banks of the Suez,* p. 131, combines the two conversations into one.

90. So Bar Tov, *Dado,* vol. II, p. 98. Adan, according to his own account, was reading the situation far more pessimistically and failed to understand what Southern Command was so happy about.

91. Ibid.

92. Adan, *On the Banks of Suez,* pp. 123–126.

93. Adan, *On the Banks of the Suez,* pp. 135–136. According to another account, Adini, who saw Amir withdraw, asked Gabi permission to do likewise but was told to charge instead. Amidror, "The Fist Disintegrates," p. 32.

94. Tavor, "The Longest Day," p. 19.

95. See Adan, *On the Banks of the Suez,* pp. 124–127. This episode with its ruinous effect on morale is also described in Kedar, *The Story of "Mahatz" Battalion,* p. 20. As signals NCO with the battalion that was to be assigned to Adan, he was able to follow the entire exchange on radio.

96. Adan, *On the Banks of the Suez,* pp. 156–157.

97. The commander of this battalion later claimed he had received no orders, and Adan in his memoirs does not directly contradict him. See M. Talmai, "The 8th October of Asaf Yagouri" (Hebrew), *Maariv,* 7.2.1975, pp. 4–6, 45.

98. Adan, *On the Banks of the Suez,* p. 140; A. Yagouri, *To Be with Them, They're All Mine* (Hebrew) (Tel Aviv, 1979), pp. 12, 72–75. Attacking over the same terrain where Adini had previously been defeated, though without knowing it, Yagouri was easily targeted by the Egyptian artillery and destroyed.

99. U. Millstein, "The Day That Was: The 8th of October" (Hebrew), *Maariv,* 7.2.1975, pp. 10–11, and Z. Schiff, "Notes on the 8th of October" (Hebrew), *Haaretz,* 7.2.1975.

100. Adan, *On the Banks of the Suez,* pp. 148–151.

101. Agranat Committee's Report, 30 January 1975. The "Peter Principle" refers to a system under which a man climbs the ladder of an organization on the basis of his performance in the previous position instead of his suitability for the new one.

102. Some mathematical calculations concerning the quality of the Israeli soldier, compared to his Arab opponents, in 1967 and 1973 may be found in T. N. Dupuy, "The Arab-Israeli Conflict: A Military Analysis," *Strategy and Tactics,* no. 90, Jan./Feb. 1982, pp. 39–48, 57. By the time Israel invaded Lebanon in 1982, however, the quality of its junior officers had deteriorated markedly, with the result that optional control had

313

to be replaced by very strict drill. The results were unimaginative tactics and a drastic decline in comparative performance.

103. On the Golan Heights, where personal relations were much better, no such problems appeared.

104. By comparison, the commander at the Golan Heights spoke to his superior only three to four times a day, and then mainly to ask for news from other fronts. (Interview with Lieutenant General Rafael Eytan, Tel Aviv, 29 April 1982.)

105. Some systems that come to mind are the All Source Analysis System (ASAS); the AN/TPQ-37 artillery locating radar; the Remotely Piloted Vehicle/Target Acquisition/Designation System; and, outside the United States, the various target acquisition radars and remotely piloted vehicles operated by the Israelis in Lebanon.

106. See P. T. Rhona, "Weapon Systems and Information War" (Seattle, Wash., 1976), especially pp. 10–14. This paper argues, persuasively, that information flows within any given command system constitute so many vulnerable spots waiting to be jammed, overloaded, or spoofed by the enemy.

7. THE HELICOPTER AND THE COMPUTER

1. A World War II P-51 Mustang fighter bomber, for example, cost $50,000, the F-4 Phantom in 1965 around $1,000,000.

2. This and all subsequent figures are from H. Wool, *The Military Specialist* (Baltimore, 1968), chap. 3.

3. This attempt to measure complexity is naturally offered only as a rough guide. For a discussion of the relationship between an organization's size, its level of technological development, and its complexity see R. M. Marsh and H. Mannari, "Technology and Size as Determinants of the Organizational Structure of Japanese Factories," *Administrative Science Quarterly,* 26, 1981, pp. 35–37.

4. See van Creveld, *Fighting Power,* especially chap. 12.

5. This instability and its results are well documented in R. A. Gabriel and P. L. Savage, *Crisis in Command: Mismanagement in the Army* (New York, 1978).

6. W. C. Westmoreland, *A Soldier Reports* (Garden City, N.Y., 1976), pp. 296–297.

7. On the reorganization of the Pentagon under McNamara see C. W. Borklund, *Men of the Pentagon* (New York, 1966), p. 215, and J. Raymond, *Power at the Pentagon* (New York, 1964), p. 293.

8. L. Hazlewood, J. J. Hayes, and J. R. Bronwell, "Planning for

Problems in Crisis Management: An Analysis of Post 1945 Behavior in the U. S. Department of Defense," *International Studies Quarterly,* 21, 1977, pp. 75–106.

9. See Gissin, "Command, Control and Communications," pp. 196–200.

10. T. M. Rienzi, *Vietnam Studies: Communications-Electronics 1962–1970* (Washington, D.C., 1972), p. 57.

11. J. H. Hay, *Vietnam Studies: Tactical and Material Innovations* (Washington, D.C., 1974), p. 82.

12. After many years during which teleprinter speeds had been frozen at 100 words per minute, new equipment permitting speeds of up to 3,000 words per minute was introduced during the late 1960s.

13. Wool, *The Military Specialist,* p. 42.

14. These and subsequent figures are from Rienzi, *Communications-Electronics,* p. 159.

15. On the techniques and assumptions of systems analysis as practiced in the Pentagon during these years, see A. Enthoven and K. Wayne Smith, *How Much Is Enough? Shaping the Defense Program, 1961–1969* (New York, 1971), especially pp. 10–30 and 45–47.

16. See for example G. Palmer, *The McNamara Strategy and the Vietnam War* (Westport, Ct., 1978), pp. 3–18. For a balanced but nontechnical assessment of the technique by one who helped originate it see S. Zuckerman, "Judgement and Control in War," *Foreign Affairs,* 40, 1962, especially p. 205 ff.

17. This is true even according to those who did try to use the method in Vietnam. J. Ewell and I. A. Hunt, *Sharpening the Combat Edge: The Use of Analysis to Reinforce Military Judgement* (Washington, D.C., 1974), p. 233 and passim. When he moved from division to corps command, Ewell says, the method lost most of its usefulness.

18. Enthoven and Smith, *How Much Is Enough?,* pp. 270–306. On the role of the OSA see also T. C. Thayer, *How to Analyze a War without Fronts: Vietnam, 1965–1972* (Washington, D.C., 1972), passim; and Palmer, *The McNamara Strategy,* chap. 4.

19. See B. M. Jenkins, "The Unchangeable War," RAND Paper RM-6278-ARPA (Santa Monica, Cal., 1972), pp. 8–9.

20. It was only in May 1968, after endless infighting, that a compromise was worked out under which sorties by Marine Corps aircraft were divided between the Marines and MACV on a 30 percent/70 percent basis.

21. D. Kinnard, *The War Managers* (Hanover, N.H., 1977), pp. 59–63. Nevertheless, standard operating procedures for air-ground cooperation

called for the Army to submit detailed requests for support (to include target location, type of target, friendly troop situation, and so on) at 1000 hours each day for the next day. Such long lead times were impossible to maintain, with the result that the plan existed in name only and sorties were routinely diverted at the last moment.

22. See Westmoreland, *A Soldier Reports,* pp. 75–77; and G. S. Eckhardt, *Vietnam Studies: Command and Control* (Washington, D.C., 1974), pp. 61–63.

23. *The Pentagon Papers,* ed. Senator Gravel (Boston, n.d.), vol. IV, p. 395.

24. Asked how he felt about Westmoreland's monthly campaign plans, one corps-level U.S. commander responded, "I never read them, they would only confuse me." Kinnard, *The War Managers,* p. 58.

25. E. B. Ferguson, *Westmoreland: The Inevitable General* (Boston, 1968), chap. 1, describes the routine.

26. Rienzi, *Communications-Electronics,* p. 169.

27. Fighter-bomber pilots, for example, were encouraged to take the shortest, rather than the safest, route to the target. Gissin, "Command, Control, and Communications," pp. 297–300.

28. Westmoreland, *A Soldier Reports,* pp. 185–186.

29. D. A. Starry, *Vietnam Studies: Mounted Combat in Vietnam* (Washington, D.C., 1978), pp. 181–182.

30. Ibid.

31. *The Pentagon Papers,* vol. IV, pp. 530, 531.

32. J. A. McChristian, *Vietnam Studies: The Role of Military Intelligence, 1965–1967* (Washington, D.C., 1974), pp. 34–37.

33. Rienzi, *Communications-Electronics,* pp. 27–29.

34. J. J. Tolson, *Vietnam Studies: Airmobility* (Washington, D.C., 1973), pp. 128, 200.

35. FUSA After Action Report, 23.2–9.5.1945, annex 8.

36. Rienzi, *Communications-Electronics,* p. 81.

37. By "information pathology" is meant the inability of organizations to obtain a clear, timely picture of their surroundings and their own functioning, owing to structural defects. See H. L. Wilensky, *Organizational Intelligence: Knowledge and Policy in Government and Industry* (New York, 1967), especially chap. 3.

38. Rienzi, *Communications-Electronics,* p. 161.

39. Paradoxically, the proliferation of high-secrecy communications was coupled with the free use of radio in the field regardless of security, a situation that is perhaps best understood as an instinctive attempt on the part of the troops to get through the information pathologies.

40. W. Scott Thompson and D. D. Frizzel, *The Lessons of Vietnam* (New York, 1977), pp. 179–180.

41. Tolson, *Airmobility*, pp. 165–179.

42. Compiled and kindly given me by Dr. David Thomas, Washington, D.C.

43. The preliminary planning for the Entebbe rescue operation was actually carried out by the then chief of staff, General Gur, on his own initiative and before he was even told what the sudden summons to the prime minister was all about. Y. Rabin, *Memoirs* (Tel Aviv, 1977), vol. II, pp. 525–526.

44. Clausewitz, *On War*, vol. I, pp. 95–97. The word "strategy" derives from the Greek *stratos*, meaning "army" or "host." From this comes *strategos*, a general, *strategia*, his post or term of office, sometimes also meaning "generalship," and *strategema*, a ruse of war.

45. One of the first attempts to understand warfare in such terms is J. F. C. Fuller, *Armament and History* (New York, 1945).

46. Ironically, body count was first introduced by MACV in an attempt to convince skeptical journalists that its reports of "victories" were accurate. This did not prevent it from turning into a highly unreliable indicator and the butt of every kind of guided and misguided criticism. See Kinnard, *The War Managers*, pp. 68–75.

47. See Thayer, *How to Analyze*, pp. 854–855.

48. It has been claimed that, even as late as 1968, there were only some thirty "experts" on Vietnam in American universities, of whom perhaps twelve possessed a thorough knowledge of the language.

49. The obvious remedy—dividing incidents into those initiated by friendly forces and those initiated by hostile ones—would not work, since a drop in, for instance, enemy-initiated incidents might mean (again, among several other things) either that he was too weak to attack or that he was too strong to need to.

50. All these examples are from Thayer, *How to Analyze*, passim.

51. Ibid., p. 722; and *The Pentagon Papers*, vol. IV, pp. 456–458, 468–469, 478.

52. D. R. Palmer, *Summons of the Trumpet* (San Rafael, Cal., 1978), pp. 143–144; M. Mylander, *The Generals* (New York, 1974), p. 194; Kinnard, *The War Managers*, pp. 55–56; Hay, *Tactical and Material Innovations*, p. 84; Scott Thompson and Frizzel, *The Lessons of Vietnam*, pp. 176–177; Bradford and Brown, *The U.S. Army*, pp. 236–237.

53. R. Thompson, *No Exit from Vietnam* (London, 1969), p. 136.

54. Nevertheless, watching a battlefield from the air is by no means the same as experiencing it from the ground, a fact that many a contemporary commander would do well to remember.

55. Westmoreland, *A Soldier Reports*, pp. 269–271.

56. Newsmen in Vietnam were provided with free military transportation on the basis of space available.

57. P. Braestrup, *Big Story: How the American Press and Television Reported and Interpreted the Crisis of Tet 1968 in Vietnam and Washington* (Boulder, Colo., 1977), vol. I, p. xxix.

58. One proposal for an alternative chain of command is put forward by S. L. Canby, B. Jenkins, and R. B. Raincy, "Alternative Strategy and Force Structure in Vietnam," RAND Paper D 19073 ARPA (Santa Monica, Cal., 1969), appendix A, pp. 29–37. Here it is suggested that the span of control of battalion and brigade should have been increased to five and divisions all but eliminated, resulting in a more flexible command structure and reducing the information flow.

59. Rienzi, *Communications-Electronics*, p. 157.

60. For some figures on the waste involved, such as seventy-five bombs and $400,000 to kill a single enemy soldier, see *Life* magazine, 27.1.1967, and the *New York Times*, 7.12.1967. Even then, of course, it might be argued that many of those killed were not enemy troops at all and that the results of killing them were, if anything, counterproductive.

61. Significantly, U.S. performance in terms of enemy troops killed versus ordnance expended improved dramatically after Westmoreland was replaced by Abrams and a halt was called to large-scale search and destroy operations. See D. S. Blaufarb, *The Counterinsurgency Era: U.S. Doctrine and Performance* (New York, 1977), p. 254.

8. CONCLUSION: REFLECTIONS ON COMMAND

1. *The Histories*, ix.12.7–10.

2. *On War*, vol. I, p. 75.

3. See J. D. Steinbrunner, *The Cybernetic Theory of Decision: New Dimensions of Political Analysis* (Princeton, N.J., 1974), especially pp. 327–342, for an exceptionally penetrating discussion of the effect of cognitive factors on the way that information is processed by the human mind.

4. For some of the logical problems involved, see M. I. Handel, "Intelligence and Deception," *Journal of Strategic Studies*, 5, 1982, p. 164.

5. In 1939–1945 the German Wehrmacht was able to fight World War II—and, from a strictly military point of view, fight as well as any force in history—with only 3 percent of all troops in staffs of various kinds. By 1975, the proportion of *Führungstruppen* in the West German Bundeswehr had risen to 14 percent.

6. The idea that uncertainty governs the structure of organizations is

known as the contingency theory of organization. See J. Galbraith, *Designing Complex Organizations* (Reading, Mass., 1973), especially chaps. 1 and 2.

7. Creativity, psychologists believe, consists of putting things together in new and unforeseen ways. Conversely, the precision associated with formal communications systems is achieved by limiting the number of ways in which things can be put together and preventing new ones from arising. See the analysis in J. F. Crovitz, *Galton's Walk* (New York, 1970), especially pp. 98–102.

8. See for example P. Mallorie, "Command, Control, Communications," *NATO's Fifteen Nations,* 27 July 1981, pp. 42–45.

9. J. R. Rowland, "Combat Readiness: Fifty Percent," *Armor,* May–June 1982, pp. 42–43. If this system is combined with one in which subordinates are independent, moreover, not even the loss of this headquarters need lead to disaster.

10. For a good discussion of technological determinism see L. Winner, *Autonomous Technology* (Cambridge, Mass., 1977), especially chaps. 1–3.

WORKS CITED

Though this study is based on a large number of sources in fields as diverse as classical history and computer science, the following list includes only those works quoted in the notes. The sources are listed alphabetically without regard to the period to which each belongs and also without regard to whether the work is primary or secondary, published or archival, a "serious" scholarly study or newspaper gossip.

Adan, A., *On the Banks of the Suez* (n.p., 1980).

Adcock, F. E., *The Greek and Macedonian Art of War* (Berkeley, 1957).

Agranat Committee Report (Hebrew), *Haaretz,* 30.1.1975.

Alban, J. R., "Spies and Spying in the Fourteenth Century," in Allmand, C. T., ed., *War, Literature and Politics in the Middle Ages* (Liverpool, 1976).

Albrecht, O., "Kurze Geschichte des militärischen Karten- und Vermessungswesens bis zum Anfang des ersten Weltkrieges," *Fachdienstliche Mitteilungen des . . . Militärgeographischen Dienst,* pp. 3–34.

Allen, R. S., *Lucky Forward* (New York, 1947).

Allgemeine Militärische Zeitschrift, 1855, nos. 27–28, 73, 74; 1859, nos. 39–40, 41–42.

Alombert, P. C., and Colin, J., *La Campagne de 1805 en Allemagne* (Paris, 1902).

Amidror, B., "Firing from the Hip" (Hebrew), *Haolam Hazeh,* 20.8.1975, pp. 8–9, 43–44.

——— "The Fist Disintegrates" (Hebrew), *Haolem Hazeh,* 25.6.1975, pp. 32–33, 35.

———— "A Foolish Plan" (Hebrew), *Haolem Hazeh,* 1.6.1975, pp. 14–15, 46.

———— "Gorodish's Error" (Hebrew), *Haolem Hazeh,* 26.2.1975, pp. 18–19.

———— "The Mitla: The Fire Trap" (Hebrew), *Haolem Hazeh,* 9.10.1974, pp. 16–17, 26.

———— "The Race for El Arish" (Hebrew), *Haolem Hazeh,* 18.12.1974, pp. 10–11, 26.

Ammianus Marcellinus, *Historiae* (London, 1950–1952).

Anderson, J. K., *Military Theory and Practice in the Age of Xenophon* (Berkeley, 1970).

Appianus, *Roman History* (London, 1958–1964).

Arrian, *Anabasis* (London, 1964–1966).

Ashworth, T., *Trench Warfare 1914–1918* (New York, 1980).

Athenaios, *Deipnosophists* (London, 1927–).

Balck, W., *Development of Tactics—World War* (Fort Leavenworth, Kans., 1922).

Barker, T. M., *The Military Intellectual and Battle: Raimondo Montecuccoli and the Thirty Years War* (Albany, N.Y., 1975).

Bar Kochva, B., *The Seleucid Army* (London, 1976).

Barnett, C., *The Swordbearers* (London, 1963).

Bar Tov, H., *Dado: Forty-Eight Years and Twenty Days* (Hebrew) (Tel Aviv, 1977).

Basta, G., *Il governo della cavalleria leggiera* (Frankfurt am Main, 1612).

Beaumont, R. A., "Command Method: A Gap in Military Historiography," *Naval War College Review,* winter 1979, pp. 61–63.

Beer, S., *Brain of the Firm* (New York, 1972).

Beha ed Din, *Life of Saladin,* in C. W. Wilson, ed., *Palestine Pilgrims' Texts Society* (London, 1897), vol. XI.

Belden, T. G., "Indications, Warning and Crisis Operations," *International Studies Quarterly,* 21, 1977, pp. 181–190.

Bellum Africanum (London, 1964).

Bellum Civile (London, 1966).

Bellum Hispanicum (London, 1958–1964).

Berenhorst, C. H. von, *Betrachtungen über die Kriegskunst* (Osnabrück, rprt. 1972).

Bernhardi, T. von, *On War of Today* (New York, 1972).

———— *Tagebuchblätter* (Leipzig, 1897).

Bidwell, S., *Modern Warfare* (London, 1973).

Blaufarb, D. S., *The Counterinsurgency Era: U.S. Doctrine and Performance* (New York, 1972).

Blume, H., ed., *Die Führungstruppen der Wehrmacht* (Berlin, 1937).

Blumenson, M., ed., *The Patton Papers* (Washington, D.C., 1961).

Blumenthal, K. von, *Tagebücher* (Stuttgart, 1902).

Boehm, H. von, *Generalstabsgeschäfte: Ein Handbuch für Offiziere aller Waffen* (Potsdam, 1862).

Bonnal, H., *La Manouevre de Iéna* (Paris, 1904).

Borklund, C. W., *Men of the Pentagon* (New York, 1966).

Bourcet, P., *Memoires historiques sur la guerre que les Francois ont soutenue en Allemagne de puis 1757 j'usqua en 1762* (Paris, 1797).

────── *Principes de la guerre des montagnes* (Paris, 1775).

Bourrienne, M., *Memoirs of Napoleon Bonaparte* (London, n.d.).

Boutarice, E., *Institutions militaires de la France avant les armées permanents* (Paris, 1863).

Bradford, Z. B., and Brown, F. J., *The U.S. Army in Transition* (Beverly Hills, Cal., 1973).

Braestrup, P., *Big Story: How the American Press and Television Reported and Interpreted the Crisis of Tet 1968 in Vietnam and Washington, D.C.* (Boulder, Colo., 1977).

Brauer, H. C., "Die Entwicklung des Nachrichtenverkehrs," diss., Nuremberg, 1957.

Bronsart von Schellendorff, P., *Der Dienst des Generalstabes,* 3rd ed. (Berlin, 1893).

Bucholtz, "Uber die Tätigkeit der Feldtelegraphen in den jüngsten Kriegen," *Militär-Wochenblatt,* 1880, no. 41, pp. 742–747.

Bundesarchiv/Militärarchiv, Freiburg i B, files Msg 101/206, Ph 3/53.

Cäncrin, *Über die Militärökonomie im Frieden und Krieg* (St. Petersburg, 1821).

Caesar, C. Julius, *The Gallic War* (London, 1946).

Canby, S. L., Jenkins, B. M., and Raincy, R. B., "Alternative Strategy and Force Structure in Vietnam," RAND Paper D 190973 ARPA (Santa Monica, Cal., 1969).

Chandler, D., *The Art of War in the Age of Marlborough* (London, 1976).

────── *The Campaigns of Napoleon* (London, 1963).

Charteris, J., *At GHQ* (London, 1931).

Cicero, Marcus Tullius, *Ad Atticum* (London, 1967–).

────── *Ad Familiares* (London, 1967).

Cipolla, C. M., ed., *The Fontana Economic History of Europe,* vol. 4 (2) (London, 1973).

Clausewitz, C. von, *On War* (London, 1962).

Codman, C. R., *Drive* (Boston, 1957).

Cole, H. M., *The Lorraine Campaign* (Washington, D.C., 1950).

Correspondance de Napoléon Premier (Paris, 1863–).

Corvisier, A., *Armies and Societies in Europe, 1494–1789* (Bloomington, Ind., 1979).

Craig, G. A., *The Battle of Königgrätz* (London, 1966).

Creveld, M. van, *Fighting Power: German and U.S. Army Performance, 1939–1945* (Westport, Ct., 1982).

——— *Supplying War: Logistics from Wallenstein to Patton* (London, 1978).

Crovitz, H. F., *Galton's Walk* (New York, 1970).

Cruickshank, C. G., *Elizabeth's Army* (Oxford, 1966).

Dayan, M., *Diary of the Sinai Campaign* (London, 1966).

——— *Story of My Life* (London, 1976).

Delbrück, H., *Geschichte der Kriegskunst im Rahmen der politischen Geschichte,* vol. I (Berlin, 1921).

Dickinson, H., "Survivability—Key Ingredient for Command and Control," *Military Affairs,* November 1981, pp. 19–25.

Dio Cassius, *Roman History* (London, 1914–).

Diodorus, *Deipnosophists* (London, 1946–1957).

Dixon, N., *On the Psychology of Military Incompetence* (London, 1976).

Dolav, A., "The 8th of October of General Gonen" (Hebrew), *Maariv,* 7.2.1975, pp. 23–27.

Domaszewski, A. von, *Aufsätze zur römischen Heeresgeschichte* (Darmstadt, 1972).

Duffy, C., *Borodino: Napoleon against Russia, 1812* (London, 1972).

Dupuy, T. N., "The Arab-Israeli Conflict: A Military Analysis," *Strategy and Tactics,* no. 90, Jan./Feb. 1982, pp. 39–48, 57.

——— *Elusive Victory: The Arab Israeli Wars, 1947–1974* (New York, 1978).

——— *The Evolution of Weapons and Warfare* (Indianapolis, 1980).

——— *A Genius for War* (London, 1977).

Eckhardt, G. S., *Vietnam Studies: Command and Control* (Washington, D.C., 1974).

Edmonds, J. E., *France and Belgium, 1916* (London, 1932).

Ellis, J., *The Social History of the Machine Gun* (London, 1973).

Engels, D. W., *Alexander the Great and the Logistics of the Macedonian Army* (Berkeley, 1978).

——— "Alexander's Intelligence System," *Classical Quarterly,* 54, 1980, pp. 327–340.

Enthoven, A. C., and Wayne Smith, K., *How Much Is Enough? Shaping the Defense Program, 1961–1969* (New York, 1971).

Erfurt, W., *Der Vernichtungssieg, eine Studie über das Zusammenwirken getrennter Heeresteile* (Berlin, 1938).

Essame, H., *Patton: A Study in Command* (New York, 1974).

Evans, P. W., "Strategic Signal Communications ... the Operations of the German Signal Corps during the March on Paris in 1914," *Signal Corps Bulletin,* 82, 1935, pp. 24–58.

Ewell, J., and Hunt, I. A., *Sharpening the Combat Edge: The Use of Analysis to Reinforce Military Judgement* (Washington, D.C., 1974).

Eytan, R., interview with M.v.C., Tel Aviv, 29 April 1982.

Fain, A. J. F., *Manuscrit de Mil Huit Cent Treize* (Paris, 1824).

Farrar-Hockley, A. H., *The Somme* (Philadelphia, 1964).

Ferguson, E. B., *Westmoreland: The Inevitable General* (Boston, 1968).

Fink, R. O., *Roman Military Records on Papyrus* (n.p., 1971).

First U.S. Army After Action Report, National Archives, Suitland, Md.

Firth, C. H., *Cromwell's Army* (London, 1962).

Fischl, H., *Fernsprech- und Meldwesen im Altertum* (Schweinfurt, 1904).

Fix, T., *Militair-Telegraphie* (Leipzig, 1869).

Fletcher, G. R. L., *Gustavus Adolphus and the Thirty Years War* (New York, 1963).

Foerster, W., ed., *Friedrich Karl von Preussen, Denkwürdigkeiten aus seinem Leben* (Stuttgart, 1910).

Fontane, T., *Der deutsche Krieg von 1866* (Berlin, 1871).

Foucart, J. P., *Campagne de Prusse* (Paris, 1887).

Francesky, E. von, *Denkwürdigkeiten* (Bielefeld and Leipzig, 1901).

Fredericus Rex, *Werke,* vol. 4, *Militärische Schriften,* ed. G. B. Holz (Berlin, 1913).

Friedjung, H., *Der Kampf um die Vorherrschaft in Deutschland 1859 bis 1866* (Stuttgart, 1898).

Froissart, J., *Chronicles* (London, 1968).

Frontinus, *Strategamata* (Leipzig, 1855).

Fuller, J. F. C., *Armament and History* (New York, 1945).

―――― *Generalship: Its Diseases and Their Cure* (London, 1937).

―――― *The Generalship of Alexander the Great* (London, 1958).

Gabriel, R. A., and Savage, P. L., *Crisis in Command: Mismanagement in the Army* (New York, 1978).

Galbraith, J., *Designing Complex Organizations* (Reading, Mass., 1973).

Galili, E., "Raphia, 217 B.C.E., Revisited," *Scripta Classica Israelica,* vol. III, 1976–1977, pp. 52–126.

Gascouin, J. E., *L'evolution de l'artillerie pendant la guerre mondiale* (Paris, 1920).

Gavish, Y., interview with M.v.C., Tel Aviv, 7 February 1982.

Generalstab des Heeres, Heeresdienstvorschrift 300, *Truppenführung* (Berlin, 1936).

Giehrl, H., *Der Feldherr Napoleon als Organisator* (Berlin, 1911).

Gies, J., *Crisis 1918: The Leading Actors, Strategies and Events in the German Gamble for Total Victory on the Western Front* (New York, 1974).

Gissin, R., "Command, Control, and Communications Technology: Changing Patterns in Combat Organizations," Ph.D. diss., Syracuse University, microfilm, 1979.

G.L.W., "Der grosse König im Grossen Krieg," *Allgemeine Militär-Zeitung*, 1870, nos. 7 and 8, pp. 49–51, 57–59.

Goerlitz, W., *Der deutsche Generalstab* (Frankfurt am Main, 1950).

Gomme, A. W., *A Historical Commentary on Thucydides* (Oxford, 1970).

Graves, R., *Goodbye to All That* (London, 1957).

Greenfield, K., *The Organization of Ground Combat Troops* (Washington, D.C., 1947).

Gröner, W., *Der Feldherr wider Willen* (Berlin, 1931).

———— *Lebenserinnerungen* (Göttingen, 1957).

Gur, M., "The Experiences of the Sinai" (Hebrew), *Maarachot*, October 1966, pp. 17–22.

———— "The IDF—Continuity versus Innovation" (Hebrew), *Maarachot*, March 1978, pp. 4–6.

Haasler, R., and Goebel, H., "Das Unbehagen am technologischen Fortschritt in den Streitkräften," *Wehrwissenschaftliche Rundschau*, February 1981, pp. 36–41.

Handel, M. I., "Intelligence and Deception," *Journal of Strategic Studies*, 5, 1982, pp. 122–154.

Harmand, J., *L'Armée et le soldat à Rome de 107 à 50 avant notre ère* (Paris, 1967).

Hay, J. H., *Vietnam Studies: Tactical and Material Innovations* (Washington, D.C., 1974).

Hazlewood, L., Hayes, J. J., and Brownwell, J. R., "Planning for Problems in Crisis Management: An Analysis of Post 1945 Behavior in the U.S. Department of Defense," *International Studies Quarterly*, 21, 1977, pp. 75–106.

Heermann, O., *Die Gefechtsführung abendländischer Heere im Orient in der Epoche des Ersten Kreuzzugs* (Marburg, 1887).

Henderson, G. F. R., *The Science of War* (London, 1881).

Herodotus, *The Histories* (London, 1961–1966).

Herzog, C., *The War of Atonement* (London, 1977).

Hewitt, H. J., *The Black Prince's Expedition of 1355–57* (Manchester, 1958).

Hittle, J. D., *The Military Staff: Its History and Development* (Harrisburg, Pa., 1961).

Horowitz, D., "Flexible Responsiveness and Military Strategy: The Case of the Israeli Army," *Policy Sciences,* vol. I, 1970, pp. 191–205.

Illan, M., "The Use of Surprise in the Sinai Campaign" (Hebrew), *Maarachot,* October 1966, pp. 23–27.

International Institute for Strategic Studies, *The Military Balance, 1973–1974* (London, 1973).

—— *The Military Balance, 1981–1982* (London, 1981).

Irvine, D. D., "The Origins of Capital Staffs," *Journal of Modern History,* 1938, pp. 161–179.

Jähns, M., *Geschichte der Kriegswissenschaften* (Berlin, 1889).

Jenkins, B. M., "The Unchangeable War," RAND Paper RM-6278 ARPA (Santa Monica, Cal., 1972).

J.L., "Méthodes de commandement de Napoléon pendant les guerres de l'Espagne," *Revue Historique,* 44, 1911, pp. 458–493, and 45, 1912, pp. 57–90, 235–263, 450–453.

Jomini, H., *Précis de l'art de la guerre* (Osnabrück, 1973; reprint of the 1853 edition).

Kedar, B. Z., *The Story of "Mahatz" Battalion* (Hebrew) (Tel Aviv, 1975).

Keegan, J., *The Face of Battle* (London, 1976).

Kessel, E., *Moltke* (Stuttgart, 1957).

—— ed., *Graf Alfred Schlieffen—Briefe* (Göttingen, 1958).

Kiggel Papers, file iv/3, Liddell Hart Centre for Military Archives, King's College, London.

Kinnard, D., *The War Managers* (Hanover, N.H., 1977).

Koch, O. W., and Hays, R. G., *G-2: Intelligence for Patton* (Philadelphia, 1971).

Kraft zu Hohenlohe-Ingelfingen, K., *Aus meinem Leben 1848–1871* (Berlin, 1897).

Krieg, T., *Wilhelm von Doering, ein Lebens- und Charakterbild* (Berlin, 1898).

Kromayer, J., *Antike Schlachtfelder* (Berlin, 1931).

Kromayer, J., and Veith, G., *Heereswesen und Kriegsführung der Griechen und Römer* (Munich, 1928).

Kuhl, H. von, *Der deutsche Generalstab in Vorbereitung und Durchführung der Weltkrieg* (Berlin, 1920).

Kuhl, H. von, and Bergmann, A. von, *Movement and Supply of the German First Army during August and September 1914* (Fort Leavenworth, Kans., 1935).

Labisch, A., *Frumentum Commeatesque, die Nährungsmittelversorgung der Heere Caesars* (Meissenheim an Glan, 1975).

Las Casas, *Mémorial de Sainte Hélène* (Paris, 1869).

Lesquier, J., *Les institutions militaires de l'Egypte sous les Lagides* (Paris, 1911).

Lettow-Vorbeck, O. von, *Geschichte des Krieges von 1866 in Deutschland* (Berlin, 1895).

Lewal, J. L., *Tactique des ravitaillements* (Paris, 1881).

Liddell Hart, B. H., *Deterrent or Defence* (London, 1960).

—— *Strategy* (New York, 1967).

Loewe, V., *Die Organisation und Verwaltung der Wallensteinischen Heere* (Freiburg i B, 1895).

Lot, F., *L'Art militaire au Moyen Age en Europe et dans le Proche Orient* (Paris, 1946).

Ludendorff, E., *My War Memoirs, 1914–1918* (London, n.d.).

—— *Urkunden der Obersten Heeresleitung über ihre Tätigkeit 1916/18* (Berlin, 1922).

Luttwak, E. N., *The Grand Strategy of the Roman Empire* (Baltimore, Md., 1978).

—— *Strategy and Politics* (New Brunswick, 1980).

Luttwak, E. N., and Horowitz, D., *The Israeli Army* (London, 1975).

McChristian, J. A., *Vietnam Studies: The Role of Military Intelligence, 1965–1967* (Washington, D.C., 1974).

Macksey, K., *Guderian, Panzer General* (London, 1976).

Mck Saltzman, C., "The Signals Corps in War," *Arms and the Man*, 46, 1909, unpaged.

McLuhan, M., *The Gutenberg Galaxy* (New York, 1969).

Mallorie, P., "Command, Control, Communications," *NATO's Fifteen Nations*, 27 July 1981, pp. 42–45.

Marsh, R. M., and Mannari, H., "Technology and Size as Determinants of the Organizational Structure of Japanese Factories," *Administrative Science Quarterly*, 26, 1981, pp. 33–57.

Marshall-Cornwall, J., *Haig as a Military Commander* (New York, 1971).

Meir, G., *My Life* (London, 1975).

Melzo, L., *Regole militare sopra il governo et servitio particolare della cavalleria* (Antwerp, 1611).

Merling, *Die Telegraphentechnik in der Praxis* (n.p., 1879).

Messenger, C., *The Art of Blitzkrieg* (London, 1976).

Middlebrook, M., *The First Day on the Somme* (New York, 1972).

Miksche, F. O., *Blitzkrieg* (London, 1944).

Military Review, November 1981.

Millar, F., "Emperors, Frontiers and Foreign Relations, 31 B.C. to A.D. 378," *Britannia*, 13, 1982, pp. 1–23.

Miller, G. A., "The Magical Number Seven," *Psychological Review*, 63, 1956, pp. 81–96.

Millis, W., *Military History* (Washington, D.C., 1961).

Millstein, U., "The Day That Was: The 8th of October" (Hebrew), *Maariv*, 7.2.1975, pp. 10–11.

Moltke, H. von (Jr.), *Die deutsche Tragödie an der Marne* (Potsdam, 1934).

——— *Erinnerungen, Briefe, Dokumente* (Stuttgart, 1922).

Moltke, H. von (Sr.), *Militärische Werke* (Berlin, 1892–1912).

Müller-Löbnitz, W., *Die Sendung des Oberleutnants Hentsch an 8–10 September 1914* (Berlin, 1922).

Mylander, M., *The Generals* (New York, 1974).

Nanteuil, H. de, *Daru et l'administration militaire sous la Révolution et l'Empire* (Paris, 1966).

National Archives, Suitland, Md., files RG 94-2046, RG 94-10823.

Oesterreichische Militärische Zeitschrift, 2, 1861, no. 2.

Oman, C., *A History of the Art of War in the Middle Ages* (London, 1937).

Onasander, *The General* (London, 1962).

Overbeck, B., *Das königliche Preussische Kriegsheer* (Berlin, 1862).

Oxford English Dictionary, vols. 8, 10 (Oxford, 1933).

Palmer, D. D., *Summons of the Trumpet* (San Rafael, Cal., 1978).

Palmer, G., *The McNamara Strategy and the Vietnam War* (Westport, Ct., 1978).

Parker, G., *The Army of Flanders and the Spanish Road 1567–1659* (London, 1972).

Parkinson, N. C., *In-Laws and Outlaws* (London, 1962).

Patton, G. S., *War as I Knew It* (London, n.d.).

Paulys Real Encyclopädie der Klassischen Altertums-Wissenschaft (Stuttgart, 1957).

Peek, E. D., "The Necessity and Use of Electrical Communications in the Battle-Field," *Journal of the Military Service Institution of the U.S.*, 49, 1911, pp. 327–344.

The Pentagon Papers, ed. Senator Gravel (Boston, n.d.).

Perjes, G., "Army Provisioning, Logistics and Strategy in the Second Half of the 17th Century," *Acta Historica Academiae Scientiarium Hungaricae*, 16, 1970, pp. 1–51.

Philip, A. de, *Etude sur le Service d'Etat Major pendant les Guerres du Premier Empire* (Paris, 1900).

Philo of Byzantium, *Poliocertia* (Berlin, 1920).

Picard, E., and Tuetey, L., eds., *Unpublished Correspondence of Napoleon I* (New York, 1913).

Plato, *The Laws* (London, 1965).

Plutarch, *Alexander* (London, 1959).

——— *Crassus* (London, 1959).

———— *Pelopides* (London, 1959).

————, *Sertorius* (London, 1959).

Polybius, *The Histories* (London, 1922–).

Poschinger, M. von, *Kaiser Friedrich in neuer quellenmässiger Darstellung* (Berlin, n.d.).

Praun, A., *Soldat in der Telegraphen- und Nachrichtentruppe* (Würzburg, 1965).

Prince, A. E., "The Payment of Army Wages in Edward III's Reign," *English Historical Review,* April 1944, pp. 137–160.

Pritchett, W. K., *Ancient Greek Military Practices* (Berkeley, 1971).

Procopius, *Anecdota* (London, 1953–1954).

Quimby, R. S., *The Background of Napoleonic Warfare* (New York, 1957).

Rabin, Y., "After the Great Maneuvers" (Hebrew), *Maarachot,* August 1960, pp. 6–9.

———— *Memoirs* (Hebrew) (Tel Aviv, 1977).

Ramsay, A. M., "The Speed of the Roman Imperial Post," *Journal of Roman Studies,* 15, 1925, pp. 60–74.

Raymond, J., *Power at the Pentagon* (New York, 1964).

Reichsarchiv edition, *Der Weltkrieg* (Berlin, 1921–).

Reinhardt, H., "Grosse und Zusammenstellung der Komandobehörden des deutschen Feldheers im II. Weltkriege," U.S. Army Historical Division Study P 139 (n.p., n.d.).

Rhona, T. P., "Weapon Systems and Information War" (Seattle, Wash., 1976).

Rienzi, T. M., *Vietnam Studies: Communications-Electronics, 1962–1970* (Washington, D.C., 1972).

Riepl, G., *Das Nachrichtenwesen des Altertums* (Hildesheim, 1913; rprt. 1972).

Riesman, D., "The Oral and Written Traditions," in E. Carpenter and M. McLuhan, eds., *Explorations in Communication* (Boston, 1960), pp. 109–116.

Rowland, J. R., "Combat Readiness: Fifty Percent," *Armor,* May–June 1982, pp. 42–43.

Ruppenthal, R. G., *Logistical Support of the Armies* (Washington, D.C., 1953).

Rupprecht, Crown Prince of Bavaria, *Mein Kriegstagebuch* (Munich, 1922).

Safran, N., *From War to War* (New York, 1969).

Savary, R., *His Britannic Majesty's Army in Germany during the Seven Years War* (Oxford, 1966).

Saxe, M. de, *Rêveries on the Art of War* (Harrisburg, Pa., 1947).

Schall, W., "Führungsgrundsätze in Armee und Industrie," *Wehrkunde*, 14, 1965, pp. 10–18, 75–81.

Schiff, Z., "Notes on the 8th of October" (Hebrew), *Haaretz*, 7.2.1975, p. 15.

———— *October Earthquake: Yom Kippur, 1973* (Tel Aviv, 1974).

———— "Tactical Intelligence Difficulties in Disseminating Information" (Hebrew), *Haaretz*, 14.2.1975, p. 2.

Schlichting, S., ed., *Moltkes Vermächtniss* (Munich, 1901).

Schlieffen, A. von, "Der Feldherr," *Gesammelte Schriften* (Berlin, 1913), vol. I, pp. 3–10.

Schmettau, Graf von, Jr., *Lebensgeschichte des Grafen von Schmettau* (Berlin, 1806).

Schwarte, M., ed., *Die Technik im Weltkrieg* (Berlin, 1920).

Scott Thompson, W., and Frizzel, D. D., *The Lessons of Vietnam* (New York, 1977).

Ségur, P. de, *Un aide de camp de Napoléon, 1800–1812* (Paris, 1873).

Sella, A., "Soviet Training and Arab Performance," *Jerusalem Post Magazine*, 8.2.1975, pp. 6–8.

Semmes, H. H., *Portrait of Patton* (New York, 1955).

Showalter, D., "A Modest Plea for Drums and Trumpets," *Military Affairs*, February 1975, pp. 71–73.

———— "The Retaming of Bellona: Prussia and the Institutionalization of the Napoleonic Legacy 1815–1876," *Military Affairs*, April 1980, pp. 57–62.

Skelton, R. A., *Meister der Kartographie* (Berlin, 1973).

Smail, R. C., *Crusading Warfare, 1097–1193* (London, 1976).

Starry, D. A., *Vietnam Studies: Mounted Combat in Vietnam* (Washington, D.C., 1978).

Steinbrunner, J. D., *The Cybernetic Theory of Decision: New Dimensions of Political Analysis* (Princeton, N.J., 1974).

Sternhall, Z., "Hamutal as an Example" (Hebrew), *Haaretz*, 2.2.1975, p. 2.

Stoffel, *Rapports militaires, 1866–1870* (Paris, 1871).

Strong, K., *Men of Intelligence* (London, 1970).

Tacitus, Cornelius Nepos, *Annales* (London, 1966).

Talmai, M., "The 8th of October of Assaf Yagouri" (Hebrew), *Maariv*, 7.2.1975, pp. 4–6, 45.

Tarn, W. W., *Alexander the Great* (London, 1936).

———— *Hellenistic Military and Naval Developments* (New York, 1968).

Tavor, E., "The Longest Day" (Hebrew), *Haolam Hazeh,* 11.12.1974, pp. 18–19, 22.

Temporini, H., ed., *Aufstieg und Niedergang der Römischen Welt* (Berlin, 1974–).

Teveth, S., *The Tanks of Tamuz* (London, 1969).

Thaer, A. von, *Generalstabsdient an der Front und in der OHL* (Göttingen, 1958).

Thayer, T. C., *How to Analyze a War without Fronts: Vietnam, 1965-1970* (Washington, D.C., 1972).

Thiebault, P., *Manual des adjutants généraux et des adjoints employés dans les états majors des armées* (Paris, 1806).

Third U.S. Army After Action Report, National Archives, Suitland, Md.

Thompson, I. A. A., *War and Government in Habsburg Spain, 1560-1620* (London, 1776).

Thompson, R., *No Exit from Vietnam* (London, 1969).

Thucydides, *The Peloponnesian War* (London, 1962–).

Thun, H., *Die Verkehrs- und Nachrichtenmittel im Kriege* (Leipzig, 1911).

Thurbon, M. T., "The Origins of Electronic Warfare," *Journal of the Royal United Services Institute,* September 1977, pp. 56–62.

Tolson, J. S., *Vietnam Studies: Airmobility* (Washington, D.C., 1973).

Tooley, R. V., *Maps and Map Making* (London, 1952).

Tournés, R., "Le GQC de Napoleon Ier," *Revue de Paris,* May 1921, pp. 134–158.

Tout, T. F., *Chapters in the Administrative History of Medieval England* (Manchester, 1937).

Vaché, *Napoléon en Campagne* (Paris, 1900).

Vagts, A., *A History of Militarism* (Toronto, 1959).

Vegetius, *Epitoma Rei Militaris* (Leipzig, 1885).

Verbruggen, J. F., *The Art of Warfare in Western Europe during the Middle Ages* (Amsterdam, 1977).

Verdy du Vernois, J. von, *Im Grossen Hauptquartier, 1870/71* (Berlin, 1895).

―――― *Im Hauptquartier der Zweiten Armee, 1866* (Berlin, 1900).

Vizthum von Eckstädt, K., *Die Hauptquartiere im Herbstfeldzug 1813 auf dem deutschen Kriegschauplätze* (Berlin, 1910).

Voights-Rhetz, K. von, *Briefe aus den Kriegsjahren 1866 und 1870/71* (Berlin, 1906).

Wallach, J. L., *Kriegstheorien, ihre Entwicklung im 19. und 20. Jahrhundert* (Frankfurt am Main, 1972).

Wartensleben, H. von, *Erinnerungen* (Berlin, 1897).

Watson, R., *The Roman Soldier* (New York, 1969).

Wavell, A., *Soldiers and Soldiering* (London, 1953).

Webster, G., *The Roman Imperial Army* (London, 1969).

Welch, J. A., "Some Random Thoughts on C^3," in Tsokos, C. P., and Thrall, R. M., eds., *Decision Information* (New York, 1979), pp. 339–354.

Westmoreland, W. C., *A Soldier Reports* (Garden City, N.Y., 1976).

Westphalen, C. H. P. von, *Geschichte der Feldzüge des Herzogs Ferdinand von Braunschweig Lüneburg* (Berlin, 1859).

Wheeler-Bennett, J., *The Nemesis of Power* (New York, 1967).

Wheldon, J., *Machine Age Armies* (London, 1968).

Wijn, J., *Het Krijgswezen in den Tijd van Prins Maurits* (Utrecht, 1934).

Wilensky, H. L., *Organizational Intelligence: Knowledge and Policy in Government and Industry* (New York, 1967).

Winner, L., *Autonomous Technology: Technics out of Control as a Theme in Political Thought* (Cambridge, Mass., 1977).

Wohlstetter, R., *Pearl Harbor: Warning and Decision* (Stanford, Cal., 1962).

Woods, E. L., *A History of Tactical Communications* (Orlando, Fla., 1945).

Wool, H., *The Military Specialist* (Baltimore, Md., 1968).

Wust, H., and Himburg, L. F., *Das militärische Führungssystem* (Frankfurt am Main, 1974).

Xenophon, *Cyropaedia* (London, 1943).

——— *Hellenica* (London, 1918).

——— *Lacedaimonum Politeia* (London, 1968).

Yagouri, A., *To Be with Them, They're All Mine* (Hebrew) (Tel Aviv, 1979).

Zanthier, F. W. von, *Versuch über die Märsche der Armeen, die Lager, Schlachten und die Operations-Pläne* (Dresden, 1778).

Zeev, "The Entire System Was Creaking" (Hebrew), *Maarachot*, April 1979.

Zeller, R., *Planungs- und Führungssystem* (Regensburg, 1978).

Zuckerman, S., "Judgement and Control in War," *Foreign Affairs,* 54, 1962, pp. 196–212.

INDEX